THE
MAYORS

The Chicago Political Tradition

Edited by Paul M. Green and Melvin G. Holli

SOUTHERN ILLINOIS UNIVERSITY PRESS
Carbondale and Edwardsville

For Sharon and Betsy

90 89 88 87   4 3 2 1

Library of Congress Cataloging-in-Publication Data

The Mayors.

Bibliography: p.
Includes index.
1. Mayors—Illinois—Chicago–Biography. 2. Chicago
(Ill.)—Politics and government.   I. Green, Paul
Michael.   II. Holli, Melvin G.
F548.25.M39 1987   977.3'11'00992   86-20240
ISBN 0-8093-1336-7

The paper used in this publication meets the minimum requirements of
American National Standard for Information Sciences
– Permanence of Paper for Printed Library Materials, ANSI Z39.48-1984.

CONTENTS

Contents

PLATES

PREFACE

This book was conceived as an effort to provide a political roadmap for the past century, charting where Chicago has been with its principal executive office, the mayoralty and its leading occupants, and where it may be going in the future. We have omitted some of the lesser mayors who served in the period after the Great Fire of 1871 (Heath, Roche, Cregier, Washburne, Swift, Hopkins, and Carter Harrison I, whose substance and style can be seen in Carter II) but covered all of the movers and shakers who have occupied City Hall. Much of the city's dynamic and turbulent political history is surprisingly poorly known even to Chicagoans, who pride themselves as experts on the byzantine labyrinth that honeycombs and undergirds Chicago politics. Most of the "historic" knowledge of politics seldom extends further back than the Richard J. Daley era or stretches beyond the memory span of those who think, write, and talk about politics in the Windy City. We hope this distillation of Chicago's mayoral history will help to fill at least a part of that hiatus and enable Chicagoans to see their present in an historical perspective.

Many debts were incurred in the process of putting together such a book. First we wish to thank the contributors, who wrote freshly commissioned pieces which appear here for the first time (with the exception of the Richard J. Daley selection, a revision of an earlier work). We would also like to thank the Illinois Humanities Council and the Chicago Historical Society, who funded and hosted the first draft of this book which was presented on 2 December 1985 at an all-day conference. Thanks also go to former Mayor Jane Byrne, to Mayor Harold Washington and members of his staff, and to a crew of lively political commentators and writers who squeeze out more interpretation per column inch or fifteen-minute broadcast than any in the nation: Basil Talbott (Chicago *Sun Times*), Sharon Alter (William Rainey Harper College), Milton Rosenberg (WGN Radio–Extension 720 and the University of Chicago), and Robert Starks (Northeastern Illinois University). We would also like to acknowledge the aid of a sharp-minded group of critics who helped significantly in shaping some of the ideas in this book: Louis Masotti (Northwestern University), Paul McGrath (Northwestern University), and Phil Krone (political consultant).

THE
MAYORS

I.

JOSEPH MEDILL: CHICAGO'S FIRST MODERN MAYOR

David L. Protess

Joseph Medill is not often remembered for his term as Chicago's first chief executive after the Great Fire of 1871, despite the historical importance of his regime. Medill's years as mayor were largely overshadowed by his other occupations. For most of the second half of the nineteenth century, Medill ran the Chicago *Tribune*. During those years, he played a seminal role in the development of the national Republican party and was instrumental in the making of the Lincoln presidency. Between 1871 and 1873 Medill also attempted to run Chicago. He proved to be less successful as the city's twenty-first mayor than as a newspaper publisher and political kingmaker. Nonetheless, his term as mayor was vital to the establishment of Chicago's unique political tradition.

In many respects, Medill was a contemporary urban mayor. His administration was preceded by more than three decades of mayors who were ceremonial figureheads, single-mindedly dedicated to promoting economic expansion during their two year, parttime terms. Medill, on the other hand, was able to expand considerably the authority of the mayor's office. Medill's increased power was accompanied by increased burdens for handling a variety of major conflicts and crises, many of which have persisted to the present time.

The legacy of the Medill mayoralty is in its precedent-setting efforts to manage complex urban problems. His administration was pressured to spend and to save, to be more efficient and more democratic, to distribute spoils and to establish a meritocracy. At the same time, it endeavored to mediate among interest groups with markedly different visions for the city.

While seeking to cope with these conflicting pressures, Medill presided over the city's first "reform" administration.[1] He also rebuilt the city with fireproof buildings, established its public library system, and used his self-generated mayoral charter to revamp the police and fire departments. More important than his ideological stamp and tangible accomplishments, however, was Medill's unprecedented willingness to *attempt* to govern the city. In the course of this effort, Medill went beyond the "transition mayor" status conventionally assigned to him [2] and became the first mayor of the city's modern political era.

Joseph Medill's Chicago

The City after the Fire

In 1871, Chicago was the fastest growing city in the country. As the result of a massive influx of immigrants in the previous decade, Chicago surpassed Saint Louis in population to become the fourth largest American city. According to the 1870 census, half of the city was foreign-born, with one of every six Chicagoans being a native of Germany. Chicago's changing demographic picture made for rivalries that would affect profoundly the political landscape of the city for more than a century.

These conflicts were temporarily put aside when fire devastated the city in October of 1871. In three days, four-fifths of Chicago burned. Thirteen thousand two hundred dwellings were destroyed, leaving 350,000 people homeless. The city was in a state of financial ruin.

Chicago's elected representatives were ill-equipped to handle the crisis. Mayor Rosewall Mason's formal authority was virtually nonexistent, while the forty members of the city council were too disorganized and preoccupied with the plight of their own businesses to be able to assume a leadership role. City Hall was one of many official buildings that burned to the ground, forcing the city's decision-makers to meet in temporary headquarters. The city treasury was quickly bankrupt by the effort to provide relief to the homeless and clean up the ruins.

With less than one month remaining before the November election for city officeholders, a coalition of business and civic leaders led by Carter Harrison decided to slate Joseph Medill for mayor on a bipartisan "Citizens Fire-Proof" ticket. The choice of Medill was not surprising. His life had been devoted to public causes. Trained as an attorney, he had gradually abandoned the practice of law to become a newspaper editor and publisher in Cleveland in the early 1850s. Medill's newspaper generally supported Whig party candidates and principles. However, he became increasingly disillusioned with the Whigs after their defeat in the national election of 1852. In 1854, Medill spearheaded the move to create a probusiness, antislavery political organization that he named the Republican party.

In the 1850s, Medill moved to Chicago and became editor and part-owner of the Chicago *Tribune*. He used the voice of the *Tribune* and his personal lobbying ability to convince the new Republican party to nominate Abraham Lincoln for President. Medill campaigned vigorously for Lincoln and became the first Republican president's close advisor and confidant. Locally, he was a delegate to the Illinois Constitutional Convention in 1869. In 1871, he served as a member of the first U.S. Civil Service Commission. In each position, he exhibited strong, tough-minded leadership traits; he made decisions with ideological fervor but was not incapable of compromise.

Despite his commitment to public affairs and dedication to Chicago, Medill proved to be a reluctant mayoral candidate. The supposedly fireproof Tribune Tower was virtually destroyed by the blaze, and Medill devoted almost all of his energy to the continued publication of his newspaper. Further, Medill resisted the overtures of Harrison and the other because he believed that "the powers of the mayor were so restricted that he did not amount to much more than a figurehead."[3]

Consequently, Medill initially declined the nomination for mayor. Undeterred, the leaders of the coalition applied constant pressure on Medill to head their ticket. After several days, he finally agreed to accept the nomination on the condition that the Illinois legislature would enact a new city charter that would greatly expand the powers of the mayor's office. Typical of his autocratic style, Medill's acceptance speech threatened that "if it [the legislature] rejected the bill then I would feel at liberty to resign the office and slip down and out; but if the amended charter bill became a law I would serve to the best of my ability."[4]

Medill's opponent in the election was Charles C. P. Holden, the alderman of the Tenth Ward and president of the city council during the Mason administration. Holden was nominated by a poorly organized local Democratic party whose main support was in the city's predominately immigrant wards. Following a two week campaign, Medill overwhelmingly defeated Holden by a vote of 16,125 to 5,988. The Fire-Proof candidates for city treasurer and city collector were also victorious. Significantly, however, seven aldermanic candidates supported by the Democratic party were elected, providing an incipient core of opposition to Medill's programs by one-third of the city council.[5]

The Medill Regime

As mayor, Joseph Medill inherited a crisis that was unprecedented in Chicago's history. His term of office was affected profoundly by the emergency conditions of 1871 and 1872. Nonetheless, Medill's mayoral programs helped to mold the city's postfire environment as much as they were circumscribed by the conditions of the times.

Medill's policies emerged from his efforts to manage a variety of paradoxical tendencies in the life of Chicago after the fire. The roles Medill played in handling five such dilemmas were particularly significant for shaping the character of his administration. First, in performing a "ministerial" role,

Medill sought to expand the authority of his office to cope with severe urban problems, while being mindful of the prerogatives of the city council and numerous other governmental units. Secondly, as a "developer" he was responsible for rebuilding the city, while conserving its scarce resources. Thirdly, in the role of "kingmaker" Medill was faced with the dilemma of advancing the careers of partisan loyalists or establishing procedures for nonpolitical merit appointment. Fourthly, as a power "broker" he had to mediate between patrician and immigrant groups who were fighting for control of the city. Fifthly, Medill as "imagemaker" had to manage the press and other public forums to develop a persona that appealed to different and often incompatible urban interests. Most significantly, Medill's willingness to assume these roles created leadership themes that have persisted through the mayoral regimes of the twentieth century.

The Ministerial Role. The first issue that Medill attended to after the election was his ability to govern. Since the duties of city officials were defined entirely by state law, Medill devised a strategy to convince the Illinois legislature to modify the existing city charter to increase mayoral authority. Even before he assumed the office of mayor on 4 December 1871 Medill appointed the well-respected Judge Murray F. Tuley to draft a "Mayor's Bill" for submission to the Springfield lawmakers in their next session.

Medill and Tuley used several arguments in lobbying for the new law: it was needed to allow for efficient executive response to the emergency conditions in the city; it was to be a temporary measure, not to extend beyond Medill's two year term of office; and it would not preempt the existing authority of the city council. After considerable arm twisting, the state of Illinois enacted the Mayor's Bill on 9 March 1872.[6] Medill was relieved of having to act on his campaign promise to resign in the absence of its passage, and he immediately rewarded Judge Tuley's efforts by making him the city's corporation counsel.

The new charter established the modern day authority of the mayor's office. The mayor was provided with the following new responsibilities:

—To appoint all nonelected city officials, with the advice and consent of the city council;
—To remove all nonelected city officials, while only having to inform the city council of the reasons for the removal;
—To serve as the presiding officer of the city council;
—To appoint the standing committees of the city council and to serve as *ex officio* member of those committees;
—To veto any ordinance, including all or part of an appropriations ordinance, with a two-thirds vote of the city council necessary to override the veto;
—To exercise special police powers, including the authority to license, regulate, and maintain order in the city.

4

In Medill's inaugural address, the new mayor made it clear that he would not hesitate to use the powers of his office to make Chicago work. In this first speech to the city council, he attacked aldermanic budgeting practices, the pervasive presence of spoils and corruption, and the inability of city government to prevent and cope with the conflagration. He promised "a complete overhauling of all expenditures in all departments of the city," warning that "the services of hundreds of persons now on the pay-rolls can be dispensed with. . . ." "Good government" was Medill's answer to Chicago's problems, and he outlined an array of programs that he believed would achieve it.[7] In doing so, Medill asserted a strong leadership position from the outset of his regime, and directly challenged those aldermen who might resist his efforts to change the direction of city government.

Despite the adversarial tone set by his inaugural address, Medill's first year in office met with a minimum of formal legislative resistance. The city's atmosphere of crisis and the broadness of his electoral coalition allowed him to implement many of his programs. Further, Medill chose to gradually and cautiously use his expanded authority during 1872, always recognizing the Council's legislative prerogatives and generally working toward the establishment of a stronger executive in city government.

While he vetoed an historically unprecedented eleven council ordinances in his first year in office, most dealt narrowly with specific "wasteful" financial practices. None of the vetoes was overridden. He also was successful in obtaining council approval of his appointments and removals, in part because the magnitude of the former fell far short of his inaugural threats.

His expanded ministerial responsibilities included the appointment of members to the newly constituted Chicago Board of Education and of commissioners of the city's first public library. His selections were unanimously approved by the council. When the new city charter went into effect on July 1, Medill sidestepped the potential aldermanic resentment of his takeover as their presiding officer by allowing the council to choose a series of acting chairmen. He good-naturedly told the council that a hearing impairment would prevent him from serving effectively in that capacity.

In performing a ministerial role in the first part of his administration, Medill was often preoccupied with intergovernmental issues. In addition to his effort to obtain the Mayor's Bill from the state, he lobbied furiously for financial aid to Chicago. Illinois law prohibited the direct appropriation of funds to the city. However, Medill convinced the legislature to pass a special act to reimburse Chicago for $2.9 million it had expended on the state-owned Illinois and Michigan canal.[8]

Medill also pressured the national government for assistance. While grants-in-aid did not yet fall within the domain of the federal government, Medill used his numerous contacts in Washington as he had in Springfield to obtain other means of support. In Medill's third month in office, he wrote to Vice-

President Schuyler Colfax urging the passage of a tariff rebate bill that would increase the supply of inexpensive materials needed to rebuild the city.[9] The legislation ultimately passed despite the strong opposition of organized lumber interests. Medill also coordinated the city's national relief effort, convincing President Grant to send a one thousand dollar contribution and collecting more than five million dollars in gifts and loans from individuals and cities from around the world.

At the end of his first year in office, Medill had managed to stabilize the city's fiscal affairs. He negotiated a budget with the city council that put the city "in better condition than before the Fire." [10] In his annual message to the council, Medill thanked the aldermen for their cooperation and expressed special appreciation to Tenth Ward Alderman Lester Bond, who was Chairman of the Finance Committee. He reviewed the traumatic events of the previous year and "look[ed] back to that dark and dismal time with a shudder." [11] In fact, the troubles of his regime were really only about to begin.

The second year of Medill's administration proved to be filled with turbulence as the mayor attempted to expand upon his ministerial duties. At the first meeting of the city council, Medill announced that for the first time he would exercise his power under the Mayor's Bill to select the chairmen and members of the council committees. Most of those chosen to top posts of important committees were Medill loyalists; aldermen from the immigrant wards received lesser consideration.

In the first three months of 1873, Medill vetoed five council ordinances. The vetoes included an important appropriations bill and an effort by the council to purchase a school lot that Medill believed was under the sole control of his board of education. In addition, Corporation Counsel Tuley was instructed to provide legal opinions to the council on why they did not have the authority to hire additional police officers or prevent the mayor's removal of police board members.

As the year progressed, council votes became increasingly divided. While the growing opposition was not sufficient to override the mayor's legislative initiatives, several of his personal choices were rejected for the first time. Moreover, Medill's move to shake up the police department met with effective aldermanic resistance.

By mid-1873, the mayor and council were at loggerheads over the city's licensure and appropriations powers. In a major dispute that will be discussed in detail later in this article, the council challenged the mayor's authority to revoke saloon licenses. The council also rejected Medill's proposals to cut budgetary spending. The mayor responded by using his line item appropriations veto repeatedly, and the council in turn made their first successful efforts to override most of the vetoes.

Medill had never experienced such direct challenges to his authority. He began to suffer from a variety of ailments that were related to the burgeoning conflicts over city government.[12] In August, Medill decided to take an extended European vacation. In accordance with the city charter, he informed the council that he would "be absent from the city for an unspecified length of time," requiring the aldermen to "appoint an 'Acting Mayor' to serve during my contemplated absence."[13] In a close vote taken on the same day of Medill's announcement, the council elected Lester Bond (Tenth Ward) to be the city's first acting mayor. Medill did not return to the city until 1874, and Bond completed the remainder of his term of office.

How may this dramatic turn of events be explained? First, Medill's initial successes were due in part to the traditional honeymoon period afforded most elected chief executives. The emergency circumstances under which he took office undoubtedly contributed to the postponement of opposition to his regime. This opposition increasingly crystallized as the crisis eased, allowing the underlying social conflicts in the Chicago of the 1870s to surface.

Moreover, the nature and timing of the controversies coincided with a major shift in Medill's performance of his ministerial role. In the first year of his regime, Medill was able to maintain a sense of equilibrium between the mayor's office and other governmental agencies. In the second half of his term in office, however, Medill's policies infringed upon the prerogatives of the council, the Police Board, and even the Illinois legislature. In the name of efficiency, Medill engaged in actions that were perceived to be antidemocratic.

In sum, Medill's ministerial efforts ultimately failed when he attempted to autocratically govern Chicago as if it were the Chicago *Tribune,* and he was its editor. In this light, the city council's vehement opposition to a move by the state legislature to reenact the Mayor's Bill can be understood. By a vote of 34 to 2, the Council resolved in 1874: "that we are unalterably opposed to the enactment of any law which shall continue in operation for one second beyond its lease of life that pestiferous relic of the Medillian era, the 'Mayor's Bill.'" Medill's personal inability to maintain his broad but obviously fragile electoral coalition proved fatal to his administration and eviscerated the ministerial responsibilities of Chicago mayors for years to come.

The Developer Role. Despite the brevity of Medill's term of office, his administration was able to affect profoundly the physical landscape of the city. As in the performance of his ministerial role, Medill faced significant conflicts in his efforts to rebuild Chicago after the fire. Following the precedent of three decades of mayoral leadership, Medill was pressured to support a policy of unregulated development. At the same time, his electoral promises as a "Citizens Fire-Proof" candidate and his conservative fiscal views led him to consider adopting a more cautious strategy.

In his first inaugural address, Medill responded to Democratic party leaders and special interest groups who wanted to provide relief to the homeless by immediately constructing pine buildings with paper and tar roofs. He argued that: "If we rebuild the city with this dangerous material, we have a moral certainty, at no distant day, of a recurrence of the catastrophe. . . . The outside walls of every building hereafter erected within the limits of Chicago, should be composed of materials as incombustible as brick, stone, iron, concrete or slate." [15] He recommended the immediate appointment of a special committee of the city council to draft a new building code for the city that complied with this mandate.

On 12 February 1872, the council by a vote of 26 to 6 passed an ordinance that prohibited the construction of wooden frame buildings inside the city limits. Within this regulatory limitation, Medill presided over a period of construction that was unparalleled in the city's history. During the first year after the fire, over $45 million was expended on the erection of ten thousand new buildings. By the end of Medill's mayoral term, historians commented that "a stranger visiting the city would not have imagined, from anything he could see, that any disastrous event had ever occurred." [16]

While most of the construction was for private dwellings, Medill was also concerned with public development projects. In August 1872, Medill proposed the construction of a new City Hall and County Building to be built on the site which it currently occupies. In addition, the new Chamber of Commerce building was completed and dedicated by Medill on the first anniversary of the fire. Finally, Medill's administration proposed and implemented the use of the present-day decimal system for numbering city streets (with State and Madison at the vortex.)

Nonetheless, public opposition to Medill's development initiatives quickly surfaced in various forms. As the city council debated the new fire code, a large demonstration of citizens calling for immediate construction of frame housing disrupted the meeting and resulted in its adjournment. Later, Medill was forced to use his veto power for the second time when the council voted to allow the completion of frame buildings that were already in the process of construction. Medill's veto message expressed sympathy for the builders and the homeless they sought to help, but refused to tolerate any exception to his fire regulations. When the Council later attempted to circumvent Medill's policy by passing an ordinance that permitted the limited construction of frame buildings, Medill used his veto power once again. Such disputes increased in frequency over the course of his term, although the basic provisions of the code were never successfully challenged.

A second dispute related to Medill's performance of his developer role centered on the use of the city's fiscal resources. Medill stated repeatedly that he was unwilling to rebuild the city at the expense of sound financial practices. In his first year in office, Medill moved the city from the verge of bankruptcy to a nearly balanced budget. This process did not occur without political costs.

The mayor and aldermen frequently locked horns on the expenditure of public money for neighborhood improvement projects. In February 1872, Medill vetoed an ordinance for the curbing and paving of a long stretch of city streets because it would place "an additional burden . . . upon the now over-burdened city treasury." [17] The single largest number of Medill's vetoes were explained by his interest in fiscal rationing. When he item-vetoed a porkbarrel appropriations ordinance in July 1873, the council had had enough; the aldermen rebelled with their first veto overrides.

Medill also proved to be as parsimonious in his social welfare policies as he was in his bricks-and-mortar programs. In April 1872, the mayor asked the Chicago Relief and Aid Society to return to their traditional practice of caring only for the sick, aged, and infirm. Further issues of stoves, furniture, bedding, and clothing to victims of the fire were ceased. Later in the month, hundreds of widows protested the change in policy to the mayor, but it took a city council ordinance to alter the system of providing relief. [18]

In sum, Medill's administration produced an amalgam of development programs. His regime broke with tradition by attempting to balance the conflicting pressures to spend and to save. Where trade-offs were necessary, it is clear that regulated development and fiscal conservatism were more desirable to Medill than uncontrolled economic expansion. In this respect, Medill's role as developer was more akin to a Chicago mayor of the 1980s than a nineteenth century chief executive.

Kingmaker Role. One of Medill's most difficult tasks as mayor was to select employees for public service. His role as kingmaker proved to be laden with conflicts and paradoxical choices. On the one hand, Medill was committed to the principle of merit appointment. The antispoils movement was sweeping the nation, and Medill's *Tribune* was one of its leading voices. Medill himself served as one of the first federal civil service commissioners. On the other hand, Medill as mayor had to face certain pragmatic realities. The use of partisan political criteria in government hiring was endemic to the city by the 1870s. Significant numbers of aldermen of both political parties benefitted by the use of the spoils system. As mayor, Medill was in the tempting position of being able to expand upon his own sphere of influence by exercising the new appointment powers of the Mayor's Bill.

Personally, Medill was no stranger to partisan political intrigue. He had played the role of kingmaker frequently on the national political scene. Medill was both a Lincoln partisan and benefactor. And he was part of an unsuccessful effort to have the Republican party nominate Horace Greeley instead of Ulysses S. Grant for president in 1872.

In performing his kingmaker role as mayor, Medill's ambivalence was often apparent. As a reformer, he took steps that virtually removed spoils from the Chicago Fire Department. [19] He made similar efforts with the Chicago Police Department. Medill's first formal communication to the council after his inaugural address provided for the election of police constables. He also fired the incumbent police superintendent and replaced him with a "good government"-oriented chief from outside of the city. [20] Medill's initial appointments to the new library and school boards were considered to be blue ribbon candidates whom the council approved without resistance.

As a pragmatic politician, Medill also proved to be sensitive to local political realities. He proposed no formal ordinance or program to eliminate the spoils system from the city. In fact, he generally tolerated the practice by the city's aldermen. Medill never made good on his inaugural threat that he would "dispense with" hundreds of city employees whom he believed were payroll-padders.[21]

Medill could be politically heavy-handed in his own right. He repeatedly juggled members of the police board when they differed with his policies, replacing them with political loyalists. In the second year of his term, the council rejected several of the mayor's nominees to boards and commissions on the grounds that they were more loyal to Medill than capable of holding public office.

On balance, Medill went further than any previous mayor to implement the goals of civil service reformers, while not neglecting partisan considerations in hiring public employees. Several years after his regime, he perhaps best summarized his philosophy of personnel selection by stating: "Change the heads [of departments], but let the subordinates alone, if they are expert and faithful, is the Golden Mean that should be adopted in the Civil Service and let their performance depend upon their honesty and capability."[22] In articulating and performing his role as kingmaker, Medill had once again adopted the complexities of modern day mayoral administrators.

The Broker Role

Perhaps the most challenging of Medill's mayoral roles was to mediate between the competing patrician and immigrant social classes. It also proved to be his most problematic effort. While Medill often was able to manage the demands of many specialized interest groups, he ultimately was unable to achieve peace between the city's most powerful warring factions. The struggle between Anglo-Saxon and ethnic groups was an important undercurrent in Medill's dispute with the city council, and significantly contributed to the untimely end of his regime.

To some extent Medill was a victim of urban demographic trends. As mentioned previously, his mayoral term occurred at a time when Chicago was divided almost equally between patricians and immigrants. Clearly, however, the latter were increasing at an exponential rate and becoming highly organized politically. Differences in customs between the social classes and among immigrants themselves accelerated the mounting tension.

Nonetheless, Medill managed in general to keep the conflict off of the city's governmental agenda during his first year in office. He accomplished this in a variety of ways. First, Medill used the atmosphere of crisis after the fire to pull together the traditional adversaries. He coordinated the relief effort with the assistance of all leading factions and made certain that each part of the city was receiving necessary assistance.

Second, he used his appointment power to ensure a fair representation in city government of immigrants and patricians alike. In July 1872, he selected library commissioners and members of the board of education from among leaders of the various groups, although some Irish spokesmen complained that they had been unfairly excluded.[23] He also allowed the city council, itself an ethnically heterogeneous body, to continue to sponsor city jobholders from their neighborhoods.

Third, Medill attempted to accommodate the different views and social customs of the city's residents. In this effort, the temperance issue became the most difficult and significant problem for him to manage. On the one hand, the patricians strongly supported measures to close taverns early on weekdays and to enforce the existing Sunday closing laws. On the other hand, most immigrant groups supported limited regulation of saloons. The latter included many Germans, a mainstay of Medill's Republican constituency.

For awhile, Medill successfully mediated between these factions by offering compromises and making promises to both. To appease the patricians, he fired the highly tolerant Police Superintenent W. W. Kennedy and replaced him with Elmer Washburne, a law-and-order former warden of the Joliet penitentiary. The police were ordered to crack down on public drunkenness and crime in the vicinity of saloons. Medill, a teetotaler himself, also spoke publicly of his "hatred for drunkenness."[24] At the same time, he was unwilling to support proposals to limit further the hours that taverns were open and instructed the police not to enforce the Sunday closing law. In September 1872, when petitioned by his police board to support tavern-closing initiatives, he expressed sympathy for their position but called the measures "impractical" and "discriminative." He claimed that there were not enough Chicago policemen to enforce any such law in an evenhanded manner.[25]

In sum, Medill played his role as broker effectively during the first year of his administration. However, as his term of office progressed, the demands of each side became more organized and strident, with the temperance issue becoming the focal point of their dispute. By the fall of 1872, Medill's tightrope had become almost impossible to walk.

In October, German saloonkeepers organized a mass meeting to oppose the growing demands for new restrictions on the sale of alcoholic beverages. They passed a resolution, which was submitted to the city council, calling all such efforts unconstitutional and threatened to "support only those candidates for public office [who] are known to favor our views."[26] The same month, Police Superintendent Washburne submitted a draft ordinance to the council requiring taverns to close at eleven p.m. instead of midnight. When the council tabled the ordinance, the stage was set for a battle to control the police department.

On the first anniversary of Medill's assumption of the duties of mayor, the police board suspended Superintendent Washburne for "negligence of duty, incompetency and disobedience of the orders of the Board."[27] The underlying issues in the dispute were Washburne's increase in the length of police shifts and his protemperance initiatives. Medill could no longer avoid taking action. He responded to the removal of his police chief by firing two members of the police board and replacing them with Medill and Washburne loyalists. When antitemperance aldermen challenged the mayor's authority to shake up the board without providing adequate reasons for his actions, Medill retaliated by using the Mayor's Bill to deny them key council committee posts. In March 1873, the newly constituted police board and the reinstated superintendent again proposed the passage of an eleven p.m. tavern closing ordinance. This time, the mayor lent his support to the ordinance, which was finally passed by a heavily divided council in April. On April 23, the superintendent on behalf of the mayor finally issued an order to the police to enforce the Sunday closing law.

At this juncture, there was no turning back for Medill. In May, various immigrant groups formed a People's party coalition opposed to the Medill regime. In early June, the Mayor took two actions that sealed the fate of his administration. First, following a police crackdown on taverns he revoked the licenses of ten saloonkeepers for failing to obey the Sunday closing law. When the council passed a resolution challenging his authority to take this action, Medill vetoed the measure. Second, the mayor vetoed a council ordinance that would have restored the closing times of taverns to midnight. While the aldermen from the immigrant wards did not have sufficient votes to override the vetoes, they had made it clear that the remainder of Medill's regime would be filled with acrimony and strong legislative resistance.

By August, Medill was physically and emotionally unable to complete his term and announced his decision to leave the city. Politically, he was no longer able to play the vital role of brokering disputes. The changing conditions of city life had made political decision making a "zero sum game," replacing the politics of mediation and compromise. When ultimately forced to choose, Medill had supported the patrician cause that was consistent with his background and ideological perspective. Having done so, he was personally incapable of backing down or taking steps to defuse the controversy.

While Medill recovered in Europe, Chicagoans in the next municipal election voted overwhelmingly for every candidate on the People's party ticket. Harvey D. Colvin was elected as the city's new mayor. Defeated were candidates of the Law and Order party, an offshoot of the Citizens Fire-Proof coalition. Shortly thereafter, Elmer Washburne resigned as police superintendent and the city council asserted its control over police department affairs. The city was moving into a new era of immigrant-dominated machine politics.

The Image-maker Role. In performing his various roles as mayor, Medill appreciated the importance of projecting a positive image to his constituency. He was, by training, both a journalist and a politician and was sensitive to how the public viewed his performance during his tumultuous regime. Consequently, he made a concerted effort as mayor to manage the flow of information about city affairs.

While in office, Medill remained active in the management of the *Tribune* and made certain that the coverage of his administration was favorable. Concerned about expanding his sphere of press influence as well as about the appearance of a conflict of interest, one of Medill's first actions in office was to approve the designation of the Chicago *Evening Post* as the city's official newspaper and the Chicago *Staats-Zeitung* as its foreign language newspaper of record. At various points, he arranged for stories to be published that were supportive of his candidacy for congress and even for president. Medill was also fond of providing lengthy public explanations for his actions as mayor. His inaugural address was one of the most detailed in the city's history, and he made a similar speech to the council at the end of his first year of office that enumerated his accomplishments. Almost all of the actions he took on ordinances were accompanied by mayoral messages, with his explanations for vetoes being especially detailed. These actions were reported verbatim by the three above named newspapers.

Nonetheless, Medill did not escape problems in the performance of his image-making role. As social and political conflicts began to flourish in the city in 1873, managing the press's portrayal of his regime became more difficult. Medill's city treasurer was accussed by the *Staats-Zeitung* of improperly investing city funds for personal gain. The German newspaper seized upon the alleged scandal as a means of discrediting Medill's temperance policies and later even suggested that he left office "to escape moral responsibility and public censure."[28] While these charges later proved to be unfounded, they lingered and became an important issue in the November municipal election.

Further, an enduring paradox existed between Medill as a public figure and as a private person. While Medill publicly projected the persona of a political man intent on exerting influence in all areas of public life, he was privately a very sedate and dour individual who felt uncomfortable in the presence of most people. As one historian put it: "Medill valued his time too highly to waste a second chatting with a friend. One result was that he had no close friends at all."[29] He dressed out of fashion and disdained smoking, drinking, and other social customs of the times. He seemed to be most at ease when barking orders from his editor's chair at the *Tribune*. (He had an "obsession with power,"[30] another historian concluded.)

Medill's public policies sometimes reflected his personal contradictions. He was quick to advocate war, yet lost his brother in the Civil War and complained to Lincoln that too many Chicagoans were being drafted to fight.[31] He was a leading abolitionist, yet was openly racist and stated publicly that "In future wars . . . we will not be so careful about spilling the blood of niggers."[32] As indicated earlier, his actions on patronage and temperance were often contradicted by both his public and private behavior.

In conclusion, Medill's performance of his role as image-maker was as complex as his other roles. His concern with the press's coverage of his regime distinguished him from all of his predecessors.[33] His mixture of successes and failures in managing the press is consistent with the experience of contemporary urban mayors. In these ways, Medill's term of office may be described as a watershed in the city's political history. The mayor's strong but highly enigmatic personality blended with the complicated circumstances of the times to create a multifaceted regime that contributed immeasurably to the richness of Chicago's political tradition.

The Medill Legacy

When Joseph Medill returned to Chicago in 1874, he scarcely recognized the city he had left the previous year. Some of the limitations he had imposed on the city's physical development had been lifted by the Colvin administration, and thousands of new structures of every kind had been erected. Governmentally, the balance of power had shifted from the mayor to the city council, with the aldermen from the immigrant wards wielding considerable influence. Politically, the spoils system flourished once again, even in the police department where Medill's reform efforts had been quickly undone. Chicago had become an open city in which saloons and vice flourished.

Had the Medill administration proved to be a failure? In the short run, at least, it is fair to conclude that Medill had fallen far short of his mayoral objectives. His decision to leave office before the end of his term was a tacit acknowledgment of his inability to govern the city at even the most minimally acceptable level. In the long run, however, the Medill mayoralty had a profound and lasting impact on the city. It marked the first time that a Chicago mayor had asserted a broad claim of executive authority. While the move in 1874 to reenact the Mayor's Bill was resoundingly defeated, the formal and informal powers of the office were gradually restored by the Illinois legislature and the practices of Medill's twentieth-century successors. The modern authority of the mayor's office is clearly derived from the regime of Joseph Medill.

More importantly, Medill's *use* of mayoral authority established policy-making precedents that have become a routine part of the contemporary urban agenda. Medill was the catalyst for moving the pendulum of economic growth towards a more stable position, for introducing merit appointment practices to city government, and for attempting to manage the city's social problems. Regardless of the short-term outcome of these initiatives, they raised issues that have preoccupied each of Chicago's mayors over the past century.

Medill's influence on the movement of the urban pendulum persisted well beyond his mayoral regime. In 1874, he purchased a controlling interest in the Chicago *Tribune* with a loan from businessman Marshall Field. As the newspaper's editor-in-chief for most of the remainder of the nineteenth century, Medill remained involved in local public affairs. His *Tribune* became the leading midwestern Republican journal, crusading for municipal reform and against the manifestations of machine politics and the trade union movement. The former mayor's interest in economic development led him to return briefly to public office in 1893 as a member of Chicago's World's Fair planning committee. Two years later, he witnessed the achievement of a longstanding goal when the Illinois legislature passed the state's first civil service law.

On 17 March 1899, Medill died in San Antonio, Texas, at the age of seventy-five. Before his death, Medill assured that his political perspective and family tradition would persist well into the twentieth century by turning over control of the *Tribune* to his son-in-law, Robert W. Paterson. He also spent time during his last years grooming his third grandson, Robert R. McCormick, for an eventual leadership position in the newspaper.[34] Outspoken to the end, Medill wrote a short editorial on the day before he died that McCormick took to the San Antonio telegraph office. It appeared in the *Tribune* the following morning, in the same issue that announced the news of his death.

At the first city council meeting after Medill's death, Chicago's aldermen passed the following memorial tribute to his mayoral leadership:

> As Mayor . . . he rendered conspicuous service to this municipality in its highest office. . . . The Mayor's Bill, embodying the reforms which he suggested, enabled him to give the city a systematic, efficient and successful administration. . . . Among the good things accomplished by the administration of Mayor Medill was the complete divorcement of the Fire Department from politics and a similar temporary divorcement of the Police Department therefrom[35] and the establishment of the Chicago Public Library.[36]

To be sure, the city council that expressed these sentiments was a very different one from the legislature presided over by Joseph Medill, but one that was a direct outgrowth of the political tradition that he established.

2.

CARTER H. HARRISON II: THE POLITICS OF BALANCE

Edward R. Kantowicz

For a man who served five terms as mayor of Chicago, a man whose father before him had also served five terms, one who lived on well into his nineties, and who wrote not one but two autobiographies, Carter H. Harrison II is remarkably little known or remembered in Chicago. No monuments or memorials commemorate him. (Harrison Street is named for President William Henry Harrison, a distant relative, and Harrison High School for Carter H. Harrison I.) No scholar has written his life. When I viewed his grave on a historical tour of Graceland Cemetery, the guide simply identified him as, "the mayor who closed down the whorehouses." As we shall see, whorehouses did play a large role in his career, but he deserves to be remembered for more than that.[1]

Harrison's lack of recognition is partly due to the general historical amnesia of our time. In addition, Richard J. Daley so dominated recent Chicago politics, both in fact and in myth, that any politician predating Daley has fallen into the background. Above all, though, Carter Harrison's relative obscurity is due to his style of leadership. Neither a flamboyant politico nor a crusading zealot, Harrison combined some of the qualities of both boss and reformer, thus blurring his image and making him hard to define. In short, Harrison practiced the politics of balance; he was a harmonizer and a unifier.

The politics of balance may sound boring, the stuff of safe-and-sane conservatism; but nothing could be further from the truth. In fact, maintaining a political balance in a rapidly growing, factionalized city is a highly dynamic, even daring act. The English writer G. K. Chesterton, in discussing what he called the "romance of orthodoxy," described the Catholic Church as "a huge and ragged and romantic rock, which, though it sways on its pedestal at a touch, yet, because its exaggerated excrescences exactly balance each other, is enthroned there for a thousand years."[2] The politics of balance is like that, with city hall rocking violently from one seemingly impossible point of equipoise to another. No one performed this balancing act, this juggling extravaganza, better than the Carter Harrisons, father and son.

The Age of Harrison

Chicago politics, for thirty-five years before the outbreak of World War I, may be termed the Age of Harrison.[3] The Harrisons won ten of the seventeen mayoral elections held during that period, each of them serving five terms. Yet, though a Harrison reigned as mayor more often than not, he did not control the politics and politicians of Chicago. No organization like the Tammany machine in New York, or the Daley machine later in Chicago, dominated the scene; Chicago politics was a bipartisan jungle of rival bosses and factions. The Harrisons owed their success to personal skill and charisma, not to the support of a disciplined machine. They were able to accommodate, with amazing dexterity and flexibility, the explosive growth and bewildering diversity of Chicago at the turn of the century.

Chicago's growth was astounding. When Carter Harrison I was first elected mayor in 1879, the city held nearly a half million inhabitants; but it was in many ways an overgrown village. The city's physical limits stretched from Fullerton Avenue on the north to 39th Street on the south, and west from the lakefront to Crawford (now Pulaski) Avenue; but much of the land within those boundaries still lay vacant.[4] Carter II grew up during the 1860s and '70s in a semirural atmosphere at Ashland Avenue and Jackson Boulevard, "with cows, horses, goats, chickens, [and] turkeys" in the backyard. Young Harrison remembered skating on the frozen prairies west of his home in wintertime; he and his boyhood chums could "sweep over the smooth unmarked ice to Riverside, a good ten miles distant." The elder Harrison avowed that in 1879 "there were not ten miles of paved street in the whole city over which a light vehicle could move rapidly without injury to wheel or axle."[5]

By 1915 when the younger Harrison left office, Chicago extended out nearly to its present borders and housed over 2,400,000 people. The *City Manual* published during Harrison's last mayoral year reported 1,800 miles of paved streets, 914 miles of streetcar tracks, 155 miles of elevated railway tracks, and 313,667 buildings which, the *Manual* remarked, "upon being placed side by side . . . would make one continuous line of homes extending from New York to San Francisco."[6]

Just as striking as this rapid growth was the city's startling diversity. Immigrants from every country in Europe poured into the city looking for work in its steel mills, foundries, slaughterhouses, tanneries, and rail yards. A full 77 percent of Chicago's population in 1900 were immigrants or the children of immigrants. The Germans and the Irish formed the two largest ethnic groups, but the Poles were increasing in numbers rapidly, eventually making Chicago the largest Polish city outside of Warsaw. Scandinavians, Bohemians, Lithuanians, Italians, Russian Jews, and many others added to the mix. Each of these groups clustered in highly segregated enclaves, centered around their churches or synagogues, their shops, and their ethnic fraternals.[7]

The city was fragmented along class and geographic lines as well. As streetcars and rapid transit lines stretched to the horizon, the largely native-born, Anglo-Saxon middle class moved out to the periphery, leaving the inner wards to the immigrant working-class. The customs, habits, values, and lifestyles of the Protestant middle class differed sharply from those of Catholic and Jewish immigrants. Under the influence of repeated evangelical revivals, Chicago Protestants campaigned against liquor and vice and strove to keep Sunday sacred and quiet. Catholics and Jews saw nothing immoral in beer, wine, or spirits and believed in celebrating the Lord's Day in more lively fashion.[8]

Turn-of-the-century Chicago, then, was a divided, segregated city comprising gold coast and slum, semisuburban retreat and teeming immigrant ghetto, slaughterhouses and counting houses, red lights and blue noses. In 1914, Chicago counted 1,077 churches and over 7,000 saloons.[9]

Carter Henry Harrison I was an old-fashioned city booster who wedded his fortunes to the growth of this brash, boisterous boomtown. He unblushingly called the city "his bride." The elder Harrison had been born on a Kentucky plantation on 15 February 1825. His family traced its Southern lineage back to the colonial Virginia of John Smith and Pocahontas. A Protestant but no Puritan, Harrison imbibed liberal attitudes and acquired a wide-ranging knowledge of people and languages on two extensive journeys through Europe and the Near East as a young man. Finding plantation life too slow, he took his young wife north in 1855 in search of fortune and frolic. After visiting St. Louis and Galena, the couple settled in Chicago, sold their Kentucky property, and invested the proceeds in Chicago real estate. "A buyer rather than a seller of real estate," Harrison invested for the long term; thereafter, the city's growth also meant the growth of his fortune.[10]

Drawn into political life after the great fire of 1871, Harrison served a term as county commissioner, then two terms in congress. His congressional service was distinguished mainly by a flamboyant, spread-eagle style of oratory. Returning to the city to run for mayor in 1879, he was elected to four consecutive two-year terms. He retired in 1887 and went on a sixteen month world tour. His attempt at a mayoral comeback in 1891 fell short, but in 1893 he won a final term, just in time to host the World's Fair. Admirably suited by his broad-minded attitudes and wide travels to greet visitors from all over the world, Harrison made a perfect World's Fair mayor.

Harrison cut a dramatic figure throughout his mayoral years. Readily identifiable by the black felt slouch hat he wore constantly, he crisscrossed the city's dusty streets on his white mare, often at a full gallop. He held court for the public in City Hall daily and applied himself in a businesslike fashion to the financial and administrative details of his office, restoring the city's credit by a policy of retrenchment during his first term. The city's first fulltime professional politician, he built a personal following of loyal retainers, particularly among the saloonkeeper-politicians. Holding decidedly broadminded views on gambling, liquor, and prostitution, Harrison never attempted to enforce Sunday closing ordinances or any other blue laws that the city council might pass. A rip-roaring stump speaker, able to discourse off-the-cuff for hours and utter a convincing phrase or two in nearly every European language, Harrison appealed forcefully to immigrant voters. Throughout his mayoral years, he combined the support of the business classes with the working masses, though the press, the Protestant pulpit, and the evangelical middle class usually opposed him.

During his final term, however, his optimistic Chicago boosterism united the city behind him. On Saturday, 28 October 1893, in the waning days of the fair, he greeted the mayors of cities from all over the United States with a final soaring speech:

> Genius is but audacity, and the audacity of the wild and woolly west, and of Chicago has chosen a star and has looked upward to it and known nothing that it cannot accomplish. This is a city that was a morass when I came into the world 68½ years ago. . . . What is it now? The second city of America. . . . I intend to live for more than a half century[!] and, at the end of that half century London will be trembling lest Chicago shall surpass her.[11]

That evening, at his home on Ashland Avenue, Harrison was shot to death by a disappointed office-seeker, Patrick Eugene Prendergast. One of the city's ethnic newspapers summed up perfectly the administrations of this optimistic city booster: "His career was a series of dramatic incidents enveloped in a haze of festivities."[12]

What we might call today the "Chicago-fest mentality" served Carter Harrison I admirably, but it would not suffice for his son, who faced even greater challenges and more complicated times.

Carter Henry Harrison II was born on 23 April 1860 in a house at the corner of Clark and Harrison Streets, on the first parcel of land his father bought in Chicago.[13] When only six months old his family moved to the semirural surroundings of the west side prairies, an area lightly settled by a number of Kentuckians, all engaged in land speculation. Harrison's mother never loved the city as much as his father did, so in 1873 she took young Carter and his sister and brother for an extended stay in Germany. Carter studied three years in a German *gymnasium*, returning in 1876 after his mother's death. The public school authorities in Chicago did not know how to evaluate his unorthodox educational background and temporarily refused him admittance to high school. So he enrolled at the Catholic prep school run by the Jesuit Fathers, then called St. Ignatius College, and took the equivalent of his high school and undergraduate schooling there. From 1881 to 1883 he attended his father's *alma mater*, Yale, and received a law degree.

The young Harrison of Chicago, newly emerged from Yale, resembled in many ways the young Theodore Roosevelt of New York, his close contemporary in age. Like Roosevelt, who wrote in his autobiography, "My father was the best man I ever knew," Carter Harrison idolized his wealthy, handsome father. Both young men traveled extensively in Europe, learned their French and German firsthand, and attended the best schools (Roosevelt attended Harvard). Neither really needed to work for a living, and therefore each spent a good deal of time "finding himself." Teddy headed West in the 1880s to punch cows and write history, whereas Harrison spent that decade knocking about Chicago, writing poetry, and practicing journalism under the pseudonym Cecil H. Harcourt. His poetry was of the "ode to spring" variety—"Winter's furious power is past, Sing the merry measure!"[14] Both Roosevelt and Harrison abandoned the gentlemen's callings of their birth and background for the hurlyburly of politics. Roosevelt put the matter strikingly:

> The big business men and lawyers told me that politics was low . . . that I would find them run by saloon-keepers, horsecar conductors, and the like, and not by men with whom I would come in contact outside. . . . I answered that if this were so it merely meant that the people I knew did not belong to the governing class, and that the other people did—and that I intended to be one of the governing class.[15]

Harrison's plunge into low politics came easier, for he had already met saloonkeepers and horsecar conductors in his father's house.

There were, of course, many differences between Roosevelt and Harrison. The future president was a Republican and the mayor's son a southern Democrat. Harrison lacked TR's boundless energy, his bellicose temperament, and his "ninety-pound-weakling-body-builder" mentality. In fact, Carter Harrison enjoyed a far more stable, balanced personality. Yet both men were well-bred, somewhat effete patricians, who plunged into the rough and tumble of politics in a turbulent era and gave as good as they got. Had Harrison not been caught between five political chieftains at the 1904 Democratic Convention, he might have opposed Teddy Roosevelt as Democratic presidential candidate that year, rather than the forgettable Alton B. Parker.[16]

Despite the failure of his long-nourished presidential ambitions, Carter Harrison II's background suited him perfectly for a career in Chicago politics. A Protestant by birth, educated in Germany, at Irish-Catholic St. Ignatius, and at Waspy Yale, he was nearly a balanced ticket all by himself. His wife, Edith Ogden Harrison, was a Louisiana belle of cultured, aristocratic habits who acquitted herself well in the parlors of the Potter Palmers and Marshall Fields.

She was also a Catholic and raised their two children as Catholics. Harrison felt equally at home in a poker game with party hacks or at a reception on the Gold Coast or in the Art Institute. He lacked his father's platform oratory and flamboyant style, but he was a good-looking, athletic man with a trim mustache, a handsome face, and a strong personal presence. "He was admired by men and adored by women." Like his father, he cultivated a businesslike administrative image, championed the rights of workingmen to enjoy a glass of beer on Sunday, and tossed off appeals to every immigrant nationality in the city. But when he entered politics in 1897, he also developed reform credentials which attracted some of the Anglo-Saxon middle class. Balancing and juggling Chicago's rival political factions, reaching out to diverse constituencies throughout the expanding city, Harrison served four consecutive two-year terms as mayor from 1897 to 1905 and a final four-year term from 1911 to 1915.

A Reform Boss

Carter Harrison was, in his fashion, a progressive reformer. This news would have startled some of his contemporaries, and it does not represent the consensus opinion of present-day historians. The uncertainty about his reform credentials is largely due to the wide variety of reformers and the amorphousness of turn-of-the-century progressivism. Many different kinds of reformers pursued many separate reform causes in a broad, diffuse movement of civic betterment. Harrison championed some of these reforms but not others. Furthermore, he allied his brand of reform with a motley crew of ward bosses and immigrant politicos, further blurring his image. Relying on machine-like methods to win elections but pursuing many reform goals, Harrison might best be labeled a "reform boss." [17]

The progressive movement on the urban scene encompassed three broad categories: moral reform, political reform, and what could be termed socioeconomic reform but which I prefer to call civic reform. Moral reform represented the evangelical Protestant impulse at its purest, attacking the immoderate use of liquor and attempting to repress gambling, prostitution, and all other forms of vice and crime. Political reformers fought the evils of bossism, graft, and patronage, and proposed to run city governments in a more businesslike, efficient fashion through a civil service system and a nonpartisan city council. Civic reformers attempted to use the power of government to make urban life more humane and comfortable, extending city services rapidly to keep up with urban growth. Ideally, they believed that city governments should own and operate all essential utilities ("sewer socialism" it was called), but if that was impossible, they insisted that private contractors not exploit the city but provide honest, efficient service and pay a just compensation for any profits or privileges they secured. [18]

In Chicago, each of these reform causes exploded on the scene in a sensational manner. The assassination of Carter Harrison I in 1893 by a disappointed office-seeker galvanized local civil service reformers. Just as the murder of President James Garfield under similar circumstances had led to passage of a national civil service law, so too Harrison's death prompted the Illinois legislature to prescribe the merit system for most city and state employees.[19]

Moral reform found its champion in William T. Stead, a crusading English journalist who published a sensational book, *If Christ Came to Chicago*, in 1894. Stead's expose left no doubt that the Lord would be displeased at the open vice and crime of Chicago's First Ward. "The Levee" was an unofficial title for several centers of gambling and prostitution in and around the Loop which the elder Carter Harrison had left unmolested. Stead found that the Nineteenth precinct of the First Ward, covering Dearborn Street, Custom House Place (today Federal Street), and Clark Street between Polk and Harrison, contained thirty-seven brothels, forty-six saloons, and eleven pawnshops. Two First Ward bosses, a Laurel and Hardy-like pair named "Bathhouse" John Coughlin and Michael "Hinky Dink" Kenna, presided over these dens of iniquity. Stead's revelations led to a series of mass meetings in Chicago and the founding of the Civic Federation to attack the evils of vice and crime.[20]

Economic or civic reform received its impetus from a series of sensational grafting scandals during the administration of Mayor John Hopkins, elected to fill out Carter Harrison I's unexpired term. Businessmen spread large amounts of money ("boodle" it was called) around the city council to buy lucrative street railway and utility franchises. In 1895, for instance, the council passed the Ogden gas ordinance, creating a new gas company whose major stockholders included Mayor Hopkins and his political ally, Roger Sullivan. The clear intent of this ordinance was to "sandbag" legitimate companies into buying out Ogden Gas's franchise rights. Repeated boodle ordinances prompted a movement to drive out the grafters, to insist on adequate compensation for franchise privileges, and to secure municipal ownership and operation of public utilities.[21]

These sensational events, occurring between the death of Carter Harrison I and the election of his son in 1897, defined the reform issues in Chicago for a generation—the prohibition of liquor and the repression of vice and prostitution; political honesty, the merit system, and nonpartisanship; and municipal ownership of utilities or, at least, adequate compensation paid by private business for the grant of public privileges. Carter Harrison II did not favor moral reform; he waffled a good deal on political reform, often trying to play both sides of the street; but he stood steadfast on issues of civic reform, blocking many audacious franchise grabs and introducing numerous small civic improvements.

During his first four terms, Harrison refused to join the aroused forces of moral reform. Like his father before him, he held a live-and-let-live attitude towards drinking, gambling, and the "social evil." Harrison knew that the European immigrants opposed the prohibition of liquor and that many respectable men who signed on as moral reformers at Stead's mass meetings privately patronized the Levee. He considered gambling and prostitution necessary evils which never could be suppressed. So he championed "personal liberty," the right to drink beer or liquor without undue restrictions, and pursued a policy of "segregated vice," restricting the brothels and gaming houses to a few small areas where they would be out of sight of respectable people but under police surveillance. When the downtown business district encroached too closely on the Old Levee that Stead had inspected, Mayor Harrison pressured the underworld elements to move. In 1903, they set up a new Levee between 18th and 22nd Streets along State and Dearborn, where it remained for a decade. Harrison's policy of segregated vice served him well politically. It placated middle-class sentiment for a time by keeping open vice out of respectable neighborhoods, it pleased those who indulged themselves in the fleshpots, and it earned the political loyalty of First Ward bosses Kenna and Coughlin. Until the very end of his career, the First Ward bosses furnished Harrison's most dependable political support, marching thousands of flophouse residents to the polls at every election to vote for the mayor and the candidates he supported.[22]

Despite his father's shocking murder by a spoilsman, Harrison never adopted a consistent position on civil service. He recognized the value of the merit system for municipal administration but did not wish to apply it until he had cleared out holdover Republican officeholders. So in his first term of office, his corporation counsel found numerous loopholes in the law, and Harrison took the opportunity to reward loyal Democrats. Later in his tenure, he spoke more favorably of the merit system, even going so far as to publicly apologize to two Republican civil service commissioners he had removed. On other political reform issues, he proved more straightforward. The Civic Federation had spun off another reform organization in 1896, the Municipal Voters' League (MVL), which worked for the election of honest aldermen on a nonpartisan basis. An honest politician himself, Mayor Harrison encouraged the MVL and worked hard to form an honest, unbought majority in the city council. In 1902, he caucused with the president of the MVL and representatives of both political parties to appoint city council committees on a nonpartisan basis. Harrison also championed other political reforms, such as home rule for municipalities, direct primaries, and referendum votes on public policy questions. Ever the juggler, he tried to satisfy political reformers whenever he could but still reserve the power to reward his friends.[23]

Harrison's progressivism stood out most clearly on the complex of social and economic issues I have termed civic reform. The mayor highlighted the essential point of civic reform in his 1905 annual message: "From the very beginning I determined that during my service as mayor no private use of public property should be allowed without requiring just and adequate compensation to the community for the privilege." If anyone wanted a favor from the city, whether it was permission to hang an awning over the sidewalk or to rip up the streets to lay streetcar tracks, the individual or corporation should not have to bribe aldermen but rather should pay a just and equitable fee into the city treasury. In pursuit of this principle, Harrison vetoed numerous utility franchises bought with boodle. Only one of his vetoes was ever overridden, the notorious Commonwealth Electric ordinance of 1897, which created a dummy company that promptly sold out to the Edison Company. But in 1900, when Messrs. Hopkins and Sullivan tried to duplicate this success with an ordinance permitting Ogden Gas to sell its franchise to other companies, Harrison made his veto stick. The Sullivan crowd had to wait until 1906, when Harrison was out of office, to cash in Ogden Gas.[24]

Besides this negative type of civil reform (stopping boodlers), Harrison introduced small, unspectacular, but useful improvements in the city's environment. One of the most important was railroad track elevation. As the nation's transportation hub, Chicago was crisscrossed by railroad tracks, all of which crossed the city's streets at grade level and exacted a frightful toll on human life due to frequent collisions. In 1892, before Harrison took office, the city began pressing railroad companies to elevate their tracks on embankments and eliminate grade crossings, but only a few miles of track were elevated in the next five years. At Harrison's urging in 1897, the city council appointed a special committee on track elevation, with a fulltime engineering expert, John O'Neill, to expedite the work. In Harrison's first six years, 286 grade crossings were eliminated and fifty-five miles of mainline track were elevated. In accord with the politics of balance, track elevation served several purposes. It not only ended the carnage in the neighborhoods through which railroads ran, it provided an estimated 115,000 jobs, all at no cost to the city.[25]

Harrison often needed someone else to pay for his civic improvements, for the state and county governments—usually controlled by Republicans—kept Chicago's finances on a short leash. Harrison's comptroller found that the city's area had increased 420 percent between 1888 and 1900 and its population 110 percent but that its tax revenue had increased only 35 percent. Harrison employed numerous stratagems to stretch these slender resources. In 1900, he declared that the outmoded center pier bridges in the Chicago River were obstacles to the free flow of water which the Sanitary District was legally mandated to maintain, so the Sanitary District should pay to replace them with modern bascule bridges. In 1899, he appointed a Small Parks Commission to open playgrounds in crowded immigrant slums. Lacking firm legal authority or adequate funding, the commission appealed to private philanthropists to donate vacant lots for parks. To provide wintertime play opportunities, Mayor Harrison, recalling his childhood skating on the open Chicago prairie, offered a free permit and free city water to any landowner who would flood his property for a skating rink. Sixty such rinks opened in the winter of 1900.[26]

Harrison squeezed out a tiny appropriation to open a Municipal Reference

Library and establish a Bureau of Statistics. Progressive reformers believed in gathering and broadcasting comparative urban statistics as a means of improving city government and building up a civic spirit. Harrison's Bureau of Statistics published an annual *City Manual* which combined encyclopedic statistics with stories of Chicago's growth and progress. The *City Manual* provided a more sophisticated, updated variety of urban boosterism than the elder Harrison's rip-roaring speeches. Harrison's successor gutted the Bureau of Statistics and cancelled the *City Manual*, but the Municipal Reference Library survived.[27]

The Traction Wars

Above all else, Carter Harrison II earned his reputation as a reformer by his firm and successful stand in Chicago's traction controversies. ("Traction" was the standard phrase used to describe electric streetcar companies. The name derives from the traction method of powering cable cars. Though cable cars were swiftly replaced by overhead electric trolleys in the 1890s, the name stuck.) The traction issue was a long and complex wrangle which kept Chicago politics in turmoil for decades. The first street railway franchises, permitting private companies to use the public streets and carry passengers at a profit, were granted by the Chicago City Council in 1858 for a period of twenty-five years. Then in 1865 a corrupt state legislature passed the infamous ninety-nine year act over the governor's veto, extending the corporate rights of streetcar companies to a total length of ninety-nine years. Widespread doubt about the constitutional validity of this act, however, kept a cloud of uncertainty hanging over the companies' traction rights. In 1883, when the original franchises expired, Harrison I worked out a compromise which simply extended the companies' rights for another twenty years but deferred settlement of the ninety-nine-year question. This bequeathed the whole problem to the next generation, led, as it turned out, by his son.[27]

In the meantime, however, streetcar lines and elevated roads had expanded to all corners of the city; and a new actor appeared on the scene in the person of traction magnate Charles Tyson Yerkes. The very prototype of a robber baron, the model for Theodore Dreiser's novel *The Titan*, Yerkes came to Chicago from Philadelphia in 1881 and began buying up streetcar lines in 1886. He planned to unify all the lines in the city into one grand system and enrich himself enormously in the process. He succeeded admirably in the second aim, amassing a fortune estimated at $29 million in 1896, but numerous obstacles slowed his unification schemes.[28]

By 1896, Yerkes controlled the streetcar lines of the west and north sides and he decided to settle the extent of their privileges with one grand ordinance of the state legislature. Senator John Humphrey, an obscure legislator from rural parts of Cook County and evidently a Yerkes stooge, introduced a series of bills early in 1897 extending Yerkes's franchises for fifty years and granting minimal compensation to the city. Yerkes's efforts to ram the Humphrey bills through the legislature with a liberal application of boodle blew up in his face due to the reform ferment which had been brewing in the mid-90s.

The thirty-six-year-old Carter Harrison, newly elected primarily on the strength of his father's name, jumped into the Humphrey Bill controversy and made the traction issue peculiarly his own. He raced to Springfield in the company of reform aldermen and helped lobby enough votes to defeat the Humphrey Bill. Yerkes then changed tactics and had another rural stooge, Representative Charles Allen of Vermilion County, introduce a bill which authorized city councils to grant fifty-year franchises. The Allen Bill passed, so the struggle shifted to the Chicago City Council.

Yerkes let the situation cool awhile, going off to Europe for eighteen months, but on 5 December 1898 he had a fifty-year franchise extension introduced in council. Mayor Harrison called on the citizenry to surround City Hall at the next council meeting and publicly vowed, "If Yerkes can pass an ordinance over my veto I'll eat my old brown fedora." At the December 19 council meeting, Harrison killed the fifty-year franchise without a veto. Employing a parliamentary stratagem, he buried the ordinance in a friendly committee, winning the roll call by a single vote. Harrison's live-and-let-live policy on the vice issue had already paid dividends, for "Bathhouse" John and "Hinky Dink" Kenna, the Lords of the Levee, voted with Harrison against Yerkes. They decided to avoid Yerkes's big boodle and stick to their protected vice rackets. Harrison helped win a major civic victory by abandoning moral reform.[29]

It may be objected that Harrison exercised no real leadership during the Yerkes fight but merely followed the wave of public opinion in opportunistic fashion. There's no doubt he hoped to capitalize politically on the issue, but had his motivation been totally cynical, he wouldn't have taken so strong and visible a stand. He not only opposed the fifty-year franchise extension, he vowed to fight any franchise extension, no matter how favorable the terms appeared, until the legislature repealed the Allen Law. His stubbornness paid off; it was repealed in 1899.[30]

Yerkes left the city permanently after his Allen Law defeat, but the traction issue did not go away. The major streetcar franchises all would expire in 1903 and the companies were sure to assert their ninety-nine-year rights under the old 1865 law. Most reform organizations favored a swift and early settlement with the several streetcar companies while Yerkes's memory was fresh in the public mind and the companies were on the defensive. Had Harrison been a mere opportunist, he would have followed this line of least resistance. Instead, he dug in his heels and delayed a final settlement of the traction controversy.

For the rest of his first four terms, Harrison pursued a firm and consistent traction policy, but it was a complex policy not easy to communicate to the public. He expressed it most clearly in a special message to the city council on

6 January 1902. He highlighted five essential conditions which the public interest demanded in any traction settlement: a definite and marked improvement in the speed, comfort, and safety of streetcar service; adequate compensation to the public for franchise rights; an unequivocal legal waiver of any supposed ninety-nine-year rights; provision for the city to purchase and operate the streetcar lines at some future date; and the referral of any final settlement to a referendum for popular approval. Harrison did not believe the city had enough money or expertise to buy out the traction companies immediately and proceed to a municipally owned and operated transportation system; but he wanted to be sure the city possessed the legal authority to do so at a future date. Therefore, he stalled any franchise extension until the state legislature granted Chicago this authority. He pointed out shrewdly, "It is easier to stop than to pass legislation. Give the companies what they want and they will successfully block Chicago's attempt to get what the citizens want." Finally, in 1903, the legislature passed the Mueller Law, authorizing any city in the state to own and operate street railways.[31]

Harrison was now ready to settle the traction question; but the companies asserted their ninety-nine-year rights, as expected, and litigation dragged on until 1907 when the Illinois Supreme Court finally overruled the ninety-nine-year franchise act. In the meantime, public dissatisfaction built up against Harrison's delaying policy, a widespread movement for immediate municipal ownership sprang up, and Harrison decided to retire in 1905. Judge Edward F. Dunne, another reform Democrat, was elected on a platform of immediate municipal ownership. Dunne, however, failed to leap through all the financial and legal hoops of municipal ownership, and the city council finally negotiated franchise extension ordinances with the existing streetcar companies in 1907.[32]

The "Settlement Ordinances" of 1907 vindicated Carter Harrison's traction policy. They embodied his politics of balance by striking a compromise, with something for everyone. The streetcar companies agreed to rehabilitate and upgrade their rickety cars under the direction of a Board of Supervising Engineers, thus providing tangible benefits to the riding public. Municipal ownership advocates were placated with a clear option for the city to purchase the lines at any time. The companies were guaranteed a 5 percent return on capital, but all profits over and above that amount were split 55 percent to the city and 45 percent to the companies. Finally, in accord with Harrison's long-standing policy, the ordinances required popular approval, which was granted at a referendum in April 1907. The long traction controversy was finally settled, largely on the terms Harrison had held out for. The settlement, of course, was far from perfect. It did not deal with the elevated lines or with the possibility of digging a subway, and eventually it was outmoded by the rapid rise in automobile use and the resulting drop in transit ridership. Yet the traction settlement did provide improved transit service and adequate compensation to the city for at least ten years after its passage.[33]

Harrison's firm stand against Yerkes in the traction war and his honest, if sometimes inconsistent, cooperation with political reformers of the Municipal Voters' League earned the mayor some often grudging but significant backing from business and middle-class reform groups. In the midst of the Allen Law uproar, a Chicago newspaper summed up his reform appeal: "We may thank our stars for the presence in the mayor's office of an honest man with a club."[34] In addition, his cosmopolitan background and liberal views on personal liberty earned him consistent immigrant support. The Poles of Chicago, for instance, gave 73 percent of their votes to Harrison in his first four elections.[35] Finally, Harrison's unholy alliance with "Hinky Dink" and "Bathhouse" delivered a dependable, controlled vote of flophouse denizens which often made the difference in close elections. The Harrison coalition, then, embraced the immigrant nationalities, the Skid Row wards, and many thousand middle-class independents and Republicans. The only groups in the city that he spurned were the big boodlers—Yerkes, Roger Sullivan, and the Ogden Gas crowd—and the moral reformers. Eventually, these two groups brought him down.

Harrison Loses His Balance

Harrison's balance had begun to totter toward the end of his first four terms. His complex traction policy frustrated the more ardent reformers, and a vocal movement for immediate municipal ownership swept Judge Dunne into office. Harrison had a valid personal reason for withdrawal—he needed to move his son to California for his health—but he probably could not have won reelection had he stayed in town. He returned briefly in 1907 but could not secure the party nomination. Then in 1911 the city scheduled its first direct mayoral primary, and Harrison won an extremely narrow victory over exmayor Dunne and Roger Sullivan protégé, Andrew Graham. The faithful First Ward bosses produced Harrison's 2,000 vote margin in the primary.

The progressive movement in Chicago rose to a crescendo in the mayoral election of 1911. Much had happened while Harrison was away. Daniel Burnham had issued his bold Chicago Plan of civic betterment in 1909, with its striking vistas of broad boulevards, green parks, and sparkling lakefront facilities. A University of Chicago professor, Charles E. Merriam, serving his first term as a reform alderman, had headed a 1909 inquiry into municipal finances which unearthed multiple scandals. In 1910, a growing agitation against the segregated vice district led Republican Mayor Fred Busse to appoint a vice commission, chaired by Episcopalian Dean Charles T. Sumner, to investigate conditions in the Levee. Then at the end of 1910, alderman-professor Merriam had announced his candidacy for mayor and had swept to a surprising victory in the Republican primary.

Harrison's campaign against Merriam in the 1911 mayoral election was a model of successful progressive politics in a diverse, divided, polyglot city.[36]

28

He got on the reform bandwagon right away, adopting Burnham's visions as his own, but he carefully avoided the dynamite threatening to go off in the vice commission and thus cemented his normal First Ward alliances. To keep the immigrant vote, he branded Merriam as a prohibitionist, fronting for blue-nosed, silk-stocking bigots in Hyde Park. Above all, he learned from his own experience and kept his reform appeals simple and concrete—"We plan to wage this fight on the theory that public utility corporations should be our servants instead of our masters. I believe the gas company can sell its product at not more than 70 cents for 1000 cubic feet." Seventy-cent gas gave Harrison a specific, easily understood issue he could sell in every ward of the city, to immigrant and Wasp alike. Whenever possible, he portrayed himself as an experienced, pragmatic reformer and Merriam as a bookish, impractical professor. Harrison won a narrow victory; but it proved to be his "last hurrah" as his carefully balanced coalition fell apart during his final term.

Just after the election the vice commission dynamite exploded. The lords and ladies of the Levee had overplayed their hands by too openly flaunting their illegal activities. Bathhouse John's outrageous First Ward Balls and the elegant debauchery of the Everleigh Club brothel had earned Chicago a nationwide reputation for sin and decadence. Dean Sumner's vice commission produced a hard-hitting expose of the "social evil" in all its aspects, counting over 1,000 brothels, 1,800 pimps and madames, and at least 4,000 prostitutes in the Levee, raking in an annual revenue of $60,000,000. The commission called for an end to protected vice and a policy of total repression. Mayor Harrison stalled for time, hoping to retain his First Ward allies by letting the public clamor cool down. In October 1912, he took the highly visible and symbolic action of closing the Everleigh Club but proceeded no further. Then the following year, a lame-duck Republican states attorney, John E. Wayman, forced his hand by sending his own agents to close down the remaining brothels in the Levee. Belatedly, Harrison sent in city police to join the crackdown. Once launched on the new policy of repression, Harrison went all the way. He fired his police chief, reorganized the department, and sent the police crashing into the Levee for a final series of raids in 1914. Hinky Dink and Bathhouse, who had long furnished Harrison his staunchest support, abandoned the Mayor and joined Roger Sullivan's wing of the party.[37] Harrison and Sullivan were archenemies. Notorious for his boodle ordinances in the city council, Roger Sullivan was a businessman-politician who had become a rich man selling the Ogden Gas franchise to Peoples Gas in 1906 for six million dollars. Yet Sullivan was also a shrewd and skillful politician who quietly forged many bosses and factions together into the nucleus of a Democratic machine. Only the personal popularity of Harrison and Sullivan's own noxious reputation prevented him from dominating the Democratic party in Chicago.

By the second decade of the century, however, so much had happened in Chicago that Sullivan's gas ring reputation had begun to fade, and he had nearly convinced the voters that he was a statesman. Sullivan wanted badly to end his career in the U.S. Senate, and he devoted all his energies to obtaining the senate nomination in 1914. Had Harrison retained his usual sure-footed balance, he might have made a deal with Sullivan, and the machine leader's forces would easily have compensated for the loss of the First Ward bosses. Washington was far away and it might not have cost Harrison too much to support Sullivan's senate bid. But Harrison's hatred for Sullivan had become a vendetta; his opposition to civic boodlers was absolute. So he desperately, and unsuccessfully, tried to block Sullivan's nomination. It came as small comfort that Sullivan lost the general election to a Republican.[38]

By the end of his four-year mayoral term, Carter Harrison was physically worn down, frustrated, and politically isolated. His uncharacteristic foray into moral reform had alienated his First Ward allies but had earned him no new adherents, for the crusading ministers didn't vote in Democratic primaries and didn't trust Harrison anyway. Roger Sullivan had gathered together anyone dissatisfied with Harrison and was ready to unseat the mayor in 1915 with a loyal lieutenant, Robert A. Sweitzer. Sweitzer, a Catholic of mixed Irish and German parentage, even cut into Harrison's immigrant support and handily defeated the mayor in the 1915 primary. Harrison exited bitterly. Years later, he wrote, "I had the sentiment but Sweitzer had the sediment."[39] Roger Sullivan and his allies were better at winning nominations than elections; Sweitzer went down to defeat in the 1915 mayoral election at the hands of Republican William Hale "Big Bill" Thompson.

A Civic Patriot

The multiple administrations of Carter Harrison II are surrounded by paradoxes and might-have-beens. Harrison was a realist, willing to take the world as it was and tolerate many sordid realities. He never entertained illusions about his unsavory political allies. Harrison once asked Hinky Dink about his flamboyant partner, "Tell me, Mike, do you think John is crazy or just full of dope?" Kenna replied, "To tell you th' God's truth, Mr. Mayor, they ain't found a name for it yet."[40] Nor did the five-time mayor repent his tolerant views on vice. Late in life, he often remarked, "Is Chicago . . . more moral or a better place to live in today than was the Chicago of 1893? Under pressure in 1914 I closed the red light district. . . . My action did not end the evil, it merely scattered it . . . and brought it close to the homes."[41] His two autobiographies present a somewhat world-weary, I've-seen-everything-in-my-day self-image.

Yet he had an idealistic side as well. He loved Chicago—glorying in the title of "Chicago's first native-born mayor"—and enjoyed city life—sharing the dream of fellow-progressives Frederic Howe and Tom Johnson for a kind of civic renaissance. Harrison's 1902 traction message expressed his progressive civic vision:

I admit today with many others that municipal operation [of the transit lines] under present conditions would not today be desirable. But he who fails to see it will be desirable even before the time limit of the franchise extension . . . expires is not keeping abreast with the times. The improvement in the personnel of your own Honorable Body [the city council, reformed by the MVL] so marked in the past few years, shows the tendency of the times. . . . Why should we on the threshhold of the new century bind ourselves with the same shackles with which our fathers bound themselves. . . .[42]

To read Carter Harrison's mayoral messages and the pages of the *City Manual* he inspired is to imbibe the optimism of a new century, of a generation that believed the city was "the hope of democracy."[43]

Had all five of his terms been of four-year duration, relieving him of the continual reelection burden; had he more consistently opposed the spoils system and improved the quality of civic administration more than he did; had the automobile not wrecked his dream of comfortable, efficient public transit; had the Levee denizens not flaunted their activities quite so extravagantly and brought about his downfall, perhaps the civic renaissance might have come about. Instead, Chicago wound up with Big Bill Thompson, Al Capone, the refurbished Roger Sullivan Democratic machine, and an international reputation for crime and corruption.

The most frequent criticism of Carter Harrison, both in his own time and by later historians, was his failure to lead the city vigorously enough. Historians use such phrases as "lackadaisical," "easygoing," "slipshod" in describing him.[44] During his final term, the public became impatient for more visible signs of action in implementing the Burnham plan, just as earlier they had chafed at his policy of delay on the traction issue. The mayor defended himself against these charges in his final message to the city:

Captious criticism has been directed at the supposed failure of this administration to do things. There are two ways of doing things. Things may be done slowly but right. Things may be done in a hurry . . . and a generation be caused to suffer because of what has been done. If a great work is to be done right, more time will be required for the planning than in actual construction.[45]

Chicago suffered no lack of leaders early in this century. Indeed, the city was bursting with energy. Daniel Burnham, Jane Addams, Walter Fisher of the MVL, and many others were all "making no little plans" for Chicago. What the city government required was a balancer, a harmonizer, a unifier, someone to focus all this energy and keep it from exploding. Carter Harrison succeeded in this task until his fifth and final term.

A more valid criticism concerns Harrison's failure to perpetuate or institutionalize his civic vision. Political control and civic policy can be perpetuated in only two ways, by building a political machine or by entrenching a professional civil service bureaucracy. Harrison did neither, so his politics of balance proved impermanent. He had no real successor. His legacy, therefore, was a memory of civic patriotism and city unity.

The *City Manual* for 1913 captured the spirit of Harrison's tenure in office:

> It was local patriotism, civic pride, that moved Saint Paul on a forever memorable occasion to exclaim, "I am a citizen of no mean city. . . ." Should every intelligent inhabitant of Chicago adopt these his noble words as his own, the resulting increase of pride in the city would be prodigiously great.[46]

And Harrison himself provided his best epitaph: "I have always been a little in advance of public opinion in Chicago. It is true I have not been so far ahead the people could not see me."[47]

3.

EDWARD F. DUNNE: THE LIMITS OF MUNICIPAL REFORM

John D. Buenker

For two tumultuous years between April 1905 and April 1907, Chicago was widely regarded as "the most radical city in America," one presided over by a "socialist" mayor who loaded his administration with "long-haired friends and short-haired women." The chief executive who evoked such furor was a fifty-two-year-old, former Cook County circuit court judge with no previous executive experience, a devout Catholic and devoted family man whose announced intention was to be remembered as the father of thirteen children and municipal ownership of the transit system. Although Edward F. Dunne's crusade for "immediate municipal ownership" failed for a complex of reasons, many of his own making, it did help force a resolution of the issue that had dominated Chicago politics for over a decade, leaving the city with a greatly improved transit system.[1]

In a broader view, the Dunne administration tried, with some success, to make government responsive to the concerns of several hitherto under-represented constituencies, such as organized labor, consumer groups, social workers, teachers, and intellectuals, and to promote the welfare of the middle and working classes in the areas of utility regulation, tax equity, education, and environmental protection. By the same token, Dunne forged a political coalition that, for a time at least, combined elements of the "old politics"—parochial, partisan, nonideological, and ethnocultural—with those of the "new"—issue-oriented, nonpartisan, candidate-centered, and reliant upon mass communications. Most importantly, his failure to achieve municipal ownership and to gain reelection clearly delineated the limits of reform politics in a city that was so fragmented, on the one hand, and so dominated by the business ethic, on the other.

Charges of radicalism or socialism notwithstanding, Dunne was squarely in the mainstream of municipal reform, usually dubbed "social reform" or "urban liberalism," that stressed sharing political power with the lower social orders, support for organized labor, toleration of ethnocultural differences and human weakness, and the expansion of urban services at costs affordable to all city dwellers. Although not as nationally renowned as Tom Johnson of Cleveland, Hazen Pingree of Detroit, Samuel "Golden Rule" Jones or Brand Whitlock of Toledo, or Mark Fagan of Jersey City, Dunne corresponded regularly with these luminaries, shared speech platforms with them, and contributed articles to the same "progressive" journals. He was a prominent member of several prestigious, municipal reform organizations and was a frequent speaker in major cities, especially on the topic of municipal ownership of utilities. From 1913 to 1917, he earned national recognition for his advocacy of numerous progressive measures as governor of Illinois, the only Chicago mayor to achieve that office.

The sources of Dunne's urban liberalism are complex but relatively easy to identify. His Irish-American identity, continuously reinforced by his leadership role in Irish causes and organizations, gave Dunne a lifelong empathy with the disadvantaged and the oppressed. Equally important was his belief in "Catholic social liberalism," a world view founded on a corporatist conception of society that stressed the interdependence of social classes, the responsibility of the more fortunate for the less, moderation in the acquisition and use of all earthly goods, a fair price, a just wage, and prohibition against usury. His Irish Catholic identity not only informed Dunne's judicial decisions and political utterances but also constituted an emotional and rhetorical link to the ethnocultural groups who were his staunchest supporters. In a vital sense, Dunne was Chicago's first "co-ethnic" mayor, the first to be "of" one of the city's substantial minorities and to serve as a conduit between his compatriots and mainstream institutions.

Dunne's ethnocultural orientation was reinforced and broadened by his legal education and by his fourteen years as a Chicago attorney and thirteen years on the circuit court bench. As a jurist he enjoyed a national reputation as a "people's judge," a defender of the underdog, and a foe of those who misused wealth and power. His outlook was further developed through his continuous association with almost every progressive cause of the day with a virtual "who's who" of Chicago social critics, independent radicals, activist intellectuals, settlement house workers, and labor leaders. Finally, it was given political structure by his leadership role in the most liberal wing of the Democratic party, that committed to William Jennings Bryan and Illinois Governor John Peter Altgeld.[2]

The rise and fall of Dunne as mayor was inextricably intertwined with the fortunes of municipal ownership (MO) of the transit system, a struggle that contemporary political scientist John Fairlie observed rivaled "in duration and intensity the Trojan War."[3] Dunne's blending of advanced Catholic social thought and populist Democracy convinced him that "the people were the ultimate repository of wisdom and goodness and that the public weal has to be constantly guarded against the machinations of predatory private interests." The granting of long-term franchises to "traction buccaneers," he charged, was to give them control over "the streets which belong to the people of Chicago." Summing up the case against privatism, Dunne accused the transit company owners of "corruption of public officials, the stealing of private property, favoritism in the selection of employees, strikes, inefficient service, exhorbitant charges, and insolence toward and defiance of the public."[4]

Dunne's conviction that municipal ownership (MO) could eliminate these evils was based upon a comparison of Chicago with MO cities that he derived from his 1900 tour of Europe and from data contained in expert studies. Dunne cited reams of statistics in support of the contention that European cities with MO provided superior service at significantly lower rates and with little of the corruption or labor strife that characterized the granting of franchises to privately owned utilities. Although his data seemed overwhelmingly persuasive to many, critics replied that they were misleading because European cities were generally more spatially compact, had long traditions of public responsibility, and enjoyed a measure of home rule denied to American cities. Nonetheless, Dunne indicted the Chicago system for its high costs, dirty cars, congestion, and lack of seating room for the average straphanger.[5]

Dunne also contended that "the wages paid by publicly owned companies are always higher than those paid by private companies," thus minimizing labor strife and strikes. Because he believed that a goodly portion of the fare went to pay inordinately high profits on watered stock, Dunne argued that it would actually be possible to raise wages while lowering fares. With no franchises to grant in exchange for graft, he insisted, the major source of municipal corruption would be virtually eliminated. To the charge that MO would create a bonanza of patronage jobs, he replied that while the privately owned gas and transit utilities were manned largely by political appointees, the municipally owned water utility was run almost entirely by civil service appointees. Although Dunne's MO speeches and writings used the transit system as a point of departure, the evidence and examples were usually selected from the entire range of public utilities, making it clear that he favored universal municipalization.[6]

As public frustration with the traction stalemate increased, Dunne gained in popularity and stature by advocating what seemed to many to be a workable plan to achieve immediate municipal ownership. Brushing aside technicalities and complexities, he boldly asserted that the Mueller Law "empowers the city which desires to own and operate public utilities to condemn the property and franchises of existing companies and, under the eminent domain act, hail them to court and compel them to surrender their property at fair cash value to the people." Dunne insisted that the city should immediately cease all negotiations with the companies and grant them only short-term three month extensions upon their current franchises. Once the voters approved application of the

Mueller Law to Chicago, he continued, the city should fix a fair market value for the companies' property and franchises and raise the necessary purchase price operating revenue, and funds for rehabilitation through the issuance of street car certificates.[7]

Publicly, at least, Dunne made no concession to the argument that the certificates might well be invalidated by the courts on the grounds that the legislature had no authority to exempt them from the constitutional limitation on the city's indebtedness. To those who contended that investors would not purchase certificates of such questionable validity, he replied that previous investors had purchased badly inflated transit company stock primarily because of the value added by the possession of twenty year franchises. Would not investors place at least equal value on franchises possessed by the city in perpetuity, he asked, especially if the municipality pledged itself to retain the five cent fare until the certificates were paid off at interest? In addition, they could earn five percent interest as opposed to the three percent paid by banks on savings deposits. Within ten years, Dunne concluded streetcar certificates would be paid in full, and the people would own the system.[8]

Dunne's emergence coincided with a sharp decline in the political fortunes of Carter Harrison. Harrison's renomination chances were severely imperiled by organized labor's endorsement of immediate municipal ownership (IMO) to which Harrison was cool and by the bitter factional fights that marred the Democratics county, state, and national conventions in 1904. The combination of Harrison's challenge to Hearst's presidential candidacy in 1904 and his seeming vacillation on MO cost the mayor the publisher's support. Withdrawing as a candidate for reelection, Harrison persuaded the council to submit the tentative ordinances, which Dunne condemned vehemently, to a referendum at the upcoming mayoral elections.[9]

Dunne, who proclaimed his mayoral candidacy in January 1905, was an outspoken leader for immediate municipal ownership. In 1903, he moved his large family back into the city from River Forest. On 26 June 1904, at a picnic of Democratic faithful, Dunne blasted Harrison for betraying the party's pledge to MO. In December, Dunne denied rumors that he planned to run as an independent, stating that he was a lifelong Democrat. About the same time, former Judge William Prentice of the Chicago Federation of Labor threatened to run as an independent MO candidate unless Dunne secured the Democratic nomination. In an open letter to the people of Chicago on 15 January, Murray Tuley, a distinguished jurist and Dunne mentor, styled MO as a struggle for control of the city's streets between Wall Street and the people and averred that the only hope of victory was for the Democrats to nominate a mayoral candidate "who would inspire confidence throughout the city in his determination and ability to carry out the municipal ownership policy for which he would stand." Tuley opined that any possible Republican candidate would be too committed to privatism to fill the bill and that an independent candidate would have little hope of success.[10]

Just eight days later, Dunne announced that Tuley's letter had led to delegations from thirty-three of the city's thirty-five wards urging him to run for mayor and that he was willing to accept the nomination as a public duty. Explaining that he would not resign his judicial seat until he began campaigning, Dunne pledged that he would accept no corporate contributions, even if "it may be that the campaign will have to be conducted from the street corners." Although the Harrison-controlled, Democratic Central Committee refused to endorse anyone, Dunne had the enthusiastic backing of Bryan-Altgeld and Hearst Democrats and organized labor and at least encountered no overt opposition from the Sullivan-Hopkins faction or from such powerful ward bosses as Mike Kenna, John Coughlin, Johnny Powers, John Brennan, Stanley Kunz, and Ed Cullerton. Most bosses were motivated either by a desire to punish Harrison for his cooperation with a good government crusader or by a recognition that Dunne was a likely "winner." Their attitude was probably best summarized in a statement that a *Chronicle* reporter attributed to City Sealer James Quinn in late February 1905: "I care nothing for municipal ownership. I'm for Judge Dunne. I have a good job in city hall and I'd be a fool to oppose him. Another reason I'm for him, I'm for an open town, I want to see North Clark Street like it was in the old days." In his acceptance speech, the candidate insisted that he agreed to run "chiefly . . . for putting into actual operation the principle of municipal ownership and operation of the streetcars of Chicago." [11]

In an apparent effort to blunt the appeal of Dunne and IMO, the Republicans nominated John M. Harlan, the maverick who had run on an MO platform in 1897. Since then Harlan had moderated his position significantly, first supporting the tentative ordinances and then hedging on MO saying "when the city shall be legally and financially able successfully to adopt it." Although some reformers campaigned for Harlan, many of his 1897 supporters switched openly to Dunne, including Clarence Darrow, Louis Post, Jane Addams, and Donald Richberg. The Non Partisan Harlan Club, organized by Harold Ickes, Raymond Robbins, Graham Taylor, and William Kent, supported Harlan because of his demands for a new city charter and in protest against Dunne's alliance with the Democratic ward bosses. Significantly, Harlan's major support came from sources that had previously opposed him—the business and financial community, the regular Republican organization, and the GOP press—or from such good government groups as the Municipal Voters League (MVL) and the Civic Federation that opposed IMO. [12]

Despite his inexperience in the rough and tumble of electoral politics, Dunne's campaign was an ingenious blending of traditional ethnocultural, partisan, pragmatic, ward-based politics with ideological appeals to independent voters through the press and political action committees. In a speech to Democratic ward leaders on 10 March, Dunne praised them as the officers of "the Democratic army of Chicago, 175,000 strong" and as practical men who knew their duties far better than he did. Because their party was committed to municipal ownership, however, Dunne insisted, it had been elevated to a higher plane, one where there could be no Dunne, Hopkins, Harrison, Sullivan, or Hearst men, "but only municipal ownership Democratics." At the same time, he emphasized the need to reach the fifty thousand independent voters "that will side with the party that is in the right" and who held the balance of power. He admonished party leaders to "go out and get the stragglers . . . and get their votes." [13]

To mobilize the party faithful, Dunne held Democratic rallies in every ward and made partisan and ethnocultural appeals. Even though several ward bosses were running for reelection, Dunne generally refrained from endorsing or opposing them unless they took a forthright position on IMO. In the Nineteenth Ward, where John Powers was a vocal critic of the policy, Dunne supported independent Democrat Simon O'Donnell, who was committed to IMO, but refrained from attacking Powers himself. In the end, the Nineteenth was Dunne's best ward, giving him better than a 3,900 vote plurality, while Powers edged out O'Donnell by just over 400 votes. In the First Ward, where Hinky Dink Kenna urged his supporters to vote for the judge because he was going to give the streetcars to the people, Dunne responded with an effusive endorsement of one of the most notorious Gray Wolves. The First Ward voters gave Dunne more total votes than did any other and a plurality of 3,800. Since Kenna's plurality was more than 5,600, it is clear that Dunne benefited from being the organization candidate. Dunne's elaborate praise of Hinky Dink prompted the Republican press and the good government organizations to argue that IMO was a spoilsmen's plot. To placate the Harrison faction, Dunne agreed to replace his candidate for city treasurer, John Traeger, with Fred Blocki. Where expedient, he also traded low-level patronage for support of IMO. [14]

But Dunne also proved himself to be an adept practitioner of ideological, independent politics. His closest advisors were Bryan-Altgeld Democrats, labor leaders, social reformers, intellectuals, or leaders of the Municipal Ownership League (MOL) or of the Municipal Ownership and Referendum League (MORL), and it was from that pool that he later made most of his high-level appointments. His decision to make the campaign on the single issue of IMO (Immediate Municipal Ownership) was designed primarily to appeal to voters who would have been largely immune to or incensed by ethnocultural or partisan appeals. Similarly, Dunne's refusal to resign his judicial position reinforced his image of independence and his stature as a highly educated, successful professional. To supplement the organizational and mobilization efforts of the ward organizations and to reach progressive Republicans and independents, Dunne supporters relied upon a series of volunteer political action clubs designed to demonstrate the support of various segments of society for IMO. City-wide, his candidacy was pushed by the MOL, MORL, and the newly formed MO Campaign Committee. Most of the volunteer political action clubs were organized by occupation, sex, ethnic group, geography, or some combination thereof, and illustrate Dunne's attempt to weave together elements of the old and the new politics. [15]

The success of that strategy was borne out on 4 April 1905 when Dunne defeated Harlan by a vote of 163,189 to 138,671. His vote total was almost 7,000 more than Harrison's best effort in 1901, and over 17,000 better than the latter's 1903 showing. Dunne carried twenty-two wards, all but one of which were on the Near North Side or in the core city bounded by North Avenue on the north, 55th Street on the south, South 46th Avenue or Kedzie on the west, and the lakefront north of 12th Street on the east. The latter was the traditional Democratic bastion, included the bailiwicks of the major ward bosses, contained the city's major industrial and commercial areas, and was inhabited primarily by working and lower middle-class Irish, Germans, or southern and eastern Europeans. The Near North Side was more of a swing area, containing some of the city's wealthiest and poorest residents and a mixture of normally Republican and Democratic ethnic groups. In the seventeen core Democratic wards, Dunne's political affiliation and/or ethnocultural ties were more important than his stand on IMO, as he outpolled the latter by totals ranging from 150 to over 3,500. In the most boss-dominated wards, Dunne's margin over IMO averaged better than two to one and he ran significantly behind the Democratic aldermanic candidate in about half those districts. In the Eighteen and Nineteenth, however, Dunne significantly outpolled Brennan and Powers as well as IMO, indicating that Dunne the partisan ethnic reformer was a formidable candidate. Apart from the First and Nineteenth wards, his strongest showing came in the city's largest Irish-Catholic community, where Dunne polled about two-thirds of the mayoral vote and ran about 1,300 votes ahead of IMO. In the Near North Side wards, Dunne received about the same vote totals as had Harrison in 1903, ran between 500 to 1,000 votes ahead of IMO, and won largely due to a drop-off in the usual Republican vote. In the far southeast Eighth ward, Dunne ran 250 votes ahead of Harrison's 1903 pace and outpolled IMO by just under 500.[16]

By contrast, Dunne's role as the transit companies' severest critic benefited him significantly in most of the thirteen largely peripheral, normally Republican wards carried by Harlan. Except for the Second, Third, and Fifteenth, these were virtually suburban wards inhabited primarily by upwardly mobile Yankees or second- and third-generation Americans of British, Scandinavian, German, or Irish descent. Their higher socioeconomic status reinforced the normal Republic proclivities of the Protestant residents and undermined the Democratic loyalties of many of the Irish and German Catholics. The Second and Third wards contained the city's largest concentration of blacks, who joined Yankee, Scandinavian, and German Protestant voters in keeping the districts solidly Republican. The Fifteenth was predominantly Jewish and Scandinavian and located in the zone of emergence where the inner city flowed into the periphery, making it a natural swing ward. Eleven of these thirteen wards were the only ones in the city where IMO received more votes than did Dunne. By contrast, the inner city, staunchly Republican Second and Third wards were the only ones where Dunne outpolled IMO and lost. In every Harlan ward save the Fifteenth, Dunne improved upon Harrison's 1903 total by margins ranging from 200 to 1,200 votes.[17]

Although it was clear that Chicago voters preferred Democrat Dunne to Republican Harlan for mayor in 1905, it was much less certain what they wanted him to do about the transit problem. The three propositions on the advisory ballot were worded in such a way that IMO supporters could only vote against some alternative course of action. On the question of whether the council should pass the tentative ordinances, they voted in the negative by 150,785 to 64,391. They were even more emphatic in rejecting the granting of any franchise to the Chicago City Railway Company and in instructing the council not to grant any franchise to any railway company. Since Dunne had made his entire campaign on IMO and since the correlation between his vote total and that of IMO was upwards of 90 percent, it was reasonable for the victorious candidate to claim an overwhelming mandate.

Although Dunne had tried all in his power to make the election a referendum on IMO and had engineered what seemed to be a smashing victory, there was still ample room for opponents to deny that he had received a clear mandate. But the vote against the tentative ordinances was nearly 30,000 more than that by which the voters approved IMO and 2,500 less than that by which they favored adoption of the Mueller Law in 1904, indicating that many may have viewed IMO primarily as a threat. Adding to the confusion was the fact that in such banner GOP wards as the Third, Sixth, and Seventh, the voters rejected the tentative ordinances by margins ranging from 1,700 to 4,200 and then overwhelmingly reelected aldermen who were members of the city council's Committee on Local Transportation (CLT) and staunch advocates of regulation. Finally, the support of such Gray Wolves as Kenna for IMO was highly tenuous at best, while several other Democratic aldermen who were indifferent to or hostile toward the prospect had been reelected.[18]

Dunne as Mayor

While the calibre of his appointments to top level administrative positions was perhaps the highest of any city administration in history, Dunne left them largely to their own devices and provided little coordination or communication. Because these were men and women of exceptional intelligence and expertise but little previous governmental experience, they frequently clashed with bureaucrats, politicians, and the mayor himself. As Jane Addams astutely observed, Dunne believed that if "citizens representing social ideas and reform principles were appointed to office, public welfare must be established." To his credit, Dunne later admitted that he "made some serious mistakes in taking the advice of some of those who had my confidence" and that he "left political matters to a large extent to be taken care of by men I trusted, but who were not adept in politics."[19]

Even though he had promised "immediate" municipal ownership and had momentum on his side, Dunne delayed for nearly three months before submitting his MO proposal to the CLT. While part of this delay was due to a teamsters strike that occupied much of his time and energy, a great deal of it was consumed by travel and speech—making statements on the benefits of MO. Dunne further alienated the CLT by ignoring much of its expertise and relying instead on outside advisers supplied by Hearst, Johnson, and other MO advocates. This tendency even led him to send for a traction expert from Glasgow, Scotland, who turned out to be both the wrong man and an unfriendly witness, to Dunne's embarrassment.[20]

Finally, Dunne fluctuated greatly in his plans to achieve MO and in his relations with his various traction advisers. His first message to the CLT contained two proposals, a city plan that called for Chicago to construct and operate its own system and a contract plan that contemplated the creation of a private corporation headed by five prominent citizens to build, acquire, and operate a system. When the council refused to adopt either plan, the mayor, with the help of several of the Gray Wolves, secured authorization to conduct a referendum on the policy of using Mueller certificates to purchase the existing lines. When the voters gave him that authority but failed to bestow upon the city the right to operate the system, Clarence Darrow resigned as City Corporation Counsel and was replaced by Walter Fisher. Dunne then proposed to CLT chairman Charles Werno that the city enter into an agreement to purchase the system and to build new lines out of a sinking fund created by sharing in all company profits above 5 percent. When Fisher negotiated such an agreement, Dunne found it so filled with "jokers" that he vetoed the so-called settlement ordinances, fired Fisher, and based his reelection campaign on rejection of the ordinances and a continued battle for MO. This apparent vacillation, along with his other shortcomings, convinced some ardent MO advocates that Dunne bungled their golden opportunity and allowed his opponents to portray him as a quixotic dreamer.[21]

But even had he done everything right, it is highly unlikely that Dunne or any other Chicago mayor could have achieved IMO. Neither as mayor nor as party leader did he have sufficient clout to overcome significant opposition. Constrained by a two year term and with limited patronage, he had little leverage with which to compel recalcitrant aldermen. He had no real recourse other than popular appeal if the council refused to act favorably upon his recommendations, while aldermen could override his veto with a two-thirds vote. Nor could Dunne derive much clout from his status in the Democratic party, where he was at most the leader of only one faction. He never gained control of either the city or county central committees and failed to forge any solid alliance with the Harrison or Sullivan-Hopkins factions. Real power lay with the ward bosses, who functioned autonomously, and Dunne commanded the consistent loyalty of only about one-third of the Democratic aldermen.[22]

Dunne's IMO efforts were further damaged by the intrusion of other issues that distracted his time and energy, alienated some supporters, and gave additional ammunition to his opponent. The first of these was a paralyzing teamsters strike that gripped the city for the first hundred days of his administration. A firm supporter of organized labor and a beneficiary of its political support, Dunne refused to call in the militia or take any other steps to break the strike. He spent long hours mediating between the union and the Employers Association, but was unable to effect a settlement. In the end, the union capitulated, costing Dunne some labor support, while his handling of the matter gave credence to conservative charges that he was both a prolabor radical and an incompetent chief executive.[23]

The opponents of IMO were also able to make a great deal of political capital out of Dunne's efforts to reform the school board. While judge, Dunne had ruled in favor of a Chicago Teachers Federation (CTF) suit forcing the State Board of Equalization to collect the full amount of taxes from the city's corporations in order to raise teacher's salaries. The CTF gave him strong backing in 1905. As mayor, Dunne appointed such reformers as Addams, Post, Robins, and Dr. Cornelia DeBey, a physician prominent in social work, to the school board, along with labor leaders and educators. Although they often disagreed among themselves, the Dunne appointees generally supported such radical causes as the creation of teachers councils to evaluate performance, restrictions on the powers of the superintendent, teacher unionization, higher salaries, and attacks on the "textbook trust." Most radical of all was their unsuccessful effort to break the long-term leases of school property at low rentals that several corporations, especially such newspapers as the *Tribune*, had cajoled out of a cooperative board in 1895. Not surprisingly, these efforts earned Dunne the violent condemnation of most Chicago newspapers, with the *Tribune* denouncing his appointees as "freaks, cranks, monomaniacs, and boodlers."[24]

Even more damaging were Dunne's efforts to cope with the highly explosive liquor issue. His Irish Catholicism mandated a preference for personal temperance over legislated prohibition and he understood the role that the saloon played in the social and political life of ethnic, working-class neighborhoods. He was also aware that no Democratic politician could afford to risk the political consequences of making concessions to antisaloon sentiment. But the reformer in him also recognized the abuses that occurred in the city's more disreputable saloons and the political and police corruption that attended their operation. Accordingly, he trod a middle course between moral reform and toleration that ended by alienating elements in both the dry and wet camps. Specifically, he proposed to enforce the Sunday closing ordinance and to raise the license fee from $500 to $1000, especially for those saloons deemed to be disreputable. The revenue engendered by the latter policy was also designed to finance the hiring of a substantial number of new policemen to improve the general quality of law enforcement. At one point, he pursued a policy of revoking the licenses of 104 disreputable saloons and restoring them if they cleaned up their act, but the state legislature prohibited the restoration of revoked licenses. His police even went so far as to close one of the Kenna's saloons for a time.[25]

None of this was enough for the Sunday Closing League and other anti-saloon groups who forced a grand jury investigation of the administration and the police. It was far too much, however, for the Liquor Dealers Association, the saloon keepers, ward bosses, and many of their patrons who vowed revenge in 1907. Anton Cermak, the rising Czech-American politician, formed the United Societies for Local Self-Government, a multiethnic organization that claimed over two hundred thousand members pledged to "personal liberty" and heavily financed by the liquor industry. Cermak worked for the defeat of his fellow Democrat, Dunne, in 1907 because Republican candidate Fred Busse advocated a wide-open city. The *Tribune* reported that an irate worker condemned Dunne at a union meeting because "he has closed the saloons and dance halls and everything. He has sacrificed everything for municipal ownership." There can be little doubt that the liquor question cost him votes in both the dry and wet camps, especially among the latter. It mattered little to many Chicagoans who owned the trolley cars if you couldn't ride them to and from your favorite saloon.[26]

More significantly, Dunne failed to achieve IMO because his philosophy presented a direct challenge to the values and interests of the city's power brokers. Each of these, from slightly different perspectives, were too firmly committed to privatism to acquiesce in an innovation that struck at the very heart of that system. Although the ward bosses publicly supported MO when it was to their advantage, they were too canny not to realize that it would mean an end to the practice of exchanging franchises for money, jobs, and other economic and political considerations. While some astute business leaders acknowledged that the system was corrupt and inefficient and adversely effected the city's economic climate, nearly all of them felt that the answer lay in better-managed, or at most regulated, private enterprise. The mainstream newspapers generally reflected this viewpoint since their publishers were a part of the business community. Ironically, the moderate reformers who populated the MVL, CLT, and Civic Federation opposed MO on the grounds that it created a patronage bonanza and increased political corruption, while the ward bosses opposed it in the belief that it would destroy the bonanza that they already had. Throughout the entire transit crisis, the moderates remained consistent in their preference for regulated private enterprise and in their strategy of using MO as a lever to achieve consolidation, regulation, and a share of the profits for the city.[27]

Finally, Dunne failed to achieve IMO because it is highly unlikely that a majority of Chicago voters ever unequivocally supported the notion, despite the apparent evidence of the various referenda. About 20 percent of the city's eligible voters failed to vote at all, and about one-third of those who did ignored the referendum questions, meaning that close to one-half of them never expressed any opinion. In all the referenda from 1902 to 1906, the pro-MO vote fluctuated between a low of 110,225 on the 1906 question of issuing Mueller certificates to a high of 152,135 on the 1905 question of denying a franchise to any railway company. Conversely, opposition to these propositions steadily grew from a low of 27,998 in 1902 to a high of 110,323 who voted against municipal operation of the transit lines in 1906. Apparently, the more "real" that MO became, the more reservations it raised among the voters.

When the issue was fairly clearly joined in 1907 between regulated private ownership and continued agitation toward MO, the total vote reached nearly 300,000 (compared to about 170,000 in 1902) and those who voted chose the settlement ordinances 165,846 to 132,720. It seems reasonable to accept the judgment of contemporary political scientist Arthur Bentley who argued that middle class voters supported MO when regulation seemed impossible and regulation when MO seemed stymied, while working class people followed the lead of their union officials and politicians. The election returns seemingly corroborated the findings of a *Tribune* poll whose respondents overwhelmingly believed that settlement meant improved service while rejection promised only delay and further agitation. There seems little reason to doubt that tens of thousands of Chicagoans concurred with one of the poll's respondents that as long as the service was improved significantly, it was all the same who got the nickel.[28]

The three-sided struggle over MO among the Dunne administration, the city council, and the transit companies raged on during most of the mayor's two-year term. As the 1907 mayoral election approached, Dunne again demonstrated that he was better at electoral politics than he was at the administrative or legislative variety. He skillfully quashed a Harrison challenge to his renomination by courting the Sullivan-Hopkins forces and a few ward bosses. On 21 February, Dunne won the primary of the Democratic convention for mayor 624 to 259 over Harrison, carrying the peripheral wards and those controlled by Powers, Sullivan, and former Harrison Lieutenant Robert Burke. Ominously, though, Harrison won the First Ward of Kenna and Coughlin, Loeffler's westside domain, and the predominantly German Near North Side, always a Harrison stronghold. Many wards bosses were incensed by Dunne's reformist policies and his public stance in favor of civil service. Perhaps more importantly, he now seemed a likely loser.[29]

The Dunne-dictated platform committed the party to defeat of the settlement ordinances and lauded the administration's accomplishments. Campaign strategy, however, consisted of stressing MO in those wards where it seemed to benefit Dunne in 1905 and emphasizing party loyalty and the mayor's personal qualities in traditionally Democratic bailiwicks. The mayor himself gave so many speeches that he eventually lost his voice, but he seemed to gain more applause when pleading his own reelection cause rather than urging defeat of the settlement ordinances. The Hearst papers were the only mainstream dailies to support his reelection and to urge rejection of the settlement ordinances, but even that was a mixed blessing. The candidate who pledged to save the city from sinister Wall Street bankers in 1905 now had to defend himself against charges that he was the tool of a radical and malevolent New York publisher. The Republican dailies kept up a steady barrage of denunciations of Dunne, while their cartoonists portrayed the mayor as a wildeyed radical riding an MO hobby horse.[30]

In an effort to placate those regulars alienated by Harlan's 1905 candidacy, the Republicans nominated Fred Busse, a German-American coal and ice dealer and professional politician. For his part, Busse endorsed settlement but concentrated his limited oratory on the need for a "greater Chicago" and businesslike government, a stance facilitated by his minor injury in a train accident early in the campaign. At that time the Republican papers portrayed the contest as an uneven one between a healthy Dunne and an injured Busse, much to the mayor's disadvantage.[31]

Much of the campaign against Dunne and for the settlement ordinances was conducted by two political action committees, the Chicago Non-Partisan Traction Settlement Association and the Straphanger League. The former was a front for the Real Estate Board and the Commercial Association, sponsors of the Chicago Plan, and it sent slick prosettlement brochures to every registered voter. The traction and liquor interests spent heavily in the campaign, with estimates ranging as high as $600,000. The Chicago City Railway Company alone spent $350,000 in promoting settlement. A sizeable portion of the money was spent in Democratic wards whose bosses had declared in favor of settlement and a wide-open town.[32]

The election of 2 April 1907 marked the end of both Dunne's mayoral career and MO. Busse outpolled Dunne 164,702 to 151,779, while the settlement ordinances were adopted 167,367 to 134,281, meaning that the Republican candidate trailed settlement by about 2,500 votes, while Dunne ran almost 17,500 ahead of the position he advocated.[33] The correlation between Dunne's showing and opposition to the settlement ordinances was about 90 percent. The prosettlement vote carried twenty-four wards and swept the entire lakeshore, everything south of 55th Street, and everything north of Van Buren, except for the Near North Twenty-fourth, the riverfront Sixteenth, 55th street on the South, and those dominated by the Irish-American community. Dunne carried ten of the eleven opposition wards. In each of them he ran ahead of antisettlement opinion. Even more than was the case in 1905, Dunne's personality, ethnoreligious identity, and/or partisan affiliation earned him the votes of many who were indifferent or hostile to MO.[34]

But Dunne's defeat should not obscure his contributions to Chicago and its political tradition. Although the 1907 election and referendum was primarily a realization of the moderate reformers' policy and probably reflected the viewpoint of the majority of Chicagoans, it is hard to see how that end could have been accomplished without the pressure generated by Dunne's IMO crusade. Emboldened by Grosscup's partial upholding of the eternal monopoly laws in 1904, the transit companies were reluctant to accept even the tentative ordinances, let alone the 1907 settlement. In collaboration with the Gray Wolves, Dunne's IMO advocates prevented further negotiations with the companies in 1906 and forced a referendum that resulted in the authorization of purchase by Mueller certificates and the prohibition of further franchise extentions. Almost simultaneously, the administration's legal counsels persuaded the Supreme Court to overrule Grosscup and invalidate most of the companies' claims under the ninety-nine-year laws. It was only at that point that the companies were willing to entertain serious consideration of regulation and consolidation.

Dunne's Werno letter outlined many of the terms later included in the settlement ordinances, and his later opposition was largely responsible for forcing the intense public debate that dominated the early months of 1907. Finally, his opposition to settlement clearly joined the issue and motivated unprecedented participation in the April 1907 referendum. None of this is to suggest that the adoption of the settlement ordinances was the outcome of any conscious design on Dunne's part. He was absolutely committed to MO and was even more convinced that any delay was a betrayal of the goal. Dunne's role in achieving regulation and consolidation was clearly unintended but nevertheless highly significant.[35]

Nor were Dunne's achievements by any means limited to his part in forcing the traction settlement. The central focus of his administration was on regulating of the rates and service of public utilities, with an eye toward eventual municipal ownership. It was clear from his speeches and writings that Dunne saw municipalization as the ultimate solution for all utilities; he backed a provision granting such authorization proposed by the charter commission. Typically, Dunne demanded more regulation than the city council was willing to endorse. In late April 1905, the new mayor led the Committee of Fifty, composed of moderate reformers and radical Democrats, to Springfield to lobby for the passage of a law permitting the city to regulate gas and utility rates. When the legislature passed the gas rate legislation, Dunne immediately asked the city council to reduce the price from the prevailing $1.00 per cubic foot to 75¢. His position was strengthened when the voters approved a public policy referendum permitting the city to sell surplus electricity and to fix rates for the supply of gas and electricity by private distributors. After the gas companies claimed that they could go no lower than 90¢, the administration filed suit to open their books. When the city council passed an 85¢ ordinance, Dunne vetoed it on the grounds that the rate was unfair and excessive, only to have the council override.[36]

Dunne also fought with the council and won an estimated 25 percent reduction in electrical rates as well as scaled-down telephone rates. Charging that

$175 a year for unlimited telephone service was exorbitant, the Dunne administration convinced the Illinois Supreme Court to mandate a $125 rate. Dunne used such tactics as opposing franchise extensions and threatening to invite rival companies to force even lower rates and greater efficiency in service. Because the city owned and operated the water utility, it was considerably easier to effect rate reduction for most consumers. This was accomplished by raising the rate for larger corporations from 4¢ per 1,000 gallons to 7¢ and correspondingly lowering the household rate from 10¢ to 7¢.[37]

The Dunne administration's legal department, headed by corporation counsels J. Hamilton Lewis, Clarence Darrow, and Glenn E. Plumb, focused on corporate privileges, and won its most famous victory when the Supreme Court's rejected the "eternal monopoly" laws. Dunne's legal department also bore down on tax evasion by wealthy corporations and persuaded the state Board of Review to examine the valuations and assessments of several estates and corporations, resulting in the recovery of nearly $2 million in revenue. The city health department vigorously pursued enforcement of health and environmental codes, nearly doubling the number of prosecutions during the first year. Spurred by the publication of *The Jungle* and the resultant passage of the federal Meat Inspection Act, the department confiscated ten million pounds of decayed and diseased meats and cooperated fully with U.S. inspectors in enforcing higher standards. However, the administration's efforts at curtailing the smoke from factories was considerably less effective.[38]

Other city departments also concerned themselves with consumer protection and business regulation. The city sealers' office waged a highly publicized campaign to eliminate dishonest weights and measures that cost customers millions of dollars per year. Building department head Peter Bartzen, a young and enthusiastic Dunne appointee, ruffled important feathers with his aggressive inspection and code enforcement policies. His department revoked numerous building permits and shut down several businesses for code violations. Bartzen's most famous exploit was the closing of Marshall Field's department store during two business hours for fire escape violations.[39]

Equally controversial were the activities of the public works department, headed by Joseph Medill Patterson, scion of *The Tribune* family who had deserted his rock-ribbed Republican upbringing to work for Dunne. He insisted upon open and honest bidding on all public works projects and sought to enforce civil service regulations in what was perhaps Chicago's biggest patronage machine. He compounded the latter by bringing assistant street commissioner and Sixth Ward committeeman Frank Solon up before the Civil Service Commission on charges of demanding campaign contributions of city hall employees. Solon's dismissal was one of the major incidents that contributed to the ward bosses' dissatisfaction with administration patronage practices. Following another of Dunne's favorite notions, Patterson vigorously pursued the collection of rents from corporations utilizing public streets, sidewalks, and tunnels. After ten months in office, Patterson resigned, praising Dunne's crusade for municipal ownership, excoriating waste, delay, and graft in government and business, and announcing his conversion to socialism.[40]

With the exception of MO itself, the Dunne administration's greatest challenge to the status quo came over the school board. Nowhere was the design to make government more representative of new constituencies more evident. In defending his appointments from the almost hysterical attacks of his critics, Dunne contended that "labor and middle class people are better able to determine what is good for their children than the merchants club." Not surprisingly, his controversial appointments were vigorously endorsed by Margaret Haley, president of the CTF, who deemed it "the most remarkable Board of Education I have ever known in Chicago or any other city," one that "so clearly saw so far ahead that it took hold of the large problems of the school." And, she added, "never did we have a board so opposed by the newspaper." Much of the latter's ire was attributable to the Dunne appointees' efforts to make them pay more for their long-term leases of school property, an action largely responsible for the *Tribune*'s charge that the mayor had packed the board with freaks, cranks, and boodlers. Dunne promptly called for a grand jury investigation and filed a one hundred thousand dollar civil suit against the paper. The grand jury returned no indictments but commended Dunne as an "honest public official," while the *Tribune* published a qualified retraction. Although the Dunne appointees achieved only minor successes, such as increase in teacher salaries, they aimed at decentralization and democratization of the school system and a drastic curtailment of the superintendent's powers.[41]

Dunne and the Chicago Political Tradition

The Dunne administration mounted the most serious challenge to the existing order ever managed in Chicago. It organized and operated municipal affairs for two years with officials recruited largely from the ranks of "outsiders." Although failing to achieve municipal ownership of the transit system, it applied much of the pressure that forced the companies to accept consolidation and regulation. It forced significant rate reductions from nearly all of the city's utility companies and induced many of them to pay rentals for use of public throughfares. It championed the right of teachers and parents to play a major role in the determination of educational policy. It brought the power of the state down upon some of the city's wealthiest corporations and estates, forcing them to pay delinquent taxes. By collecting rentals, delinquent taxes, and fines and by raising saloon license fees, it produced the largest surplus in the city's history. Taken as a whole, the Dunne administration's effort merited its leader's description of "militant civism."[42]

Yet it is still Dunne's failure to achieve MO and reelection that provides us with a distinct sense of the limits of political reform in Chicago. The successful reformer must not only be an effective practitioner of electoral politics, but also proficient at administrative and legislative politics. Dunne was not and clearly failed either to forge a coordinated administrative machine or to lobby his program through the city council where his approach was too confrontational.

Even if Dunne had been an effective administrator and legislative leader, however, he would still have been defeated by the fragmented nature of Chicago's life and by the realities of power. The strong council-weak mayor system severely inhibited any positive action by the latter and the virtual autonomy of individual aldermen and municipal departments exacerbated the problem. This fragmentation was also reflected in the factionalism of the party structure that severely undermined party discipline.

Dunne's frontal assault on privatism attacked the business and financial community's belief in its right to manage its own affairs, to make as much money as possible, and to use public property for private gain, values generally shared by the majority of Chicagoans. It was also an assault on the practice of exchanging franchises and contracts for jobs, money, and other favors that was the politicians' life blood. Dunne had tried to innovate faster and to push policy further than his predecessors but had run his administration aground when he reached the limits of municipal reform.

4.

FRED A. BUSSE:
A SILENT MAYOR IN TURBULENT
TIMES

Maureen A. Flanagan

Mayor Fred A. Busse's political personality may be suggested by the fact that during the entire mayoral campaign in 1907 he gave no speeches, made no campaign appearances. This was due partially to circumstance. At the start of the campaign, while returning to Chicago from Washington, Busse was seriously injured in a train wreck. Although he was then confined to bed under doctor's orders, one gets the impression from reading the newspapers that the accident was a rather fortuitous event: had he really wanted to, or if the Republican party had wanted him to, he might have risen from his bed of pain and gone speechmaking a few times. However, as one observer of the campaign cogently remarked of the accident, "this relieved him from the necessity of a speechmaking campaign, which would not have been at all to his liking. He rarely talks in public."[1] Busse's public reticence in the long run was to prove a handicap, especially given the bombastic style of Chicago politics at the time, but in early 1907 he was precisely what the Chicago Republicans were looking for. He was a solid Republican with no hint of scandal; a party man who promised to be amenable to promoting the party line; and a German with the potential to attract some ethnic voters away from the Democrats.

Fred Busse was born in Chicago in 1866 to German immigrant parents. His father was a small businessman engaged in hardware, and the son took a similar business path. After working in his father's hardware business for a time, Fred moved into the coal business, ultimately becoming president first of the Busse-Reynolds Coal Company and then of the Busse Coal Company. He joined the Republican party and entered the political arena in 1891 at age twenty-five. Over the next two decades, he carved for himself a solid, if not spectacular, political career. He was elected to his first public office in 1891, that of town clerk of North Chicago. After serving as a court bailiff and deputy sheriff for a time, Busse broadened his political aspirations and went into state politics. First, he held two terms in the Illinois House of Representatives in 1894 and 1896 and then followed with his election in 1898 as state senator from the Twenty-first District. After serving his four-year term as senator, he was elected state treasurer in 1902. Four years later, President Roosevelt appointed Busse postmaster of Chicago, a position he occupied until his election as mayor of Chicago in April 1907.

During his tenure in these public offices, Fred Busse did little to draw attention to himself as anything other than a competent officeholder, a man who made himself available to his constituents, and one who had made few enemies. Although he was the political boss of the North Side faction of the Republican party in the city, he was relatively unsullied by political graft and corruption, being neither a flamoyant political boss nor a practitioner of the more flagrantly corrupt aspects of the machine politics of the day. And his personal life, if dull, was above reproach. Until he married in 1908 at the age of forty-two, he lived at home with his parents. Newspaper accounts during the campaign are full of references to his mother fending off reporters and well-wishers who would invade her son's convalescent room. Moreover, while he was by no means the darling of the liberal reform element of the Republican party, he was an uncontroversial figure to whom few men would object openly, a factor that enabled the party to display a unity of purpose that otherwise would have been impossible behind other potential candidates.

And in 1907 the Republicans wanted to present a united party to the voters. In that year, the party thought it stood a good chance of regaining the mayor's office—a seat it had not controlled in well over a decade. The incumbent mayor, Edward Dunne, had alienated many Chicago voters either by being too wishy-washy or, from the opposite perspective, too radical on some important municipal issues. Moreover, the factions of the Democratic party were not in line firmly behind Dunne, and this interparty feuding gave the Republicans hope that their rivals would not be able to make a strong showing at the polls. This mayoral contest was especially important to the Republicans first of all because the winner would serve the first four-year term in that office. But they also wanted to have their man in office because the next four years promised to be critical ones for determining the shape of Chicago's future development.

Chicago, in 1907, was in the throes of the reforming spirit of the Progressive Era,[2] and the perception in the city was that whoever occupied the mayoral seat, and by extension his party, would exert tremendous influence over the outcome of these reforms. A new municipal charter that could centralize the powers and configuration of Chicago's government would be put to a referendum of Chicago voters; the proponents of municipal ownership of public utilities were promising an all-out campaign to achieve their goal of transferring utilities, especially the municipal transit systems, from the hands of private entrepreneurs to the city; the financing and direction of the public school system was in open dispute among the city's residents, particularly in regard to the composition, powers, and selection of the board of education; and the question of liquor regulation had become a hot issue not only within the city, but in the relations between the city and the state.

As a personality Busse pales in significance when set against contemporaries Carter Harrison and William Hale Thompson, both strong, flamboyant individuals who between them spent twenty-five years in the mayor's office from 1897 to 1931. Nor can Busse be easily described as machine or reform; he is one of those Progressive Era figures who falls between the cracks in the definitions, both an ethnic machine-oriented politician, and a businessman comfortably backed by the most reform-minded, antimachine businessmen of the Republican party. But, because the issues at stake in the first decade of the twentieth century were never satisfactorily resolved, they continue to be controversial problems today: the school system, mass transit, the structurally noncentralized municipal government.

So with its nonloquacious candidate safely confined to bed, the Republican party assumed complete control of the mayoral campaign and turned it into one of the more scurilous Chicago mayoral races, not an easy task for a city that has seemed to specialize in dirty politics. By all accounts of the 1907 mayoral race, the single, most rancorous issue, and one that caused much anguish for the Dunne forces, was that of traction reform. Under Chicago's existing system, the municipal government granted franchises to private companies to build and run transit lines in the city. By the turn of the century, Chicagoans clearly agreed among themselves that the franchise system, as it then functioned, was hopelessly corrupt and unable to provide sufficient or affordable public transportation. But Chicagoans did not agree on how to remedy the situation. They split into two distinct camps. There were those people who wanted to accomplish reform by tightening municipal regulation of franchises: issuing them for twenty years instead of the prevailing fifty year grants, setting more rigorous regulations on construction and provision of services, and making the traction companies pay more compensation to the city in return for their right to use municipal property. Opposing these proponents of regulation were those residents who believed that the franchising of public utilities itself was the problem and thus believed that regulation would never sufficiently guarantee adequate and affordable public services. These people, instead, advocated direct municipal ownership and operation as the only viable solution.

The issue of regulation versus municipal ownership had intruded heavily into the two previous mayoral contests of 1903 and 1905.[3] First Carter Harrison and then Edward Dunne had supported the idea of immediate municipal ownership, but once elected neither man carried out his campaign pledge. Now in 1907 the traction issue was again a focal point of the mayoral campaign, particularly because the existing franchises had expired and some decision had to be made about how to continue furnishing public transit. Dunne helped insure his defeat by turning several flip-flops on the issue. Although he had promised municipal ownership in 1905, soon after taking office he had appointed Walter Fisher as his official traction advisor. Fisher was committed to moderate franchise reform, and he and Dunne agreed to the course of renegotiating the existing franchises to receive better terms for the city than they had managed in previous franchise agreements. However, no sooner had Fisher accomplished this and presented new traction agreements to the city council for approval, than Dunne repudiated Fisher and the agreements. Labeling them neither sufficiently protective of the rights of the people who had to depend on public transit nor remunerative enough to the city, he vetoed the agreements after they had passed the city council and renewed his earlier call for immediate municipal ownership.

In the ensuing uproar over Dunne's about-face, the Republican party saw its opportunity to move back into city hall and they determined to get as much political mileage as possible out of the issue. Party leaders believed that the people had grown so tired of unfulfilled promises and political wrangling on this issue while at the same time watching public transit services continue to deteriorate in the city, that they could be swayed to vote for the man who promised to settle the problem once and for all by signing the pending traction agreements which Walter Fisher had negotiated. To this end they hoped that by agreeing unanimously upon Fred Busse as their candidate and by tying together Busse's election with the ratification of the agreements, their man would win the election.

The fight over traction reform was more than a disagreement over the proper means to reform, for it contained within it fundamentally different views of city life and good municipal government. It was this aspect of the issue, and of other municipal issues also as we will see, that made them so controversial and helped turn the 1907 mayoral campaign into a mudslinging affair. To many Republicans, the traction problem was a business matter to be settled by businessmen sitting down together and hammering out the best deal for all concerned—that is, for all the businessmen concerned. Speaking at a Busse campaign rally, state Attorney General William H. Stead ridiculed any other means to reform as absurd. "The one thing needed in the present crisis," he said, "is plain, everyday common sense and business judgment." Underlying this stance on traction reform was the ideological position that the business of the city was to accommodate business and that traction service should have as its main objective the enhancement of business. The campaign arguments of party leaders and their citizen supporters on this issue, therefore, stressed that business needs should always take precedence over any other municipal needs or desires since business made the city. Hence, as a proponent of moderate reform, Republican Alderman Milton Foreman dismissed opposing arguments that the renegotiated franchises did not bring in sufficient revenue to the municipal government by saying "what do we care whether the city makes $1 or $1 million out of the deal? The thing we are vitally interested in is keeping a straight spine by getting a seat." Or, as one Chicago banker put it most succinctly, "the building up of a new street car system is absolutely indispensable to the business life of the city. It would pay the people of Chicago to spend almost any amount of money and upon almost any terms to create an adequate transportation system for themselves in the shortest possible time."[4] For the Chicago business community, the compensation to the city negotiated in traction franchises was far less important than getting new franchises that promised to provide the kind of transit system that it desired, running over the routes that it declared the most desireable.

Many supporters of Mayor Dunne, on the other hand, could not agree with these arguments. For them, municipal ownership was not just a way of operating a mass transit system; it was also an ideological view opposed to the perspective of those persons favoring franchises. Municipal ownership contained the possibility of the people themselves, rather than just businessmen, having a say in the crucial decisions to be made about the transit system: where and when, for instance, traction lines would be built and how much the fares would be. As one of Dunne's backers put it, "If the voter is for private corporate control of the streets and street railways . . . he should vote for the election of Mr. Busse for mayor."[5] Many voters in the city were sympathetic to this argument, fearing that, in fact, the Republicans were in league with the companies currently holding traction franchises with the purpose of getting the best deal for the businessmen involved rather than for the people of the city.[6] These suspicions could only have been furthered when one of the franchise holders, the City Railway Company, announced pay raises for its employees if the traction agreements were ratified, "the way for which was paved by James Pease of the Republican county central committee and other friends of Mr. Busse."[7] Nor could they have been much comforted by Busse's record on traction. As a state representative, he had voted to extend the ninety-nine years the traction franchises of the notorious Charles Yerkes who had steadfastly refused to increase the number of streetcars on his routes in Chicago, saying it was "the straphangers who pay the dividends." Busse only reversed his stand two years later when the outraged public threatened to unseat at the next elections anyone who voted for franchise extensions again. Busse's supporters preferred not to bring up his original vote, or at best to attribute it to his newness in office.[8]

In this campaign, as was their wont with the numerous other current municipal issues bedeviling Chicago, the Republicans refused to acknowledge any legitimate opposition to their position. The Chicago *Tribune*, the strongest supporter of the Republican cause among the city's dailies, day after day during the campaign viciously ridiculed Dunne and anyone supporting him. Headlines such as "Hysteria Rules Demo[crat]-M[unicipal] O[wnership] Camp," "Chicago Suffers by Dunne Fiasco," "Dunne 'Loses' Use of Voice, But Abuses Opponents," were matched against ones saying "Busse a Fighter: Credit to City" and "Busse Managers Stick to Issue; Better Traction and Clean City Urged, While the Dunne Followers Sling Mud." The political cartoons did much the same: the "mild-mannered" Busse was depicted reading in his sick bed while Dunne supporters, all dressed in black with masks over their faces, sneak up to throw buckets of mud on him.[9] Every speech made by Dunne, every statement issued by him or his campaign, was mercilessly ridiculed; to read the *Tribune* accounts of his campaign, hardly a person ever showed up for his campaign appearances. All the while, Busse was safely tucked away in his bed, never having to face the public, a delightful situation for the Republican campaign committee that as much as possible answered any Democratic challenges to its candidate by referring indignantly to the poor man laid up in bed just wishing that he could respond in person, but alas it could not be.

Other daily newspapers at times gave more measured coverage to the campaign, but the *Tribune* coverage helps expose the underlying political tensions within the city in 1907 that were in fact central to determining the outcome of the elections and subsequent reform proposals. A tone of political hysteria emerges from its pages, conveying the sense that at least some Republicans held Busse's election essential to reverse a trend in Chicago toward radical municipal government. In a poll conducted among real-estate men during the campaign, one respondent urged Busse's election because it would "settle for many years the question as to whether the long haired men and short haired women are going to rule and ruin this town." The same sentiment was echoed by Thomas D. Knight, who, when presiding over a meeting of the Republican businessmen's Hamilton Club, declared the club to be against the "long haired management of city affairs." In cartoons, Dunne and his "cronies" were seen hanging out the City Hall windows, all wild-eyed and long-haired.[10] Partially this hysteria was a legacy from Haymarket and the confrontations with the radical labor movement of the 1870s and 1880s. It also reflected the fears of more conservative Republicans that Dunne's reelection might guarantee municipal ownership and other municipal reforms that would reshape the city in ways to which they were unalterably opposed. Certainly Edward Dunne himself was too upright a figure, a man who had been a respected Circuit Court Judge and would later be elected governor of the state, to merit the scurrilous attacks on him either on the basis of his personality or any ties to machine politics.

That these political tensions were more than those of reformers versus machine politicians, or matters of political personalities, is apparent too in other aspects of the Busse candidacy and campaign. Time and again, moderate Republican businessmen reformers proclaimed themselves nonpartisan, promoting only what was good for the city as a whole, claiming that if their candidates were elected there would be no more machine politicians, no more trading political patronage and political favors for votes. Many historians have accepted their claims more or less at face value, but in doing so they miss some of the inherent contradictions between these claims and actual political practices. The Republicans excoriated Dunne as a machine hack, a man engaged in vote buying and using his position to force municipal employees to work for his campaign. But Busse was also a machine politician, and the Republicans had to confront counter-accusations of Busse's vote buying. How they did so makes some interesting reading. While Dunne was accused of scandously and corruptly buying votes, Busse was a man who "just simply helps the sick and poor and lightens the load of poverty" by giving out jobs, money, and coal (he owned a coal company) to his North Side constituents. Pursuing this line of reasoning, the Republicans lauded their candidate for "more instances of the Postmaster's kindness to the needy" as told to them by Mrs. Busse, who confirmed that money and coal had been sent personally by her son to needy constituents. Letters of support sent to Busse were proffered as evidence of Busse's kindness; never was their any acknowledgment that there just might be a connection between his "gifts" and votes. In one such letter, a man wrote to Busse: "I received your letter of the 21st today. You say in your letter that a mutual friend has told you that I was friendly to your candidacy. Well I don't see how I can be otherwise. Don't you remember 3 years ago when I was going to be put out of my house . . . and I went to see you and you let me have $8.50? . . . I think this is a good reason why I should do all I can to help your election." [11] Evidently, Democrats bought votes; Republicans acted kindly towards the needy. [12]

In Chicago in 1907, Republicans of most every variety, including the liberal reformers, backed a machine politician because it suited their purposes. Better, they believed, to have a machine politician of their own who basically supported their political program, than Edward Dunne, a man who in fact was not closely aligned with machine politics, but was of the wrong party and stood on the wrong side of most municipal issues from them. Chicago Republicans were every bit as partisan as Chicago Democrats, and had been for the past decade. [13]

On election day, Dunne could not overcome the handicaps of a divided party and the uproar over the traction issue. Fred Busse was elected mayor, although not by as wide a margin as the Republicans had been predicting in the last days before the voting. While they thought a margin of 30,000 to 40,000 was a safe bet, their candidate actually won by a little over 13,000. That Dunne had won his own election by 24,000 votes two years prior, however, gives some indication of how far he had fallen in the public's esteem. Busse and the Republicans took office in a buoyant mood that, however, was not destined to last the year. They had promised to resolve with their business expertise the central issues of the time, including the traction issue. Their failure to resolve these issues would prove quickly to be their undoing because they could not understand the depth of conflict among Chicago residents.

One of these issues—a dispute that had been brewing for more than a decade—was the question of how to run the public school system. Proper Republican businessmen had been horrified by Edward Dunne's appointments to the board of education, among the most distressing of whom—from the businessmen's perspective—were Raymond Robins, a social worker, and Louis Post, newspaper publisher, member of the radical Independence League, and proponent of the single tax. Furthermore, the growing influence of the Chicago Federation of Teachers, led by Margaret Haley, had made these same businessmen apoplectic. The broad issue at stake in the school question was whether the schools were to be run by an all-powerful superintendent, hopefully a businessman who would order the system around sound business principles with finances as the highest priority, or whether the community as a whole, and the teachers, were to be given a greater measure of control by replacing the currently appointed board with an elected one, and by according the teachers' union more say in the overall educational policy of the school system. Dunne's school board pointed in the latter direction. This combined with the results of a nonbinding public policy referendum wherein the voters registered their overwhelming favor of an elected board and the increasingly vociferous rhetoric and actions of those citizens favoring an elected school board to alarm thoroughly the Chicago business community. During the mayoral campaign, the Republicans characterized the board of education as composed of "avowed single taxers and socialists," undertaking "one constant case of wild experiments and crank ideas," and run by "a preponderance of people with excessively progressive notions." What was needed, Republicans and businessmen said, was "a good, straight, hard headed businessman like Mr. Busse to straighten out the muddle."[14] But a hard-headed businessman was precisely the last person many Chicago residents wanted to see running the schools because they had spent the last several years fending off what they believed was the attempt of "business interests" to take control of the schools away from the people.[15]

Although Busse had said little on the issue of schools during the campaign, almost immediately upon taking office, he set about ousting ex-Mayor Dunne's appointees, first by requesting the resignations of twelve members (at the time there was a total of twenty-one members to the board of education) and threatening to remove them anyway if they failed to meet his demand. Among the dismissed were, of course, Raymond Robins and Louis Post, and two members of the Chicago Federation of Labor, John Sonsteby and John Harding. The *Tribune* hailed the move as one that would "give the control of the city school system into the hands of a board dominated by a practical and capable business element"; Busse, his usual reticent self, refused to comment on what he was doing or why.[16] Several of the board members refused to resign quietly, threatening legal actions against the mayor, but within two weeks Busse prevailed. His new appointees were what his opponents had expected: all business and professional men, they included John Morrow, chairman of the Merchants' Club school committee, the businessmen's group that was promoting the antithesis of what the Chicago Federation of Labor (CFL) wanted from the school system, and Severt Gunderson, "a warm, personal friend of Mayor Busse." The CFL denounced Busse's moves as a giant step toward making the public schools "a cog in the capitalistic machine, so that the children may reach manhood's estate content in a condition of abject servitude."[17]

Within days of his election, Busse had also to confront the problems posed by a proposed new municipal charter then awaiting ratification by the state legislature, which if passed would go to a referendum of Chicago voters. The Republican party, most especially its reform element, very much wanted this charter. Under its provisions, the municipal government would be reorganized administratively and fiscally in ways that they favored. They were, however, facing a stiff challenge to their charter from within the city from citizens and Mayor Dunne, who labeled it a charter designed to hand over control of the city to businessmen and the Republican party and one that failed to remove the influence of the state legislature from municipal affairs.[18] Heavy opposition was voiced also by ethnic voters in Chicago who feared the proposed charter would result in the imposition of Sunday closings of saloons and other state antiliquor laws in Chicago. This fear was especially strong among Chicago Germans, who the year previously had organized an umbrella ethnic organization, the United Societies for Local Self-Government, to help secure antiprohibition guarantees in the new charter.[19] The United Societies had not succeeded in this objective. Candidate Busse, the Republicans believed, was the right man to smooth over the difficulties. First of all, he staunchly supported the charter and the party felt it could count on him to remain firm on this issue. Beyond this, he had the distinct advantage that he was a German himself and could be expected to talk to his people in ways to allay their fears. During the mayoral campaign he did just that, promising the United Societies that if its membership voted for him he would go to the legislature and seek relief for Chicago from state liquor laws, separate from the proposed charter.[20]

Busse attempted to fulfill that pledge and journeyed to Springfield to ask the state legislature to pass separate antiprohibition bills for Chicago to accompany the new charter legislation. But when the legislature refused to consider such new liquor laws for Chicago, Busse refused to turn against the charter, and until the municipal referendum in mid-September of 1907, Busse worked to secure its ratification. In doing so, he alienated many of his German supporters, especially in the last days of the charter campaign when, in an uncharacteristic outburst for the usually quiet mayor, he accused the United Societies of being in league with the brewing industry to stop the charter and threatened to implement Sunday saloon closing himself if the charter failed.[21] A week later, he followed this blast with his pronouncement that "the best citizenship in this community approves the Charter," an insulting statement that surely won over none of the charter's opponents.[22] Despite the Republicans' hopes for success and Busse's work for the charter, the voters of Chicago rather soundly rejected it in September of 1907. For the next two years, Busse remained at odds with the United Societies and others of his former ethnic supporters on the issue of charter reform. He grew increasingly suspect in their eyes in 1909 when they believed him willing to make deals on new charter legislation with Republican state legislators who were trying to impose stricter liquor laws on Chicago.[23]

As the charter had failed in 1907, so too did attempts to revive charter reform in 1909, and Busse and his party remained linked in the minds of many voters to a measure that they had strongly opposed. Busse changed the school board, but he could not stem the continuing criticism and bitterness of which of the citizenry toward a maneuver that they believed was intended to make the schools the personal preserve of the business community. Even before the new traction franchises could be put into effect, the railway companies were saying they could not meet the terms they had negotiated with the city in these franchises,[24] an announcement that deepened the cynicism those residents favoring municipal ownership felt toward businessmen and franchises.

By running Fred Busse in 1907, the Republican party had made a practical, short-term choice: he was the man who could put them back into the mayor's office. That the reformers of the party could back a machine politician and that Busse in turn could support municipal reform measures desired by these reformers, blurs the distinctions between machine and reform politicians and turns them into ineffective categories through which to try to understand Chicago politics of the early twentieth century. Nor is it enough to assign voter behavior either to ethnic or machine sympathies. The municipal issues at stake during this time were critical factors in determining political races and the fortunes of the parties. What happened to the school system or to the public transit system were every bit as important to many voters as were the ethnic background or promises of political patronage coming from certain candidates. The "radical" Edward Dunne lost the mayoral nomination in 1911 to Harrison by only 1,500 votes and there were still those in the city urging his renomination on the basis of his support for municipal ownership.[25] The deep feelings aroused by these issues during the campaign did not disappear afterwards, and they helped insure that Busse and the Republicans would make little headway in Chicago politics at this time. Busse's continuing support of the causes of the Republican businessmen eroded much of his hitherto natural constituency. Moreover, Busse's refusal, or inability, to act the part of a politician proved as much of a liability to his party once in office as it had been an asset during the campaign. A small-time office holder and presumably capable administrator and businessman, he had not the personality nor the temperament to lead a complex urban center such as Chicago.

In the long run, then, Busse's term in office did little to enhance the party's position in municipal politics. The party itself remained split between machine factions and a liberal progressive wing, seemingly unable to find tenable ground to stand on in appealing to the voters as it fluctuated between its two wings. In early 1911, when the Republicans had to decide on a candidate, Busse was his usual uncommunicative self, saying nothing about whether he planned to put himself in for renomination. While the party leaders waited for word from him, the reform element of the party decided to put up as candidate Charles Merriam, a professor at the University of Chicago and as a member of the city council, a noted liberal reform Republican. Busse finally declared his intention to retire in a short written statement to the party, ending his mayoral career as silently as it had begun. The way was open for Merriam to win the Republican nomination. Against him, the Democrats nominated the formidable Carter Harrison. Merriam and the Republicans went down to defeat, losing to Harrison by seventeen thousand votes.[26] It was the last hurrah of the liberal progressive wing of the Republican party; the only Republican mayor for the rest of the century would be William Hale Thompson, a politician who could play the game of machine politics with the best of them.

5.

BIG BILL THOMPSON: THE "MODEL" POLITICIAN

Douglas Bukowski

The Honorable James E. Watson, Republican from Indiana, found himself in impressive company. Fellow senators William Borah, Robert LaFollette, and George Norris all were present, and, minding tradition, they consented to Watson's request to insert a magazine article into the Congressional Record. And so "Shall We Shatter the Nation's Idols in School Histories?" by Mayor William Hale Thompson of Chicago became part of the legacy of the 70th Congress. Later, the United States Printing Office made Thompson's remarks available in pamphlet form.[1]

It was fitting that the thoughts of Big Bill Thompson should reach the shelves of Harvard and the University of Chicago if only because his career thrived on contradiction. Thompson was the machine politician first elected on a harmony ticket with two Bull Moose Progressives, the nationally discredited figure courted by presidential candidates, and the alleged ally of Al Capone the Justice Department never prosecuted. After Thompson's death in 1944, the Federal Bureau of Investigation discreetly examined his safety deposit box in search of stolen securities, but J. Edgar Hoover could no more "catch" Thompson than did a generation of Chicago reformers and Democrats. When he was defeated for a fourth term in 1931, Big Bill bequeathed the electorate a final contradiction. For the next half-century, Chicagoans elected mayors who followed policies established by Thompson towards blacks, ethnics, and labor, the business and reform communities, and organized crime. Even Richard J. Daley was beholden, if not for a campaign style, then for the Thompson-fashioned image of the mayor as big builder.[2]

For the most part, critics have dismissed Thompson as a creature of the 1920s, more related to style than substance. He is the fat demagogue who appealed to the Germans and Irish with his tirades against the king of England.

His contributions are of the type cited by Daniel J. Boorstin, a member of the go-getter decade who laid the foundation for all of Capone's undertakings. The FBI, in a report on Chicago politics, was impressed enough with Harold F. Gosnell that it cited his *Machine Politics, Chicago Model* to note that Thompson was so much buffoonery. (The bureau did not read Gosnell closely; he over-stated Thompson's mayoralty by eight years.) Accurate enough in themselves, these views ignore the social and political tensions Thompson exploited during his career, and they reduce the era's politics to rote stimulus-response. Rather, Thompson is best understood from the same perspective Joel Tarr used in his study of Big Bill's mentor, William Lorimer. The Blond Boss, Tarr discovered, was a politician who attracted both the laborer and the businessman. If Thompson never learned the value of precinct-level organization from Lorimer, he did grasp the importance of coalition politics.[3]

The early Thompson was a fairly conventional politician. He faced Judge Harry Olson of the Municipal Court in the 1915 Republican primary. Olson had the organizational backing of ex-Governor Charles Deneen and the support of such Progressives as Jane Addams and Charles Merriam. Still, Thompson won. Rather than a Lorimer protégé, voters saw a candidate who was physically attractive, spoke well, and knew the value of a good campaign song: "We want a cleaner city where the good can thrive and shine." In contrast, Olson came off as a drab reformer. With women about to vote in their first mayoral election, he could do no better than praise the "sense of economy" they would bring to public life. As a model of good government, he held out the meatpacking industry. Thompson won by 2,325 votes with the largely black Second Ward contributing a 6,800-vote margin, but there was more to Olson's defeat than race. With what the *Tribune* termed a "laboratory exactness and chill efficiency," Olson transformed Thompson into an attractive candidate.[4]

With the help of manager Fred Lundin, Thompson carried that new-found legitimacy through the general election. He picked his words well as he promised a "square deal" for all party factions, Progressives included, and had Deneen and Edward Brundage—a second GOP factional leader—named to his managing committee. While Merriam refused to lend support, Thompson appealed to the middle-class and reform vote by promising to fight the excessive rates charged by Peoples Gas Company. In a show of factional support, Harry Olson and Charles Deneen spoke for the party candidate.[5]

The Democrats failed to match that unity. Incumbent Carter Harrison II lost to County Clerk Robert Sweitzer in a primary one part movie, the other theatre. Harrison experimented with a campaign movie-short; Sweitzer preferred opera. He likened Harrison to Pooh-Bah from Gilbert and Sullivan's "The Mikado," as a man driven more by family pride than a sense of civic responsibility. What Sweitzer won, as Democratic leader Roger Sullivan warned him, was the right to lose. Particularly, the Democrats outwitted themselves in their appeal to the ethnic vote. During the primary, a Harrison lieutenant charged that Sweitzer was a German who chose membership in the Ancient Order of Hibernians over that of any organization from his own ethnic group. To prevent Thompson from reviving the issue and to minimize damage from the inevitable whispering campaign over his Catholicism, Sweitzer released the German Fatherland letter. The leaflet was intended for distribution in German neighborhoods, but once the Republicans discovered and reproduced it, the letter found a new audience. "You, your relatives and friends can be of great assistance to Germany and Austria next Tuesday by electing Robert M. Sweitzer . . ." took on an unintended meaning in Polish Downtown and Czech Pilsen, where sensibilities had been rubbed raw by World War I.[6]

The letter worsened ethnic friction already present in Democratic ranks. During the primary, Congressman Adolph Sabath charged that Sweitzer was an anti-Semite who called City Hall a synagogue because of the number of Jewish workers. The remark was not forgotten in the name of party unity. The leaflet was a measure of the Democrats' inability to appeal equally to all groups.[7]

Running with Progressives Charles H. Sergel for treasurer and John Siman for clerk, Thompson won by 148,000 votes. Contrary to legend, he did not begin looting the city treasury. Instead, he played the role of advocate of (relatively) good government. The emphasis remained on the middle class. In one of his first moves, Thompson thanked the *Tribune* "for the fair manner in which you gave me an opportunity" to present his candidacy and principles. Thompson chose for police chief Captain Charles C. Healey, who claimed he had never tasted liquor in his life. Thompson also acted on his promise to fight Peoples Gas by choosing a select committee of aldermen; when the committee decided on Merriam ally Donald R. Richberg as counsel, Thompson accepted. Charles Wacker was impressed—and politic—enough with the new mayor to pledge the support of the Chicago Plan Commission in furthering projects in accordance with the Burnham Plan. By the summer of 1915, the Thompson administration was promising a $3.7 million economy drive and the dismissal of one hundred overaged officers from the police department. The "new" Thompson was in full evidence after the steamship Eastland capsized in the Chicago River. The mayor left the Panama-Pacific Exposition in San Francisco to direct relief efforts, and he led a funeral procession of five thousand through Lawndale, home of many of the drowning victims.[8]

At first, Thompson was not particularly interested in the support of organized labor. His policy was shaped by middle-class interest and bias. When a traction strike shut down public transportation in June 1915, he helped mediate a quick settlement. In doing so, he realized which groups most used the els and trolleys; the page-one thanks in *Chicago Commerce* magazine could not have come as a surprise. Yet Thompson made it clear he was no friend of labor. When Sidney Hillman and a delegation representing striking garment workers went to city hall that autumn, the mayor refused to see them. The group came to protest police action against pickets. Thompson's explanation of his inaction in this labor dispute, that his participation "would set the precedent of wild agitation and murder," was not meant for a working-class audience. The strike lasted three months.[9]

Thompson was as hostile to union activity among municipal employees. At a time when officers received the same pay as they had in 1912 and were expected to work a 365-day year, Thompson's police chief suspended four officers for trying to revive a patrolmen's benefit society. It was part of the same attitude displayed for nearly two years toward the city's teachers. In August 1915, school board member Jacob Loeb, a Harrison holdover, forced passage of a measure that forbade school employees from belonging to unions. The board hoped this "Loeb Rule" would weaken if not destroy the Chicago Teachers' Federation, and Thompson gave his support. He contended, "City employees should be prohibited from organizing to operate against the municipal government. I am opposed to it for such a movement can bring no good." Instead, he urged the schools to support efficiency and the 3 Rs.[10]

Again, it was a move calculated to elicit the support of a group like the Illinois Manufacturers' Association, which approved of Thompson's stand "because the Teachers' Federation is controlled by union labor." When the federation's Margaret Haley secured an injunction against the measure, Thompson allowed the board in June 1916, under newly elected president Jacob Loeb, to pass a second antifederation rule in the guise of an employee tenure measure. The board quickly dismissed sixty-eight teachers, thirty-six of them federation members. The teachers were forced to leave the Chicago Federation of Labor in the spring of 1917 before the state would pass legislation protecting them against the Loeb measures.[11]

A mayor who settled traction strikes and fought teacher organizations naturally would move in another area of middle-class concern, the saloons. For years the city had celebrated a Continental Sunday in violation of state law. The Sunday hours of the Columbian Exposition in 1893 encouraged the practice, which was a tradition in the city's growing German and Catholic neighborhoods. From the time of his election, Thompson was pressured by temperance groups to comply with the law. On the first Sunday of October 1915, he did. There was little the estimated 7,150 establishments that were closed could do to stop him. Saloon owner and alderman Bathhouse John Coughlin tried the pen ("I never dreamed that such a day would ever come to pass/When you and I would be deprived of friendship's social glass") without success while Anton Cermak resorted to more direct action. As secretary of the United Societies, Cermak released a pledge Thompson had made to the antiprohibition group during the campaign that he would not enforce the closing laws. Cermak hoped the disclosure would make Thompson appear as a political hypocrite or weakling. Instead, it demonstrated Thompson's abililty to withstand criticism when in tune with his constituency.[12]

Thompson emerged from the 1916 Republican Convention as a national committeeman from Illinois. The committeeship represented the epitome of Thompson, the conventional politician. Winning city hall, he had a power base for dealings with other party factions. Downstate political leaders soon realized the importance of Thompson's strength in Chicago. Senator Lawrence Y. Sherman needed help for his favorite son candidacy; Frank Lowden, who first supported Thompson for mayor in 1900, wanted the nomination for governor. Both figured in his election as committeemen. "Do not forget," Chicago banker and Republican leader Charles Gates Dawes wrote Sherman, "that unless it is prevented by unwise conduct in little things that Thompson, if he handles himself right, is a coming man."[13]

Ultimately, it was a series of "little things" that ended the conventional phase of Thompson's career. Critics charged that Corporation Counsel Samuel Ettleson was little more than a spokesman for the utilities while in early 1916 two city officials resigned in protest of civil service abuses. One of them, Dr. Theodore Sachs of the Municipal Tuberculosis Sanitarium, committed suicide. His suicide letter, addressed "To the People of Chicago," became a campaign staple against Thompson. With the release of a report claiming the mayor had made 9,200 temporary civil service appointments within his first five months in office, the good government forces gathered at the Auditorium for a protest rally in March 1916.[14]

Thompson knew that few elections were decided on civil service. Still, his critics understood his new image was by no means secure, and they proceeded accordingly. As early as September 1915, the press reported that the new mayor had racial problems. Blacks and Italians clashed, allegedly the result of the increased black presence on city work gangs; black employment figures were reported for the various city departments. Thompson was forced to make a public defense of his hiring practices to a rally of black supporters at the Coliseum. He spoke of "my duty to do what I can to elevate rather than degrade any class of American citizens." Blacks and whites could draw differing conclusions from the mayor's words and the size of the audience (15,000). Shortly after the rally, aldermen found bogus notices in their mail boxes for a new play, "Uncle Tom's Cabin," featuring Thompson in the lead and advisor Fred Lundin in the role of Simon Legree. The time of performance was four years.[15]

As Democratic state's attorney, Maclay Hoyne did more than satirize; he generated indictments. Running for reelection in 1916, Hoyne combined race and vice in a blow against the mayor. In the weeks before the November elections, Hoyne raided City Hall in search of evidence concerning a vice scandal. The raid led to the indictment of Police Chief Charles Healey on charges of being part of a gambling conspiracy. Two months later Hoyne lodged similar charges against Oscar DePriest, the city's first black alderman and a Thompson ally. The trials gave Hoyne the chance to portray black Chicago as most whites were inclined to see it—as a center of vice and corruption—and link Thompson to that image. Despite the use of 1,470 phone tap conversations as evidence in the Healey trial, Hoyne lost both cases to Clarence Darrow. Still, Thompson's reputation was tarnished. The middle class did not want its police chief using a private line to conduct gambling "business." [16]

If Thompson were less ambitious, he could have recovered from the Healey scandal; American participation in World War I and his desire for national office would not allow it. Ironically, until the declaration of war by Woodrow Wilson, Thompson seemed to support American foreign policy. He was the first Chicagoan to enroll in a civilian training course at Fort Sheridan, and he helped coordinate Chicago's preparedness parade, a typical Thompson production of 130,000 participants marching through downtown. [17]

In part, his stand on the war can be traced to one of the most astute observations made by a city politician: "Chicago is [in April 1917] the sixth largest German city in the world, the second largest Bohemian, the second largest Norwegian and the second largest Polish." The good mayor always trod carefully in matters of ethnicity. Yet Thompson's criticism of the war—it never reached the level of formal opposition—was based on more than simple nose-counting in the city's precincts. Thompson was a smart enough politician to sense that a majority of Chicagoans, particularly the new immigrants whose homelands were controlled by the Central Powers, would support the war, as would the city's elite. Rather than go along with that majority and in the process blunt the criticism of his administration, Thompson gambled on an issue that transformed his career. He did it because he wanted to be a United States senator, and he thought he saw something in the vote in Congress on 5 April 1917. Of the fifty votes cast against the war in the House of Representatives, six came from the Illinois delegation. [18]

The mayor intended to project himself as an Illinois LaFollette, at least to the extent his personality would allow. In one of his first moves, Thompson released a public letter warning that Chicago and the nation faced starvation if too much food was diverted to Europe. He urged Congressional action and offered his own interim solution, a city garden program. He again appealed to national self-interest in his remarks on the draft. Opposing it "until the life of the republic" itself was threatened, the mayor contended the danger would come from Mexico before it would Europe. Further comments on the war appeared in Thompson's unofficial newspaper, *The Republican*. The paper struck a Populist pose in its remarks on the war. Woodrow Wilson, Wall Street and the commercialized press, Thompson's critics, caused American involvement in the war. "The industrial and commercial rivalry between Great Britain and Germany was not our fault; and we were not especially interested in their respective pretensions to power and predominance in old world politics." It was a common *Republican* refrain. By summer 1917, Thompson and his paper together regularly cited Washington's Farewell Address, the Wilson administration's violation of free speech, and the "fat contracts" of war profiteers. [19]

Thompson balanced his wartime remarks with repeated promises of a greater Chicago. A month before the war, architect Jarvis Hunt released two plans, one for a combination monorail-subway system and the other Thompson's proposal for lakefront development. There would be offshore islands, a twenty thousand-capacity town hall set in Grant Park, and two more commercial-recreational piers, like Municipal [Navy] Pier. Although nothing came of either idea, Thompson had set a precedent with the lakefront idea: He recast a part of the Burnham Plan and offered it as his own. He would not be the last mayor to do so.[20]

Like Thompson, Charles Wacker of the plan commission publicized civic projects during the war. As a businessman and supporter of the war, Wacker had no particular affection for the mayor. Wacker fought for the continuation of public works in wartime because he was a true believer in the Chicago Plan; that Thompson held office was incidental. Wacker publicly defended his position. "How are we to develop a strong, virile and capable people?" he asked. The Wacker solution lay in better housing and more playgrounds, parks, and beaches. Wacker also helped in the fight to continue work on the Michigan Boulevard link. Writing to Frederic A. Delano—an original member of the Chicago Plan Committee—of the capital issues committee of the Federal Reserve Board, Wacker argued that the project constituted an important part of the national war effort because it facilitated traffic and, by extension, the movement of war material and because it connected the city with Fort Sheridan and the Great Lakes Naval Base.[21]

When Thompson gave his third annual message to the city council in May 1918, he avoided the war to focus on such construction projects as 12th Street and Ogden Avenue. The mayor needed these successes since his other actions, e.g., the refusal to extend a formal invitation to the visiting Marshal Joffre (on the claim that it was the duty of the city council) and the hostility shown Liberty Bond salesmen at City Hall during the first loan drive (Thompson explained he wanted to avoid the appearance of coercing city employees to buy bonds) expended political capital. Still, these were minor incidents when compared to the meeting of the People's Council of America for Democracy and Terms of Peace. Thompson allowed the antiwar group, which included Crystal Eastman and Socialist Victor Berger, to come to the city in September 1917 even though it had been denied permission throughout the Midwest. Governor Frank Lowden was unmoved by the argument of the corporation counsel that there were no grounds for barring a meeting. Lowden ordered Chicago Police Chief Herman Schulttler to stop it. After police dispersed the first meeting, representatives of the group appealed to Thompson, who again granted permission (as he avoided phone calls from Lowden). The governor dispatched a detachment of the National Guard from Springfield by train, but the People's Council held its session. It was not the only controversial appearance of antiwar spokesmen in the city. A well-known group of radicals such as Victor

Berger, Emma Goldman, Big Bill Haywood, and Morris Hillquitt all appeared without incident.[22]

The federal government did not move directly against Thompson. When the Hearst papers printed the remarks of an assistant district attorney that the Joffre snub could lead to an investigation, Assistant Attorney General Samuel Graham demanded a report; the assistant denied the statement. Rather than an investigation, the Justice Department kept a file. It included Thompson senate campaign literature and the transcript of a mayoral strategy session held in a room—which was bugged—at the LaSalle Hotel. The file did not, however, lead to any prosecution of the mayor. Rather than risk an incident, the government allowed the problem of Chicago's loyalty to work itself out, which it did. Nationalistic Poles and Bohemians helped by pressuring the school board to stop German instruction and the use of the "Kaiser-page" in the grammar school speller and to rename Bismark School. The press reported approvingly of these actions, and the *Tribune* began a Kaiser-page referendum. Those who found "The Kaiser in the Making"—the lesson on page 154 of the speller— offensive were encouraged to rip it out and mail it to the board.[23]

Self-styled patriotic organizations also joined in the cause of insuring wartime loyalty. The National Security League undertook a variety of activities, including the expulsion of Thompson from its executive committee. The American Protective League (APL) assumed a less public posture. Claiming over 6,100 active members by the Armistice, the APL provided the federal government with information that, in the words of the league's first president, "the Bureau of Investigation has generously intimated could hardly have been secured from any other source." The league helped index the names of 18,000 registered German aliens, conducted a daily average of twenty-five character checks for federal authorities, and detained some 200,000 men in a Slacker Drive conducted in July 1918. The superintendent of the Chicago division of the Bureau of Investigation credited the APL with doing 75 percent of the government's investigative work in the region during the war.[24]

Thompson accepted the constraints imposed by the prowar groups. Utilizing the school board, he found it easier to give off informal signals that he was not a dangerous politician. Immediately after the People's Council incident, the board dropped the Kaiser-page; Bismark School became Funston School in March 1918. A virtual boycott by students made German-language instruction a moot point. Mindful that his rhetoric on war profiteers would not help his Senate campaign, Thompson allowed the board to join with the Chicago Association of Commerce in 1918 to offer an adult Americanization program. These gestures could not stop criticism of Thompson—it had become a given in the newspapers—but they did succeed as damage control. The Germans could content themselves with the knowledge that Thompson had fought the good fight for them while the prowar groups had the satisfaction of getting their way on the school issue.[25]

The mayor faced Congressman Medill McCormick in the 1918 primary for the United States Senate seat. Rather than avoid it, Thompson made an issue of his own loyalty. His campaign material was intended to convince the doubting: "I love but one flag—Old Glory! I love but one country—the United States of America, which is your country and my country." To preserve it, he proposed a foreign policy guided by Washington's Farewell Address and the Monroe Doctrine; any government official sacrificing the national interest was to be impeached and removed from office. For domestic policy, Thompson promised to respect Constitutional rights and to fight for a protective tariff and an excess war profits tax. "The Truth About William Hale Thompson" included the words of Washington, Jefferson, Webster and Lincoln. On the front cover of the pamphlet were two crossed American flags; on the back, a picture of Thompson with a Shriners' pin on his lapel.[26]

Although he campaigned statewide, Thompson had little chance of victory. Primarily, he was the victim of timing. Had the election been held a year earlier, when there was still doubt over the wisdom of American participation in the war, he would have had a chance, but with the Allies close to victory, Illinois Republicans had little reason to register a protest vote. Medill McCormick exploited the mayor's vulnerability. Before a crowd at Cubs Park, he demanded the votes of loyalists against the "faint-hearted, the pacifists, the defeatists, the IWW, the Copperheads, the American Bolshevik" and all the others who intended to make the United States into another Russia. The *Tribune* contributed to the loyalist din by classifying the mayor with such Progressives as Robert LaFollette, Charles Lindbergh, Sr., and Henry Ford. They belonged together because "Bolshevism in Wisconsin, pacifism in Minnesota, peace-arkism in Michigan, [and] Thompsonism in Illinois, all have sought to divert attention from their records by shrieking against 'war profiteers.'" McCormick won by just under 60,000 votes although Thompson carried Chicago by 18,000.[27]

If the defeat frustrated Thompson and his national ambitions, it also liberated him. He no longer had to play the conventional politician. Since it was impossible for him to attempt further agreement with party leaders like Edward Brundage, Charles Deneen, and Frank Lowden, Thompson instead embraced the radical image his opponents had fashioned of him. Shriner pins and Sunday closings became irrelevant along with any semblance of the conventional. As he sought renomination for a second term as mayor in the winter of 1919, Thompson could have *The Republican* run an article on Irish independence by the president of De Paul University, or he could blame Donald Richberg, as lawyer for the city council gas committee, for the high cost of gas. It simply took an abundance of political nerve. Thompson's shift away from middle class politics also reflected a demographic change. During the 1920s, the area outside Chicago grew at a rate double the city's. Chicago was less Wasp middle class, at least politically. Reformers Harold Ickes and Donald Richberg might not have liked that change, but they were already suburbanites.[28]

Judge Harry Olson and Charles Merriam faced Thompson in the 1919 mayoral primary. Olson was as inept as before, with the promise of "an administration of good, clean and honest housekeeping" and an interest in eugenics that would not appeal to blacks or ethnics. Merriam positioned himself as the real alternative to Thompson. Returned from army service in Italy, the former Hyde Park alderman was convinced he could win without a strong organization. He cast himself as Captain Merriam, the concerned war veteran who would return democracy to local government with a platform combining business and social reform. City hall would be run efficiently and, with the use of a postwar reconstruction commission and increased home rule powers, compassionately. According to the Merriam campaign literature, Chicago had a courageous friend: "I may be standing with my back to the wall, but I do not intend to forsake the men and women who have asked me to lead this fight, nor to desert the claims of Chicago at this critical moment." [29]

If the primary constituted his critical moment, Merriam failed with a campaign that resembled that of any political opportunist. He revived the issue of Dr. Theodore Sachs' suicide, publicized the support of E. O. Hanson (a Chicagoan whose brother as mayor of Seattle had won momentary national fame for opposing a general strike), and allowed a sailors' and soldiers' vigilante club to intimidate Thompson campaign workers downtown. With a campaign speech that warned against the "Hohenzollern cult of power" in city hall, Merriam showed he could sound like Thompson if not win like him. Merriam's defeat— 67,000 votes behind Olson, 106,000 behind Thompson—ended his political career. [30]

As they had in 1915, the Democrats found party unity impossible. When Roger Sullivan slated Robert Sweitzer a second time, State's Attorney Maclay Hoyne declared an independent candidacy. His executive committee included Clarence Darrow, Donald Richberg, and the suddenly popular E. O. Hanson. Labeling his two opponents the "gasocracy" for their alleged ties to utility interests, Hoyne added a twist to the 1915 Fatherland letter. He reprinted it as a leaflet and included facsimiles of old German-language Thompson and Sweitzer campaign buttons. Between the buttons, Hoyne inserted, "This is the sort of Appeal to Race Prejudice that is a Slur on American Citizenship." The voters disagreed. Thompson, whose speeches ranged from advocating Irish independence to the free trade policies of Grover Cleveland, defeated Sweitzer by 21,000 votes, thanks in large part to the 111,000 votes Hoyne attracted. [31]

Almost half of Thompson's victory margin came from the black Second Ward. Still, the vote did not reflect an ideal relationship. Earlier 1915, the Thompson campaign claimed that Robert Sweitzer as county clerk had ignored the tearful pleas of a mother—who was white—when he issued a marriage license to boxer Jack Johnson to marry the woman's daughter. The charge failed to damage the Republicans, testament both to the strength of the South Side organization of George F. Harding and Congressman Martin B. Madden and to the inability of Democrats to attract black support. There was continued cause for dissatisfaction with Thompson. The symbolic value of Thompson's banning "Birth of a Nation" diminished as the movie managed to play in 1915 and again during the next two years. Thompson also showed himself willing to exploit race prejudice for political advantage. On the grounds that it wanted to lessen conflict at the integrated schools, the school board sent out letters in July 1918—in the middle of the mayor's senate primary campaign—to ask some 350 blacks the best means of achieving voluntary segregation. A delegation of black leaders informed Thompson there was none. He was forced to disavow the scheme, and, instead, school segregation continued along de facto lines.[32]

Yet, despite periodic reports—particularly before elections—that the "better element" in the black community was about to abandon Thompson, there was little choice for blacks in the 1920s. If a Louis B. Anderson or Robert R. Jackson wanted to run for alderman, he had to work with the mayor's white South Side allies. Had the Democrats been willing, they could have challenged that strength by cultivating the support of *Chicago Defender* publisher Robert S. Abbott. In 1926, Abbott publicly endorsed party leader George Brennan for the Senate over the Thompson choice of Frank L. Smith, and the *Defender* printed—in Polish—a speech Abbott gave that year to a Humboldt Park crowd of 50,000 on the celebration of the 150th birthday of Polish hero Thaddeus Kosciusko. Still, no change came in the Democratic attitude toward blacks until 1931.[33]

To his credit, Thompson never denied his identification with the black community. By his last term, 14 percent of the city's legal department, including six assistant corporation counsels, was black while the number of black patrolmen in the police department rose from 50 in 1914 under Carter Harrison II to 137 in 1930. If there was civil service abuse in the process, and there was, it did not end with Thompson. After Anton Cermak's election, Leonard D. White of the University of Chicago was appointed to the civil service commission. White kept his friend Charles Merriam informed of his experiences in city hall. Among White's problems was the hostility his fellow commissioners showed when he attempted to post an eligibility list for the public works department. They complained it was "full of Thompson niggers."[34]

The race riot of 1919 has been interpreted as a violent turn of the struggle over jobs, housing, and public accommodations, with the black vote in that year's mayoral election a contributing factor. The riot was that, as well as a manifestation of ethnic anxieties. Versailles did not bring peace to Central Europe or independence for Ireland. Rather, news from Warsaw, Vilnius, and Dublin brought frustration to the immigrant neighborhoods; signs of friction between ethnic groups was evident long before the riot. When a group met on south Halsted in May 1918 to urge the formation of a Polish republic which would include Poles, Lithuanians and Ruthenians, the *Dziennik Zwiazkowy* blamed the breakup of the meeting on Lithuanian Bolsheviks. In its coverage of the meeting, the *Lietuva* condemned "Polonized Liths" present who were interested in little more than imitating Polish barons; the paper found the disruption appropriate in light of Polish "intrigues against Lithuania." A year later, in June 1919, speakers at the Lithuanian National Congress meeting in Chicago charged that Polish Prime Minister Ignace Paderewski was using the Polish army to oppress Lithuania.[35]

In the case of Chicago's Poles and Jews, the argument moved from the editorial page to the streets in June and July 1919. Antagonisms arose over the issue of pogroms in Poland. The *Narod Polski* dismissed the stories; the *Jewish Courier* ran eyewitness accounts. Some 25,000 people marched downtown in late May to protest the situation in Poland. That was followed by an incident in early June, when another 8,000 people gathered around the intersection of 12th Street and Kedzie in the Jewish section of Lawndale to fend off a rumored invasion of 5,000 Poles. No onslaught occurred, but 250 police had to be stationed in Douglas Park to keep the peace. Then, in early July, Poles on the Southeast Side took to the streets. The story that a Jewish grocer had killed a Polish boy filled Buffalo Avenue with a crowd bordering on 3,000. Two days before the riot, the *Courier* reported—with satisfaction—that eighteen Poles had been fined for their part in the incident.[36]

Like the more recent immigrants, Chicago's Irish were concerned over events in the old country. In April 1919, former mayor and governor Edward F. Dunne left with a group to visit Versailles to appeal to the American peace delegation on the status of Ireland. By the time Dunne returned in early July, his efforts and his report on British atrocities against the Irish were widely covered. In the same week Jews in Lawndale prepared to fight with Poles, the Irish crowded into the Auditorium for an independence rally. Mayor Thompson and De Paul University President Rev. Francis X. McCabe both attended; the audience hissed at the mention of Woodrow Wilson's name. Later in the month, De Paul awarded an honorary degree to Irish nationalist Eamon De Valera. Visiting the city in mid-July, De Valera spoke at Cubs Park and drew a crowd of 25,000 which included Dunne and Thompson. When he presented De Valera to the city council, the mayor introduced him as the president of the Irish republic.[37]

If De Valera's visit did not hasten Irish independence, it did add to the city's emotional strain that summer. By the end of July, the situation worsened with the beginning of a series of strikes. On the eve of the riot, an estimated 250,000 workers either were threatening action, on strike or locked out by employers. Police on strike duty (500 by midmonth) weeks earlier had considered a joint walkout with firemen over salaries. When violence began on July 27, it proved impossible to contain. The rioting was fueled in part, as William Tuttle has shown, by racial tensions. Blacks also made for victims of transference. A white Chicagoan living close to the black belt could not easily prevent a pogrom, guarantee the independence of Lithuania or Poland, stop a Black and Tan, or break the British naval blockade to feed relatives in Hamburg. But if the conditions were right, as they were after the stoning and drowning of Eugene Williams off 29th Street Beach, he could find a violent release or cheer on those who had. The emotion preceding the riot was so deep and peculiar to the summer of 1919 that a similar incident the following June did not cause a repeat. Two white men, one a sailor, were shot and killed at 35th and Prairie during a parade of the black separatist Star Order of Ethiopia. In the summer of 1920, the South Side remained peaceful.[38]

Thompson's reputation survived the riot without serious damage. Critics failed to exploit the controversy over his delayed call for the National Guard, in part because Frank Lowden was in Chicago negotiating a traction strike settlement when the riot began. With the mayor and his police commissioner returning from a frontier celebration in Cheyenne, Wyoming, Lowden missed the opportunity to repay Thompson for his handling of the People's Council meeting two years earlier. Thompson came out of the riot strong enough politically to stop Lowden's favorite-son candidacy at the 1920 GOP convention. As city hall convention delegates spread stories that the governor had misspent campaign funds in Missouri, Thompson added dramatic effect by resigning as a delegate rather than vote for the "tainted" Lowden. Although he initially favored Hiram Johnson, the mayor came around to the candidacy of Warren G. Harding. After the obligatory trip to Marion, he predicted greatness for the Ohio senator.[39]

The city went Republican in the November election. The Democrats again proved themselves unable to maintain party unity. Two days before the election, the rally in Grant Park was not for James Cox but Terence McSwiney, the lord mayor of Cork who died after a seventy-five-day hunger strike; the meeting at the Coliseum, where Edward Dunne spoke and a representative for George Cardinal Mundelein gave the prayers, included cheers for "Ireland's greatest friend," William Hale Thompson. After the election, the mayor learned the advantages of having a friend in the White House. In 1921, the *Tribune* named Thompson and others in a $2.9 million suit to recover city funds paid to real estate experts who figured property values for land used in municipal construction projects. At the request of Chicago congressman and city hall ally M. A. Michaelson, President Harding instructed the Justice and Treasury Departments not to assist the newspaper in its suit. Thompson, however, received more favorable treatment from Washington in his libel suit against the *Tribune*. Asked to give a deposition in the case (which involved Thompson's treatment in the wartime press), William M. Offey, a former superintendent of the Bureau of Investigation, declined on grounds of confidentiality. Later, Attorney General Harry M. Daugherty refused to allow *Tribune* attornies to view Bureau of Investigation files that might pertain to the paper's defense. (The suit was dismissed after a mistrial.) The Harding administration even allowed the mayor some fun at the expense of its most popular cabinet member, Secretary of Commerce Herbert Hoover. Thompson told the renowned internationalist that he should embrace a policy of "America first" and "renounce the foxhunting nobility of Europe."[40]

Despite the indictment of confidant Fred Lundin in 1922 on charges of conspiring to defraud the school system of $1 million, Thompson endured. Clarence Darrow deflected testimony on the $133 potato peelers the school board purchased under Lundin, and, for a third time, the attorney kept a Thompson ally out of prison. Thompson had to sit out the 1923 election, but his successor, the Democrat William Dever, made possible his comeback in 1927. The new mayor set out to give the city actual good government—a professional cabinet, a school board free from politics, and a police department devoted to enforcing the law. When he ran for reelection in 1927, Dever had the enthusiastic support of such Republicans as Sewell Avery, John V. Farwell and Julius Rosenwald. He also lost to Thompson by 83,000 votes. Neither Dever nor party head George Brennan understood the city as well as Thompson.[41]

The Democrat's defeat was not due solely to Prohibition. Dever did antagonize ethnics and Anton Cermak by trying to enforce the 18th Amendment, but that was not his only mistake. Dever consistently alienated his natural constituency. His appointment of A. A. Sprague was typical. Sprague had been one of the early members of the Citizens' Committee to Enforce the Landis Award. The group formed in 1921 to police an arbitration decision by federal judge Kenesaw Mountain Landis in a wage dispute between contractors and the building trades. The decision that committee members Thomas E. Donnelley and Julius Rosenwald found worth defending included a 10 to 36 percent wage cut; provisions against strikes and lockouts; and the right to use nonunion labor and materials. The committee took the decision a step further when it warned that any trade not accepting the award would be declared open shop. To force compliance, the group offered contractors and property owners insurance, guards, and, most importantly, nonunion labor. The committee declared fifteen trades to be open shop, which led to the establishment of a trade school and employment bureau. By 1925, the committee had placed seventy-five thousand workers on jobs, with twenty-five thousand brought in from outside the city. The committee was so successful that it was forced to ask participating contractors to help defray the cost of a $43,000 transportation bill, the result of paying train fare for recruits.[42]

In 1927, the citizens' committee took credit for $400 million in construction work. Landis Award projects included the Allerton Club and the Edgewater Beach Hotel, the theology and medical buildings at the University of Chicago, and the Joseph Bond Chapel and Chicago Theological Seminary, also on the university campus. As mayor, Dever could not do much to oppose the group; the open-shop drive was as much a part of the 1920s as the speakeasy. But as a card-carrying member of the tanners and curriers local of the American Federation of Labor, he did not have to appoint Sprague or be photographed breaking ground at the building site of a Landis Award contractor. To do so simply was not good politics for a Democratic mayor.[43]

Dever's efforts at reforming the schools were no better. Allowed to make seven school board appointments in his first month in office, Dever chose five members of the Chicago Association of Commerce. The board set about to select a superintendent free from politics. It chose William McAndrew from out of the New York City system. A former Chicago teacher, McAndrew reduced the advisory role of faculty by abolishing teachers councils. Popular for over a decade, the councils gave teachers a sense of participation in system policy making. Forcing through the junior high school and the "platoon" systems and the use of intelligence testing, McAndrew made little effort to explain the changes. He appeared to be another Jacob Loeb.[44]

Thompson only benefited from Dever's problems. Returning to active politics in 1926, he joined those Republican factions opposing Charles Deneen's slate in the party primaries. Thompson did not disappoint. Senator William Borah accepted his invitation to deliver a Washington birthday address against the World Court, and his own speeches helped turn a party primary into a referendum on America First and Big Bill Thompson. The anti-Deneen forces won, and Chicago Republicans knew who would be running for mayor again.[45]

Dever rested in Biloxi, Mississippi, before the February 1927 mayoral primaries. While there, he noted the polite manners of black children and complimented the schools for work well done. The remark, intentional or not, set the level of Democratic strategy in the general election. A series of vice raids on the South Side in March netted one thousand arrests, all of them black; Dever explained it was part of an effort "to give the decent colored people a chance to vote and have their votes counted properly." Party leader George Brennan predicted that voters never would allow the city to be run by the black belt or hoodlums. For music, the Democrats hired a calliope to play "Bye-Bye, Blackbird" downtown. Nor did all the independents and reformers who supported Dever avoid such race baiting. Former state's attorney Maclay Hoyne charged that Thompson caused the 1919 race riot while Raymond Robins, a veteran of the settlement house movement and Bull Moose candidate for the Senate in 1914, told listeners Thompson was "talking 'America First' and acting 'Africa First.'"[46]

A masterful campaigner, Thompson had little problem turning the Democratic attacks against Dever. He warned that the police "cossacks" who rounded up blacks could just as easily move against Jews, Poles, and Germans; these were groups that who some idea what the term meant in its European context. Where Dever posed as an upholder of the law, Thompson cast him as the head of a police force more interested in "fanning mattresses for pints or breaking in your doors" than in protecting the ordinary citizen. If Brennan wanted to label him a lawbreaker, Thompson accepted. He opened an address to a group of society women with the greeting "My hoodlum friends" and received the attention desired.[47]

Then came the classic Thompson. A rally could include charges against anyone: Sewell Avery, the "biggest tax dodger in America" and a Dever supporter; the Independent Republicans for Dever, a "gold coast committee of absentee landlords" that Thompson claimed was spending $10,000 a day in advertising against him; and Arthur Schlesinger, Sr., whose *New Viewpoints in American History* Thompson quoted to listeners as so much British propaganda taught at a disloyal University of Chicago. The demagoguery was not merely overkill; it served a vital purpose. Without a strong precinct organization, Thompson had to be outrageous enough often enough to command the respect of both party leaders and the voters. The strategy worked. After the Republican primary, the Brundage and Deneen factions had no choice but to accept him, just as Herbert Hoover, preparing for 1928, felt the necessity to visit a victorious Thompson four days after the election.[48]

With the vote counted, a group of Thompson supporters crowded the Louis XVI Room of the Hotel Sherman to sing "Bye-Bye, Dever." The ex-mayor was not the only one about to retire from local politics. He was joined by the Chicago business community. After 1927, the city's leading businessmen no longer concerned themselves greatly with local politics. They realized the voters no longer cared who business leaders endorsed for political office. The Independent Republicans for Dever Committee constituted a last stand for the business vision of good government in Chicago. The group started with a budget of $500,000 but was forced to halve that amount on two occasions. Worse, its full-page advertisements for Dever in the newspapers became unintended endorsements of Thompson, at least for labor. Seven of the twenty-four committee members whose names appeared at the bottom of the ad also belonged to the Citizens' Committee to Enforce the Landis Award. The Dever appreciation banquet held the month after the election showed how quickly Chicago businessmen were abandoning politics. The dinner did not raise enough to cover the cost of a commemorative bust and testimonial book.[49]

Thompson did not merely pay off political debts in 1927; he set precedents which endured for the next fifty years. During the election, he received the support of policemen and teachers—as well as Margaret Haley of the Teachers Federation—and the neutrality of the Chicago Federation of Labor. In return, he stopped a practice revived under Dever of surprise field checks for patrolmen, and he removed William McAndrew as school superintendent. Oscar F. Nelson, a vice-president of the federation of labor and a Republican convert, became the Thompson floor leader in the city council. Labor leaders also were appointed to positions for distributing patronage in the board of education and city hall. Where labor encountered a politician hostile to their cause in 1915, they found a mayoral ally in 1927.[50]

So too did organized crime. The estimates of the campaign contribution from Al Capone to Thompson range from $100,000 to $260,000. However, Capone was not alone in trying to buy influence with public officials during the 1920s in Chicago. Even such noted reformers as Julius Rosenwald, chairman of Sears and Roebuck, made substantial offers of stock and cash to help reform candidates reach their virtuous goals.[51]

The Capone money raises an intriguing question: Why didn't it lead to some type of prosecution? If local officials did not want to attempt it, the federal government could have intervened. Prosecution for income tax evasion seems as applicable to Thompson as Capone, yet no mention is made of the money in Thompson's Justice Department files. Regardless of the amount, though, Thompson did formalize the link between city government and organized crime when he paid off another political debt and chose Daniel A. Serritella as his city sealer. Until his death in 1967, Serritella was suspected for having ties with organized crime in the city. His trial in 1931 on charges of conspiracy to defraud the public of $54 million by shortweights did not end the relationship between criminals and Chicago officials.[52]

Thompson managed to keep attention away from crime for nearly a year after the election. His victory cruise down the Mississippi coincided with the spring floods. He quickly announced the formation of a relief committee and convened a flood control conference in Chicago in early June. The meeting attracted a number of national politicians—including Senators Smith Brookhart of Iowa and Pat Harrison of Mississippi—and helped publicize the problem. It also provided Thompson with another platform. America First took on more than King George. Farm relief, inland waterways, and national flood control all became part of the full measure of Big Bill Thompson's Americanism. During the summer of 1927, Thompson spread his message on a speaking tour that covered the Great Plains to the West Coast. By the time he reached Los Angeles, Thompson had made Boulder Dam as much a part of America First as his opposition to the World Court.[53]

Thompson's California itinerary included a rest at San Simeon. By 1927, the mayor had befriended publisher William Randolph Hearst. Although his papers had opposed Thompson in his first two elections, Hearst in time found the mayor to be something of an isolationist soulmate. They both worked for Hiram Johnson in the 1920 GOP Convention, and, by 1923, Hearst's *Herald-Examiner* was lamenting the loss of a progressive Republican the caliber of Thompson when he decided against running for a third term. Hearst's coverage of Thompson was in sharp contrast to that of the *Tribune* and *Daily News*. The mayor developed statesmanlike qualities not only in Chicago but in Hearst papers nationwide. San Franciscans reading their *Examiner* found in Thompson a "captivatingly democratic, ready witted and far visioned type" of leader the country needed. That paper and the New York *American* ran the same editorial on Thompson's 1927 victory, and both coasts were able to read how

Thompson's first two terms were a "golden age" for Chicago public works. Where other papers and the wire services reported on the Chicago textbook controversy as high—or low—comedy, Hearst accorded it serious treatment with a signed editorial, "Undermining of Patriotism Not a Cause for Laughter," to the editor of the Baltimore *American*.[54]

Thompson began the civil service proceedings against Superintendent McAndrew on returning to Chicago from his speaking tour. The mayor may have gotten the idea for the showcase "trial" from an incident in 1926. The Chicago *Defender* led a protest of blacks against a school text, *Community Life and Civic Problems*, by Howard Copeland Hill of the University of Chicago. The book contained a passage which, while praising Booker T. Washington, noted his constant struggle with blacks to "change their shiftless ways and become industrious citizens." Even with a defense of the work by sociologist Robert Park, school officials agreed to changes. Still, the book continued to offend. Following the 1927 election, Victor Olander, secretary of the Illinois Federation of Labor, wrote to Thompson ally Oscar Nelson to complain of the book. Olander was no friend of the new administration; he was a leader of the Dever labor committee in the election. What offended Olander was the selection in Hill on state police, "propaganda which has no proper place in any text book except to be exposed as propaganda."[55]

By combining the proceedings against McAndrew with repeated charges that the superintendent allowed the use of school books filled with British propaganda, Thompson knew he had created an appealing issue. Chicagoans could pick and choose from the "trial" testimony and Thompson's remarks. Germans, Irishmen, and Poles might focus on the charge that the history books of the McAndrew era slighted the contributions of immigrant groups to the Revolution; teachers could enjoy McAndrew's public humiliation; and labor might smile over the charges leveled against the University of Chicago. A place that used Landis Award labor certainly could be guilty of treason. The papers cast Thompson in the worst possible role, that of book burner, but there were too many disaffected groups in the city to care. A delegation of Chippewa, Navajo, Sioux, and Winnebago Indians visited Thompson during the controversy to present him with a petition: "We ask only that our story be told in fairness." If they could not get fairness there was always revenge, and American Indians, European immigrants, blacks and organized labor did not particularly care what motivated Thompson to give them satisfaction.[56]

Thompson wanted to establish a national American First Foundation, and he played with the idea of using the radio to broadcast citizenship lessons. Both ideas died after the results of the 1928 GOP primary. The homes of Charles Deneen and his choice for state's attorney were bombed, and, the remarks of Senator James Watson notwithstanding, the press dubbed it the Pineapple Primary. The bombings and the murder of a black Deneen precinct worker were blamed on Thompson, and allies Governor Len Small and State's Attorney

Robert E. Crowe were defeated for renomination. The vote broke Thompson politically and physically. The defeat in itself was not as great as the papers made it. In 1921 a Thompson judicial ticket was rejected also, despite a careful campaign. The difference was that in 1921 Thompson defied his critics and repaired the political damage; in 1928, he suffered a nervous breakdown. He did not recover until the end of his term. Meanwhile, the city drifted through the St. Valentine's Day Massacre and the Great Crash. When he recovered, all Thompson could offer was something on the level of William Randolph Hearst Day. The October 1930 event brought fifty thousand to Soldier Field, but it did not help teachers get their paychecks on time.[57]

The 1931 election was a watershed in Chicago politics. Anton Cermak defeated Thompson and began the Democratic domination of city government. Still, Democrats changed few of those policies Thompson had established by his last term, including his hostility to the reform community. Thompson's three terms—and the identification of reformers with the unpopular William Dever—caused the political atrophy of Chicago reformers. In 1930, Donald Richberg wrote Clarence Darrow for his help in opposing a traction ordinance the mayor favored. Darrow spoke for more than himself in his response: "I couldn't go into the fight without going into it thoroughly and I don't want to undertake the work of it all. You know I am old and tired." With the election of Franklin Delano Roosevelt, the city's leading reformers found themselves welcome not in city hall but Washington. Charles Merriam went to the National Planning Board; Harold Ickes became Secretary of the Interior; and Donald Richberg joined the National Recovery Administration. Later reformers who faced the choice of political frustration at home or political reward in Washington often chose the latter.[58]

Running against Thompson, Cermak did not repeat the Democratic mistakes of 1927. Instead, he took out an ad in the *Defender* to encourage blacks to "Come and Hear the Truth" when he spoke at Wendell Phillips High School. Cermak did not appoint a black to the school board as the ad promised he would, but the rally marked the realization by Democrats that blacks would have to be included as part of the party. The later success of Edward J. Kelly in transforming blacks into Democrats may be traceable to Thompson. As president of the South Parks Board in the 1920s, Kelly had to be responsive to a black community that had become politically skilled. When he failed, he could expect to be corrected. In 1926, the park board voted against erecting a memorial to the black veterans of World War I on the grounds that it would create a traffic problem. A group of blacks, including Aldermen Louis Anderson and Robert Jackson, protested to the board. To emphasize the importance of the memorial to blacks, the group visited the board on the most revered of holidays for Chicago's Irish, St. Patrick's Day. The board changed its vote, and Kelly learned an important lesson in racial diplomacy.[59]

Thompson also instructed Democrats on matters of ethnicity. The German

Fatherland letter, Irish independence, and the McAndrew history texts all were issues that exposed the Democrats' inability to appeal adequately to the various ethnic groups. When he defeated Dever in 1927, Thompson damaged the leadership of George Brennan as Democratic party head. When Brennan died the following year, the Irish were unable to perpetuate their control of the party. Instead, it passed to the Bohemian Anton Cermak, who treated the balanced ticket as something more than a necessary evil. In 1931, Thompson promised to "load that city hall up with Poles" if he were reelected. He aimed his pitch well. Poles long had felt slighted by the Democrats despite their party loyalty. However, with Cermak in control of the party, there was no defection en masse to Thompson because Cermak had seen fit in 1930 to allow the reslating of Judge Edmund K. Jarecki, the popular but controversial Polish politician who controlled the county election machinery. Poles repaid Cermak in the mayoral election by giving him 70 percent of their vote. If Democratic party leaders failed to recognize the political aspirations of another voting bloc in 1983, it was because they either forgot or ignored the lessons Thompson and Cermak taught their predecessors.[60]

The image of mayor as big builder may be Thompson's most enduring legacy to Chicago politics. Thompson pushed through the Michigan Boulevard link, which transformed a back street into Boul Mich, and he erected enough bridges, streets, and municipal buildings to have himself compared to both Baron Haussmann and Napoleon III. The nature of the builder image has changed with administrations. For Ed Kelly, it encompassed the various Works Progress Administration projects during the Depression; for Martin Kennelly, the legal framework for urban renewal and the construction of much of the expressway system; and for Richard Daley, the master ribboncutter, the image ranged from paving new runaways at O'Hare Airport to paving the alleys of the neighborhood of Gage Park. What remained constant, however, was the realization that concrete, poured in great quantities and with equal fanfare, went a long way in silencing critics.[61]

Thompson committed an uncharacteristic blunder in 1931 when he used trucks broadcasting "canned music." Union musicians were upset to be denied work even if it was on a truckbed, and at least one Thompson truck had its signs stripped off. The Democrats were left alone because they made an agreement with the musicians' union not to use recorded music. The episode showed that the overt anti-union atmosphere of the 1920s was dead and politicians would have to treat organized labor with care. The Citizens' Committee to Enforce the Landis Award disbanded in 1929 after the state supreme court ruled against it in a suit first brought by union carpenters, whose trade had been declared open shop. The recognition Thompson granted labor in his last term and the experience of millions of Chicagoans during the Depression transformed Chicago into a real union town; later mayors treated labor with the same respect Thompson learned to use. Richard Daley's father was a sheet metal worker, another of the trades declared open shop by the Citizens' Committee. As mayor, the son made sure city hall never abused the old trade of the father or any segment of organized labor.[62]

As much as anyone, Harold Ickes had a sense of what William Hale Thompson was about. The two shared a passion for Chicago Republican politics, although from opposite sides. Of his longtime antagonist, Ickes wrote in his *Autobiography*, "He was the Huey Long of his time and locale—without Huey's brains, however." If Ickes was right, Chicago got off lucky. In his three terms, Thompson had determined how city hall would deal with blacks and ethnics, businessmen and labor leaders, gangsters and reformers. To rephrase Paddy Bauler, Chicago wasn't ready for Big Bill with brains.[63]

6.

WILLIAM E. DEVER: A CHICAGO POLITICAL FABLE

John R. Schmidt

Once there was a mayor of Chicago named William E. Dever. He built great public works, removed politics from the city schools, revitalized municipal government, cut waste, and ran the gangsters out of town. Not once was there even the hint of scandal in his administration. He became well-known throughout the land, and some spoke of him as the country's next president. At the end of four years, he was soundly defeated for reelection by a loudmouthed lout who had barely avoided imprisonment for his outrageous misconduct in the same office.

So much for good government. To anticipate Paddy Bauler, Chicago evidently wasn't ready for reform in 1927. Like any cliché, this interpretation is grounded in truth. Dever did not give the public what they wanted, so they voted him out.

There is a bit more. Dever's story is not merely the case of a naive do-gooder misreading the mind of the electorate. It is a tale of many things: the decline of personality politics, the rise of the Chicago Democratic machine, the emergence of the urban ethnic voter—and, of course, the triumphs and travails of Chicago reform. Coming as it did at the juncture of these developments, the Dever administration played a significant role in the evolution of the Chicago political tradition. Certainly it is one of the more interesting episodes in the city's public life. Even Paddy Bauler might appreciate it.

I

William Emmett Dever was born in Woburn, Massachusetts in 1862.[1] His people were what is charmingly referred to as "lace curtain Irish." Patrick Dever, his father, owned one of the area's largest tanneries; his mother, Mary, was the daughter of Martin Lynch, one of Boston's early Irish ward bosses. William was the oldest boy in a family of eight children. He attended the Woburn public schools through the ninth grade, then quit to enter the family business.

He did not want to spend his life in his father's shop. At twenty William was on the road with a friend, working his way west through various tanneries as far as Wisconsin. By twenty-five he had married a New York state girl named Kate Conway, returned to New England for awhile, then set out for Chicago, where he had heard the tanners were earning twenty-four dollars a week. He arrived in the city in August 1887.

The Devers settled in West Town, a gritty workingman's community a few miles northwest of downtown along the Milwaukee Avenue car line. William took a job at a tannery on nearby Goose Island. An ambitious young man, he also began attending night classes at the Chicago College of Law. He graduated in 1890 and began a new career as a neighborhood lawyer.

He entered politics reluctantly. During the 1890s, Dever began to participate in the political discussion groups at Chicago Commons, the local settlement house. Settlement director Graham Taylor was a leader in the Municipal Voters' League and the general clean government movement. Reverend Taylor detected potential in the young lawyer with the lantern jaw and tried to talk Dever into running for alderman. Dever put him off, pleading the press of his legal practice. But Taylor was persistent, and Dever finally agreed to run as a reform Democratic candidate in 1900. He lost. Two years later, Taylor was ready to try again. By now Dever had gotten the political itch, and was anything but the unwilling candidate. He waged a spirited campaign that attracted the attention of Mayor Carter Harrison II. Harrison liked what he saw and threw his support to Reverend Taylor's candidate. This time, Dever won easily.

Dever spent eight years as alderman from the Seventeenth Ward. Almost from the beginning, he was one of the city council's most visible and most influential members. He championed the causes of honest government, improved schools, more parks and playgrounds, bigger and better public works. When Edward Dunne won the mayoralty in 1905, Dever became floor leader of the new mayor's unsuccessful fight to achieve municipal ownership of the city's transit lines. The alderman also flirted with the idea of higher office, running for state's attorney and judge, and seriously considering a shot at the mayoralty. Through it all he kept his close ties with Chicago Commons and the reform movement, while remaining a partisan Democrat.

In 1910, he moved up another notch. The squabbling factions of the Chicago Democratic party came together to produce a "harmony ticket" that year. Alderman Dever was slated for judge of the county circuit court. The fragile party alliance broke down soon after the election, but by then Dever was safely on the bench. There he would remain for the next dozen years, still in politics, though now removed from the daily trench warfare.

Of Dever's service on the court, little need be said. His cases were a mixed lot. Probably the most publicized was the sensational fraud trial of ex-Senator Lorimer. Still, most of Dever's decisions were hardly newsworthy, and his name began to appear in the papers less and less. The periodic "Dever for Mayor" booms—heard often during his years as a fighting alderman—grew infrequent, then stopped.

As Judge Dever passed his sixtieth birthday, he was well-settled. He had built a solid, unspectacular career in local politics, not notably different from the careers of a hundred other men. His was a comfortable situation of prestigious obscurity. Dever had become an elder statesman—meaning he had reached a political dead end.

Then it all changed.

II

Some people lead events, others are led by them. Dever's emergence in 1923 was the latter case. He became mayor of Chicago by being the right person in the right place at the right time.

A bit of background is in order.[2] As far back as anyone could remember, Chicago's political parties had been fragmented. Democrats versus Republicans did not tell the story. There were Harrison Democrats, or Deneen Republicans, or Lorimer Republicans, or Dunne Democrats, or any of a half-dozen subparties at a given time. It was the age of personality politics, a decentralized arrangement based on loyalty to a factional leader. No single king reigned over this urban feudalism. The factions fought among themselves, frequently and bitterly. Alliances were only temporary. They shifted often.

Roger Sullivan had set out to make matters different. Just after 1900, this Democratic ward boss began putting together a coalition he hoped would eliminate internal strife and simplify the business of winning elections. He started with a narrow, Irish-flavored clique on the city's West Side. Very gradually, however, Sullivan was able to convince various ethnic and factional chieftains of the benefits of unity. Enlighted self-interest was a persuasive recruiting incentive, especially among the younger men who were not greatly concerned about personal fealty or national identification. Sullivan's alliance grew and prospered. By the early 1920s, most of the city's prominent Democrats had affiliated with his multiethnic organization.

Still at large was a small band of irregulars led by Carter Harrison and Edward Dunne. The two former mayors had once been on an equal footing with Roger Sullivan, each man controlling about a third of the local Democratic party. As the Sullivan organization expanded, Harrison and Dunne had seen their followings slip steadily away. They now held only a shadow of their former influence, and continued to be wary of the Sullivan brand of centralization. Yet the Harrison-Dunne group retained some importance. They held the party's pedigree for respectability. They also had an uncanny knack for attracting publicity.

The task of wooing this bloc fell to George Brennan, a genial former school-teacher who became party leader on Sullivan's death in 1920. Until the Harrison-Dunnites could be won over, the organization was incomplete, Democratic unity unconfirmed. Nor, for that matter, could the new boss's place in the center chair be secure. Brennan needed a unifying factor, something to bring his party together and cement his own position as leader. As the 1923 city elections approached, he stepped up his search for the missing piece to the puzzle.

Reform was in the air that winter. A few days before Christmas of 1922, a group of high-powered clean government advocates gathered at the City Club for a forum on the coming mayoral race. Led by Reverend Graham Taylor and Mrs. Kellogg Fairbank, a Social Register novelist who dabbled in politics, the reformers organized themselves into the Non-Partisan Citizens Mayoral Committee. Their stated purpose was to lobby the two major parties for an honest alternative to William Hale Thompson, the large Republican who had occupied the mayor's office since 1915. "Big Bill" Thompson had long captivated the city with his distinctive political style of blarney, buffoonery, and shouting; but after eight years, his act was getting stale. Worse still, Thompson's administration had grown notably corrupt. New scandals seemed to be uncovered daily. The Non-Partisan Committee was determined to be rid of Thompson. To this end, they planned to study the mayoral possibilities in each party, then issue a list of five or ten men they could support.[3]

It was at this point that George Brennan began to take an interest in the reformers' activities. Brennan had no particular mayoral candidate in mind for his party— though it was a case of having too many hopefuls, not too few. He welcomed any suggestion that might help narrow the field. So when the Non-Partisan Committee published its list of seven endorsees, Brennan was pleased to find the name of Judge William E. Dever included. Dever, he recalled, had been separately touted by such diverse people as George Sikes of the Municipal Voters' League, William L. O'Connell from the Harrison-Dunne bloc, and Harold Ickes of the Progressive Republicans. Their common argument was that Dever could unite the Democratic party while giving the city honest, efficient government. What was especially intriguing to Brennan was that Dever was being pushed forward by both the Harrison-Dunne faction within the party and the Republican/Independent reformers on the outside. He decided to have dinner with the judge.[4]

The two men hit it off well. More important from a practical standpoint, they found they could work together politically. When talk got around to the mayoral election, Brennan indicated that he was considering Dever. He said he would not attempt to unduly influence the new mayor's decisions, but did expect a promise that the mayor would not use his patronage powers to build his own political machine. Dever thought this a reasonable arrangement and said he would abide by it. The spheres of authority were thus set; other details could be worked out later. Though he made no immediate offer to Dever, Brennan was convinced he had found his man. A quick consultation with the organization hierarchy confirmed that no one had any great objection to the judge. The next day William E. Dever was officially announced as the regular Democratic candidate for mayor of Chicago.

Dever was the ideal candidate for George Brennan's purposes. The judge was intelligent, articulate, and had a reputation for honesty. As an old Harrison-Dunne man with friends among the regulars, he could bring the party together. As a sitting judge, he did not have a long, controversial political record to defend. The fact that Dever had a limited personal following was also attractive to Brennan—it was unlikely that the new man might quickly build enough power to take over the organization himself. Finally, Dever was popular with reformers and independents. He could attract these influential, well-advertised citizens into the Democratic fold.

As has been said, Dever's personal role in securing his party's nomination was minor. He had been mentioned as a possible mayor for nearly twenty years, but there was little reason to think the lightning would finally strike in 1923. His friends and admirers advanced his candidacy. When the main chance came, Dever made the necessary accommodation. He had built a career based on honesty, hard work, and good relations with all groups. Circumstances had combined to make a man with his résumé the logical Democratic candidate.

Incumbent mayor Thompson was not eager to joust with the Democrats' new champion. Within a week of Dever's slating, Thompson bowed out of the contest. The feuding Republican factions took their fight into an open primary. Finally emerging from the confusion was Arthur Lueder: businessman, federal postmaster, and favorite son of the GOP's McCormick-*Tribune* bloc. Lueder was the direct opposite of Thompson—a dignified, soft-spoken gentleman of executive skill and personal integrity. Like Dever he had been endorsed by the Non-Partisan Committee. His nomination established a scenario unique in Chicago politics. For the first time, the candidates of both parties would wear the face of reform.

Reform may make for efficient government, but it does not always provide exciting campaigns. The 1923 mayoral contest was deadly dull. The candidates agreed on nearly everything. Both men attacked the excesses of the Thompson years, vowing to give the city an honest, thrifty administration. Both promised to take the schools out of politics. Both declared for law and order. In fact, the only notable difference between the nominees appeared to be on the transit issue. Dever came out squarely in favor of municipal purchase of the traction companies, while Lueder merely promised to "study" the matter.

From the start momentum was in the Democrats' favor. The party rallied behind Dever. Carter Harrison made the keynote speech at the campaign's kickoff luncheon, and Edward Dunne cut short his Florida vacation to return home and stump for his former protegé. The Brennan regulars, meanwhile, performed with their customary professional competence. Over on the Republican side, the story was different. The GOP remained divided into at least three factions—if not hostile to one another, then surely indifferent. Thompson sulked in his tent and would not work for Lueder. As for the reformers and independents, they moved as a group to the Dever camp. Many of them took an active role in the campaign as the Independent Dever League. Though they recognized Lueder as an able man, the reformers frankly preferred Dever. Experience was the reason. As Harold Ickes put it, "Why waste time . . . educating a novice when the trained executive and experienced municipal statesman is already at hand?"[5]

The campaign moved on, with no debates, little disagreement, and few fireworks. During the last week, some of the local bigots awoke to the fact that Chicago might soon have a Catholic mayor—something of an innovation for the city—and began a whispering offensive against the Democratic nominee. Antipapist broadsides appeared in Protestant neighborhoods. By now, however, it was too late to matter.

Big Jim O'Leary, the gambling king of the stockyards, closed his election book with Dever a 1–7 favorite. Big Jim knew a winner when he saw one. Dever crushed Lueder by 105,000 votes. He carried thirty-two of the city's fifty wards. His plurality was concentrated in the Democrats' traditional stronghold, ten inner-city ethnic wards; he also made major inroads among black and Jewish voters. Lueder won the usually Republican middle-class wards on the city's rim, though Dever ran strongly in these areas as well.

In 1923 Dever had an appeal that crossed ethnic, factional, and party lines. He was not closely identified with any particular section of his party; the public vaguely viewed him as a "reformer." He had been the perfect standard-bearer around whom George Brennan could gather the diverse elements of his grand alliance. He had stayed in the spotlight, run a tight campaign, and managed to avoid any divisive controversies. Party organization did the rest. Not surprisingly, he won a great victory.

III

Dever read the election returns as a mandate. The voters were tired of the policies of the past and wanted change. The new mayor would give it to them. He saw his administration as a chance to do "something big, something worthwhile, . . . something definite in the service of the city." As one newspaper put it, Dever planned to give the people a "new deal."[6]

And so reform came to Chicago. Restoring public trust in government was a major task facing the mayor. Dever started at the top, assembling a strong cabinet of accomplished individuals. (He also treated political considerations deftly: his appointees were a nice mix of reformers, Brennan regulars, and Harrison-Dunnites.) To promote efficiency and tighten management, he initiated a complete survey of metropolitan government. Meanwhile, he revamped the city personnel system. Thompson had skirted civil service regulations by putting temporary workers into merit positions, then reappointing them each time their sixty-day commissions ran out. Dever scheduled new examinations, obtained a pool of test-qualified applicants, and fired the Thompson temporaries. Over two thousand jobs were thus restored to civil service status.

The public schools were also targeted for reform. The system had become a national disgrace under Thompson, with political interference and financial mismanagement merely the most obvious of many failings. Here Dever got lucky. Through an administrative slip, he received early resignations from eight of the eleven members of the school board. The mayor was then able to fill the board with his own people—a progressive, businesslike, independent-minded group considered one of the finest school boards in the city's history. Dever promoted education throughout his term. He backed the board's efforts to obtain more money, using his influence to promote the cause and improving tax-collection procedures to get the funds more quickly. Still, in day-to-day matters, he kept his campaign promise. He left the schools alone.

Reform came to law enforcement. For chief of police, Dever chose Morgan A. Collins, an "honest cop" who had risen from the ranks to command the tough Chicago Avenue district. The police force was in a state of near anarchy at the time. With the full backing of the mayor, Chief Collins moved swiftly to bring order and discipline back to the department. He called in district commanders, gave them their instructions, then demoted anyone who would not carry out his policies. To fight corruption, he broke up a number of suspected cliques with wholesale transfers. Collins hired hundreds of new patrolmen, many of them exservicemen whose integrity and devotion to duty he believed in. At the same time, the chief began a series of flashy raids on gambling dens and sporting houses. First reports indicated that Chief Collins's programs were succeeding.

Reform came to the public works arena. Thompson had done grand things in this field, earning the nickname "Big Bill the Builder." He had also spent lavishly, and most of his projects came in with big bills of their own. Dever shared Thompson's booster spirit; he also knew he could do the job cheaper. During Dever's four years in office, construction boomed. The mayor opened parks, beaches, public bathhouses, and more schools than any previous administration. The south branch of the Chicago River was straightened in preparation for railroad terminal consolidation and land development south of the Loop. Dever built roads: Wacker Drive, the northern extension of Ogden Avenue, a new section of Lake Shore Drive. He established the city's first full-fledged air terminal, the present Midway Airport. He also began plans for a world's fair to celebrate Chicago's "century of progress" birthday in 1933. Through it all, he kept a close watch on spending, making sure the taxpayers got their money's worth.

Finally, there was transit reform. During the campaign, Dever had declared that solving the public transport problem would be the most important job for the new mayor. Service on the Chicago Surface Lines had grown shoddy and increasingly expensive. With CSL's franchise expiring in 1927, Dever intended for the city to buy out the company; also on his shopping list was Chicago Rapid Transit, which ran the elevated lines. Twenty years after Dever had fought for it at the side of Edward Dunne, Municipal Ownership would finally become a reality. So in the first days of his administration, the mayor opened negotiations with the transit carriers. Meanwhile, he mapped plans for service extensions and the city's first subway.

Dever was still busy getting his programs off the ground when a series of events unfolded that were to have a profound effect on his administration. During the evening of 7 September 1923, two bands of bootleggers became involved in a shootout at a South Side cafe. One man was killed. Scarcely a week later, another gun-battle erupted between the same gangs, with two more men left dead. Territorial rivalries in the lucrative illegal liquor business was said to be the cause.

Although Prohibition had been part of the federal Constitution for over three years, it was widely ignored in Chicago. Most residents opposed the law; the police rarely bothered to enforce it. From the first, William E. Dever himself had been a "wet"—a person committed to the repeal of Prohibition. However, when he became mayor, Dever could see more closely that bootlegging payoffs were corrupting the police and public officials. As a former judge, he also believed that neglect of one law breeds disrespect for all laws. The South Side shootings convinced the mayor that the liquor situation had gotten out of hand. Personal feelings must be set aside. He would have to step in and set things right.[7]

Dever convened a summit conference of all the appropriate city, county, state, and federal law-enforcement officials. After securing their support, he announced an all-out drive against bootlegging. Then he unleashed Chief Collins's new shock-troops. Hundreds of violators were arrested, underground breweries smashed, and four thousand saloons padlocked. Next, the mayor moved against drugstores, soda parlors, and other legitimate businesses which sold intoxicants as a sideline. Dever lifted the licenses of 1,600 of these establishments, effectively driving them out of business. Appeals to courts or to friendly aldermen proved useless: the mayor was acting within his prescribed executive powers. The crackdown continued. By the end of 1923, barely a hundred days after the cleanup had begun, Chicago was being proclaimed the driest big city in America.

The Great Beer War made Dever a national celebrity. All over the country, journalists took time out from local affairs to examine the remarkable happenings in Chicago. The larger publications dispatched reporters to the city to observe events firsthand. Magazines printed feature articles on Dever, and the mayor was even cajoled into telling his story in a syndicated essay. At the Democratic National Convention of 1924, the new hero received a few complimentary votes for president and was seriously discussed for vice president. Though he missed on that one, the mayor was still riding high. A few months after the convention, John D. Rockefeller, Jr., and other wealthy Eastern industrialists tendered Dever a special banquet in New York. No Democrat had been honored by a similar group in that city since the days of Grover Cleveland, one writer noted. Mayor Dever had "unquestionably [become] a prominent candidate for the Democratic nomination in 1928."[8]

The mayor was always careful to state that he was "not a Prohibitionist." He said that he had begun his Beer War to preserve the integrity of the law. He told one gathering that he knew Prohibition was a bad law, but was enforcing it strictly so that the people would get fed up and force Congress to repeal it. Dever knew his stand was politically risky. Despite the large majority of Chicagoans who opposed Prohibition, the mayor was willing to gamble that the people would support his methods. They did for awhile.[9]

Trouble developed just when it appeared the cleanup had been successful. Part of the problem was that early success. Before Dever came along, there had been plenty of trade for everyone in the illegal liquor business. Violence had been rare: the South Side shootings had been an exception to the general rule of peace. Now that the city was drying up, the bootleggers were driven into more direct competition for the business that was left. Fresh bloodshed was the result. By the beginning of 1925, a major gangland war had broken out, bringing spectacular killings and lurid headlines.

Nor had enforcement worked as planned. Other politicians and government agencies were not as vigorous in carrying out the law as were Chicago's mayor and police chief. County officials had a particularly permissive attitude. As a result, many of the liquor traders simply removed themselves from Dever's jurisdiction by moving their operations past the city line—making bootlegging one of the first industries to flee the central city for the suburbs. Back in Chicago, meanwhile, Chief Collins had still not gained complete mastery over his police force. Political influence and bribery remained strong at many station houses. Ward politicians and police captains who disagreed with the enforcement program cut new deals with bootleggers. The old ways had not been unlearned.

The second half of Dever's term is a story of breakdown. Much of what he had sought to build in his first two years came crashing down around him. The mayor was reduced to conducting a holding action, trying to salvage what he could of his ruined plans. He did not accept this role meekly; he could still react to events with his customary feistiness and vigor. But the initiative no longer seemed to be his.

The grand political alliance that had swept Dever into office was showing cracks. Some strain on the coalition was to be expected—unity was an unnatural state for Chicago's factionalized, feuding parties. What was remarkable was that George Brennan's fledgling machine hung together as well as it did.

The Harrison-Dunnites drifted away early. Within a year of Dever's inauguration, they were fielding a rival ticket in the state primaries. They felt they were not getting a fair share of the political spoils from the regular organization. For years, Sullivan and Brennan had worked to incorporate the Harrison-Dunne bloc into their alliance. Now they were whining again, and Brennan concluded that they weren't worth the trouble. He let them go their own way.

A far more serious concern was the uneasiness within the regular ranks. Disagreement with Dever's Prohibition enforcement was the cause. Most of the Democratic committeemen were partisan, active wets; so was Brennan himself. In the first days of the mayor's Beer War, they had put aside their personal feelings and rallied behind Dever for the sake of party unity. Only Anton Cermak had spoke out against the enforcement program. But as the violence escalated and the mayor remained steadfast and the voters grew restless, more and more ward leaders were heard to grumble about the Dever crusade.

For these men, the mayor's mishandling of the Prohibition matter indicated that he was growing away from the people. Some of them believed that Dever's continuing fraternization with the reformers might be the problem. It was as if the mayor had forgotten his own roots. "It is all right for a Republican to go heavy on that reform stuff, but . . . a Democrat doesn't fit into a fanatical reform picture," one alderman observed. "Silk-hatting the LaSalle Street crowd is all right if you are one of them; but to give the impression that you've gone over to the silk-hatters after you've been raised under a fedora is fatal in politics in Chicago." [10] The mayor was losing credibility with those groups which should have formed his strongest power base.

Reflective of this mistrust is the fate of Dever's transit reform plan. By the end of 1924, the city and the two main carrier companies had reached agreement on a purchase price and method of municipal takeover. The package was to be submitted to the voters at the coming spring election. Although there was opposition to the settlement in some quarters, the referendum was rated a tossup, with the plan expected to carry. What happened was a surprise to nearly everyone. The Dever Plan was rejected by a margin of over one hundred thousand votes. The outer wards which had been cool to the transit package went against it, as expected. But the inner-city organization wards, which the mayor had counted on to carry the day, failed to deliver the votes. Some of them even voted a majority against.

Perhaps Dever had simply submitted a bad plan. Yet an analysis of the voting pattern suggests that certain committeemen may have "knifed" the Dever package. Once again, Prohibition was the reason. The ward leaders were trying to send the mayor a message. Even before the referendum, one wet politico had warned: "Now watch our smoke—if he puts his traction plan up to the people, we'll defeat it." [11] And so Dever's most treasured reform program was lost.

The Prohibition issue was not the only place where Dever's stubborn idealism cost him. The public schools had once more become involved in controversy. The mayor's board of education had hired the distinguished New York educator William McAndrew as superintendent of schools. Though the appointment was highly praised, the new superintendent soon antagonized populace, politicians, and teachers with his administrative revisions, his curriculum innovations, and his glacial personality. The teachers particularly objected to McAndrew's moves against their informal teacher councils. They enlisted several prominent labor and political chieftains in their cause and called upon the mayor for help.

Dever was in a difficult spot. The teachers had backed his candidacy in 1923; most of the party organization was sympathetic to them. The mayor realized that McAndrew was making matters worse through his personal style and had an associate privately speak to him about diplomacy, public relations, and other useful arts. However, Dever had pledged not to interfere with the schools. So he issued a statement saying as much, adding the hope that "cooler heads will prevail." This was not good enough for the teachers. Margaret Haley, leader of the largest faculty union, delivered a blistering denunciation of the mayor for his failure to intervene in the McAndrew dispute. For the rest of his term, Dever could count on the city's public school teachers as his adversaries.[12]

Despite his periodic intransigence, Dever remained a practical politician. When "moral issues" like law enforcement or keeping politics out of the schools were not involved, the mayor could compromise. His traction plan is one example of this art: though it had shortcomings, it was probably the best municipal ownership package that could have been hammered together at the time. Or when a fight was not worth the trouble, Dever could give in. Consider his attempts at budget reform. After trying to curb departmental spending by having the mayor's office draw up the city budget, it became evident that the city council would fight to keep this traditional privilege. So Dever simply allowed the old system to continue. He knew that he did not have the political clout to enforce his will. Rather than wage a symbolic war with the council over who had what power, he merely instructed his department heads to cut financial corners as best they could.

As his term entered its final year, the mayor began to express doubts about the wisdom of Prohibition enforcement. He appeared before the U.S. Senate hearings on the Volstead Act in the spring of 1926. To those who knew him only as the great enforcer of dry ordinances, his testimony must have been surprising. Dever told the senators that Prohibition had become the number one political issue in Chicago, affecting the election of aldermen, judges, and every public official. He himself had to spend too much time on the matter, time better spent on building bridges or clearing land for parks. "I find myself immersed in it . . . from morning to night," he said. "It is almost impossible to give anything approaching good government along general lines [because] this one subject presses so strongly upon our attention."[13]

He continued to make his doubts public. The liquor question was like a toothache, he told the city hall press corps—the pain makes you neglect your more important business. In a Rockford speech he compared the problems caused by the dry law to those created by slavery before the Civil War. Prohibition was a "tremendous mistake," the mayor said, and he would do "anything . . . to correct it." He also wrote another magazine article, this time for the *Atlantic Monthly*. In it Dever suggested that Congress set up a special commission to make a comprehensive, objective study of the whole liquor issue. He also made a significant concession. Once he had declared that an unpopular law could and should be enforced, if only to speed its repeal. Now he admitted that his policy had not worked. "The wise legislator in a democracy will not attempt to impose a law, however desirable in the abstract, that will not receive general support of the people," Dever wrote. "Men cannot be brought to support a policy that they believe to be oppressive and unjust."[14]

The people, it seemed, would sooner disobey a bad law than follow procedures and petition for a redress of grievance. Sometimes politics did not operate the way the textbooks said. Yet even with this knowledge, Dever still carried on his determined enforcement of the Prohibition Amendment until the day he left office. The law was the law. And there remained a good deal of strict constructionist judge in the mayor of Chicago.

IV

Dever was not anxious for a second term. He was tired of the browbeating from all sides, his health was not good, he had numerous offers of lucrative employment. Many of the wetter Democratic commitment would be glad to be rid of him. In the end, however, he agreed to run once more.

Duty was the reason—duty to his party and to his city. As George Brennan saw matters, the mayor was the Democrats' strongest candidate. Dever had the advantages of incumbency and a creditable record in office. He had the best chance of attracting independents and straying Republicans. He could also preserve his own party's unity. Although Dever was controversial, the ward lords would probably be persuaded to rally around a sitting mayor; if Dever dropped out, there might be a free-for-all primary that could rip the party apart.

At the same time, the mayor felt his work was unfinished. He had spent too much of his first term on police matters. He still had to sort out the transit mess, continue his public works projects, and move on with governmental reorganization. Perhaps a second term would be better. In any event, as business leader Julius Rosenwald warned him, he had to save the city from Big Bill Thompson.

Thompson had, indeed, emerged as the leading Republican candidate. Big Bill had spent his years of exile hatching various plots, pausing for such widely-publicized diversions as launching a safari in search of a tree-climbing fish and holding a political debate with a pair of caged rats on a Loop stage. Now he was back. The public had evidently forgiven or forgotten the scandals of Big Bill's earlier regime. He easily swept the Republican primary and squared off against Dever.

The 1927 mayoral campaign has achieved legendary status in the annals of Chicago politics. Most of this repute stems from Thompson's antics. Early in the contest, Big Bill decided to revive the splendidly vague campaign plank that had served him well in the past, the issue of "America First." Nobody could argue with him on that one—especially when he found a convenient target in school superintendent McAndrew. It seemed that McAndrew had once made some disparaging remarks about *The Spirit of '76* and other nationalistic works of art; meanwhile, his allies on the school board had promoted various "unpatriotic" history texts. There were other sins as well, too numerous to mention here. When all these facts were put together, and combined with the superintendent's curriculum innovations, a clear pattern emerged—or so Thompson claimed. A giant international conspiracy was at work. McAndrew was a British agent dispatched by King George. His purpose was to corrupt the minds of impressionable American schoolchildren, paving the way for the King's reconquest of his former colonies. Fortunately, Big Bill had uncovered the plot just in time.

Thus did William Hale Thompson embark on a crusade to save Chicago from the British monarch. Big Bill roamed from rally to rally, ranting against King George, McAndrew, and that "left-handed Irishman" Dever who had brought all this treason about. And while he moved among the voters, his sensitive political nose began to sniff out another issue: Prohibition. He began to hammer away at Dever's enforcement record, and hammer hard. He noted that the current administration had closed down "businesses" all over the city. When he was elected, Thompson pledged, he would reopen all the places Dever had closed and put in ten thousand new ones. If anyone doubted what kind of businesses Big Bill had in mind, he gave it to them straight—"I'm as wet as the Atlantic Ocean!" he roared.[15]

The Democrats fought back as best they could. Brennan called in the troops and sent them off to battle. Joining the party soldiers were many prominent independents and reform Republicans who feared the consequences of a Thompson restoration. Dever's supporters countered Big Bill's bombast with some artillery of their own. Brochures were mailed, advertisements printed, campaign orators sent into the neighborhoods. Voters were reminded of Thompson's past failures, his dubious record contrasted with Dever's honesty and accomplishment. Dark hints were also raised about Big Bill's friendship with utilities magnate Samuel Insull. Meanwhile, four of the city's six daily newspapers announced they were backing Dever.

The mayor himself came out on the stump. He appeared ready for one of his old, sedate judicial campaigns or a rerun of the bland mayoral contest of 1923. He said that he would engage in a polite debate on issues of substance, a "decent, friendly discussion without malice or sensationalism." He dismissed Thompson's pronouncements as sheer "blarney" and refused to get into a shouting match with his opponent. Nor would Dever do anything to compromise the dignity of his office. When it was discovered that the mayor still held membership in the tanners' union, some Democratic strategists suggested dressing their candidate in overalls and photographing him at one of the old tanneries on Goose Island. Dever vetoed the idea. He said that he would not descend to Thompson's level. He would win on his own terms.[16]

Most of the others involved in the election did not share Dever's ideals. In its final weeks the campaign grew more desperate and dirty. Republican bigots resurrected the anti-Catholic propaganda that had been used against Dever in 1923. The Democrats trotted out the race issue; Thompson was a great friend of the city's black community, and his opponents claimed his election would bring about "Negro supremacy." Both parties charged the other side with preparing to use chicanery and force to steal the election. It was known that gang chief Al Capone was actively supporting Thompson's cause with both money and "campaign aides."

Dever's campaign never seemed to catch fire. Thompson seized control of the contest early and did not relinquish it. The Democrats were put on the defensive. They spent much of their energy reacting to Thompson's agenda. The mayor's case got lost amid all the rhetoric. "Dever and Decency," his followers beseeched. To which one cynic replied, "Who the hell is attracted by decency?"[17]

Early newspaper and street corner polls showed Dever trailing Thompson. The election returns confirmed the predictions. Thompson won by 83,000 votes, taking nearly 52 percent of the total. Dever polled 43 percent, with third-party candidate John Dill Robertson getting the rest. The Democratic ticket suffered serious erosion in the party's stronghold: the white, working-class, inner-city wards. Though Dever captured a majority of the ethnic vote, he did worse than usual for a Democratic candidate. He also lost the black vote to Thompson by a margin of better than 10 to 1. Dever did pick up a notable number of votes in the traditionally Republican Wasp areas along the lake shore. However, these gains were not enough to overcome the other defections.

The news of Dever's defeat stunned the nation. Over the next months, the Chicago election became a hot topic for newspaper and magazine articles. How had America's best mayor been beaten? A few observers blamed the nature of the city itself: such behavior was just what could be expected from Chicago. Most analysts, however, attributed the result to Thompson's extraordinary skills as a campaigner. Big Bill had "hypnotized" the voters, one writer claimed, and Dever could not snap them out of it. Thompson knew what the people wanted: entertainment. Dever, on the other hand, had tried to jam virtue down

the public throat. The mystery was not that Dever had lost, concluded Elmer
Davis of *Harper's;* the mystery was how he had gotten 430,000 votes.[18]

There was also talk of conspiracy. Rumor claimed that Dever's reelection
had been sabotaged by Cermak and the wetter ward bosses, with or without
Brennan's complicity. Sixty years later the talk still goes on, and it is impossible
to confirm or deny it. What evidence there is argues against the conspiracy
scenario. Throwing the mayor to the wolves was not the practical approach.
Cermak may not have liked Dever, but his own ambitions were more likely to
be thwarted by putting Thompson in the mayor's chair. As for Brennan working against his own candidate for some "bipartisan deal," how could the party
leader have improved on what he already had? The Democratic organization was simply better off with Dever reelected than by taking a chance on
Thompson building his own machine. Dever himself never suggested he had
been double-crossed; he always considered he had been treated fairly. To argue
that he was beaten by Democratic turncoats is also giving the fledgling machine
more power than it had at the time. The mayor lost because he was less popular
than Thompson. That much is undeniable, and all else is speculation. Perhaps
the party did not work especially hard for Dever in 1927. But it is more logical
to assume that the lethargy was the result of voter hostility, not its cause.

Chicago Democrats had sought power in 1923 by assembling a coalition of
ethnic and factional elements. Dever was slated in order to hold the party together while attracting the votes of the reform bloc. He succeeded and was
elected mayor. But in reaching for the new groups, the party was pulled away
from its traditional center of support. The multiethnic coalition began to come
apart. By 1927, Dever's brand of politics had become a force for division, not
unity. Brennan had thought Dever was the man to play it both ways, one who
would be a bridge between the foreign stock and the old stock. He had mis-
calculated. The organization would have to try something else.

V

After his defeat, Dever retired from public life, taking a job as a bank executive. Within two years he was dead from cancer. The city mourned its former
mayor with a magnificent funeral. Political associates reminisced about him.
The newspapers and drugstore journals commemorated his passing with editorial testimonials on his nobility of character. There was a public school and a
water-intake crib three miles out in the lake named for him, and then he was
forgotten.

In the years since his death, Dever has remained unknown—or at best, im-
perfectly known. Putting his career in perspective requires the explosion of a
few myths. For one thing, Dever was not a wide-eyed, inexperienced reformer.
He was a professional politician and a party regular. He played the game well,

he made deals, he got along. Dever was no hack; he retained his ideals and worked to carry them out. But first of all, he was a politician.

His election was not a grassroots uprising against an entrenched machine. In 1923, both Chicago parties were still battling their hereditary factionalism. The local clean government crowd wanted to deliver the city from the clutches of Big Bill Thompson and was inclined to accept nearly anyone who could accomplish the fete. George Brennan read the situation shrewdly, then put forward a candidate the reformers were comfortable with. When Dever won, his "reform" victory was actually part of the consolidation of the local Democratic organization. In fact, the slating of a blue-ribbon, squeaky-clean candidate worked so well that the machine would return to the practice in later years, from Martin Kennelly through Paul Douglas through two Adlai Stevensons.

Dever was a symbol of unification—the new Democratic order wrapped up in one blue serge suit. He brought together the regulars and the Harrison-Dunnites while charming the reform bloc. He was also the symbol of the new breed of urban ethnic politician. Though Dever was a straight Irish Catholic, he was a step up from the old, one-dimensional figure of "Paddy the Mick," the provincial saloonkeeper politician. Party chiefs Sullivan and Brennan had long been developing talented young men of varied background who might aspire high and go far: Catholics and Jews of many national pedigrees, and even a Bohemian Protestant. When Dever broke through in 1923, it was indication that the new peoples had achieved decisive political prominence.

Once in office, Dever recognized his role as a "respectable ethnic." He often told Knights of Columbus suppers or other such gatherings that he would show the critics a Catholic could govern wisely. He tried to avoid any hint of favoritism, and was so scrupulous that a few Catholics complained the mayor was not being fair to his own people. His Prohibition policy also reflects this concern for appearances. Dever thought the dry law was ridiculous and knew that defending it would be politically dangerous—yet he embarked on the most ambitious enforcement program in the country. He said he was preserving the dignity of the law. Once again, Dever seemed to be advertising his official scruples, demonstrating that an Irish Catholic could have the same high public standards as a Wasp Brahmin.[19]

Prohibition finished him off, of course. It cut at the heart of his party, for Dever could not get the ethnics to accept his way of dealing with the problem. "Personal Liberty" was a sacred concept to them. To have the police sniffing around for something as trivial as a glass of beer was a reminder of the oppression they had fled. This was not what America was supposed to be. In a very real sense, the mayor was betraying their dreams. No matter how much he accomplished in other areas, no matter how persistently he courted the ethnic voters, the seeds of mistrust were sewn. They would flower in 1927.

Dever should have won reelection that year—not necessarily because he was the better man, but because he had the better political apparatus behind him. Democratic unification had been accomplished by 1923, with Dever becoming the first "machine" mayor of Chicago. The infant organization was strained mightily during his administration. It hung together, and was reasonably healthy at the end of four years. Dever's defeat was a rejection of his policies and him personally, not a repudiation of the organization concept. The return of Big Bill Thompson was merely the last hurrah of the old style of personality politics. By 1931, this last vestige of Chicago's feudal age would be swept away.

What of William E. Dever himself? Studs Terkel referred to the mayor as "the Calvin Coolidge of Chicago politics." Perhaps Jimmy Carter would be a better comparison. Dever was an honorable man of fundamental decency. He helped heal old wounds when such skills were needed, and he restored public trust in his political office. He also made the people feel guilty when they wanted to feel good. He earned their admiration and probably their respect, but not their love or friendship—and in the end, not their votes. What he lacked as a political executive was showmanship and a sense of nastiness. At some other period he might have had more success in doing his elected job; but then the odd conjunction of political stars that propelled him into prominence would not have been at hand. Dever was either the right man at the wrong time, or the wrong man in the right job. Such is the comedy of our politics. And the tragedy.

7.

ANTON J. CERMAK: THE MAN AND HIS MACHINE

Paul M. Green

Anton J. Cermak was Chicago's first and only foreign-born mayor. No man in Chicago political history had a more controversial and complicated political career than "Tony" Cermak. To some Cermak was a gruff bully who consorted with mobsters and hooligans while others viewed him as a political genius and friend of the ethnic poor. Cermak's life and political style reflect the contradictions and turmoils that epitomize Chicago's political tradition. His slow and difficult rise up the city's power ladder, his transformation from slugger to statesman, make him the last street politician to reach city hall.

Cermak was the consummate ethnic politician. According to his biographer, Alex Gottfried, "Cermak made Chicago Czechs and Chicago Czechs made Cermak."[1] However, Tony Cermak was not ethnocentric in his politics. Rather, he rose above his own ethnicity and prevailing nationality conflicts to construct the city's first truly multiethnic political machine. His life story reflects in the words of H. K. Barnard the saga of a man striving to become accepted as both "The new American and the new Chicagoan."[2]

In terms of personality Cermak was not a choirboy. In Chicago political parlance he was known as an "intimidator" who was capable of unleashing a violent and terrifying temper. His large and heavy-set physique coupled with his capacity for anger made many a foe and subordinate fear Cermak's physical strength as much as his political prowess.

Cermak was a poor public speaker who "appeared to take pride in his own absence of polish."[3] Reminiscing about his experiences with the mayor, one old-timer bluntly stated "Cermak was not a very nice man."[4] Yet this man who trusted few people, who was not a good mixer or back-slapper, and who generated loyalty through ethnic attachments and shrewd political deals emerged as boss of Chicago. Why? The simple truth is that Anton J. Cermak was a political survivor who eventually outlasted his old opponents and outsmarted his new ones.

The Early Days

Cermak was born on 9 May 1873, in a Bohemian village fifty miles from Prague. His family were Hussites (followers of the early fifteenth century Czech Protestant reformer John Huss), but Cermak would eventually marry a Catholic and raise his children as Catholics. One legendary Chicago political tale reveals that Cermak, a lifelong Protestant, calculated that having a Catholic family would be a huge political benefit in the heavily Catholic Chicago Democratic party—or put another way, "how many precincts could John Huss carry?"[5]

Cermak's family immigrated to America in 1874, settling in Chicago at 15th and Canal Streets. Later they moved to Braidwood, Illinois, a small coal mining town fifty miles southwest of Chicago. Young Cermak was a big strapping lad who had a very limited elementary school education. Ironically, one of his teachers was George Brennan, a man who would precede Cermak as Chicago's Democratic leader in the 1920s.

By the turn of the century, Cermak's family moved back to Chicago finding a home in the heavily Bohemian west side. Here is where Cermak constructed a political base strong enough to support him in various political campaigns for the next three decades. In return, Cermak would identify thoroughly with his Bohemian brethren. He acted as their voice expressing their hopes and concerns on various social and political issues. Cermak, like other successful Chicago mayors, never moved from his community even as his own political and economic fortunes rose. Loyalty given/loyalty received sums up Cermak's relationship with his Bohemian constituents; he never let them down.

Cermak's move into politics was almost inevitable. After dabbling in various business enterprises—including his occupation as teamster (horse and wagon) which would give his future political enemies the ammunition to label him "Pushcart Tony"—the ambitious Cermak was elected to the Illinois state legislature. After serving four terms in Springfield, he was elected Chicago alderman in 1909, municipal court bailiff in 1912, and after shuffling back to alderman in 1919 following an unsuccessful county sheriff candidacy, he was elected president of the Cook County Board of Commissioners in 1922.

Cermak's early career illustrates not only his knack for political survival but also the quagmire known as Chicago Democratic politics. As mentioned in earlier chapters, the local Democracy was split at least three ways: Carter H. Harrison II, Roger C. Sullivan, and Edward F. Dunne were factional party leaders more intent on beating each other than in defeating Republicans. Given his ethnic and geographic situation, Cermak joined the more multinational

Harrison forces rather than the heavily Irish Sullivan troops or the reform-minded Dunneites. Aiding his choice was the fact that Harrison was mayor for much of the early part of the twentieth century—thus giving Cermak control of many of the jobs and services he needed to satisfy his constituents.

Using his organization skills, Cermak turned his Twelfth Ward into the best Harrison area in the city. In the 1911 mayoral election, Cermak's Bohemian voters gave Harrison his largest ward margin in Chicago. Cermak was rewarded for his efforts with various plums including the honor of selecting the city's new assistant prosecuting attorney—a young lawyer and fellow Czech named Otto Kerner.

Using his physical skills, Cermak quickly became known as a "stand-up guy" who would not shy away from a personal confrontation. At the 1915 Democratic party's judicial convention (the new primary law had not ended all nominations by convention), Cermak engaged in his famous one-on-one stand-off with Timothy J. Crowe, a young, tough, upcoming West Side leader. Both Cermak and Crowe were opposing factional spokesmen and following a series of personal jibes, Cermak simply told Crowe to step out into the hall to settle their differences.[6] Crowe accepted the challenge and even though they were restrained by their associates, this near battle left both men bitter rivals for the rest of their lives. This event also reveals how much of the old frontier mentality remained in Chicago politics well into the twentieth century. In Mr. Dooley's words, the city's politics "ain't bean bag"—nor was it a place for the faint of heart.

Cermak also took early command of the wet/dry issue in Chicagoland. Labeled by the Chicago *Tribune* as "the wettest man in Chicago" Cermak organized the United Societies for Local Self-Government to fight for personal liberty (the right to drink on any day, but especially on Sunday). As the movement for national prohibition gained momentum in the World War I era, Cermak led a massive pro-wet parade down Michigan Avenue. Chicago Democrats were overwhelmingly wet, and it was this issue that gave Cermak instant political entry into other ethnic circles.

The 1920s

Two themes emerged in the 1920s which aided Cermak in his quest to become both Democratic party leader and Chicago mayor. First, in the early 1920s a group of new-breed Democratic politicians exploded on the Chicago political scene. Their arrival coincided with the coming of Prohibition and the demise of the traditional saloon keeper politicians who for decades had dominated the local Democracy. The new-breed politicians were better educated and more professional in their demeanor than their roguish predecessors. These new-breeds shied away from old-style saloon, gambling house, and boodle enterprises and instead involved themselves in construction, law, real estate, banking, and insurance businesses.[7] Central to the new-breed personality was a willingness and a desire to coalesce into a unified political organization.

Cermak, already a politician with two decades of experience and a known exponent and practitioner of political unity, became a sturdy and tough bridge linking the personality-oriented, factional politics of the Sullivan, Harrison, and Dunne era with the organization-oriented, new-breed 1920 politics. Guided by his former teacher George Brennan, Cermak emerged as a political survivor who melded easily into the victorious Sullivan wing of the party by winning the Cook County Board presidency in 1922. His willingness to work openly with his former intraparty foes coupled with his loyalty to the dominant party leadership signaled an end to alternative routes of political power within the local Democratic party structure. Dissension and internal disputes would remain, but the framework was set. As one old-timer commented, "Cermak agreed that there was now only one Democratic party ballgame in Chicago—and he wanted to become its only pitcher."[8]

If new-breed politics would aid Cermak's party takeover, changing Chicago demographics in the 1920s would help his quest for city hall. From 1920 to 1930, Chicago's population rose by almost 700,000 to 3,376,438 residents. However, this growth is even more impressive when one examines the population spurts in suburban communities surrounding the city. There was a dual migration taking place in Chicago: (1) older Chicago Protestant families were beginning their short march to the suburbs, and (2) more recently arrived Catholic and Jewish families were moving into vacated Protestant neighborhoods. In short, it was a classic demographic case of departure and filling in.

Church membership roles reveal the parameters of this demographic shift. In the 1920s Protestant Chicago was moving out of its old inner and central city neighborhoods to better neighborhoods on the city's periphery and the suburbs.[9] A sizable group of traditional Republican-oriented Protestant voters would remain in Chicago, but evidence reveals that every Protestant denomination, except the Baptists because of new black migration, saw several of its churches close and its membership lists dwindle in many older Chicago communities.

On the other hand, heavily pro-Democratic Jewish residents jumped from their old Maxwell Street ghetto region to expanded new west neighborhoods in formerly Swedish and German Douglas Park and Lawndale. However, it is the Catholic church that best shows the ethnic and Democratic colonization of former Protestant neighborhoods. Between 1920 and 1930, over thirty new parishes were started on the city's northwest and southwest sides. The number of Catholic communicants in Chicago rose 8 percent even though some older inner city parishes showed a membership decrease.

All of this movement left 1930 Chicago as a city having nearly two-thirds of its population foreign-born or children of foreign-born. In short, the city was demographically ripe for a shrewd politician who could put together the right ethnic political mix—Anton Cermak was that man.

Cermak Takes Over the Chicago Democratic Party

More than any other city politician, Cermak recognized the impact of new-breed politics and changing demographics on the Chicago political scene. However, before "going for the hall" he shrewdly decided to secure and widen his city political base by running for Democratic party chairman.

Following Brennan's death in 1928, Cermak moved quickly and successfully to capture the top party post. Several authors have documented and analyzed Cermak's Democratic chairman victory. Most concur that Cermak won because he organized and mobilized city voters of eastern and southern European heritage around the slogan "get the Irish." [10]

Obviously Cermak used ethnic appeals in attracting support from Chicago's diverse population, and it's certain his main opponents for the top job were Irish. However, it is far too simplistic to label his quest for party boss as an interethnic showdown inside the Democratic party. On the contrary, Cermak found key Irish allies in his move to take over the party among several new-breed politicians. Men like Pat Nash and Joe McDonough saw Cermak as the vehicle by which the remaining old guard leadership, mainly Irish, could be replaced by them and others in a multiethnic power play. Commenting at the time, Boetius Sullivan (Roger Sullivan's son and a strong Cermak Irish ally) accused Cermak's foes in both parties of attempts to create a Cermak/Irish split: "A glance at the recent Democratic ticket on which appears the names of Sullivan, McKinley, O'Connor, McGoorty, Kavanaugh, and Finnegan . . . and the list of Democratic party leaders like Clark, Bowler, McDonough . . . is enough to convince anyone that [this charge] is as untruthful as it is malicious." [11]

Key to understanding Cermak's party maneuvers was the fact that he cloaked his efforts in the mantle of reform. He told the press, "The period of the backroom . . . is gone. From now on everybody in the organization will have a voice in its management." [12]

Cermak's commitment to political reform, as it was understood in the late 1920s, is somewhat debatable; but its use as a political tool, given his chief opposition, made a great deal of sense.

Blocking Cermak's path to political leadership was his old nemesis Timothy (T. J.) Crowe and his ally Martin J. O'Brien who through their patronage network at the Metropolitan Sanitary District and the party's managing committee refused to step aside for Cermak and his new breed. However, their political stars faded quickly when the infamous sanitary district "Whoopee Scandal" broke on the Chicago political scene. Besides the somewhat routine charges of corruption, Crowe, O'Brien, and their henchmen were accused of wild carousing during a business visit to New York's Waldorf Astoria Hotel.

Though Cermak would eventually allow Crowe to remain a committeeman (like Mayor Richard J. Daley—Cermak had opponents and not enemies), Crowe's leadership possibilities ended when the press labeled his New York behavior "as an astounding picture of political debauchery." [13]

Upon seizing party control, Cermak reorganized the existing Democratic political apparatus into his own image. Multiethnicity was the new guiding political principle of Chicago Democrats. The blueprint for assembling the country's last great political machine rested on the notion of depersonalizing politics between ethnic groups and individuals while stressing the joys and advantages of organizational unity. Cermak and his new-breed pals saw economic and political glory in having the string of Jewish, Bohemian, and Polish wards bursting with Democratic voters on the city's west side marching shoulder to shoulder with other Democratic voters spread throughout the rest of the city. Aided immeasurably by his allies Nash and McDonough, as well as the country's economic woes, Cermak led his ethnically integrated Chicago and county Democrats to an overwhelming victory in the 1930 elections. It was now clear that the former immigrant pushcart peddler was ready for the big prize—city hall.

Anton J. Cermak's March to the Mayor's Office

Luck is often the deciding variable in understanding why one person emerges from the political pack to achieve the brass ring. Anton Cermak certainly had good fortune in his lengthy climb to the top. From 1920 to 1931, issues, events, personalities, demographics, and even the sudden death of two new-breed rivals—County Sheriff Paddy Carr and Alderman and fellow Bohemian Joseph Kostner—all worked in Cermak's favor. Yet also during this time period, Cermak worked hard to make these advantages pay off. Most impressive were his efforts to change his public image as an officeholder from that of an old-fashioned political operative to a "master public executive."

Following his narrow loss in the county sheriff race of 1918, Cermak recognized the need to become more attractive to the middle-class and better-educated Chicago voters who had by and large rejected his candidacy. His election as county board president in 1922 gave Cermak the opportunity to demonstrate his administrative leadership and fiscal management to these outer ward voters. Cermak adopted many of the state-of-the-art image-changing techniques (the use of blue-ribbon commissions, the use of the latest technology, and the presenting of himself to the public as a workaholic) and began appearing before the leading good government clubs and associations in the city. His energy, intensity, and grasp of facts made up for his lack of oratorical skills as he dazzled audiences with his command of the issues. Even his unsuccessful but highly publicized U.S. Senate race in 1928 was a political plus—it demonstrated to one and all that Anton Cermak had become a serious and respected public figure who was capable of serving in high public office.

Cermak's evolution as a public administrator also included his acceptance of the leading reform notions concerning government efficiency and budget economy. Keying Cermak's image transformation was the public perception of his one remaining political obstacle to gaining city hall—Republican Mayor William Hale "Big Bill" Thompson. Big Bill's well-publicized governmental shenanigans, his highly questionable political activities, and his continuous war with the city's newspapers (especially the solidly Republican *Tribune*) was anathema to traditional GOP city voters. It was this group that Cermak wanted to win over or at least neutralize in any upcoming mayoral candidacy. The fact that Cermak was able to do this while organizing a political machine illustrates not only his own talent but the good fortune of having the discredited Thompson as his Republican opponent.

In 1931, it all came together for Anton Cermak as he swept into city hall, trouncing Thompson by almost 200,000 votes. In retrospect, Cermak's mayoral victory was anticlimactic given all the groundwork he had laid prior to the campaign. Cermak's campaign game plan was so complete that Thompson was made to look not only silly but totally out of date as the three-term mayor tried vainly to resurrect old issues. Cermak's political and governmental alliances left Thompson with only his black supporters, his city hall patronage, and some diehard Republicans to stem the Democratic challenge.

Even Big Bill's once mighty campaign skills were ineffective against Cermak's citywide onslaught. Thompson and his allies, hoping to create an old-fashioned Democratic party split brashly, charged that Cermak's candidacy was anti-Irish and an insult to the sons of Erin. Big Bill specifically attempted to make West Side Democratic Alderman John Clark part of his anti-Cermak campaign. Clark was no close Cermak friend and it was well known he wanted to be mayor, but Clark was also a new-breed organization Democrat who served on the county central committee. He and his fellow Irish new breeds were far too sophisticated to fall prey to Big Bill's ethnic baiting. At a monstrous Cermak rally in the Chicago Stadium, Clark ended any hopes for a Thompson victory when he answered the charges by simply saying "His [Big Bill's] only reason for bringing in my name was to engender intolerance." [14]

Anton J. Cermak: Mayor of Chicago

Cermak's mayoral term began during the depths of the Great Depression. Chicago and its citizens were hurting and it did not take long for Cermak to show he was the man in charge. In his inaugural speech, he told Chicagoans his first mayoral objective was to curb expenses and cut taxes. He spoke of improved government efficiency, proposed labor-saving devices for city departments, and demanded general costcutting through consolidation of overlapping city agencies and through centralized purchasing. What is important to note is that nothing Cermak advocated was a departure from what he promised as a candidate or what he had openly supported as county board president. It is of equal importance to note that none of these good government reform positions interfered with Cermak's political operation that was fine-tuning the Chicago Democratic machine. For it was Cermak and not Richard J. Daley who first recognized the enormous benefits of implementing the public policy "that good government was good politics—and good politics was good government."

Cermak intertwined the governmental and political process during his city hall reign. He was intent on providing services to all Chicagoans in the manner he knew best—as a ward committeeman. (Daley has been the only ward committeeman other than Cermak to be mayor of Chicago.) Individual loyalty to the city, loyalty to good government, loyalty to a community, church, or constituent was fostered and encouraged—as long as it was understood that it all fell under the mantle of the Cook County Democratic Central Committee or "the machine." As this complicated political mechanism began spreading its influence throughout the city, one fact became abundantly clear: Mayor Cermak's true power rested not on his ability to reward but rather on his ability to punish. Going against Cermak's political or governmental authority was considered heresy and not dissent and though it would take over twenty years to fully implement this incredible philosophy, it was Cermak who first made Chicagoans believe that his Democratic party was the only true and acceptable vehicle for one to practice local politics.

Economic issues dominated Cermak's mayoral term. Dollars to pay municipal employees, dollars to pay poor relief, discussions about taxes and budgets took up most of Cermak's time. And though some critics chastised him for maintaining friendships and associations with various undesirables from the Prohibition era and others called him "Cermak the dictator" as he fully exercised his power, the new mayor kept his eye on the target—a businesslike approach to solve the city's financial ills.

City council meetings were run for the first time in a professional manner. Cermak and his floor leader Alderman Jacob Arvey ended the practice of councilmen roaming the chambers holding private conversations. The mayor dramatically made this point at an early council session when he stopped the proceedings, telling the startled aldermen in unmistakable Cermakian tones "to keep their seats and refrain from talking while business is being transacted."[15]

His council foes balked at Cermak's iron rule but even his most bitter critic admitted that no previous mayor had ever possessed more detailed information about city issues than Cermak. Aldermen who challenged Cermak had to be prepared to debate the issue on specific terms with the mayor and his council team, for this administration did its homework. More than one council member itching for an old-fashioned fight based on personality and political innuendo were laid low by the mayor's use of outside experts, research reports, and blue-ribbon study commissions.

Cermak pressed his notion that he represented Chicago as he spoke on behalf of the city in Springfield and Washington. In a major pre-Christmas 1931 speech before the state legislature, the mayor called for passage of innovative and long-debated reform measures to deal with the economic woes of city and state. Charles Merriam, the eminent University of Chicago political scientist and former reform-minded GOP mayoral candidate, saw Cermak express his views on the evils of overlapping jurisdictions in Cook County and the need to revamp the local and state tax system. Imagine the chagrin of Cermak's Republican opponents and remaining Democratic foes on seeing the architect of a blossoming political machine earnestly advocating the leading reform ideas of the day.

How Did Cermak Do It?

Cermak's ultimate political genius rested on his ability to adopt and articulate traditional reform issues, make them his own while not hurting his political activities. Along with his trusted Irish pal Pat Nash (selected by Cermak to run the party following his 1931 mayoral victory) Cermak and his Democratic allies took the lead in advocating an end to waste and extravagance in local government. Like turn-of-the-century Progressive reformers, Cermak and Nash demanded that government become more effective, efficient, and businesslike in serving the public interest. However, whereas earlier reformers wanted to bypass or even abolish existing political party organizations to achieve their goals, Cermak and Nash advocated change through the political process—the local Democratic party.

They ran the party as they tried to run the city—as a business. One either delivered or was out; rewards equaled performance, and one was answerable to the board of directors, the central committee. More than anything else, Cermak wanted to show Chicago voters that a political party could run itself and a city like a profit-making enterprise using political victories and not financial success or reform as its overall goal. Above everything else, it must be remembered that Cermak and his machine henchmen did not trick or fool Chicago voters into accepting their style and method of governmental and political leadership. Cermak gave the people what they wanted and those who refused to follow him would eventually have to pay a price for their independence— political defeat or government exile.

As a mayor, Cermak wanted to control or influence every aspect of city life through either the mayor's office or the Democratic party. "Tony really saw himself as a corporate executive" said one old-time ward committeeman, "and he thought it was stupid for the top guy not to know everything that was happening." [16] Cermak's passion for detail and control extended to Chicago's public school system and its board of education. As has been shown in a recent study by Kip Sullivan, the Chicago Board of Education was one of the last holdouts to Cermak-style leadership. [17] Angered by the actions of the so-called "solid six" (incumbent board members previously appointed by Thompson), Cermak turned his wrath on the school system. He prepared massive educational cuts and teacher layoffs, making the schools a case study of retrenchment and reduction. Aided by another of his handy "blue-ribbon advisory committees" Cermak taught the educators a lesson of what it meant to defy his political wishes. And he did it all in the guise of reform and efficiency.

Other examples abound of Mayor Cermak using reform rhetoric and machine manipulation to build his control over the entire city. Two final case studies, one governmental, the other political, demonstrate the mastery of this political wizard.

Civil service reform is perhaps the granddaddy of all reform measures aimed at curtailing the evils of big city political machines. Government appointments based on "functional job requirements" rather than on political ties and personnel systems based on an individual's ability to perform (merit) rather than partisan party considerations (patronage) are beliefs long held by good government advocates. To the lengthy list of civil service true believers, one could add the name of Anton J. Cermak.

During his campaign against Thompson, candidate Cermak promised "a virile civil service commission" to undo the politicization of Chicago's employee hiring practices. Since 1910, the city's payroll had increased by 86 percent (41,000 jobs) while its population had grown by only 54 percent.[18] Once in city hall, Cermak immediately orchestrated a highly publicized effort to recruit the best civil service commission in Chicago history.

The mayor told the press and civic associations that the 1895 city civil service law (the Illinois legislature had forced the city to have civil service ten years before it passed the same law for themselves in 1905) had been largely ignored. To change this situation, Cermak once again offered Charles Merriam the opportunity to join his administration by suggesting him for the commission chairman post. Though Professor Merriam again declined a mayoral appointment, his University of Chicago colleague, Leonard D. White, the country's leading scholar in the blossoming field of public administration, accepted the same Cermak offer. The mayor completed the three-man commission lineup by selecting Richard Collins, a "silk-stocking businessman," and J. V. Geary, a quiet Democratic ward committeeman. Geary's qualifications in personnel matters paled compared to his two colleagues; but the publicity generated by the other two selections allowed him to slip silently into the third slot.

The *Chicago Tribune* was ecstatic over Cermak's commission choices, claiming that "the new board gives promise of integrity"; and it congratulated the mayor "for choosing its members with care." They concluded their ringing praise of Cermak by stating "there is no more important agency in the city than the Civil Service Commission," and after detailing how Thompsonism had demoralized professional public service in Chicago, the *Tribune* prophesized that Cermak's commission selections "were the best indication of his purpose to give Chicago good government."[19]

Cermak's virtuoso Civil Service Commission performance was a prime example of his mayoral style. Unlike his city hall predecessors who either sought to build political support by rejecting reform or by rejecting partisan political attachments in favor of reform, Cermak took the best from both worlds. He welcomed and even championed good government reform measures as long as it did not interfere with his political activities. He sought out governmental experts and gave them freedom to promote new ideas as long as he had final veto over their activities. Information was key to Cermak and he instituted the practice of placing one of his own men (e.g., Geary on the Civil Service Commission) on the various appointed boards and commissions to act as his unofficial spokesman. Given his passion for efficiency, Cermak accepted reform calls for government effectiveness, but he never took his eye off the overriding goal—political control.

Just as Cermak proved how reform parts could produce a political machine, he also demonstrated how a party could adopt a businesslike approach to government and elections. Under his direction, the local Democratic party became probably the first political organization in the country to use statistical analysis to evaluate political performance and devise election strategy.

Cermak published a local party newspaper, *The Public Service Leader*. Though its masthead labeled itself the official publication of the regular Democratic organization in Illinois, it was well known that its real focus was city hall and the Chicago Democratic party. Following the 1932 general election, Cermak ended some general local Democratic party jubilation by listing each ward organization's vote production performance in the *Leader*. According to the newspaper, the party's executive committee had formulated "a scientific mathematically exact grading of the vote getting machinery in each of Chicago's fifty wards." [20]

Rankings were listed by ward (1–50) for each office contested in the November election. Rating criteria included vote margins, turnout percentages, and the percentage of straight Democratic voters. Though the party had enjoyed an overwhelming victory in Chicago, Cermak hoped to avoid complacency by interjecting intraward rivalry for pecking order and patronage purposes. This political competition factor inside the party made *every* contest crucial to the fifty ward organizations and their respective committeemen. Perhaps the most revealing aspect of this new ranking practice was the *Leader's* bitter attack on some precinct captains for knifing (not supporting) two losing municipal judge candidates. Never before had Chicagoans seen a political party so organized for battle; but, then, again, the city had never seen a mayor like Anton J. Cermak.

Cermak's Death and the Chicago Political Tradition

As with most of his life, Cermak's death was analyzed for its political implications. Even as he lay dying in a Miami hospital, many Chicago politicians questioned whether his assassin, Giuseppe Zangara, was truly aiming at President-elect Franklin Roosevelt when he accidentally shot their mayor. Everything about Cermak was political.

Perhaps the best testimony to Cermak's lifelong dream to build an unshakable political organization took place during the selection process to name his successor. His multiethnic machine held firm under the guidance of his confidant Pat Nash and his organization regulars. Following Cermak's death, the council immediately appointed an interim mayor, Alderman Frank Corr, a little-known council member who was selected for his anonymity. Most of the process to find a permanent replacement for Cermak took place behind closed doors as party leaders met privately to find a suitable and acceptable mayoral successor. Choosing Edward J. Kelly as Chicago's next mayor was not an easy decision. Several names were discussed and debate often became heated; but once the designation was made, the organization rallied publicly behind their choice. Cermak would have been proud of the actual council vote as Republican and independent aldermen, recognizing the futility of contesting the nomination, joined organization Democrats in unanimously supporting Kelly 47 to 0.[21]

Cermak's place in the city's political tradition is a crucial one. His ability to link or bridge generational political change, his willingness to accept innovation and reform administratively, and his single-mindedness to reach the top changed the direction and style of Chicago politics. Often overlooked in Cermak's slow climb to city hall was his incredible public office and political background. He had worked in state, county, and local government and had run for U.S. Senate. He was knowledgeable about the court system and law enforcement (some critics would argue from both sides of the law). Politically, he had worked the precincts, run a ward organization, survived intraparty warfare and eventually was elected chairman of the party. Thus, Cermak was prepared to govern his adopted city from an experience base previously unparalleled in Chicago history.

In sum, Cermak was a winner. He demonstrated that if you were smart enough, tough enough, and lucky enough, you could have it all in Chicago politics. His vehicle for victory was a multinational Democratic machine which he created, nurtured, and fine-tuned. However, it must be remembered that little came easy to Cermak. This Bohemian immigrant also outworked all his rivals and in his own favorite phrase proved, "Only lazy precinct captains steal votes."

Joseph Medill (1871–73), Chicago's first modern mayor.
Courtesy University of Illinois at Chicago

Carter Harrison II (1897–1905,
907–11), ultimate practitioner of
ie politics of balance in Chicago.
*Courtesy University of Illinois at
Chicago*

Edward F. Dunne (1905–07), one of a rare breed of Chicago politicians: a reformer.
Courtesy University of Illinois at Chicago

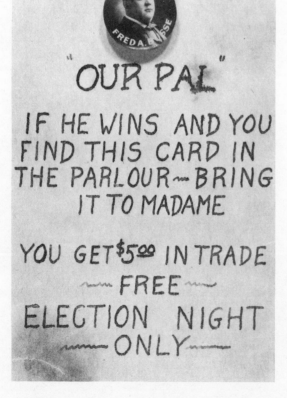

Fred A. Busse (1907–11) reflected and accepted the free and easy mora climate of turn-of-the-century Chicago.
University of Illinois at Chicago. The University Library; Lawrence J. Gutte Collection of Chicagoana

William "Big Bill" Thompson (1915–23, 1927–31) at the lever of an earth-moving machine; *right*, Public Works Commissioner Richard Wolf. Thompson began the tradition of the "builder" mayors.
University of Illinois at Chicago, The University Library; Lawrence J. Gutter Collection of Chicagoana

Big Bill Thompson launching his "America First" campaign for mayor in 1927.
University of Illinois at Chicago, The University Library; Lawrence J. Gutter Collection of Chicagoana

Chicago reform mayor William Dever (1923–27), *center,* watches his wife cast her ballot.
Courtesy Chicago Sun-Times

Mayor Anton J. Cermak (1931–33), *left,* with presidential candidate Franklin D. Roosevelt and Roosevelt's son Jimmy at a Chicago White Sox game. Cermak was beginning to appreciate the importance of federal patronage to the Chicago machine.
University of Illinois at Chicago, The University Library; Department of Special Collections

Mayor Anton Cermak (*left*) with Alderman Charles Weber in a Havana
bar during Prohibition. Cermak advertised his antiprohibition views
to approving Chicago voters.
Courtesy University of Illinois at Chicago. Urban Historical Collection

Mayor Edward J. Kelly (1933–47), *center,* appears with some members of the
Kelly-Nash machine: *right,* Senator J. Hamilton Lewis, a North Side alder-
man; *left,* Alderman Mathias "Paddy" Bauler.
Courtesy University of Illinois at Chicago

Spanning the political generations, Carter Harrison II (*1*) and Edward Kelly (*3*) flank newly elected reform Mayor Martin H. Kennelly in 1947.
Courtesy Chicago Sun-Times

Martin H. Kennelly (1947–55), the "mugwump" reformer who could not control the machine that elected him.
Courtesy University of Illinois at Chicago

Cook County Clerk Richard J. Daley administers the oath of office to Mayor Martin J. Kennelly in 1951. This power relationship would be reversed four years later when Daley would take the Democratic mayoral nomination from the incumbent Kennelly. *Courtesy Chicago* Sun-Times

Flushed with victory, a jubilant Richard J. Daley (1955–76) shakes hands in 1955 with the defeated and crestfallen Kennelly. *Courtesy Chicago* Sun-Times

Richard J. Daley, "America's last boss," exuded a twinkling Irish charm even though somewhat flustered by an affectionate Hawaiian tourist representative.
University of Illinois at Chicago, The University Library; Department of Special Collections

A young Richard J. Daley, shown here campaigning for mayor, was always ready to demonstrate his strong commitment to family values and to the neighborhoods.
Courtesy University of Illinois at Chicago

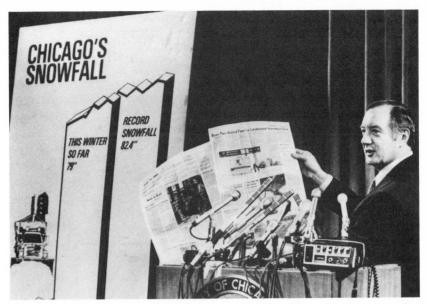

Michael Bilandic (1977–79) would be defeated by Jane Byrne and a record snowfall.
Courtesy Chicago Sun-Times

Jane Byrne (1979–83) doing what she did best: campaigning among Chicago's
upscale, professional women.
Courtesy University of Illinois at Chicago

Mayor Jane Byrne appearing with the Roman Catholic Auxiliary Bishop of Chicago, Alfred L. Abramowicz. Raised and educated with her upper-income, "lace curtain" peers in private schools, she was an unorthodox Chicago politician.
Courtesy University of Illinois at Chicago

"Fighting Jane" Byrne unleashes her campaign for the 1987 mayoral election.
Courtesy Jane Byrne for Mayor, 1987

Candidate Harold Washington (*center*) celebrating his 1983 mayoral primary victory with Jesse Jackson (*left*) and Senator Alan Cranston of California.
Courtesy University of Illinois at Chicago

Candidate Harold Washington prepares to debate Republican mayoral candidate Bernard Epton.
Courtesy Chicago Sun-Times

A smiling and photogenic Mayor Harold Washington
(1983–) was no longer an enigma to Chicago voters
by 1987.
Courtesy Office of the Mayor

8.

EDWARD J. KELLY: NEW DEAL MACHINE BUILDER

Roger Biles

For fourteen critical years spanning the Great Depression and Second World War, Edward J. Kelly ruled Chicago's city hall and its Democratic party. At a time when political machines were declining in most American cities, the reverse was true of Chicago, where Ed Kelly, with the assistance of Pat Nash, not only preserved the Democratic organization but vastly expanded its power and influence. Kelly's enterprising strategy included several elements: attracting traditionally Republican black voters to the Democratic fold, allying the machine with President Franklin D. Roosevelt's New Deal, and tapping the financial resources of organized crime. Because of these changes during the 1930s and 1940s, Kelly transformed the "house for all peoples" assembled by Anton Cermak into the political leviathan commanded by Richard Daley.

To aid him in his successful quest for the mayoralty, Anton Cermak, a Czech, assembled an ethnic coalition of Chicago Democrats including the Irish, Poles, Jews, and Germans. At the time of his death, the most likely successor seemed to be the machine's second-in-command and leader of the powerful Irish faction, Twenty-eighth Ward Alderman Patrick A. Nash. But the seventy-year old Nash demurred, citing his age and lack of interest. He did, however, exercise his authority as titular head of the party to pick the new mayor. Nash used the Democratic majority in the Springfield General Assembly to pass a state law enabling the city council to go outside its membership in choosing an interim mayor. With the support of Democratic Governor Henry Horner and the majority of his party, Nash announced his selection—Chief Engineer of the Sanitary District, Edward J. Kelly.[1]

The new mayor was a familiar figure to Chicagoans, but not as an elected public official. Born and raised in the predominantly Irish neighborhood of

Bridgeport, Kelly began working for the Sanitary District at age eighteen in 1894 and remained in its employ for the next thirty-nine years. He gained more notoriety, though, in his alternate capacity as president of the South Park Board. During his triumphant years at its helm, Kelly presided over the transformation of Grant Park from a tin can dumping ground to a beautiful adjunct to downtown. During his tenure, private citizens donated the Shedd Aquarium and the Adler Planetarium, along with the Buckingham Memorial Fountain, to the newly developing civic center in Grant Park. Kelly also supervised the construction of Soldier Field and the refurbishing of what is now the Museum of Science and Industry. As a result of these efforts, he became known as the "Father of the Lakefront." More importantly, as Chief Engineer of the Sanitary District, he awarded millions of dollars in contracts to Pat Nash's sewer contracting firms and launched an enduring friendship with the Democratic leader.[2]

When Kelly took office in 1933, Chicago continued to reel from the force of the depression. The most severe economic crisis in the nation's history devastated the Windy City which, during the worst moments, virtually ceased to function. The signs of suffering and want were everywhere. As the nation's transportation hub, Chicago attracted thousands of transients to its already sizable stable of indigents and unemployed; throngs of uprooted men and women descended upon the city hoping for work and lodging, but they found only breadlines and cardboard shacks. A shantytown had appeared at the very edge of the Loop on Randolph Street. Its residents named it "Hooverville" and its streets "Prosperity Road," "Hard Times Avenue," and "Easy Street." The municipal relief agencies strained to meet the demand for shelter—they used asylums, poorhouses, and veterans homes to house the needy—but like all departments of city government, they remained incapable of dealing with such large-scale misery.[3]

Faced with forty percent unemployment, Chicago increased its relief expenditures to $35 million in 1932. But it was not enough. Private donations, though generous, proved equally inadequate. The failure of philanthropy merely heightened the dilemma, for owing to a sordid history of fiscal mismanagement, Chicago entered the depression already on the verge of bankruptcy. As a result of a real estate assessment concluded in 1929, the state reduced the city's property valuations by over $400 million. At the same time, a large number of property owners conducted a tax strike. The failure to produce revenue meant not only that the city could afford little in the way of welfare assistance, but that it could not afford to pay its employees. For a brief period, the school board issued scrip to the teachers, but the courts ruled the practice illegal. Payless paydays followed in succession. While teachers continued to work without compensation, the city discharged many of its policemen and firemen. When local banks refused to accept any more tax anticipation warrants, Chicago was flat broke.[4]

On Ed Kelly's first day in office, the tax delinquency lists filled 260 newspaper pages. Fourteen thousand schoolteachers, not having received paychecks for several months, stormed the banks and picketed the downtown financial district. The police used tear gas to disperse the crowds and arrested scores of picketers. Undaunted, the teachers broke up public meetings and heckled the city council and school board. As many as twenty thousand high school students struck on a single day to demonstrate their sympathy for the teachers. The city's unpaid workers clamored for immediate action from the new mayor; Kelly did not disappoint them. In his first official act, the mayor signed tax warrants worth $1.7 million and dispatched paychecks to the city's teachers. The city also sent checks to the other municipal payrollers, most of whom had not been paid in months. And to ensure the availability of more funds, Kelly led an entourage of Chicago politicians to the state capital to successfully lobby for legislation enabling cities to collect rents and income taxes on delinquent income-producing properties.[5]

Recognizing the need for sustained economy, Kelly set out to trim the city's budget further. He focused specifically on Chicago's white elephant, the foundering public school system; his plan was severe in the elimination of both programs and personnel. It mandated the abolition of printing, physical education, and home economics in elementary schools, as well as printing and vocational guidance in the high schools. The program also increased teaching loads by 40 percent, shortened the school year by one month, reduced all teacher's salaries 23.5 percent, and closed all special schools and special departments. Over thirteen hundred teachers lost their jobs. Responding to an uproar from the city's educational community, Mayor Kelly defended the action as the only alternative to closing the schools altogether. Judging by the short life of the controversy, most Chicagoans agreed.[6]

In the first few months of his administration, Ed Kelly scored a number of triumphs including meeting municipal payrolls, wiping out a significant portion of the city debt, establishing good relations with the state legislature, and keeping the schools open. He enjoyed good relations with the Democratic governor; and with the new Roosevelt administration more inclined than the previous Republican one to commit federal monies to help the cities, he benefited from the availability of additional resources. If Kelly had not vanquished the depression, conditions had improved to the extent that the riots and confrontations of prior months were not being repeated. Moreover, his popularity soared as he presided over the highly successful Century of Progress Exposition and wisely extended the lucrative world's fair for a second year's run.[7]

In 1935 Kelly stood for election against an obscure Republican, Emil Wetten. The Chicago *Tribune* accurately observed: "The spirit of contest has been entirely lacking. This is recognized as the most peaceful, the most one-sided campaign since Chicago, in 1911, began naming the mayoral candidates through primaries. . . . It's all Kelly, so why talk about anything else?" On

2 April 1935, the voters elected Kelly by the greatest margin yet in Chicago. He received 799,060 votes to Wetten's 167,016 and carried all fifty wards. The defeated candidate lamented: "There isn't much to say except that the results confirm what had been repeatedly published—that the Republican party is completely disintegrated. In fact, there is no local Republican party."[8]

Pondering the 1935 election results, the New York *Times* concluded: "Why did the people of Chicago give him an unparalleled vote of confidence? Because he turned one of the worst-governed cities into one of the best-governed. . . . The floating debt has been greatly reduced and in consequence the cost of borrowed money has declined to something like a normal rate of interest. Even more dramatic has been the wiping out of the arrears in wage and salary payments of city and school employees. These are memorable achievements. . . . He is a good model of mayors and even offices of loftier title to follow." Political columnist Arthur Krock said: "Chicago still has relief problems, slums, poverty, and great groups of the unemployed. But the difference between present conditions and those in 1932 is the difference between black and white." Douglas Sutherland, director of the silk-stocking Chicago Civic Federation opined: "Mayor Kelly is giving Chicago better government than it has had in many years. He has made several strong appointments and is a man of good judgment and great strength." Indeed, praise from many quarters reflected Ed Kelly's status as one of the nation's most-heralded mayors.[9]

Along with his old friend, Democratic Committee Chairman Pat Nash, he also controlled one of the most powerful urban political machines in the nation. From the outset Kelly and Nash sought peace among the party leaders. Since a number of powerful Democrats harbored designs on the mayoralty even before Cermak's death, the prospects for amicable relations seemed dubious— especially in light of the persistent ethnic rivalries. But Kelly and Nash took immediate steps to forestall any potential difficulties by granting membership into the party's new inner circle to spokesmen for the different factions. They chose Jacob Arvey of the predominantly Jewish Twenty-fourth Ward to be chairman of the prestigious city council finance committee; Barnet Hodes, Arvey's law partner and a respected member of the Jewish community, was selected as corporation counsel for the city. The mayor appointed Polish leader M. S. Szymczak city controller and later elevated him to a seat on the Federal Reserve Board. In the city's North Side German-American community, Forty-third Ward Alderman Matthias "Paddy" Bauler and Forty-seventh Ward Alderman Charlie Weber gained increased stature in the new open-ended Kelly-Nash melting pot.[10]

Under Kelly-Nash leadership, the Chicago machine commanded the loyalty of its members because it produced at the polls and rewarded the faithful with a share of the spoils. The cobosses established clearcut standards of performance, whereby party workers advanced or were demoted according to successes or failures within their own fiefdoms. Given a certain latitutde and hope for advancement within the hierarchy, the party faithful, from ward committeemen down to precinct workers, had a reason to work hard. This system of incentives, tempered with stern discipline, was very instrumental in keeping together an uneasy alliance among disparate factions.[11]

The Democratic organization also benefited from the acceptance, if not the wholehearted endorsement, of Chicago's business community. While many of the city's wealthiest and most influential families shared a generations-old affiliation with the Republican party, they reached a comfortable arrangement with the Kelly-Nash organization. Bankers tolerated Kelly because he kept city finances in order, guaranteeing a profitable market for city bonds and tax anticipation warrants. Moreover, Kelly's dramatic success in keeping Chicago solvent between 1933 and 1935 earned him the gratitude of the LaSalle Street bankers. The mayor courted the Loop merchants by providing services for the downtown area. First-rate police and fire protection, along with prompt maintenance work on streets and sidewalks, provided everyday reminders of city hall's beneficence. Most noteworthy was the construction of the State Street subway, a boon to Loop merchants and one link in a revised transportation network designed to provide consumers with easy access to the city center. And finally, Kelly earned the plaudits of the business community through his sustained opposition to personal property and state income taxes.[12]

The Democratic machine also received the support of organized labor, despite the potentially disastrous Memorial Day Massacre of 1937. In that incident, Chicago police fired pistols into a crowd of fleeing picketers, killing ten and wounding thirty more. Kelly staunchly defended the actions of the police, but a well-publicized investigation by a U.S. Senate Committee chaired by Robert LaFollette, Jr., condemned the police action and the city's blatantly partial investigation. The Democratic leadership so feared retaliation by working-class voters that they met with CIO officials to discuss ways of improving their rapport. Kelly offered them future exemption from police interference in return for official forgiveness for Kelly's role in the Memorial Day affair. The CIO worked for the machine in subsequent elections and, amazingly, a steelworker whose eye had been shot out in the 1937 skirmish gave Kelly a radio endorsement during the 1939 mayoral campaign. Thereafter, Chicago police assumed a more circumspect stance during labor-management confrontations, and the CIO took its place among the supporters of Chicago Democracy.[13]

To a great degree the ability of the Kelly-Nash organization to command the allegiance of the various Democratic factions and the goodwill of both business and labor constituted a continuance of Anton Cermak's policies. If these had been the only accomplishments of the fourteen-year Kelly stewardship, his sole claim would have been that he preserved the status quo for his successor. However, the machine not only survived but expanded during the Kelly years as a result of three new resources tapped by his machine. The additional revenue and votes supplied by blacks, organized crime, and the New Deal enabled Chicago Democracy to thrive in the 1930s and 1940s.

Prior to the depression decade, blacks voted Republican in overwhelming numbers, but that changed dramatically during the Roosevelt years. Contrary to the belief that urban blacks switched to the Democratic party solely because of New Deal generosity, in Chicago local factors contributed significantly as well. Kelly's popularity in the black community existed independently of, and indeed preceded, Roosevelt's. Kelly set out to capture the black vote and did so by appointing blacks to an increasing number of municipal posts, by selecting them as candidates for elective offices, and by distributing government aid— first municipal and later, in much larger quantities, federal—to the ravaged South Side. Moreover, the mayor intervened on several occasions to defend the principals of desegregated housing and education.[14]

Kelly worked assiduously to present a good image to black voters and succeeded in establishing a reputation as a friend of "the Race." The mayor censored the showing of the film "Birth of a Nation" in Chicago because of its explicit racism. He honored successful black Americans for their accomplishments—making Joe Louis "mayor for ten minutes" in an elaborate city hall ceremony, for example—and made numerous personal appearances at South Side functions. "Big Red," as blacks affectionately called the mayor, attended the annual Tuskegee-Wilberforce football games at Soldier Field and endorsed Governor Horner's refusal to extradite a fugitive black man to an almost certain lynching in Arkansas. As a result of these concerted efforts, blacks supported the Democratic ticket in all elections, consistently giving Kelly a greater percentage of the vote than he received citywide.[15]

Kelly's soaring popularity in the black community first became evident in 1934 when the Democrats selected a black candidate, Arthur W. Mitchell, to contest Oscar DePriest's congressional seat from Illinois's 1st District. The popular DePriest, a three-term incumbent who was nationally renowned as the first black Republican to sit in Congress since 1901, had the endorsement of the black press, including the influential Chicago *Defender*. But with the aid of the Kelly-Nash machine, Mitchell won a narrow victory and became the first black Democratic U.S. congressman.[16]

The man who ultimately came to rule the black Democratic "submachine" was former-Republican Alderman William L. Dawson. Kelly did not start out to choose a subordinate to whom he could entrust the administration of the party's interests in the black community; he initially chose Dawson for a very specific purpose, to assume control of the troublesome Second Ward. In the words of a politician close to Dawson: "Kelly did not build Dawson by prearranged plan into the South Side boss; he made him head of the second ward, and after that Dawson just grew. In each showdown, Dawson was seen to be the better man and was supported." Eventually, his domain included not only the Second Ward but also the Third, Fourth, Sixth, and Twentieth on the South Side; as a result, he controlled an estimated quarter-of-a-million votes.[17]

Kelly's capture of the black vote proved to be a monumental contribution to the Chicago Democratic machine. Beginning in the 1930s, with the city's black population increasing and whites fleeing to the suburbs, the black vote became a precious commodity to the white politicians seeking to maintain control. The importance of Kelly's feat became evident years later, during the Daley era. In 1963, for instance, Daley lost the white vote in the city—Benjamin Adamowski gained 51 percent of the votes cast in the white wards—but carried the black vote by such an overwhelming margin that he managed to retain the office of mayor.[18]

While the black community provided votes in substantial quantities for the machine, its modest economic resources precluded contribution of another essential need, money. For that factor, the Kelly-Nash organization turned to organized crime. The mayor deplored the publicity that attended gangland killings, and to a great degree his administration restrained the rampant lawlessness of the Roaring Twenties, but gambling revenue was so important to the ward organizations that no genuine effort was launched to enforce the anti-gambling statutes. Tribute paid to the organization by the vice lords in return for protection became a vital source of funds, variously estimated at $12 to $20 million annually. A particularly prosperous handbook operator might pay up to $1000 a month, whereas for a more modest hole-in-the-wall crap game the fee might have commanded $300 per month. While rates varied by wards, gambling proprietors typically had to split their profits equally with the local political representative.[19]

The Kelly-Nash machine entrusted the supervision of the gambling revenue to each ward committeeman. A portion of the money collected went to the Democratic offices downtown, while the rest stayed in the ward to defray the expenses of campaigning and electioneering. (In the Forty-second Ward, for example, 40 percent of the money collected stayed in the ward organization, and the remaining amount went to party headquarters in the Morrison Hotel.) Ward committeemen chose police captains, who were usually placed in charge of collections. If a ward committeeman became troublesome to the organization, a new police captain would be dispatched to that district with orders to enforce the gambling laws. Thus cut off from his source of revenue, the penitent committeeman would get back in line and gambling would again flourish in the area.[20]

The Chicago *Daily News*, mindful of the vast sums of money available to the Kelly administration by virtue of its toleration of gambling, touched on an even more important factor in the mayor's decision to sanction protection for the underworld:

Cynics, viewing the mixed picture of the mayor's good financial administration in contrast with his tolerance of protected vice and gambling, are tempted to ask whether the two are not somehow related. The question arises whether it is not because the mayor has courageously denied his henchmen the opportunity to exploit the city's finances directly that he allows them to exploit vice and gambling on so lucrative a scale.[21]

But while Kelly presided over an organization saturated with graft and corruption, there is little evidence to suggest that he profited personally—at least after his elevation to the mayoralty. His apparent decision to spurn emoluments from gambling may have been the result of several considerations. Having fallen victim to an Internal Revenue Service investigation in 1933 for which he paid over $100,000 in penalties and interest, he cautiously avoided any hint of fiscal impropriety. Another explanation lay in the mayor's already healthy financial state. Since he allegedly stockpiled a fortune during the infamous "Whoopee Era" at the Sanitary District years before, he could bypass this second wave of graft. (In the sensational Whoopee Era scandal, over seven hundred witnesses testified that Sanitary District officials had stockpiled sizable fortunes from payoffs, bribes, and kickbacks. Of the eleven men indicted, several served jail sentences, and only Kelly went unpunished.) In the parlance of Chicago politics, "Big Ed already had his." Some observers suggested that Kelly's abstinence reflected a change in his character triggered by exposure to New Deal principles; this seems unlikely. Though the money generated from gambling seemed too important to the party organization to refuse, Kelly, with one eye on what would go on his gravestone, insisted upon a higher standard for himself. As one student of Chicago politics wrote, Kelly tolerated the corruption around him "in the familiar style of Irish Catholic politicians who went to mass, led lives of personal fidelity, and were not scandalized by an imperfect world." In all likelihood, all of these factors contributed.[22]

Under the aegis of Roosevelt's New Deal, the federal government also provided desperately needed financial assistance to depression-stricken Chicago. After Kelly established himself as the most powerful Democrat in Illinois with his landslide 1935 victory, federal relief czar Harry Hopkins turned his back on the mayor's rivals. Governor Horner, with whom Kelly frequently quarreled in the second half of the decade, complained that Hopkins ignored him, even refusing to return his telephone calls. Secretary of the Interior and native-Chicagoan Harold Ickes bemoaned Hopkins's "blind worship" of Kelly to President Roosevelt, but to no avail. Ickes called the Kelly-Nash organization "the rottenest crowd in any section of the United States today" and toyed with returning to his native city to run against the mayor in 1939, but his attacks failed to sever the strong ties between the Chicago machine and Washington. Hopkins went out of his way to support the Kelly administration, funneling extra money to the Chicago WPA office; in 1936, for example, he phoned that office to say, "the Treasury has suddenly found a little more money, and I don't want to put you and Ed in a hot spot. If there is any money here and it will do some good, I want you to have it."[23]

Along with Hopkins, Kelly could count on the support of Roosevelt's political right hand, Postmaster General Jim Farley. Like Hopkins, Farley ignored other Illinois politicos to focus all his attention on Chicago's mayor. One disgruntled politician told Ickes that "Farley never talks with anyone in Chicago except Mayor Kelly." To affirm their exclusive contact, Farley wrote Kelly that the Democratic National Committee would "do nothing in your County with reference to speakers or meetings without consulting Pat [Nash]." With these members of Roosevelt's inner circle favorably disposed toward him, Kelly enjoyed an enviable position. At the same time, he also benefited from a favored position with the president himself.[24]

Kelly frequently regaled Roosevelt with results of public opinion polls he conducted in Chicago and advised him on topics ranging from practical politics to foreign affairs. According to Samuel Rosenman, one of the president's speech writers, Roosevelt valued Kelly's opinions because he knew the mayor to be totally candid. Besides establishing his reputation as a sagacious politician, Kelly also made himself a worthy Roosevelt lieutenant by performing some sensitive tasks for the Democratic party. He championed administrative measures in Illinois and frequently aided WPA chief Hopkins in his struggle to compel Governor Horner and the General Assembly to assume greater financial responsibility for the state's relief program. Furthermore, Kelly used his influence on other Illinois politicians to force them into line with presidential initiatives.[25]

There also developed between the president and the mayor a mutual respect and friendship. Roosevelt not only thought enough of Kelly's political prowess to rely upon his counsel. He also socialized with him, inviting him to luncheons at the Roosevelt estate in Hyde Park, New York, and at the White House. While the president stayed on the good side of many big city bosses whose support he coveted, men like Ed Crump of Memphis and Frank Hague of Jersey City, Kelly was one of a select few who penetrated into the inner circle. Even Eleanor Roosevelt, who looked upon the urban bosses as anathema, thought enough of Kelly to defend him publicly when journalists labeled him a corrupt boss of the Frank Hague–Tom Pendergast stripe.[26]

As for Kelly, he could not have been more effusive in his praise of the president. He made "Roosevelt Is My Religion" the title of his standard campaign speech in the thirties. Privately, Kelly called Roosevelt one of the greatest Americans of all time, not to mention the country's finest chief executive. According to many Kelly intimates, the mayor became so enamored of Roosevelt Democracy that he became an avid New Dealer himself. It appears logical that a man in his position would at least pay lip service to New Deal tenets—urban bosses profited from both the nationwide success of the Democratic party and the provision of large quantities of federal funds—but Kelly genuinely seemed to embrace the spirit of liberal reform. This, of course, made the president's association with the boss more palatable.[27]

Most important, though, in explaining Roosevelt's esteem for Mayor Kelly was the power wielded by Illinois's political kingpin. Chicago was the key to carrying Illinois at election time, and the Kelly-Nash machine could deliver the necessary votes. Kelly's political achievements contrasted sharply with the stubborn recalcitrance of Governor Horner, whose relations with Washington New Dealers were as strained as the mayor's were excellent. Roosevelt cast his administration's lot with the Chicago Democrats and often opposed antimachine reformers in the prairie state. (He supported Kelly's bid to unseat Horner in the 1936 gubernatorial contest, for example.) And because of the huge Democratic vote turned out in Chicago throughout the thirties—most notably in 1936 when Roosevelt carried the Windy City by over 500,000 votes—the president's decision to back Kelly paid off handsomely.[28]

Good relations with the federal government aided the city of Chicago as well. The largess made available to Mayor Kelly enabled him to provide jobs and a modicum of relief for the city's destitute; it also made possible a number of long-overdue physical improvements in Chicago. As a result of WPA and PWA funds, the city's transportation network came to maturity with the completion of Lake Shore Drive from Foster Avenue to Jackson Park, including the Outer Drive Bridge, and the opening of the State Street Subway. Thanks to PWA funds, thirty new schools opened in the years from 1933 to 1940, and three housing projects (Jane Addams, Julia Lathrop, and Trumbull Park Homes) were constructed. Later in Kelly's mayoralty, funding from the U.S. Housing Authority resulted in the construction of several other housing projects, including the Ida B. Wells Homes, Altgeld Gardens, Frances Cabrini Homes, Bridgeport Homes, Lawndale Homes, and Brooks Homes. Kelly enlarged Chicago's antiquated municipal airport, adding four sets of dual runways so that for the first time, two planes could land simultaneously, and installed the most modern lighting system in the nation. Equally advantageous were the acres of beautiful new parks landscaped by WPA labor and the ubiquitous road and sewerage improvements. The partnership between Kelly and the New Deal indeed resulted in a major facelift for Chicago.[29]

A savvy politician, Kelly became a master at reaping political capital from the machine's New Deal alliance. In the words of one historian, "Kelly and his organization clung so tightly to the New Deal that the two seemed to be one." For federally financed work projects the mayor chose items of a highly visible and enduring nature, such as construction projects, usually with no special assessments required. The premium placed on labor inevitably resulted in overmanning at project sites, so much so that the state admitted that the use of excessive numbers of workers constituted a serious problem in Chicago. Other complaints arose about Kelly's "exploitation" of New Deal programs: critics charged that machine hacks administered federal agencies, needy citizens were threatened with the loss of relief if they failed to vote Democratic, and WPA workers had to contribute portions of their paychecks to the machine coffers. In short, good government advocates feared that the expanded federal power would be abused by the unsavory political machine wielding it in Chicago.[30]

Without question, some measure of graft existed in the implementation of the New Deal in Chicago. It could not be said, however, that the local Democratic machine received carte blanche authority to manipulate federal programs in any manner. From all indications, WPA officials insisted that the relief certification process be free from political influence. Though many party workers received WPA jobs, federal officials denied that any consideration other than need had been used to certify employment recipients. Harry Hopkins's top troubleshooter, Lorena Hickok, toured WPA projects in Chicago to see "if we were being made victims of the political spoils system." She found no evidence of widespread nepotism, and concluded that "someone apparently had put up a fight to keep politics out of this Chicago show—and pretty successfully too." Similarly, the administration of relief was relatively immune from spoils politics. While machine operatives tried to penetrate the relief apparatus, the county agencies designated to award stipends, staffed by trained social workers, maintained their independence. Director Leo Lyons wrote of his agency: "At no time has the mayor or other city officials attempted to direct the formulation of policies or the selection of personnel by the Chicago Relief Administration."[31]

In fact, the primary contribution of the New Deal lay in the financial largess it provided for the Kelly administration during the threadbare depression years. Set afloat with federal money, the city saved its own slender resources and spent great sums of federal money for the support of the indigent and unemployed. With this working capital, neither patronage nor city services needed to be trimmed. At a time when the gravest threat to the Democratic machine came from financial disaster rather than from a robust opposition party, New Deal largess assured Chicago's solvency.

Kelly's assiduous labors for Roosevelt and the special perquisites that the president granted to the Chicago machine do indeed make it seem indisputable that the Democratic organization thrived as a result of its association with the New Deal. In fact, the operation of the New Deal in Chicago contradicts many of the tenets of the "Last Hurrah" thesis, which attempts to explain the demise of big city political machines. Based upon Edwin O'Conner's novel, *The Last Hurrah*, this thesis suggests that the New Deal destroyed urban political machines by terminating the dependence of the poor upon city hall and substituting federal suzerainty. Kelly's experiences called into question the notion that the bosses were at odds with Roosevelt; clearly, the relationship between the mayor and the president was both cordial and mutually beneficial. No evidence indicates that Roosevelt set out to subvert the influence of the Chicago politicians, nor did he attempt to deemphasize the achievements of the local Democrats in favor of his own federal programs. In the 1936 battle between a "reformist governor" and a corrupt local boss, Roosevelt sided with the latter. Clearly, the ties between Chicago and Washington grew stronger, not weaker, during the 1930s. For a variety of reasons, the Kelly-Nash machine enjoyed a much more secure position than had Cermak's fledgling model on the eve of Roosevelt's inauguration.[32]

As the Democratic machine enjoyed continued good fortune, so too did its leading figure. Mayor Kelly successfully sought reelection in 1939 and 1943, making his the longest administration in Chicago history to that time. In the 1939 contest, dissident Democrats united behind the candidacy of state's attorney Tom Courtney but failed to derail the incumbent in the party primary. In the general election, the resurgent Republican party, enervated by their strong statewide showing the previous year, put forward an attractive, dynamic candidate to challenge Kelly. Dwight H. Green, an able young lawyer and reformer, had as an assistant district attorney helped build the income tax evasion case against notorious gangster Al Capone that resulted in his imprisonment. Green conducted an aggressive campaign, hammering away at the machine's underworld connections and "exorbitant" increases in the municipal tax rate. Nonetheless, Kelly managed to hold the Democratic party together— even Courtney grudgingly supported the mayor—and won by a comfortable margin.[33]

In 1943 reform-minded Democrats again attempted to unseat the mayor, but the candidacy of Alderman John S. Boyle excited even less support than had Courtney's crusade four years earlier. Lackluster Republican standard-bearer George W. McKibbin, like Wetten and Green before him, based his campaign on an all-out attack on bossism and machine politics. "Pendergast is out in K.C.," he proclaimed. "Hague, in Jersey, and Tammany, in New York, have been cleaned out. Now it is time to clean out the Kelly-Nash machine." And like his unsuccessful predecessors, McKibbin returned repeatedly to the theme of the underworld-politics connection. Despite machine apathy and overconfidence, Kelly's refusal to campaign, and the outbreak of some untimely scandals shortly before election day, the incumbent bested the challenger by a plurality of 114,000 in a very light voter turnout. The Chicago *Sun* observed:

> The reduction of the mayor's majority from that which he attained against Governor Green in 1939 thus seems no more than legitimate wear and tear, chargeable to the four years in office which intervened. In view of the heavy artillery which the Republicans leveled against him, his 54.5 percent looks pretty solid.[34]

Following his reelection Kelly devoted much of his time to grappling with the problem of the city's antiquated mass transportation system. The traction situation had plagued not only Kelly but his predecessors as well, hailing back to the first decade of the twentieth century. When Kelly became mayor in 1933 he faced a disastrous situation: Bankrupt companies had no capital to make structural improvements; streetcars averaged twenty-five years old and suffered from disrepair; and elevated trains varied in age from twelve to forty years. In all, the public transportation system, once the pride of Chicago, paled in comparison with its counterparts in virtually every other large American city.[35]

Kelly consistently affirmed his commitment to the city's purchase of a unified transit facility but balked at the asking prices of the companies. As the years passed, the mayor's unwillingness to compromise the city's bargaining position meant that a lingering problem went unsolved, and Chicago's straphangers chafed at the inaction. Finally, in 1945 Kelly offered a plan to the state which provided for a privately financed Chicago transit authority empowered to buy up all existing facilities and operate them as an independent agency. Authorized to operate in eighty-one municipalities in Cook County, the supporting agency could issue bonds, payable solely out of its own revenues, but not levy taxes. Following legislative action by the state, the city council granted the newly created Chicago Transit Authority (CTA) an exclusive franchise for fifty years. In October 1947, after selling $105 million worth of bonds, the CTA began operation in metropolitan Chicago.[36]

The creation of the CTA, a landmark in the city's development and decidedly one of the most notable achievements of the Kelly mayoralty, came at what should have been a politically propitious moment for the Democratic machine, just before the 1947 mayoral election. But the traction settlement was largely overlooked in the preelection atmosphere—unfortunately so for Kelly, who found himself in a bitter struggle to maintain control of a fractious Democratic party and to secure for himself the party's nomination for yet another term.

For years Kelly and Nash ruled effectively through a clearcut division of labor: the mayor maintained high visibility, giving speeches, cutting ribbons, kissing babies, and keeping reporters abreast of party affairs as well as city business. The reclusive Nash shunned publicity and limited himself to behind-the-scenes administrative work. More importantly, Nash occupied the role of beloved patriarch. With the trust of the politicians and a reputation for fairness and scrupulous honesty, Nash served as the great harmonizer for the party—a task he often had to undertake due to the impulsive Kelly's fiery temper. As one contemporary noted: "Pat Nash was revered by the committeemen. They adored him. . . . Had it not been for Pat Nash, Kelly would have been in trouble nine times out of ten." Nash died in 1943, and without his mediating skills to calm the tensions between rival factions, party discipline faltered as seldom before. For the first time, Democratic aldermen dared to criticize Kelly in city council sessions, and talk that the mayor did an inadequate job as party chairman since Nash's death became widespread. Arguing that doing both jobs demanded too much from the seventy-year-old Kelly, the malcontents called for a new party leader.[37]

The man chosen was Jacob Arvey. Shortly after assuming control he began conducting public opinion polls in Chicago movie theaters and commissioned one of Kelly's speech writers to canvass by telephone in order to gauge the mayor's popularity. Arvey summarized: "Well, we were still solid with the Jews, we could see, and better than even with the Negroes, but everywhere else—the Poles, the Irish even, the Germans—we were in trouble. 'Him?' they'd say. 'Are you kidding? We'd sooner vote for a Chinaman.'" The once popular Kelly had seen his esteem crumble under the weight of several damaging scandals and the failure of his administration to deliver services to the citizenry. Defalcations in the public schools, official tolerance of organized crime, an ineffective and corrupt police department, haphazard garbage collection and street cleaning, high taxes with no apparent return in municipal services— all of these shortcomings surfaced in Arvey's canvassing.[38]

Chicago's civic leaders also called for Kelly's removal, but the opposition of the better government advocates, the reformers, independents, and "goo-goos," had surfaced in each of Kelly's election campaigns. Scandals of every variety plagued the Democratic machine over the years, yet it always managed to survive. In the opinion of Arvey, however, one new issue that arose in the mid-forties crystallized public opinion against Kelly: the open housing controversy. Jealously guarding their turf, South Side whites braced to resist racial "blockbusting" and sneeringly referred to neighborhood swimming pools which blacks seemed to monopolize as "Kelly's inkwells." The mayor's repeated pledge to guarantee the availability of housing citywide to blacks galvanized the public and helped to explain the findings of Arvey's polls; the Germans, Irish, and Poles shared one thing in common—an opposition to Kelly's stand on open housing.[39]

Ultimately, the opposition within the party, not just public indignation, which had been transcended repeatedly in the past, persuaded Arvey to dump Kelly. Supporting the incumbent mayor, hazardous enough on the basis of his record, would have been disastrous without the united support of the party leadership, and Arvey, vulnerable in his new post at the head of the machine, was in no position to alienate other party dignitaries while possibly losing his first election. Kelly had to go. Ironically, Kelly's efforts to strengthen the Democratic party led to his own demise. The machine he helped make became so powerful that the mayor was no longer in complete control, and it unmade him. The days of personality politics as personified by Big Bill Thompson and others had passed.[40]

Though clearly crestfallen, Kelly remained a good soldier and campaigned strenuously, if infrequently, for the Democratic candidate, moving-van magnate Martin H. Kennelly. After fourteen years in city hall, Kelly lapsed into the role of elder statesman. Stripped of the mayoralty and the county committee chairmanship, he continued to serve in the largely symbolic role of Illinois Democratic national committeeman until his death in 1950.[41]

A few hours after Kelly passed away, Illinois governor Adlai Stevenson eulogized the former-mayor on a statewide radio broadcast. He said: "Here was a leader! Strong, adroit, and tireless, he guided the destiny of Chicago as its Mayor longer than anyone in history. . . . And he will be studied by students of American politics as a leader who was never afraid to lead." Kelly was without question an aggressive, self-confident leader. He boasted to a reporter, "I tell a million people what to think, and they listen to me because they vote for me." He exercised nearly complete control over the city council, so much so that until the last year of his tenure, never more than ten of the fifty aldermen ever dared to oppose a measure he favored. To those who railed against the Kelly autocracy, he replied: "These people look to me for leadership. To be a real mayor you've got to have control of the party. You've got to be a potent political factor. You've gotta be a boss!"[42]

As boss of the Chicago Democratic machine, Kelly not only dominated local politics and government for fourteen years but greatly expanded the strength of the organization. To a great extent, the amazing resiliency of what came to be known as the "Daley machine" was nurtured, shaped, and enlarged under Kelly's leadership. Unfortunately for Kelly, the political "monster" that he had developed turned on its master and destroyed him—thus making good on the old Chicago machine axiom: "don't make anyone who can unmake you."

9.

MARTIN H. KENNELLY: THE MUGWUMP AND THE MACHINE

Arnold R. Hirsch

He was a nice man. It is not the sort of thing one usually says about Chicago's mayors, but the description suits Mayor Martin H. Kennelly. The incongruity stems not from his personality, but rather from his accidental occupation of city hall. Unlike those who clambered to the top of Chicago's political heap by stepping on the fallen bodies of their rivals, Kennelly ascended the ladder of business success and simply found himself the most "available" candidate as the Cook County Democratic organization desperately sought respectability after Ed Kelly's forced retirement in 1947. He was thrust into a political maelstrom for which he was ill-prepared, and yet he was, most notably, the Chicago machine's political savior. His fresh face and clean image saved the Democrats from almost certain defeat. The organization subsequently survived its postwar electoral scare, utilized the time and freedom bestowed upon it by Kennelly's lax administration, seized the credit for the mayor's achievements, and finally dumped him when he no longer served its purposes.

Popular legend portrays Kennelly as a naive reformer. It is a label that flows out of the inevitable comparisons with both his immediate predecessor and his successor. Next to Edward Kelly and Richard Daley, he *did* appear to be a political babe-in-the-woods. But there is more to it than that. His emphasis on civil service reform, his crackdown on open gambling, and his frequently expressed desire to upgrade the moral tone of Chicago's government all contributed to his squeaky-clean image. And it was a portrayal that was trumpeted in the contemporary press. Not only was he the darling of Chicago's media, but after a year in office even national publications such as the *Saturday Evening Post* marveled at the city's "new moral climate."[1]

Martin H. Kennelly was as close as the Chicago machine could come to Puritan respectability. A Bridgeport-born Irish-Catholic, Kennelly could cite only his poor background as a reason for his otherwise ill-fitting Democratic affiliation; indeed, he remained a Democrat more out of inertia than conviction. He was a self-made businessman and millionaire who had left the old neighborhood for the North Side's Gold Coast. A bachelor, he lived with his widowed sister in a posh apartment that belied his humble origins. In his connections with Chicago's business community, his concerns for efficiency and respectability, and his circumspect personal life—he took only an occasional drink and that often only to prove that he was "one of the boys"—he seemed a mugwump out of season. Even sympathetic observers believed him to be, personally, a "cold fish," and if Kennelly fit any popular stereotype at all, it was not that of the glad-handing, back-slapping ward politician, but rather than of the distant, proper, civic leader.[2]

The image, however, obscures reality. Kennelly was neither naive nor a reformer. There is no question that he struck an apolitical pose, content to leave party matters in the hands of chairman Jake Arvey, while cultivating the image of an administrator concerned only with the broader public interest. If he remained aloof from politics, though, it was not out of naivete or ignorance, but because of the certain knowledge that he would be soiled if he descended into that arena. "All I have in the world is my reputation," Kennelly declared as he accepted the party's nomination for mayor, "and I don't propose to have it dirtied up in politics."[3] He had no taste for that kind of action, and his refusal to engage in the rough-and-tumble of everyday politics thus suited his inclination, philosophy, personality, and talents. And on social issues he was, simply, quite conservative, displaying none of the New Deal activism that animated Ed Kelly's administration.

Moreover, the sharp division between political and governmental authority meant that Kennelly—despite some good intentions—accomplished a good deal less than he might have desired. It also left him exposed and vulnerable to those political professionals who respected neither his intentions nor his personal attributes. Forty-third Ward Alderman Mathias "Paddy" Bauler derisively dubbed him "Fartin' Martin," and other regulars, even more indelicately, referred to his large, round features, his lifestyle, and, perhaps, his habitual flight from political combat, and christened him "the capon."[4] Obviously, Kennelly's dalliance with Chicago's Democrats was a mutually unsatisfying marriage of convenience; but it was an accommodation that each party entered with open eyes. Ultimately, Kennelly gave more to the organization than vice versa. If he received eight years worth of ribbons to cut and banquets to attend, he helped trigger a spurt of postwar development that redounded to the favor of the man who yanked the newly polished throne out from under him in 1955.

Martin Kennelly was born in 1887 in that cradle of Chicago mayors on the near Southwest Side, "practically in the shadow of the packing plants," according to his campaign biography. His father, Jeremiah, a packinghouse worker who came to Chicago from Wisconsin, died when Kennelly was two years old. His mother, Margaret, a migrant from Vermont, subsequently raised five children; Martin was the youngest. Kennelly graduated from the Holden Public School at 31st and Troop in 1901 and quickly went to work for Marshall Field and Company as a stockboy, earning $2.50 per week, including overtime. In little more than a year he left that job ("He did his work well and we found him honest," his employer wrote) and, benefiting from the tuition raised by a brother's packinghouse labor, entered De La Salle Institute, the "poor man's college" in Bridgeport. Taking the three-year commercial course that attracted many of the area's upwardly mobile Irish, he learned the ways of the counting-house rather than the slaughterhouse. After graduation in 1905, Kennelly took a job with the Becklenberg Warehouse Company, and made the moving and storage business his career. With the coming of World War I, he enlisted, served in the Quartermaster Corps, and emerged in 1919 as a captain, with enough capital to start a partnership with an older brother. With the aid of his twenty-year-old letter of recommendation, Kennelly won the Field's contract to move exhibits to the new Grant Park museum of natural history, and within a few years he presided over one of the largest storage companies in the midwest. By 1929 he helped organize a nationwide moving cooperative, Allied Van Lines, and by 1931 he assumed the presidency of the National Furniture Warehouseman's Association. Financially successful beyond his wildest dreams, Kennelly had reached the pinnacle of his professional world.[5]

Politically, Kennelly was a fringe player, generally assuming the role of silk-stocking contributor and supporter of individual candidates of his own choosing. When he took on a public role, it was usually as the concerned civic leader performing a disinterested service. Still active in local business groups such as the Chicago Association of Commerce and Industry and the Illinois Furniture Warehouseman's Association, Kennelly made his greatest civic impression during World War II. He served as president of the Army Emergency Relief Auxiliary and, most notably, chaired the American Red Cross campaign in Chicago. He raised some $44 million, refused compensation for his services, and greatly enhanced his reputation.[6]

In the narrower political realm Kennelly held only minor appointive offices on the Lincoln Park Board and the reorganized Chicago Park District. His only real political notoriety came from his support of anti-Kelly Democrats during the depression. Kennelly backed the independent Henry Horner in the bitter gubernatorial primary of 1936 and helped thwart Kelly's attempted purge of County Judge Edmund K. Jarecki two years later. Less successful, but equally telling, was Kennelly's support of state's attorney Tom Courtney in the 1939 mayoral primary against Kelly himself. But when initially presented with the opportunity to hold office himself—the mayor asked Kennelly to fill out the unexpired term of the recently expired Cook County Sheriff in 1943— Kennelly wisely declined.[7] Little did either of those Bridgeport Irishmen suspect that, within four years, the Cook County Democratic organization would again ask Kennelly to lend his beaming visage to a campaign to retain yet another tainted office—this time Kelly's own.

After fourteen years as mayor, Ed Kelly found himself on the ropes as he contemplated running for reelection in late 1946. His administration's undeniable connection to Chicago's underworld, the deterioration of the city's schools, and Kelly's aggressive efforts to bring blacks into the Democratic party had alienated Republicans, independents, and machine adherents alike—each could find something to vote against in the Kelly record. When the organization's own polls raised grave doubts about another Kelly campaign, the party leadership convinced him to step down and tabbed Martin Kennelly as his replacement.[8]

It is unclear whether Kelly himself selected his successor, although Kennelly's biographer (Biles), Jake Arvey, and the mayor's 1943 offer to the moving van executive suggest so.[9] What is abundantly clear, however, is that Martin Kennelly offered what Chicago Democrats desperately needed: respectability. Kennelly's integrity was unquestioned, his image was nonpartisan, and his independence was a matter of public record. And if, as the *Daily News* believed, the machine's embrace of Kennelly was a "desperate political necessity," Kennelly took full advantage of that desperation and accepted the mayoral nomination with no strings attached.[10]

Kennelly's statement to the slatemakers of the Cook County Democratic Central Committee on 20 December 1946 went beyond the sort of posturing that even hardened politicians could be expected to tolerate with equanimity. It was a measure of their distress that the party leaders sat quietly and handed the mayoral nomination to a man who assaulted their political faith. Displaying no sense of party loyalty, recognizing no commitment to the organization, and acknowledging no sense of reciprocity, Kennelly laid down the terms on which he would become the party's standard bearer. "I am a Democrat but I have never had any connection with your organization," Kennelly informed the central committee. "My political experience," he continued in a phrase that surely made the party regulars squirm, "has been confined to the several occasions when I supported such fine Democratic officials as the late Governor Horner, Judge Jarecki, and Thomas J. Courtney." Reaffirming his independence, Kennelly concluded, "I will have only the interest of the people at heart. If there is a conflict between personal or political considerations . . . I will decide the matter on the basis of what is good for the city and its citizens. We must get away from the idea that government belongs to a party and realize it belongs to the people. . . . I do not subscribe to the principle of "to the victor belongs the spoils." If Kennelly was pleased at receiving the Democratic mayoral nomination without encumbrances, however, he was rash in assuming that the organization was "willing to follow" his lead.[11] Indeed, the rejection of reciprocity cut both ways. The party's commitment to its candidate extended no further than his election and the denial of the feared Republican takeover. After that, all bets were off.

The Republicans exposed the tension in the civic leader/machine coalition and attacked it mercilessly. Kennelly's nomination, according to his opponent, Russell Root, was nothing more than a "deathbed repentance act" put on by a "divided and discredited" group that had "adopted a plea of 'Guilty' as its platform." Former Republican mayoral candidate George McKibben agreed and noted that even though the Democrats had put forward a new candidate, he had been selected in the "usual manner, at a secret meeting of the same old Democratic City Hall gang." Such charges might have been more effective had they not been tied to the undistinguished candidacy of a nominee foisted on Chicagoans by Governor Dwight Green's statewide Republican organization. If anyone were open to the charge of being a party hack, it was Root, not Kennelly.[12]

For his part, Kennelly parried the Republican jabs and enunciated a set of principles that was lifted whole out of the Progressive era in which he matured. He spoke of efficiency, of economy, of curbing waste, of running the city on a nonpartisan basis, and of treating public offices as public trusts. For Kennelly—as for the antimachine politicians of an earlier age—his allegiance was to the city as a whole and he viewed Chicago as a "cooperatively owned municipal corporation" in which the voters were shareholders and the alderman served as so many directors.[13] And when Republicans tried to tarnish Kennelly's image by accusing him of profiteering in the public contracts let to store polling place materials, Kennelly simply replied that he charged the city no more in 1947 than he did initially in 1923; he performed that service as a civic duty and not as a profit-making venture. Kennelly was, as his precinct workers contended with a mixture of awe and disdain, "running on his sainthood."[14]

When the dust had settled, Kennelly won nearly 920,000 votes and 59 percent of the ballots cast. "Our first concern must be Chicago's progress," he affirmed in his inaugural; "an objective which must exclude partisan politics. Let our record for the public good be our only politics."[15] The irony was that Kennelly's attempt to be nothing more than a city manager in an intensely political city government hamstrung his administration. His most lasting legacy, consequently, was not the blow he delivered to the machine, but rather the breathing space he provided for it. He saved the Cook County Democratic organization from itself, warmed the mayor's chair until a revitalized machine could safely reclaim it for one of its own, and left himself vulnerable enough so that the party had little trouble in dispatching him once his usefulness had ended. Certainly not an eager front for the organization, Kennelly, in fact, became one as he found himself besieged and out of his depth. The man who had no use for politics could not outmaneuver those who lived and breathed it.

Kennelly's administration, though, was not without a record of achievement. Indeed, in early 1954, in a speech before the State Street Council, Kennelly eyed a third term by looking back over his first seven years in office. He pointed with pride to the financial and administrative reforms enacted under his tutelage. The installation of a centralized purchasing department that met "every possible standard of efficiency and integrity" replaced the chaotic practices of earlier years. A Home Rule Commission laid the groundwork for the city's future development, and a host of other mayor-appointed committees likewise proved their value. A commission on municipal finances under civic leader Frank Sims, particularly, issued a report that independent alderman Leon Despres used "over and over again" after he was elected to the city council in 1955; it was a "fabulous job" according to Despres.[16]

Nor was the modernization of the city's administration confined to its financial affairs. The police department was similarly "streamlined and reorganized." The department brought its crime laboratory up-to-date, improved its motorized equipment, and developed contingency plans to meet every emergency. Kennelly improved record-keeping procedures and installed a new traffic system that unquestionably saved lives. And the mayor's transfer of district captains and his well-publicized crackdown on open gambling drove the most notorious operations underground or to the suburbs early in his first term.[17]

The two areas, however, that provided the most substantial support for Kennelly's reputation as a "reformer" involved the public schools and the city's civil service system. A series of investigations during Kelly's last term exposed the Chicago Board of Education as a political wasteland. Indeed, in the mid-1940s the school system served primarily as a source of jobs and contracts for the faithful and a safe haven for precinct workers between elections. The atrophy of its educational mission was so pronounced the North Central Association of Schools and Colleges threatened to revoke the accreditation of local high schools. Even before he left office, Ed Kelly consequently appointed a nonpolitical citizen's advisory committee that recommended the resignation of the board president and the superintendent of schools, and the appointment of a new board of education. Six new faces, in fact, already graced the eleven-member board and the superintendent had resigned when Kennelly was elected.[18]

Two tasks confronted the new mayor. The first involved the revision of the state law that set the school superintendent's term of office but left control of the system's business and legal affairs in the hands of the heretofore politicized board; it was a situation that made it impossible to lure a competent and independent educator to the superintendent's position. The proposal to centralize authority in the superintendent's office subsequently attracted strong opposition from those who profited from the existing arrangement, and it was one of the mayor's first jobs to smooth its passage. Margaret Hancock, vice president of the Citizens' School Committee, recalled that Kennelly brought both sides to his office and that he impressed her with his "poise and persistent good humor, and withal, the gentleness with which . . . [he] dominated the group which gradually came to terms, with concessions on both sides."[19] The bill eventually sailed through both houses of the legislature without a dissenting vote. In the appointment of Herold C. Hunt as superintendent, Kennelly fulfilled his second task. A first-rate administrator, Hunt "practically stopped" the trafficking in politically dictated contracts and jobs, greatly improved teacher morale, and directed a spurt of new capital improvements that were financed with a succession of Kennelly-backed bond issues.[20] It was a remarkable turnaround.

The appointment of a tough, efficient, nonpolitical administrator also characterized Kennelly's approach to civil service. The mayor's selection of Stephen E. Hurley, a former director of the Chicago Bar Association, to head the Civil Service Commission aroused the "bitterest kind of opposition from ward bosses who [gave] up patronage about as cheerfully as they sacrifice an arm or an eye," according to the *Tribune*.[21] While there was no wholesale firing of city workers, there was a constant, gradual erosion of politically sponsored jobs. Before he was through, Hurley's persistence and tenacity transferred some ten thousand jobs from the patronage rolls to the merit system and earned the undying enmity of the machine. One precinct captain, in an almost hysterical 1951 assessment, warned Kennelly that "Hurley . . . has wrecked the working Democrat organization" by "calling more examinations and laying off Temporary workers" on the eve of important municipal elections. The mayor, however, remained true to his mugwump faith, allowed Hurley his freedom, and raised an irreconcilable conflict of interest between his administration and the organization that gave it life. The city's progress on civil service was, in the *Tribune*'s estimation, "the brightest star in Mr. Kennelly's crown."[22]

Finally, Kennelly had the good fortune to preside over the city as it stood poised on the edge of a postwar boom. The history of his administration would also, consequently, be read in bricks and mortar. Responding to the tug of decentralization, the city provided greater access into, around, and through the Loop; the Dearborn Street subway, the Congress Street Superhighway, the Northwest Expressway, the Calumet Skyway, and the extensions of the North Outer Drive and Wacker Drive all gave evidence of that priority. Within the business district itself, the Grant Park underground garage helped accommodate the Loop to the automobile and the construction of the Prudential building heralded a new round of downtown development.[23] And in terms of the city's most pressing need—new housing—the Kennelly administration began a massive urban renewal program. The New York Life Insurance Company's investment in Lake Meadows, the planning of Prairie Shores, and the beginning of the University of Chicago's reconstruction of Hyde Park gave further proof that the city would not be willingly stripped of its middle-class population. It is not surprising that Kennelly began his 1954 "State of the City" address with a detailed recitation of his physical accomplishments.[24]

But the edifice of achievement rested on a rotten foundation. The mayor's accomplishments were weakened at every stage by political ineptitude. Kennelly's record, in fact, exemplified the abdication, not the delegation, of authority; and where the executive vacuum was filled by powerful, active forces, things did get done. But the limits and possibilities of Kennelly's administration were determined by the needs of others, particularly the Cook County Democratic organization and aggressive downtown business interests.

Kennelly's police reforms provide a striking case in point. He may have brought the department into the twentieth century technologically, but its politics remained rooted in an earlier era. Whether due to a prior, unspoken agreement with organization leaders, or simply a reflection of his political weakness, Kennelly did not touch its command structure—the network of political influence that dominated it—nor did he challenge its ties to the underworld. In part, his refusal to deal with the department's most fundamental problems may have been linked to a world view that acknowledged the inescapable reality of human frailty and elevated the habit of "looking the other way" to a local art form. It is also possible that Kennelly embodied the city's political ethos—one that defined democracy as being the open and equal access to "the fix"—although this is less likely given his frequently expressed beliefs on public morality. The bottom line, however, was that there were limits that the mayor either understood and accepted or was too weak to overcome. Before Senator Estes Kefauver's peripatetic committee on organized crime and, indeed, before the public at large, Kennelly played the comfortable role of civic booster and, however reluctantly, defended the machine's interests.

The results were the eruption of repeated scandals during Kennelly's tenure, the demonstration of his inability to maintain order, and a series of public embarrassments that undermined his administration. Payoff scandals involving Thomas Harrison and Redmond Gibbons, police captains in the notorious Hudson Avenue district in Paddy Bauler's Forty-third Ward, belied Kennelly's protestations and exposed, it appears, not his naivete, but rather his mendacity.[25] The sensational 1952 murder of Republican committeeman Charlie Gross (who was a Republican in name only) and the mob's successful expulsion of Democratic alderman and committeeman George Kells from the Twenty-eighth Ward the previous year (Kells's lieutenant, Big Jim Martin, had been gunned down to emphasize the criminals' desire that Kells not run for office again) similarly revealed the city's inability to control its own streets. The *Tribune* could only denounce the fact that Kells was "Kennelly's man" and that the mayor could not "protect him from the hoodlums."[26] Under such circumstances, Kennelly's denial of the existence of organized criminal influence in Chicago prior to the Kefauver hearings and his dogged defense of Police Commissioner John C. Prendergast proved major public embarrassments.[27]

Having rebuffed repeated calls for Prendergast's removal before the Kefauver investigation, Kennelly merely dramatized his lack of independence by his later retreat. Reacting to the prospect of selecting a new police commissioner,

Kennelly earlier had curtly rejected the Chicago Crime Commission's suggestion that candidates should be selected by a blue-ribbon citizens' committee. "The Mayor alone is responsible to the people for the police department," Kennelly asserted; and, he added, "[t]he statute makes no provision for sharing this authority with anyone." Yet the same statutory responsibility governed the mayor's selection of a new school board; and, in that case at least, Kennelly did not hesitate to share his power in order to end political "meddling." The police department, Kennelly explained—making a distinction that required a sophisticated eye wise in the ways of Chicago politics—"is an integral part of the city government administered by the Mayor." [28] It could perhaps also be added that, in 1947, the machine could no longer ignore the clamor for school reform while control of the police department occupied a more insulated position closer to the organization's heart—which, in this case, was located next to its wallet. Kennelly consequently refused to look outside the department and named Timothy O'Connor as Prendergast's successor. An honest cop, O'Connor was noted, as was Prendergast and the mayor himself, for his uncanny ability to look the other way and represented a safe choice for the organization. [29]

Kennelly's great reluctance to confront the Cook County Democratic organization could even be detected in the one area he did directly challenge it—on patronage. If Stephen Hurley's actions met Kennelly's expectations, the new civil service commissioner was hardly sustained by the mayor's willingness to do battle for him. Harassed, insulted, and repeatedly investigated by a hostile city council, Hurley resigned at one point, only to be cajoled into returning by Kennelly. Even then, however, the mayor refused to defend Hurley before the council and stood aside as the aldermen held his budget hostage. When independent alderman Robert Merriam championed Hurley's cause in budget hearings, rather than receiving praise from the mayor, Merriam caught only Kennelly's queasy lament that he "wished Steve wouldn't get into all these jams." Merriam subsequently concluded that the mayor was "a very delightful person but with no real backbone, and no real desire to fight with the organization." [30]

The Hurley episode not only revealed Kennelly's distaste, if not outright fear, of confrontation, but also his failure to support members of his own administration when they crossed swords with Democratic regulars. Both qualities surfaced again when Kennelly and a group of aldermen surveyed prospective public housing sites by bus in 1950. Met, at one point, by an angry West Side crowd, Kennelly simply told the bus driver not to make the scheduled stop; even neighborhood women in "babushkas" set the mayor to flight. [31] It was, in fact, shortly after this incident that Kennelly's corporation counsel, Benjamin Adamowski, tendered his resignation and—unlike Hurley's later recantation—this time there was no retraction. Adamowski was "shocked" by Kennelly's close cooperation with the machine-dominated council on public housing and, something of a maverick himself, he was further disappointed that the mayor did not support independent members of his own administration in their clashes with top party leaders. Adamowski said later that Kennelly "never should have been mayor of Chicago. He should have been a cardinal or monseigneur." [32]

Even more important, however, was Kennelly's willingness to let the city council—and, consequently, the Cook County Democratic organization—run its own affairs. Kelly had said earlier that, as mayor, "either you run the machine or the machine runs you." Kennelly proved his point. The budgetary squabble over Hurley's civil service commission was only symptomatic of the larger problem. In leaving the city's budget in the hands of the council's "Big Boys"—people like Tom Keane, John Duffy, and Clarence Wagner—Kennelly guaranteed that the political initiative remained with the regular Democrats. As expected, they used their power to harass their enemies and reward their friends. At one point, Stephen Hurley had to dig $1,500 out of his own pocket to cover the salaries of the "intellectuals" on his staff; on another occasion, the mayor had to dip into his private fund to sustain the Commission on Human Relations (CHR). On the other hand, Kennelly's budgetary green light and his refusal to trample on the council's domain ushered in a "golden era of mayoral permissiveness," according to Len O'Connor. Republican John Hoellen, first elected in 1947, said simply that it "was a sickening and terrifying experience to be involved in the city council in that period. Graft was rampant." Insider Paddy Bauler confirmed Hoellen's minority assessment when he told Robert Merriam that he could find but two honest aldermen at the time. The first, Bauler admitted, was young Merriam, the independent Democrat; the second, according to the forty-third Ward saloon owner, was himself—unlike the other "fakers" in the council, Bauler claimed the integrity to admit being a crook. [33] There was, in sum, no shortage of "grease" for a machine in sore need of lubrication during the Kennelly years.

Kennelly's candidacy was, of course, an open admission that the machine was in dire need of repair. And Chicago's voters turned not only to the "clean" Kennelly, but they simultaneously elected seventeen Republicans and an independent Democrat to the city council. There were enough nonorganization votes, in other words, to sustain mayoral vetoes and challenge the machine (which was itself deeply divided and factionalized) if that was the mayor's inclination. Clearly, it was not. Kennelly offered no direction to the regulars (who would have rejected it in any case) or their opposition, and meekly stood aside as machine stalwarts seized committee assignments and chairmanships. Except for Adamowski's ill-fated appointment as corporation counsel, Kennelly also generally retained Kelly's department heads and offered few alternatives there, either. [34] It was a precarious moment for the machine; one that found it fragmented, vulnerable, out of public favor, and potentially confronted with significant opposition. But the final blows never came. The "anti-machine" mayor provided the time, freedom, and wherewithal for the organization to regroup and emerge stronger than before.

If Kennelly's unique style of nongovernance proved helpful to the Cook County Democratic organization, it was also a boon for the downtown business community. Indeed, the mayor had little to do with either the conception or the execution of Chicago's urban renewal program. As was the case with the regulars in the political arena, Kennelly simply got out of the way of the Loop's economic giants and powerful institutional interests and merely lent his name to their endeavors.

Chicago's postwar reconstruction proceeded under the Illinois Blighted Areas Redevelopment Act of 1947, the Illinois Urban Community Conservation Act of 1953, and the federal legislation that was modeled on these pioneer measures: the Housing Acts of 1949 and 1954. Coming out of Chicago during the Kennelly administration, the Illinois laws were the products of years of private concern and activity. The Chicago Title and Trust Company, directed by Holman Pettibone, and Marshall Field and Company, which provided the services of Milton C. Mumford, had been working since World War II on plans to revitalize the central city. They had, in fact, drafted their own legislation before Kennelly assumed office and steered it through the legislature with the mayor's blessing shortly thereafter. When some controversial aspects of the law created a public uproar, however, Kennelly's reaction revealed how poorly he understood the measure and, indeed, Mumford concluded that the mayor "did not really know what was involved" when he agreed to its essential features. Similarly, the Urban Community Conservation Act was the product of the University of Chicago's desire to restructure Hyde Park and was the legislative handiwork of the Metropolitan Housing and Planning Council, Julian Levi, and the South East Chicago Commission. Levi recalled "dumping" the plan on the mayor's desk, and, though the conservative Kennelly remained "lukewarm" toward a law that entailed a significance expansion of government power, he did not oppose private interests he found philosophically congenial, socially acceptable, and politically useful.[35]

The mayor did little more to see the plans through. It was Pettibone and Mumford who brought in the New York Life Insurance Company to develop Lake Meadows, and, in a telling episode, the businessmen themselves had to deal directly with the city council when it threatened their designs. Ira Bach, director of the Chicago Land Clearance Commission, remembered that the chairman of a key council committee demanded a bribe as the price of his cooperation in closing a section of Cottage Grove Avenue that was vital to the project. The mayor, in Bach's words, said he "couldn't do anything about it," and Bach instead turned to Pettibone, who somehow broke the logjam in the council. Ultimately, Bach relied less on Kennelly ("who was not the strongest kind of mayor") than he did on the Republican businessman who "knew how to wheel and deal with the aldermen."[36] Little more could be expected from a chief executive who went so far as to refuse to read housing authority recommendations and related newspaper stories so that he might honestly claim ignorance when asked for an opinion.[37] Such practices were testimony both to his integrity and to the quality of his leadership.

If Kennelly had any direct impact on Chicago's postwar development, it was, perhaps, to slow its pace. Chicago's finances were strained throughout the period, and, despite the presence of a Democratic governor in Springfield after 1948, the state hardly opened its coffers to the beleaguered urbanites. Much of the coolness in the Adlai Stevenson–Kennelly relationship apparently stemmed from personal pique as the mayor resented both Stevenson's privileged background and his slating at the expense of longtime Kennelly friend Tom Courtney. And when the governor called a special session of the legislature to deal with Chicago's financial problems and convened a meeting of legislative leaders to hear Kennelly's proposals, Stevenson was appalled to learn that the mayor had none to offer. Left to his own devices, Kennelly simply "talked aimlessly" and informed the legislators that they had to develop their own plans for Chicago's benefit. After such a performance, the governor concluded that Kennelly was "hopelessly inept" and offered him little future assistance.[38]

Party chairman Jake Arvey echoed Stevenson's use of the word "inept" when assessing Kennelly's political acumen. The mayor's evident lack of skill undoubtedly flowed both from his inexperience and from his barely episodic attention to such details once in office. It was not that Kennelly ignored politics as a matter of principle as his campaign rhetoric suggested, but rather that he played the game only intermittently, usually poorly, and almost exclusively in conjunction with his own electoral fortunes. Thus it was with a transparent heavy-handedness that the "reform" mayor overrode the recommendations of his citizens' committee and retained Kelly-holdover and heavy party contributor Bernard Majewski on the school board in 1951 for fear of alienating both regulars and the Polish vote on the eve of his reelection. And in a futile attempt to impress the new party chairman, Richard J. Daley, in his hunt for a third term, Kennelly tried unsuccessfully to pressure the Chicago Housing Authority into appointing the chairman's cousin, John Daley, as its new counsel. It apparently mattered little to Kennelly that John Daley ranked 183rd out of 191 in his law school class or that he lacked the requisite experience specified by CHA guidelines. Even worse than the proposed appointment itself was Kennelly's failure to make it stick and the public embarrassment that caused the young attorney to withdraw his name. Such spasmodic attention to personal politics would prove no match for the man who spent his whole life preparing to seize the prize that had earlier fallen fortuitously into Kennelly's lap.[39]

Kennelly's subversion of the CHA for political purposes also exposed a weakness on racial issues that eventually helped to engulf his administration. Where Kelly insulated the housing authority from the political demands of the ward committeemen, encouraged its experiments in integration, and offered unswerving support to executive secretary Elizabeth Wood, Kennelly backtracked and dashed the hopes of those who believed the local Democratic party could become a truly multiracial (and not just a multiethnic) organization. His administration represented a turning point in the machine's relationship to blacks. After Ed Kelly's symbolic and substantive overtures to the black community, party leaders, with Kennelly's acquiescence and support, made certain that blacks occupied a subordinate and "safe" position within the local Democratic coalition.[40] If the full implications of that decision only became apparent during Richard J. Daley's long tenure, it was Kennelly's administration that set the course. Indeed, it was only in this context that Kennelly's billing as "white knight" had any real meaning.

None of this, of course, was apparent in Kennelly's 1947 campaign. Riding his predecessor's long coattails in the black community, Kennelly won the *Defender*'s endorsement because blacks felt it important to "continue and expand the progressive and far-reaching racial policies" of Kelly.[41] The bright hopes for Kennelly's administration, however, withered under the twin pressures of rapid black population growth and white resistance to change.

The first signs of trouble came as violence erupted in changing neighborhoods. White assaults on the black pioneers homesteading on the city's racial frontier began during World War II and plagued Kelly's last years. It was, in fact, Kelly's use of the police to protect blacks and his unqualified assertion of the blacks' right to move wherever they wished that destroyed his support within the organization and guaranteed that the machine would not reslate him.[42] The hit-and-run attacks that bedeviled Kelly, however, evolved into massive mob violence in the postwar era. Large scale rioting surrounded the CHA's Fernwood Park Homes just months after Kennelly took office in 1947, and erupted again in Park Manor and Englewood in 1949. When confronted with this reaction to black expansion, the mayor refused to reaffirm his predecessor's stand on nondiscrimination. His reaction to recurrent disorder, according to a Commission on Human Relations that openly longed for Kelly's firmer hand, consisted of little more than "appeasement and persuasion." Relations between the CHR and the mayor subsequently remained cool until the Englewood riot, when they broke down completely. Blaming the uprising on subversives, Kennelly did little to end the violence or assuage black feelings.[43]

In the aftermath of that explosion, Urban League executive Sidney Williams attacked the Kennelly administration's "ineptitude" and its "shameful failure" to protect blacks. He also called for the mayor's impeachment and organized the Committee to End Mob Violence to prod the city into greater action. Kennelly's response, it was rumored in the black community, was to use his influence in Chicago's business community to dry up white contributions to the Urban League. While it is impossible to confirm Kennelly's alleged role, the Urban League's subsequent financial distress forced it to shut down for six months and fire its entire staff, including Sidney Williams. When it opened its doors again, it had the support of the city's business leaders and, not coincidentally, a more conservative leadership.[44]

When Kennelly finally did take a stand on housing discrimination, it was to oppose an ordinance that would have banned it. Black Republican alderman Archibald Carey, Jr., introduced the measure to assure blacks that they would not be displaced by the city's slum clearance program and that they would have access to all publicly assisted housing. After its proposal, Kennelly maintained a silence that was, according to the Chicago Council against Discrimination, "interpreted not only as opposition to the Ordinance, but also as a tactic repudiation of the platform commitments of the [Democratic] party." Opposed to the architects of the city's redevelopment plans and denounced by whites fearful of any expression of black political power, Loop business elites and machine politicians stood together to defeat the Carey Ordinance. With such solid support, the debate over the measure provided one of the rare occasions when Kennelly stepped entirely out of character and took the council floor to speak against pending legislation.[45]

Ultimately, however, it was not Kennelly's leadership but the lack of it that was of the greatest significance. Under his regime the ward bosses were able to reassert themselves and, most tellingly, exploit the vacuum at the top to attack the CHA. Bereft of Kelly's protective shield, the authority was now vulnerable, and before Kennelly left office in 1955, it was transformed into a bulwark of segregation.

The process began just weeks into Kennelly's first term when the state, at the city council's request, passed a redevelopment program that gave the council a veto over locally funded projects. The legislation threw the authority into a "new relationship" with the city, and led Elizabeth Wood to anticipate "profound difficulties . . . due to the Authority's racial policy." Indeed, within months that policy led to the passage of additional state legislation that granted the city a veto over all CHA projects, even those supported by federal funds. The result was that the precedent-setting first slate of public housing sites selected under the Housing Act of 1949 was chosen by a handful of council leaders whose chief desires were to contain the city's black population and bring the CHA's building program to a halt. By the fall of 1952, Elizabeth Wood acknowledged their success and characterized the CHA as a "captive Authority." Those who looked to the mayor for help found that he had "forsaken" their goals, and was incapable of the "aggressive leadership" missing since "Mayor Kelly left office."[46]

Wood vowed to fight on, but realized that she had become a controversial figure. It was because, she said, she "made every effort to run an honest enterprise" and "tried not to discriminate." When the Trumbull Park Homes exploded in yet another racial confrontation in the summer of 1953, she found herself unable to withstand a final political assault on her independence. Demoted and rendered powerless in a reorganization inspired by one of Kennelly's "efficiency" studies. Wood attacked the hypocrisy of her superiors and their lack of resolve on racial issues. Dismissed by the authority's commissioners in 1954, Wood's removal ended the CHA's resistance to the racial demands of the city's white ward leaders. It also set the agency on the road to becoming one of the "worst" managed authorities in the country, according to a 1982 federal study, and one whose sole purpose was the "acquisition of as many Federal . . . dollars as possible for the creation of patronage jobs and financial opportunities."[47] Scandal-free under Elizabeth Wood, the CHA became a bastion of segregation and a trough for the machine.

Kennelly's difficulties were compounded by the mayor's disastrous relationship with William Levi Dawson, political overlord of the black South Side. Kennelly, who was clearly uncomfortable with blacks, never developed a political strategy to deal with them, and had no basis for communicating with Dawson who was both black and a "boss." Instead, when Kennelly dealt with blacks at all, it was through more "respectable" leaders such as the *Defender*'s John Sengstacke, the housing authority's Robert R. Taylor, and Rev. J. L. Jackson—all individuals with strong ties to the white business community. The mayor consequently isolated himself not only from the black ward organizations, but also from the black labor movement as well—despite repeated overtures from the CIO's Willard Townsend. And in his 1951 reelection bid, Kennelly kept even those blacks friendly to him at a chilly distance, organizing a committee of black leaders only in the campaign's final weeks. Dawson could not understand Kennelly's "disregard" for him or the mayor's willingness, in Dawson's view, to work with "opportunists who would go either way."[48]

Kennelly's much publicized crackdown on gambling also infuriated Dawson. The embarrassment of the Kefauver hearings in late 1950 and Kennelly's campaign for reelection in early 1951 led the mayor to prove he was "tough on crime" by raiding South Side policy wheels that were nominally under Dawson's protection. Police conducted 11,562 raids that netted 24,476 individual arrests between January 1951 and the end of March 1955. Even Kennelly's friendly biographer noted that such operations simply "became a satisfactory way for creating favorable headlines without upsetting [the larger] system of payoffs." And when Dawson tried to negotiate their differences by offering to support Kennelly's redevelopment plans, Ira Bach—who served as Dawson's intermediary in this instance—received nothing more than the mayor's characteristic "blank stare" in return. The raids continued, Dawson's opposition slowed progress on Lake Meadows, and the mayor fashioned yet another loop on his own political noose.[49]

There was also more to the gambling raids than met the eye. C. C. Wimbish, Dawson's Third Ward committeeman, was embroiled in a bitter dispute with the one-legged congressman over the division of the ward's spoils. Dawson kept a tight rein on South Side operations despite Wimbish's expectation that, as committeeman, he would rake in the "goodies." The success of Kennelly's raids subsequently owed a great deal to information provided by Wimbish, and the mayor's actions projected him squarely into the middle of an internecine political battle that challenged Dawson's dominance on the South Side. The Cook County Democratic Organization—at Dawson's insistence—later purged Wimbish and Kennelly succeeded only in alienating Dawson beyond redemption.[50]

The mayor's problems in the black community, and elsewhere, surfaced during his 1951 campaign, but they were not yet enough to deny him victory even if they did manifest themselves clearly in the returns. Kennelly lost sixteen wards in 1951, doubling the number he dropped four years before. Significantly, not only did he lose traditionally Republican wards on the far Northwest and Southwest sides, but defections could be detected in the black belt and those white wards threatened with racial transition.[51] The tally graphically revealed the racial-political dilemma of postwar Chicago: Kennelly could not protect blacks without alienating the still-dominant whites, nor could he ignore black concerns without losing the support of the most rapidly growing group in the city. Eager for a third term in 1955, Kennelly proved only that he lacked the considerable skill necessary to handle, balance, or negate the forces at work. He never had a chance.

Going into the campaign, Kennelly was burdened by a number of debilitating problems. First, his inability to defuse the city's gnawing racial tensions left both blacks and whites dissatisfied. Second, the mayor's stance on civil service and his estrangement from organized labor made his removal from office a virtual necessity for organization Democrats; indeed, party leaders decided back in November 1952 that Kennelly had to go.[52] Finally, there was the consuming personal ambition of the new party chairman, Richard J. Daley. Any one of these factors could have dashed Kennelly's third-term hopes. Any two of them would have caused certain political death. All three together produced a perfunctory four-minute interview for the two-term incumbent mayor before the organization's slatemakers and his unanimous rejection. It was a swift and sure political beheading executed by Daley's hand-picked committee. Stripped of the party's support, Kennelly was left virtually alone to face Daley and onetime ally Ben Adamowski in a three-cornered primary.

The white siege of the Trumbull Park Homes on the far South Side entered its second year in 1955 and provided the backdrop for the campaign. Violently protesting the presence of a handful of black families, the whites in South Deering faced a housing authority forced to take a public stand against discrimination, but one fearful of disorder and eager to avoid the appearance that policy was being made in the streets. The CHA consequently "froze" the number of black families in the project and watched helplessly as recurrent violence lashed the community. Kennelly, doing what he did best, stood on the sidelines and ignored black protests. Believing that the "mob violence at the project was sanctioned and stimulated by the willful failure of the city administration to end it," blacks rejected Kennelly's candidacy. Indeed, not only did the *Defender* claim that Kennelly's "cowardly handling" of the Trumbull Park disorders cost him black support, but white strategists mapping Democrat-turned-Republican Robert Merriam's race in the general election also concluded that blacks deserted Kennelly because he "failed them in the Trumbull Park situation." [53]

Faced with such dim prospects in the black community, Kennelly turned his imminent defeat there into a rout by running a campaign that openly courted white backlash voters. Having the sophistication to use stereotypes rather than slurs, Kennelly claimed that it was the vicelord Dawson who "pushed the controls in the 'Dump Kennelly' project." The daily press dutifully echoed the charges, claiming that "the notorious Bill Dawson" was the "chief architect" of the nefarious "plot." If Kennelly campaigned against "bossism" in general, he was counting on a white reaction to the prospect of being dominated by a black boss in particular. The *Defender* denounced Kennelly's transparent "race baiting" and attacked his strategy as "both dirty and dangerous." Even Claude A. Barnett of the Associated Negro Press, hardly a Dawson supporter, believed the campaign coverage in the white press "fanned racial hate," made the mayor's dumping a "racial issue," and merely served to rally even unsympathetic blacks to Dawson's cause. [54] And while there is no question that Dawson played an important role in the mayor's defeat, the perception that it was an angry Bill Dawson—stung into action by the mayor's attack on policy—who was primarily responsible for an outpouring of pliable black votes that denied Kennelly renomination merely reflects the lasting legacy of the incumbent's rhetoric and the white dailies' election coverage. The black community's dissatisfaction with Kennelly was much deeper, and its rejection of him far more profound, than such self-serving interpretations suggest.

Mobilized by the mayor's vituperative campaign and the deadly drone of disorder that echoed not only from South Deering, but from Fernwood, Park Manor, and Englewood as well, black voters marched to the polls not to vote for Richard J. Daley, but to bring down Martin H. Kennelly. The distinction is important, for Daley was able to win their support with no more than the assurance that he would place the solution of Trumbull Park's troubles "at the head of his program" and the promise that he would defeat the incumbent. Indeed, it was a measure not of Daley's political skill, but of Kennelly's, that the challenger was able to pick up endorsements from both the Chicago *Defender* and the South Deering Improvement Association at the same time. With the regular organization solidly behind him (forty-eight of the fifty ward committeemen backed Daley), the party chairman left the mayor in an impossible situation. When it was all over, Bill Dawson's five wards turned nearly 82 percent of their votes over to Daley (58,999 to 13,437) and the rest of Daley's 100,000 vote plurality came largely from a handful of inner city, machine-controlled "river" wards. [55]

142

Kennelly, however, still had one arrow left in his quiver. The general election between Robert Merriam and Daley would, the *Sun-Times* indicated in an article that projected hyperbole beyond the primary, be a showdown "between the forces of civic righteousness and the nefarious political bosses." Kennelly's endorsement in such a contest was potentially of great value, and it offered one last chance for the mayor to deliver a blow to those who had ended his career. It never came. Told by machine operatives that Merriam sought his indictment in earlier criminal investigations, Kennelly rejected Merriam's personal denial and sat out the election. If the press had little trouble distinguishing between the forces of light and darkness, Martin H. Kennelly was not similarly blessed—or, if he was, it made little difference.[56]

On the night of his primary defeat, Kennelly watched the vote roll in, shook his head, and muttered, "They're unbeatable, just unbeatable, aren't they?" It was not a thought that would have occurred to anyone just eight years before. But by 1955, with Richard J. Daley in control, they were. And they would remain so for another twenty-five years.

10.

RICHARD J. DALEY: AMERICA'S LAST BOSS

John M. Allswang

Before 1955 Richard J. Daley's name was not a household word in Chicago. His was one among a small number of well-known names in political circles, but one which received increasing media coverage from the time he became party chairman in 1953. In his mayoral debut (to what would become a twenty-one-year reign, 1955–76), Daley pushed aside Democratic incumbent Martin F. Kennelly in the primary, winning 49 percent of the vote to Kennelly's 35 percent and Benjamin Adamowski's 16 percent. Daley swept the black vote, and most of the working-class and ethnic wards, often by huge margins; he was strong where the organization was strong. Kennelly had his strength in the middle-class areas along the borders of the city; and Adamowski ran strongly mainly among the Poles. (See table 1.) Thus, Daley's victory in the 1955 primary was largely organizational rather than personal. He could take great satisfaction, however, in having been for some time an important member of that organization, to say nothing of now being its public as well as actual leader. It's possible that he never dreamed, in 1955, of how long his party leadership and his holding of mayoral office would last. But that tenure was based to a considerable degree on his own efforts and success.

Richard J. Daley was the leader of the Cook County Democratic party for twenty-three years and was mayor of the city of Chicago for over twenty. He was not only elected mayor six times, but also directed an almost endless series of successful local, state, and national campaigns in which Chicago was about as reliably and consistently Democratic as any place in the United States. The deference shown him by presidents and would-be presidents was in no way illogical, and he became a politician of real national power and importance. On the whole, he had operated on the broader sphere just as he did locally, with little concern for issues or much more for individuals—except in the important aspect of supporting those who were loyal to himself—but rather as a partisan

TABLE I

Daley Vote in Six Mayoral Campaigns, 1955–1975, and 1955 Primary

(Percentages)

Ward	1955	1959	1963	1967	1971	1975	1955 Primary
1	89	87	74	91	81	91	86
2	80	86	84	87	69	86	70
3	76	84	87	89	81	91	87
4	67	84	84	88	77	86	65
5	40	75	76	83	45	60	54
6	62	82	76	82	61	84	67
7	35	61	45	71	64	80	29
8	41	66	54	76	58	85	38
9	44	59	42	67	69	86	38
10	57	70	45	71	74	86	42
11	81	87	72	89	91	95	75
12	58	76	45	70	76	85	30
13	53	66	37	64	71	84	38
14	80	88	59	82	83	88	59
15	56	66	42	67	73	85	39
16	63	79	65	81	73	91	52
17	54	80	76	85	68	86	56
18	51	65	49	72	75	86	38
19	41	60	42	68	69	78	27
20	73	83	82	83	70	87	86
21	70	83	51	70	60	85	57
22	73	79	59	79	81	87	57
23	61	72	32	53	68	80	50
24	92	96	95	94	89	93	78
25	81	91	73	85	87	92	73
26	75	87	69	86	84	90	45
27	88	91	87	95	87	94	86
28	80	78	67	84	74	91	69
29	78	90	87	93	82	93	72
30	59	74	55	75	70	74	49
31	70	85	66	84	88	90	56
32	59	82	54	75	80	85	23
33	46	68	45	65	69	75	25
34	46	67	42	66	69	88	32
35	45	61	34	60	65	69	19
36	46	62	41	68	71	77	26
37	46	65	52	75	74	84	36
38	44	59	35	65	71	73	30
39	42	61	46	71	67	72	36
40	43	71	63	77	61	69	38
41	32	44	27	58	62	69	24
42	64	80	74	82	63	76	78
43	54	74	59	71	49	58	53
44	41	70	56	75	57	70	41
45	43	60	31	58	67	68	41
46	49	69	57	74	60	73	52
47	38	57	43	63	62	63	38
48	43	66	55	70	57	65	41
49	38	69	56	75	58	72	25
50	37	65	60	77	60	75	23
Average	55	71	56	74	69	75	49

leader who equated the success of the organization, the party, with political success generally. If this was the measure of his noninvolvement in the larger matters of the day, it was at the same time the measure of his success and his power.

I want to look at the development of his own campaigns as a way of focusing on the development of his organization and on that organization's response to the local issues and concerns of Chicago during his reign. Table 1 gives Daley's percentage of the two-party vote in his six mayoral campaigns and the 1955 primary for Chicago's fifty wards and the city as a whole.

The first campaign was the most difficult. Daley's primary victory over the not unpopular—and generally considered honest—Mayor Kennelly inevitably led to division within the party and to general charges of "bossism." Kennelly and Adamowski both refused to support their party's nominee, remaining neutral. Other Democrats, especially Assessor Frank Keenan, supported Daley's Republican opponent. Robert E. Merriam was young, bright, liberal, well connected and well supported, and ran probably the best campaign that Daley ever confronted.

Daley was never an effective speaker, and the presence of television—a force our earlier bosses never had to contend with—did create problems for him. But he had defeated Kennelly, whose television personality was good, and thus had reason to believe that organization was more effective than "presence." Beyond organizational matters, Daley campaigned on limited themes, primarily among Democrats. He told the Democratic women that women should have more public positions, he worked hard among the Poles and other ethnic groups, and he stressed to groups like the International Brotherhood of Electrical Workers that he wanted to keep the "thinking and philosophy of the Democratic Party" in control of Chicago.[2]

When accused of bossism, Daley pledged that he would resign from the party chairmanship if elected, a promise he later simply ignored. He matched Merriam generally in the vigor and activity of his campaigning. He matched him as well in allegations, responding to Merriam's charges of corruption and a "wide-open city" with his own indirect publicity of Merriam's being divorced, left wing, and remarried to a part-Negro—the particular allegation matched to the neighborhood where it would do the most good.[3] But the key element was the organization, down to the individual precinct leaders and their canvassing and promising. The organization shepherded voters in to register or to re-register if they were among those who had been purged from the polls on election day.

Like his famous father in the 'teens and twenties, Merriam railed against political corruption and the lack of law and order which the Democratic machine represented. During March, a large-scale investigation of "ghost voters" was undertaken, amidst much news of vote scandals. The inquiry was directed by County Judge Otto Kerner, who was a party man. The role of organized

146

crime was also publicized but was fairly well neutralized by Daley when he pledged a series of public hearings on crime if elected.

Most striking was Daley's brilliant triumph over a potentially very dangerous event. Alderman Benjamin M. Becker, the party's candidate for city clerk (mayor, city clerk, and city treasurer run as the only three citywide candidates in mayoralties and are almost always elected together), was cited by the Chicago Bar Association for misconduct (fee-splitting, alleged payoffs, etc.) and had to be dumped. But Daley shrewdly selected Morris B. Sachs, a popular Chicago retailer and television amateur hour sponsor and host, who had run for the position on Kennelly's ticket in the primaries. Moreover, Daley switched his own city treasurer candidate, John C. Marcin, to the clerk's position, so that the respectable Sachs could be slated as treasurer and make the public confident of the proper supervision of its monies.

Given all his problems, Daley's 55 percent of the vote over Merriam was a good showing. He did well in the more interior working-class and ethnic wards, and very well among the blacks. But the conflict with both Kennelly and Adamowski had hurt, and some work would have to be done before 1959. Indeed, 1956 made this all the clearer. In this first general election since Daley assumed the mayoralty, the Chicago Democrats did poorly in national and local contests. More disturbing than the reelection of Eisenhower, however, was the election of Adamowski, now a Republican, as state's attorney for Cook County, a position wherein he could oversee, and potentially hurt, the Democratic organization.

But Daley was not idle. Preparations for 1959 had begun on election day 1955. The organization was purged and tuned to great efficiency. And he began his successful campaign to win over the social and economic elite of Chicago and to support business and his ambitious building program. The construction of O'Hare International Airport, the expressway system, redevelopment of the area around the University of Chicago—signs were omnipresent (each of them emblazoned "Richard J. Daley, Mayor") that the city was vital and economically healthy. And during the campaign it was announced that Chicago's property tax assessments were being cut by 8 percent at the same time those in suburban Cook County were rising.

Thus even the Chicago *Tribune* felt in 1959 that his record "deserve[d] respectful consideration." And the "Nonpartisan Committee for the Reelection of Mayor Daley" and the "All Chicago Committee for Mayor Daley" included such names as William Patterson, president of United Air Lines and member of the board of governors of the United Republican Fund; Clair Roddewig, president of the Association of Western Railroads; Chancellor Lawrence A. Kimpton of the University of Chicago; and many, many more, a veritable Who's Who in Chicago.[4]

Combining this middle- and upper-class support (and money) with the organizational base among the blacks and white ethnics (he would campaign among the Swedes, Greeks, Italians, and Croatians, among others, and his ticket included one Jew and one Slav), Daley confronted the election—there was no primary contest—with confidence. The Republicans were in disarray, lacking funds and candidates. Timothy Sheehan took the Republican nomination that no one wanted and was beaten by the largest mayoral majority in Chicago history except for Kelly's in 1935: 71 percent to 29. Daley carried forty-nine of the fifty wards, missing only the Forty-first, on the Far Northwest side; and in all but two wards he did better—usually considerably so—than he had in 1955.[5]

Turnout did decline in 1959; it was 60 percent of those registered, as compared with 69 percent in 1955. (This would continue to be a characteristic of his elections.) But it was a stellar performance by any count; the Daley machine was as deeply insinuated in Chicago politics as any in the city's history.

During his second term Daley became an acknowledged Democratic leader of national importance. And his Irish Catholicism as well as his party allegiance oriented him to Kennedy in 1960. The machine's alleged vote stealing in the 1960 campaign was just Daley's way of not hedging any bets: he wanted to be sure that Illinois went Democratic, and he wanted to remove Adamowski from the state's attorney's office. He was successful in both, and the allegations of vote fraud were shrugged off as well, not only by Daley but by his supporters—from lowest class to highest, from the South Side ghetto to the rarefied air of North Shore suburbia.

The mayor confronted his third mayoral campaign with equanimity shattered a bit by the lingering effects of the famous "Burglars in Blue" scandal, which had surfaced during the 1960 election year. A captured burglar, Richard Morrison, became talkative and implicated a number of Summerdale District police officers as his accomplices. This did lead to a great deal of publicity, as well as successful prosecution of Morrison and the accused officers, which lasted through the 1963 mayoralty. Once again, however, Daley was able to turn danger into triumph; he pledged to remove politics from the police department and, after a national search had been conducted, brought in the highly respected Orlando W. Wilson as police commissioner.[6]

Try as the might, Daley's opponents were not able to turn the issue to their advantage. Alderman Leon Despres, the independent-minded representative of the University of Chicago area, writing at the time in the *Nation*, bemoaned both the corruption of Daley's Chicago and the machine's lack of interest in and support of national liberalism. But amidst his many criticisms, Despres acknowledged that "school administration is very good, and the city's finances are handled by a distinguished comptroller, streets are cleaned and repaired, garbage is collected, the water and sewage systems do their job, and assorted public works flourish."[7] What Despres did not say, and apparently did not realize, was that these were the things most Chicago voters were concerned about, not the national and ideological issues that so excited intellectuals.

Adamowski, trying to ride the prestige he had gained as exposer of the police scandal, took the Republican mayoral nomination in 1963. He was well known, now had a reputation for opposition to the machine, and had a good base among Chicago's Poles. But the police issue had been blunted by Daley's response, and it was very difficult to generate much interest in the campaign.

Daley's sources of support were pretty much the same as in 1959, with the exception of the Poles. John D. Marcin, campaigning for reelection as city clerk (and generally claimed by both Czechs and Poles, which made him doubly attractive) stressed in a speech the recognition given ethnic and racial minorities by Daley's Democrats; and Daley personally carried his campaign into the black belt, stressing what he had done for the people there. President Kennedy came to Chicago to speak in Daley's behalf and to join him in the dedication of O'Hare Airport.

Business-class support continued strong. Daley's man as new president of the county board had carefully appointed leading business and professional figures (often suburban residents who worked in the city) to various boards and commissions, as had Daley in the city, leading the *Tribune* to applaud the mayor's performance. It would have endorsed him, the paper said, were Chicago politics nonpartisan and unconnected with national parties; instead, it endorsed neither candidate, but did say that Adamowski's "capacity and temperament fall short." [8]

Adamowski, searching for an issue that would reach the front pages, raised the issue of birth control—alleging that Daley favored it. Daley denied this, and also that he had authorized the welfare department to provide birth-control devices. It was hard to persuade Catholic Chicagoans that Daley, who attended mass every morning, was anything other than a loyal Catholic. In a last desperate move, Adamowski openly came out against open housing, catering to white fears of black incursions. This Daley could not match for reasons of national Democratic policy; but he equivocated nicely enough, and it was too late for Adamowski anyway.

Daley and his running mates won, but his 56 percent was well below his 1959 performance. Turnout was higher than in 1959, continuing the trend of a negative relationship between size of Daley's percentage and size of turnout. Daley's percentage declined a bit almost everywhere in the city, but his main losses were in some—by no means all—middle-class or Republican areas (e.g., wards seven and forty-seven) and among the Poles (e.g., wards nine, thirty-three, and forty-one). That the mayor trailed his running mates for the first and only time suggests that Adamowski's personal appeal to some groups, rather than any general alienation from the machine, was the key.

That the mayor was indeed in good shape became clear four years later, in 1967. It seemed that everyone was for Daley, every newspaper in the city, business and professional groups, ethnic organizations, etc. His opponent, John L.

Waner, a businessman of Polish extraction, impressed no one. And even the beginnings of Daley's conflict with Martin Luther King during the 1967 campaign did not slow the momentum.

The mayor led his ticket, reached a new high of 74 percent of the vote, and maintained his overwhelming control of the city council. About 155,000 fewer people voted in 1967 than in 1963, a turnout rate of 64 percent; the machine's supporters were there on election day, and its detractors had been persuaded to stay home.

The machine did suffer the next year, in the violent riots and police violence attendant upon the 1968 Democratic National Convention and the ensuing Democratic defeat at both national and state levels. But the damage can easily be overestimated. Tom Wicker, writing in the *New York Times Magazine* one year later, concluded that "all America [was] radicalized" by the events in Chicago in 1968 and that Humphrey lost the election because he had not stood up to Daley. And it is indeed true that Daley's actions were vicious and insensitive. But the same newspaper's public opinion poll one day after the "police riot" found overwhelming support of the police position. And a Survey Research Center poll two months later found more people saying the police used too little violence (25 percent) than that they used too much (19 percent). Moreover, support for the police increased with the age of the respondent and decreased with educational level—in both cases suggesting that supporters of the Chicago Democratic organization were among these most likely to approve of Daley's position.[9]

That only one important group was critical of the police—the blacks—suggests the greater problem that the machine was confronting: how to reconcile the increasingly conflicting aims of the white ethnics and the blacks of Chicago. This was becoming urgent in the late 1960s, with issues like open housing, the presence of Martin Luther King in the city, and control of the police.

The resiliency of the machine was clear enough by the 1970 off-year elections, when Daley recouped his 1968 losses and the machine's vote led to a Democratic sweep of county and state offices, sending Adlai Stevenson, Jr., to the United States Senate (thus removing a potentially powerful Daley rival from the local scene). Even the state senate went Democratic for the first time in thirty-seven years. The state was set for Daley's fifth campaign in 1971.

Richard E. Friedman, former head of the Better Government Association, took the Republican nomination against Daley, but there was little evidence that he had even the support of people who were active in that association. Once again, every daily newspaper in the city endorsed the mayor. With Daley on the Democratic ticket were the now-perennial John C. Marcin for clerk and—for the first time—a black, Joseph Bertrand, for treasurer.

The mayor campaigned vigorously, once more leaving nothing to chance. On the same day he inaugurated construction of a United Steelworkers' housing complex, he also addressed the Junior Chamber of Commerce, where he was given a plaque as "Chicago's No. 1 Volunteer." He went on from there to address another middle-class group on pollution and to note in passing that Chicago was the only large American city to have an AA bond rating. He took up the issue of ill treatment in nursing homes, having initiated well-publicized law suits against some of them; and he responded to Friedman's taunts about his income with just enough information (his federal 1040 form) to blunt the issue.[10]

Holding the entire coalition together was not too easy, however. At a Polish Democratic meeting the mayor was praised for his opposition to public housing in white neighborhoods, as well as for his famous "shoot to kill" order during the 1968 riots. His remarks ignored both elements for praise; although they were central to his white working-class support, they were dangerous to black support. And he closed his campaign speaking to union and black audiences, focusing on more neutral topics: no one important was against unions, not even his upper-class supporters. But the rift between black and white was becoming increasingly disturbing.

Nonetheless the mayor carried forty-eight of the fifty wards in 1971 (two less than in 1967), and 70 percent of the vote. He led his ticket once again, but did it with the lowest turnout in thirty-six years. It could be argued that this apathy was a two-edged sword, signifying a steady erosion of the organization's base. But that could not be proved until some opposition organization found a way to involve nonvoters.

This was even clearer in 1975, when Daley won his unprecedented sixth term (the only other five-term winners, Carter H. Harrison I and II, served when the terms were for only two years). Daley's margin of 75 percent was his highest, but it was based on the lowest total vote in over fifty years and probably the lowest turnout rate in the city's history.

Daley ran this campaign amidst a number of real difficulties. For the first time in his career, his health was an important issue. Moreover, new police corruption and corruption among some of his oldest and strongest allies in politics hurt him. Even the Chicago *Tribune* and other papers that had become the mayor's most consistent supporters refused to endorse him, although this did not lead to endorsement of his opponent, Republican alderman John J. Hoellen.

The best appraisal of the campaign came from Hoellen himself, who said after the election, "It's hard to be a Republican in Chicago." It is indeed, because the declining base of the Daley organization, as seen in turnout rates, had simply increased the number of nonvoters and had redounded to the advantage of no other party or organization. As table 1 shows, Daley carried every ward in the city in 1975, with no less than 60 percent anywhere, and over 90 percent in eleven (the machine-reliable black and ethnic wards).

Some additional light on this amazingly consistent success can be sought in table 2, which gives the correlation coefficients for the Daley elections. What the table suggests, first, is an overall strong correlation among Daley elections;

TABLE 2

Correlation Coefficients (Pearson's r*) for Daley Elections, 1955–1975*

	1955	1959	1963	1967	1971	1975	Primary 1955
1955	—	.898	.700	.731	.728	.740	.838
1959		—	.842	.840	.565	.636	.795
1963			—	.952	.337	.456	.818
1967				—	.478	.573	.766
1971					—	.813	.412
1975						—	.512
1955 Primary							—

the sources of his support—and of the organization's support—remained essentially consistent over twenty years. This is as we should expect from our understanding of the development of the Democratic machine and its coalition. This is the crucial factor behind the enduring strength of any political organization, and it was the chief reason for the strength of the Daley machine.

Beyond this, however, there are some interesting variations in the table. Particularly, the last two elections (1971 and 1975) relate less strongly to the earlier heights of Daley's strength in 1959, 1963, and 1967. Their relationships are still significant, but less strong; and, interestingly, they are stronger in relation to the first election (1955), when the party was divided over the dumping of Kennelly and there was a primary contest, than in relation to the subsequent elections. Moreover, 1971 and 1975 show a considerable dropoff in strength in relation to Daley's vote in the 1955 primary. Some of this is simply the result of time and of changing population in the wards that are my basic units of analysis. The statistic is a function of the movement of each ward in the percentage Democratic relative to all other wards. Thus population changes that resulted in a ward's becoming either more or less Democratic would lower the correlation over time.

Beyond this, however, it is worth asking if there is any substance in the declining level of association seen for 1971 and 1975. For this purpose, we can isolate some distinct types of wards, representing specific population types, to observe any considerable falloff in Democratic vote among them.

In table 3, I have selected three groups of wards and merged their vote (the mean of the percentage Democratic of the several wards in each group) for an overall measure of Democratic voting for blacks, foreign-stock working-class whites, and middle-class whites. And the question, once raised, appears to be answered in the negative. The black vote remained consistently high (the falloff in 1971 will be considered below), and the working-class and middle-class white vote both increased quite steadily (the 1963 falloff being explained by the attractiveness of Adamowski to Polish voters). Thus the lower rate of association for the 1971 and 1975 elections in table 2 does seem to have resulted not from a declining party base, but simply from gradual population change, which had led to modest changes in the relative positions of the various wards.

Our table of coefficients, therefore, suggests the consistency behind the enduring strength of the Daley organization. It has not, conversely, given any evidence of important change in that support over the twenty years of Daley's leadership. More significant in this regard is the declining turnout rate that Daley experienced; this was across the board and did not undercut the Democrats' position.

Richard J. Daley, like William Hale Thompson, bossed Chicago in part because of his ability to hold onto the black vote. Behind this gross similarity, however, there are also differences. Thompson, as a renegade Republican who never controlled all of his party, needed the largely Republican blacks as his major factional support; Daley, a Democrat presiding over a united party, confronted a rapidly growing black population that had been turned Democratic by his predecessors.

With a black population of over one-third of Chicago's total population, one that had undergone important new pressures and leadership since the 1960s, the problem of the local Democratic organization was to avoid losing the political loyalties of this group to any of several alternatives. And as the late 1960s witnessed increasing tension between the major constituents of the Democratic coalition—the blacks and the immigrants and their children—while independent black leaders rose to contest the machine, it was not easy. But the Daley organization did hold onto the overwhelming majority of the black vote. It is therefore worthwhile to look at this aspect of his power more closely.

The shift of the previously overwhelmingly Republican black vote to the Democrats took place in the late 1930s, a result of the organizational drive begun by Cermak and continued by Kelly and Nash, plus the national policy and politics of the New Deal. The shift was also seen in, and to some extent led by,

TABLE 3

Daley Vote among Selected Groups, 1955–1975
(Percentages)

	Blacks	Foreign stock, working-class white	Middle-class white
1955	82	54	38
1959	89	73	57
1963	88	51	39
1967	91	72	66
1971	80	75	64
1975	91	84	74
1955 Primary	77	38	26

SOURCE: as in Table 1 Figures are mean of percentage Democratic for selected wards: blacks, Wards Two, Three, Twenty-four, Twenty-nine; foreign stock working-class white, Wards Thirty-one, Thirty-three, Thirty-four; middle-class white, Wards Thirty-eight, Forty-one, Forty-nine.

the new generation of black politicians rising at the time. Some, like William Dawson, anticipated the trend and jumped parties just in time to be part of the new movement; others first entered politics in the 1930s and 1940s, when the future was already quite clear. The Democratic organization saw the increasingly important role blacks were going to play numerically and worked to create a viable organization in the black wards.

Because of the relative poverty and the lack of sophistication of the rising number of blacks in the city, they were susceptible to traditional machine methods of attraction and needed the services which the organization would provide. New Deal welfare programs did not, as I have already suggested, change this, since local government intervened. Moreover, the Democrats were, by the 1930s, a good deal more responsive to blacks, both nationally and locally, and began to give them an increasing share of nominations and appointments—never proportionately as many as they gave to most other groups, but nonetheless more than the Republicans gave. And those at the bottom of the socioeconomic ladder are most needful of the party in power, so the blacks and black leaders needed the Democratic organization as much as the organization needed them.

The question was, as the black population of Chicago increased from about 7 percent of the population in 1930 to a third of it under Daley, whether or not there would be anything like equivalent growth in their political and economic power. And the answer was no—for reasons which largely go beyond the scope of this chapter.

I want to look first at some of the sources of black support for the Daley organization and then at some of the problems which arose in that support. The most important of those strengths was partisan—the Daley organization was the local Democratic party, and to the extent that party loyalties extended across national, state, and local lines, this was a consistent reason for black loyalty to Daley. Certainly at the national level the Republicans offered little reason for blacks to desert their Democratic loyalties. And, apart from any particular reasons of policy, the very weakness of the local Republicans and of local third parties had the same effect.

At the start, Daley's cultivation of Congressman Dawson was very important since the latter was by far the most important political leader in the old South Side black belt and the rapidly expanding West Side ghetto as well. As the Chicago *Defender* pointed out in 1955, the black vote was the key to Daley's primary victory.[11] It was also a Dawson success, both in Daley's victory and in that of Dawson's own man, Ralph Metcalfe, over incumbent Alderman Archibald Carey in the Third Ward. This election also saw the number of black aldermen increase from three to four.

By 1959 the *Defender* could argue that Daley was the best mayor Chicago had ever had, lauding him for his concern with racial problems as well as his general leadership of the city.[12] Daley's opponent, Sheehan, was criticized for being a typical Republican, failing to commit himself on issues of integration. This suggests, again, that however inadequate the Daley machine was in meeting the needs of black people, it was nonetheless better than its opponents. Voters choose only between real options, not ideal ones.

In the 1963 and 1967 elections, black support remained very high at all levels. The *Defender* consistently pictured Daley as an outstanding leader who really sympathized with black problems. The local and national Democratic party's alliance with organized labor was also useful in getting consistent support from groups like the Joint Council of Negro Trade Unionists. And black business groups responded like their white counterparts in supporting the most "building" mayor in the city's history.[13]

The organization was slowly but steadily responsive to questions of black representation. The number of black aldermen increased (to fourteen by 1971). In 1971 a black was slated for citywide office (treasurer) for the first time in history. The *Defender* in that year noted the large number of black judges, officeholders, and administrators that had come into being under Daley. Black ministers also supported him strongly in 1971, despite the rising conflict over civil rights that had marked his fourth term.[14] Thus the Daley organization was sufficiently responsive to black social, political, and economic ambitions to forestall its being undercut by Republican or black rivals. It was a minimal approach but a successful one. In 1975, for example, when a "Committee to Elect a Black Mayor" fell apart, the *Defender* noted with only moderate regret that "the time is not feasible for the election of a Black Mayor." Moreover, the paper said, despite his inadequacy on police control and housing discrimination, Daley "has done a creditable job of running the city," and deserved reelection.[15] This was not only the point of view of the black middle class, but also of the black politicians, and it explains the continuation through his sixth term of Daley's hold on black voters.

If we look more carefully at some of the conflicts which Daley had with the blacks of Chicago, we may at the same time see further indications of the extent and consistency of his success. Such conflict did exist, as was perhaps inevitable given the tremendous changes that took place among American blacks during the years that Daley was mayor. In Chicago those conflicts revolved around two major problems. First was the question of whether or not the Daley machine was sufficiently responsive to the political, economic, and racial desires of the city's black population. And second was the question of power—not so much the substance of rule but its form, the hands which were to control the destiny of the city generally and its black areas specifically. Both of these questions were divisive, but the latter related most directly to the survival of the machine itself.

One early source of conflict came from the rapid increase in size of the black community and its geographic spread, which led to a more rapid increase in the number of black wards and precincts than in that of black ward and precinct leaders and aldermen. The Seventeenth Ward on the South Side, for example, had been about 50 percent black in 1959 but rose to 90 percent by 1963. The machine supported its incumbent white alderman, despite some organized black insistence that a black man replace him. And Charles Chew, a black with support from a number of black leaders, entered the 1963 primary as an Independent Democrat and defeated the white incumbent.

Chew supported Daley's reelection in 1963 but remained somewhat outside the organization and a potential source of opposition for a while. Moreover, Daley did not really learn much from the event. True, the number of blacks slated did increase slowly—but too slowly. More important, when Daley sensed a conflict between what working-class whites wanted and what blacks wanted, he generally chose the former.

The situation shortly became more serious. By the mid-1960s disputes over school segregation and inferior black schools were more and more frequent. In 1964, conflict developed when a couple of young blacks moved down the street from Daley's home; this led to riots and counterdemonstrations for which the mayor hardly concealed his support. The next two years saw Martin Luther King come to Chicago, leading marches and protests, rent strikes, and other formal opposition to the status quo. Daley prevailed because Chicago segregation was extralegal, and time was then on the mayor's side. But it was not a complete victory. He was correct in seeing that too much compliance with black wishes would alienate his white supporters and that the only real threat was the one at the polls. But he was not right in underestimating the depth of the issues and the extent to which they might become irreconcilable. Daley, however, was motivated first by his striving for political power and second by his provincial Irish Catholicism, which led him to a dislike of blacks and a lack of sympathy with their goals. If he had to choose, he would choose his own people every time.

That most black politicians—as practical as Daley in their orientation—remained with the organization was a key factor. The black community could have been led away from the machine in the mid-1960s, but the leadership to do so did not appear. Thus in 1967 only one black, A. A. Rayner, was able to defeat the organization's choice for alderman, in this case in the Sixth Ward. It is noteworthy that both the Sixth Ward and the Seventeenth, where Chew had been successful, were relatively more middle-class black wards, where feelings of group awareness and of deprivation were more likely to exist. And Daley's 1967 campaign for reelection was as successful among blacks as among the rest of the people. He bent far enough in response to black demands to confuse his opposition in that community but never so far as to alienate his white working-class supporters. His vote in black wards remained tremendous and about as much so in the more middle-class ones (e.g., the Sixth, Seventh, and Seventeenth—see table 1) and working-class ones (e.g., Twenty and Five) as in the very poor (Two, Three, and Twenty-four).

In April 1968, as a result of the assassination of Martin Luther King, Chicago experienced violent riots, leading to Daley's famous order to "shoot to kill any arsonist or anyone with a molotov cocktail in his hand because they are potential murderers, and . . . to shoot to maim or cripple anyone looting any stores in our city."[16] His strong reaction to the riots was condemned by black leaders and the liberal press but widely supported by working-class people in Chicago. The gap was widening.

This approach was reified in Daley's response to the young radicals and the police riot later that year during the Democratic National Convention. But, as we have already seen, his actions were by no means unwelcome to most white Chicagoans. The city was becoming increasingly polarized on a basis that was by no means readily reconcilable. Daley proceeded on the logic of his political sagacity and his ethnic provincialism, to the satisfaction of no one group—and to the clear disadvantage of Chicago's blacks. But perhaps this was also about as well as anyone could do.

In one of the few perceptive things ever written on Daley, David Halberstam noted in *Harper's* shortly before the 1968 Democratic convention that the city's blacks were still very weak; their representation in government and finance, for example, was still proportionately much lower than that of any other group. (Moreover, the machine had somehow been able to separate black politicians from their group, a most unusual but crucial development.) Daley's problem was not simply political, but also ideological: he had, Halberstam argued, a rather old fashioned Roman Catholic sense of "individual sin" but no modern sense of "social sin." And he remained a Bridgeport provincial; as one black interviewee put it, "I think one of the real problems he has with Negroes is understanding that the Irish are no longer the out-ethnic group."[17]

All this was true. Daley was provincial, insensitive, and unsympathetic to the plight of urban blacks. What he gave them he gave them for political reasons; and his lack of sympathy and sensitivity made him less of a leader than he might have been. But the defense of expediency is also a real one. Had Daley really tried to deal with black problems, there is good reason to argue that he would have lost not only much of his white ethnic support but his upper-class business support as well. It was a risk he was surely unwilling to take.

Some blacks and many white liberals continued to be critical of the mayor during his fourth term. Even the generally supportive *Defender* noted during the 1971 campaign that there was more criticism of him in the black community than ever before. He refused to cooperate with the more independent and assertive black organizations like Operation Breadbasket and its controversial leader, Jesse Jackson. His housing plans were widely condemned as political and not really addressed to the problems of segregation. The Independent Voters of Illinois condemned him as "a flagrantly racist mayor," which was an exercise in liberal verbosity: few blacks belonged to the IVI or listened to it. And Jesse Jackson finally decided against a write-in campaign for himself, urging instead that blacks vote for Republican Richard Friedman.[18]

This long-term tension was not without some cumulative effect. Daley's vote did decline in black Chicago in 1971, although a black man was running on the citywide ticket. And the decline was evident in black wards at every socioeconomic and machine-controlled level. The Second Ward, the heart of the old Black Belt and Dawson's organization, declined in Democratic voting by 21 percentage points from 1967 levels; and the Seventeenth fell off by only one point less. Of the thirteen wards that might be considered black in 1971 (Wards 2, 3, 4, 5, 6, 7, 15, 17, 20, 22, 24, 27, and 29), all but two showed declines in the Democratic vote for mayor. On the other hand, all but one of these wards (the Fifth—influenced also by a large, liberal, University of Chicago vote) did go Democratic, and with majorities of 60 to 89 percent. Thus if we can argue that the events of the 1960s did lead to a gradual undercutting of the organization's black support, we must also realize that this was only partial. It suggests a basic problem that Daley did have by the end of the 1960s, but not a problem that was in any way overwhelming at the time. Moreover, the dropoff turned out to be temporary. The organization's black support in Daley's 1975 campaign was as high as it had ever been; all the black wards went Democratic, by margins that were much higher than those of 1971, and in more than half of them even higher than in 1967. But turnout continued to decline. Daley was strong among steadily declining numbers of blacks—an ominous sign, even if went unperceived at the time.

Daley had confronted a primary contest in 1975, wherein he was challenged by both a black state senator, Richard Newhouse, and a white liberal, Alderman William Singer. Citywide, the challenge was not significant, but in the seventeen largely black wards there were indications of some continuation of black opposition. Daley received 48 percent of the primary vote in those seventeen wards, Newhouse and Singer together the other 52 percent. Variation was considerable from the poorer and more machine-dependent to the more middleclass and independent. Thus Daley won 58 percent of the vote of the West Side's Twenty-fourth Ward, and 55 percent in South Side Ward Three; but he held only 49 percent in the increasingly independent Second and 44 percent in the more middle-class Ward Six.

This discrepancy between a real primary challenge for the first time since 1955 and an overwhelming general election victory points to the continuing importance of state and national politics. The Daley machine, after all, was part of the national Democratic party, which was always a major source of its strength. And its relationship to blacks was always tempered by the fact that third parties are notoriously unsuccessful in the United States, especially in a city like Chicago, where the party serves so many purposes. The conflicts of 1971 did not disappear in 1975 but were focused in the primary; after that the general appeal of the Democratic party and the obviousness of Daley's impending victory neutralized the opposition. But the relationship between Daley's Democratic organization and the blacks, however strong it was, continued to be tenuous. The problem was not so much the relative insensitivity of Daley and the other Irish rulers of Chicago's politics, but rather the quite real conflicts of interest between constituent elements of the Chicago Democratic coalition. Successful majority voting coalitions have always consisted to some degree of mutually conflicting interests; the difference here is one of degree, but of a very great degree.

It would appear that for the Democratic organization created by Cermak and honed by Daley to persist into the 1980s, it would have to find a way to pacify black demands (including a black mayor) while holding onto white working-class support and white business support, which were equally important to its previous success. This would not be easy. And Daley's holding action on this issue would not make the process easier; not, in his defense, that there was really a great deal he might have done about it.

The events immediately following Daley's death indicated both the extent to which blacks desired the party leadership and mayoralty and the extent to which the Daley machine had kept them off balance and not immediately equipped to press their demands. Black Alderman Wilson Frost's early bid for the acting mayoralty simply lacked a black organizational support in any way equivalent to the ready-made forces for the succession of Daley's people.

In considering how, precisely, Daley managed to maintain the Democratic organization in a form and strength relatively unchanged from the time of Cermak, it is important to look directly at his strategy and his tactics. In the process, I shall try to deal with the argument about the "decline of 'bossism.'"

What kept Daley and his organization in power was essentially the natural conservatism of the professional politician—his reluctance to change anything he does not have to change. And the Daley organization of the 1970s was as much like the Cermak organization of the 1930s as it could possibly be. This was the measure of his strength; perhaps in the future it will be considered the measure of his, or his successor's, weakness.

I noted at the start of this chapter the continuing role of patronage in the Chicago Democratic organization. Daley always understood the centrality of patronage to party strength and single-mindedly sought to maintain it. Thus he successfully avoided some of the most threatening aspects of the civil service laws, sometimes by such powerful devices as not scheduling examinations for long periods, or making them hard to find, or hiring "temporary" employees (who are exempt from civil service regulations) on a permanent basis. It was one of the reasons, also, why he opposed aspects of the civil rights movement—less because of the threatened rise of black people than the danger the movement implied for party control.

Likewise, with a sort of reverse patronage, he was loyal to those he appointed. People were kept in their jobs as long as there was no scandal associated with their tenure; competence was rarely insisted upon. He also remembered their names and maintained some personal contact. And like other successful bosses before him, he was loyal to his friends so long as they remained loyal to him. (The number of Bridgeport people in city government was very great indeed.) Old Hamburg Club pal Robert Quinn was made fire commissioner despite obvious questions of his competence; and the mayor never had a more loyal political supporter.

The mayor was aided by the nature of his own ambitions: he sought power, not wealth. Thus his own political career was untouched by personal scandal. At the same time, he did not expect other people to maintain a similar probity. So long as they avoided scandal and did not hurt the party, they were free to make some money for themselves. He supported county treasurer Herbert Paschen for governor until scandal attached to Paschen's use of discretionary funds became well known, and then Daley dumped him. As forgiving as he could be, he could also be apoplectic when a machine politician engaged in actions that threatened the party.

Daley was always a party man, by conviction and by practical logic. And as he used appointive patronage, he also used nominations to office. Ethnic representation continued to be basic; and if blacks, for example, did not have the proportion of representation that the Poles or Irish had, theirs nonetheless steadily increased—enough to avert major defections from the party. Within the party Daley exhibited a real knack for coopting or otherwise undercutting his opposition. Thus in 1955 he turned scandal to advantage when he added Morris B. Sachs to his ticket. And in 1970, when Senator Dirksen died, Daley was able to persuade State Treasurer Adlai Stevenson, Jr., to run for Dirksen's seat, thus slating an attractive and eventually successful Democrat for the previously Republican senatorship and removing from local affairs one of the mayor's potentially most powerful opponents. Daley used his control of the slating committee well, moving more reliable candidates to more powerful positions and less reliable ones to positions that might have civic power but were always politically less threatening.

Control of the party was most important. In 1955 he reneged on his pledge to resign as party chairman if elected mayor; it was logical that he do so. But it was through his control of the party, not his elective office, that he gained complete control of the city council—always having at least forty of the fifty votes, sometimes more. Thus the mayor, not the council, decided the budget; the mayor, not the council, decided on the legislation that ran the city.

Likewise, his control was extended to the Cook County board via his party chairmanship (he was head of the county Democratic party), giving him control as well over the great budget and power that county commissioners command. So long as the Democratic party was successful at the polls, the mayor ruled; thus success at the polls was crucial. The primary, on the other hand, was not so crucial. Since the party slate-making committee did recommend candidates for the primaries, those candidates started out with such an edge that it was extremely difficult for other Democrats to beat them. And it has been very rarely—for offices ranging from ward to national level—that a Chicago candidate other than the duly designated one has received a Democratic nomination. This obviously made it illogical for any aspiring Democratic politician in Cook County not to make his peace with Chairman Daley.

Party unity, moreover, was a universal watchword to Daley. He made his peace with downstate Democrats, controlling what he could, giving in when he had to. And he was ever loyal to the national party as well. Kennedy's election was indeed due in no small part to Mayor Daley, not so much for the votes he may have stolen as for the 89 percent turnout he delivered. The mayor worked for Humphrey in 1968, although he didn't like him. And even after his delegates had been unseated in the 1972 Democratic National Convention (a cruel blow to one who understandably saw himself as one of the party's greatest stalwarts), he worked for McGovern, whom he detested. Chicago went Democatic in 1968 and again in 1972. Small wonder, then, that Daley insisted on party loyalty from those under him; he practiced what he preached. And he could be vicious indeed to those who failed to follow this cardinal rule of politics.

Daley's political acumen was perhaps nowhere better demonstrated than in his ability to turn adversity into advantage. He not only overcame major scandals and other challenges to his control, but very often turned them around so that he emerged the hero of the piece. This was seen as early as the 1955 campaign, when he did not really suffer for having placed Becker on his ticket; rather, he was generally praised for having replaced Becker with Sachs. Likewise, in the famous "burglars in blue" scandal in 1960, Daley was able to emerge as the "reformer" who removed the police department from politics (temporarily) and defended the independence of the new police commissioner, O. W. Wilson. He was similarly lauded for freeing the city's welfare department from politics—a development, like that in the police department, that did not really happen: the welfare check remained under some machine control, as did the police department once Wilson was gone.

Probably the foremost demonstration of this phenomenon, however, can be seen in his sixth election (1975) because here, for the first time, scandal reached right into his inner organization. Indeed, the fifth term had seen numerous troubles, not least of them Daley's first serious extended illnesses in his public career: some wondered whether the mayor, now over seventy, could still handle the job. The years 1971–74 had given him sufficient reason to be ill.

In December, 1971, Otto Kerner (judge on the U.S. Court of Appeals, former governor of Illinois, chairman of the National Advisory Commission on Civil Disorders, son-in-law of Tony Cermak, and shining light of respectability in the Chicago machine) was indicted. In February 1973 he was found guilty and in July 1974 went to prison for tax evasion and perjury charges arising from his allegedly having profited from his position as governor in collusion with racetrack interests. In September 1972, County Clerk Edward J. Barrett, an institution of sorts in the machine and local politics, was indicted on charges of soliciting a $187,000 bribe for the purchase of voting machines; he was convicted in March 1973. New police scandals emerged in the fall of that year; the "depoliticization" of the department had indeed been temporary. Matthew Danaher, Daley's neighbor and closest confidant, whose job was circuit court clerk, was indicted in April 1974 on charges resulting from a $400,000 real estate scheme. One month later, Daley's floor leader in the city council and very close associate and personal friend, Thomas E. Keane, was indicted for conspiracy and mail fraud, also over questionable real estate transactions; he was convicted in October. The mayor's long-term press secretary, Earl Bush, was also forced to resign under conflict of interest charges that came to trial in 1974. And similar charges even came against the mayor's own family: his son was charged with having received favorable treatment in selling insurance to the city.[19]

Scandal and corruption had been alleged and proved among his closest political friends and aids—in his personal political family, as it were. Never had scandal gotten so close to Daley before. Moreover, there was an attractive first-term Democratic governor, Daniel Walker, who had defeated Daley's own candidate in the 1972 primary (a most unusual circumstance) and who continued openly to oppose him. Alderman William Singer, who had played a role in unseating the Daley delegates at the 1972 Democratic National Convention, announced his plans to contest the mayor in the 1975 primary. Daley had two strokes in 1974—small wonder.

Yet, as we have seen, Daley beat Singer and Newhouse in the 1975 primary; and he slaughtered Republican Hoellen in the general election. The charges of corruption never touched him personally, though a great deal of energy was expended trying to make them do so. What he could not turn to his advantage he managed to override or ride out. His control of the party and the party's support by the electorate overcame probably the greatest challenge he had faced since 1955.

One thing he could bank on in 1975, which I have already noted as being central to his control and new to "bossism," was his large-scale business leadership support. He had wooed the business community from the start: in his great building program, in getting Democratic national conventions in 1956 and 1968, in providing good police protection for private property, and in fostering an overall environment conducive to economic growth. The contractors, the banks, and the downtown businesses were pleased—not only economically, but also in terms of their sense of civic responsibility: the city appeared clean, its books were balanced, its credit rating was good, and the number of nonpolitical special commissions was legion. And this Chicago Democratic mayor was applauded and supported by the city's four essentially Republican newspapers as no Democrat had even been before. When Richard Friedman of the Better Government Association ran against him in 1971, he had found almost all of his associates on the other side.

Daley worked hard to maintain this element of support; it seemed that he had an emotional need for it as well as a political one. At times, this required that he ride roughshod over more traditional Democratic supporters, as when he chose a central location for the new campus of the University of Illinois, which required the destruction of an old, well-established inner-city community and of the venerable Hull House as well. But the urban Italians, however much they protested, did not seem all that likely to bolt the party; and in the final analysis, they did not. Other kinds of urban renewal likewise displaced the urban poor, but the political effects of all this were on balance beneficial to the machine. Not only did the business community, the upper class, and "society" applaud him and support him; not only did the industrialists and retailers and union presidents to whom he deferred, defer back to him in response; but the building and the contracts also greatly increased the patronage—via private jobs—available to the machine. Sometimes, indeed, it could provide jobs to the very people the projects were displacing. It is a complicated business to evaluate; but it was a key aspect of a political machine that survived through the 1970s.

In the immediate aftermath of Richard J. Daley's death, his machine was attacked on several fronts. Blacks, independents, Poles, and a new generation of Chicagoans have not followed the organizational leadership of the Chicago Democratic machine as they had in Daley's day. Historically, the machine's longevity was based on its ability to accommodate rapid demographic social and governmental transformations, thereby broadening its base as it modernized its service delivery. Race and the demand for new power sharing injured Daley's machine far more than any Republican opponent or independent party rival could have dreamed possible. Yet to Daley's lasting legacy—despite the mistakes, the losses, and the change in leadership—the machine lingers.

II.

MICHAEL A. BILANDIC: THE LAST OF
THE MACHINE REGULARS

Paul M. Green

Unlike most Chicago mayors, Michael Bilandic is most remembered for how he entered and exited office and not for what he accomplished as the city's chief executive. Under any circumstance, the mayor succeeding Richard J. Daley would have found the task of governing the city difficult. Daley was Chicago, and for many citizens the office of mayor died with him. Daley's genius of intertwining government and politics under his sole control left his political survivors the unenviable task of finding a replacement either to handle both tasks or two individuals who would share power. As Chicago's mayor and Cook County Democratic committee chairman, Daley had followed the old Chicago political axiom to his grave: "Don't make anyone who can unmake you." On both the governmental and political levels there was no logical heir apparent to fill the "Old Man's" shoes. However, there were many pols with itchy feet eager to assume power.

On 21 December 1976, one day after Daley's death, Michael Bilandic was one of four aldermen to meet in Daley's city hall office to discuss succession. The other three council members present were Edward Vrdolyak, Tenth Ward; Edward Burke, Fourteenth Ward; and Wilson Frost, Thirty-fourth Ward. These men, along with several key Daley aides—Tom Donovon, the city's patronage chief being the most important—would guide the mayoral replacement process. Vrdolyak, Burke, and Frost (the only black) were all powerful Democratic ward committeemen who combined personal ambition with hard-nosed political moxie in pushing themselves to the forefront of city politics. Yet it would be Bilandic who would receive the honor of replacing Daley and the responsibility of maintaining the Chicago political tradition.

Who was Michael Bilandic? A lifelong Chicago resident of Croatian descent,

Michael A. Bilandic (1976–1979)

Bilandic earned a law degree and settled in the Near Southwest Side, blue-collar Bridgeport community. What Eton's playing fields were to the English war effort, Bridgeport's streets and alleys were to Chicago's governmental leadership. Bridgeport was Daley's neighborhood, the backbone of "Hizzoner's" famous Eleventh Ward Democratic organization and the city's bungalow version of "God's Country." In 1969, Daley selected Bilandic to fill an Eleventh Ward aldermanic vacancy, thereby elevating the middle-aged bachelor attorney to instant political prominence. In the council, Bilandic, a shy and careful politician, demonstrated a sound mind and a willingness to work hard, and with Daley's approval assumed the powerful post of finance committee chairman in 1975. In his meteoric rise to political power, Bilandic was never tested politically or challenged in a fair political fight. In the end, this lack of political experience and acumen would cut short his mayoral career.

Potent political forces collided during the urgent and secret negotiations to determine Daley's successor. Frost, the council president pro tempore, asserted he was the city's acting mayor. Backing Frost's mayoral claim was the city's huge black community whose activist leaders, like the Reverend Jesse Jackson, overlooked Frost's nearly impeccable regular Democratic organization credentials. Also openly angling for the mayor's job was Northwest Side Polish alderman Roman C. Pucinski. Chicago's huge Polish community, like the black community, was frustrated at its inability to capture real power in the world's second largest Polish city. Also moving quickly into the mayoral sweepstakes was Ed Vrdolyak, a youngish, tough, and smart Southeast Side alderman. Vrdolyak—called by some the Che Guevara of Chicago politics for his leadership in orchestrating the so-called "Young Turk" aldermanic "Coffee Rebellion" against Daley's iron-fisted council control—was working the hardest and fastest to line up council support.

Beyond the constantly shifting political scenarios, two other factors complicated the mayoral selection process. First, who would fill Daley's other crucial position, party chairman? Most political players wanted to avoid a Daley-style replay where one man was both party boss and mayor. Cook County Board President George Dunne, a recognized old pro, was the leading contender for the chair—in part due to his pledge not to seek the mayoralty. Second, the city council could only select an interim mayor since state law required a special mayoral election within six months[1]—thereby raising the issue of whether the council's acting mayoral choice would be a candidate in the special election. Obviously, if the interim mayor became a special election candidate, he would have a huge advantage, for in effect he would be the incumbent mayor. Into this labyrinth of Chicago political intrigue entered Michael Bilandic, whose strengths and weaknesses combined to make him Daley's mayoral successor.

Not only was Bilandic from the right neighborhood and a Daley disciple, he was also not Irish (some ward committeemen and aldermen wanted to break the four-decade Irish hold on city hall), and he was admittedly not a very able politician. On Christmas Eve, two events cemented Bilandic's selection as interim mayor. First, he told his fellow aldermen and other city hall leaders that he would *not* be a special election mayoral candidate. Second, he and his old guard advisors (Daley's key administrative aides) worked out a council compromise with his potential rivals. Frost was made chairman of the crucial council finance committee (Bilandic's old job); Vrdolyak was made council president pro tempore (Frost's old job); and Burke retained his important police and fire committee chairmanship and was given credit for putting the deal together. As for Pucinski, he announced his special election mayoral candidacy relieved that the interim mayor, Bilandic, would not be his mayoral challenger.

The Bilandic selection as interim mayor was perhaps the old machine's "last hurrah." It was done easily and quickly, with style and old-fashioned crispness, and few Chicagoans raised any objections. The *Chicago Tribune* editorialized that Bilandic was "technically well qualified to serve as acting mayor." [2] The council vote on his selection was 45–2, with only the lakefront independent aldermen Dick Simpson and Martin Oberman questioning the process. Finally, the strength of the machine's muscle was illustrated in Frost's closing comments following the council vote. He told his black supporters who had wanted other black aldermen to nominate Frost without his consent, "Why should I be the one who takes the suicide job. I've been the mayor for eight days and it's been a difficult task. The only way I could sit in that chair is to have 25 council votes and I didn't have them." [3]

One week into his interim administration, Bilandic reversed his field with a move that would have made Chicago Bears halfback Gale Sayers proud. [4] The acting mayor suddenly announced he was open to a mayoral draft for the upcoming special election. Old-timers thought it was déjà vu as they recalled that a generation earlier Richard Daley had reneged on his promise that if he was elected party chairman, he would not seek the mayor's office. Bilandic's pledge, like Daley's promise, was quickly forgotten: an integral party of the Chicago political tradition is "never admit that you ever said never."

Bilandic's surprise announcement, coupled with Dunne's easy election as party chairman, conjured up thoughts that a new Kelly-Nash machine was on the horizon. [5] However, Chicago in 1977 was no longer an ethnic/Catholic dominated city. Its citizens and voters reflected the changing lifestyle and demographics of the previous two decades. The civil rights movement, antipatronage court decisions, the decline of political involvement, and simple white flight had eroded traditional organization power. The old pols had been lulled and misled by the ease of the Bilandic appointment. Their fight to retain power would never again go unchallenged.

Bilandic soon found himself in a mayoral primary campaign. An outraged Pucinski scoffed at the well-staged "draft Bilandic movement" that led to a party central committee endorsement. Pucinski rejected intense party organization pressure to be a team player as he told his largely Polish supporters that he was in the race to stay. The Northwest Side alderman unleashed a bitter barrage against Bilandic and the entire process as he boldly challenged the acting mayor to a series of campaign debates (Bilandic refused).

Soon another major mayoral contestant entered the arena. State Senator Harold Washington—like Bilandic, a middle-aged, bachelor lawyer—became the black community's new champion. Under-financed and under-organized and suffering from the effects of personal legal problems, Washington campaigned largely in South Side black wards. Late in the primary campaign, he told the congregation of Ebeneezer Missionary Baptist Church that "there is a sleeping giant in Chicago. And if this sleeping giant, the potential black vote, ever woke up, we'd control the city."[6] Washington's prophetic words would have to wait two more mayoral primary elections before they would become reality.

Bilandic campaigned leisurely for mayor. He ignored his primary opponents, was cool with the press, and refused to be drawn into any controversy. Bilandic wanted Chicagoans to recognize him as a competent administrator and a solid, if somewhat dull, chief executive. When a third primary opponent, the discredited former State's Attorney Edward Hanrahan, told voters to reject Bilandic because "there (was) no pepper in the city . . . (only) a b(i)land(ic) diet,"[7] the acting mayor responded by addressing a meeting of professional public administrators. Bilandic, like a suddenly crowned Prince of Wales, had to prove to all that he was a worthy successor to the departed king.

At first glance, the April Democratic special mayoral primary election was an easy Bilandic victory. He captured slightly over 50 percent of the vote, carried thirty-eight of fifty wards, and won by a comfortable 130,000 vote margin. Yet on closer scrutiny, the vote returns revealed severe cracks in the once omnipotent machine. Pucinski won seven North and Northwest Side wards while receiving over 32 percent of all the votes cast. Most interesting was the fact that his total citywide vote was almost identical to the final numbers of 1975 Daley mayoral primary challenger William Singer, a reform-minded, former alderman. Thus, in two consecutive elections, an independent lakefront liberal alderman (Singer) and a regular, northwest side ethnic alderman (Pucinski) were able to attract one-third of the Democratic primary vote. Singer and Pucinski had different power bases—thus revealing the potential for a meaningful future organization challenge by a candidate who could unite supporters from both rebel camps.

Also foreboding to organization Democrats were the Washington vote totals. The state senator won five middle-class, black Southside wards while capturing 10 percent of the citywide primary vote. His numbers, when combined with Pucinski's totals, exposed the future possibilities of a real mayoral horserace.

Three groups, Poles, blacks, and lakefront liberals, were upset with the machine, and they had demonstrated this displeasure at the most vital part of the Democratic organization's life-support system—the ballot box.

Bilandic accepted his primary triumph in a businesslike manner. He gave traditional thank-yous to the party workers, business and labor organizations, and Chicago's various ethnic communities. Though nominated under his own name, Bilandic paid special homage to the Daley family for their support as he expressed his hopes to follow in the footsteps of "hizzoner." According to Bilandic, "the standards of (city) leadership, in the past 21 years would be a great challenge for anyone." As mayor, Bilandic would never truly find an adequate method of freeing himself from Daley's memory while maintaining the proper respect for the man who was his chief patron. In almost every comparison between the two, Bilandic came out second best, thus leaving the impression in the minds of most Chicagoans that the new mayor was a stand-in and not a successor.

In the April general mayoral election, Bilandic wiped out his hapless Republican opponent, Forty-Eighth Ward alderman Dennis Block—the last GOP city council member remaining in Chicago.[8] The machine's main opponents were Democrats, not Republicans. Thus, Bilandic's easy victory was a low-turnout, low-interest affair.

What kind of mayor was Michael Bilandic? According to one public official, "Bilandic put the job of mayor on—like a comfortable bathrobe."[9]

Some years after he left office, Bilandic admitted that as mayor, "I didn't rearrange the administrative furniture."[10] In little over two years in city hall, Bilandic never overcame the notion that he was a caretaker and not the man in charge.

Administratively, Bilandic's term was not without its achievements. His good friend and eminent political scientist, the late Milton Rakove, summarized Bilandic's record as one "of accomplishment, continuity, and some forward motion."[11]

Bilandic maintained a balanced city budget, kept the city's bond rating high, and, until late in his term, reinforced the public service city tradition that "Chicago was the city that worked." Bilandic also maintained peace in the city council by using a strategy that relegated all controversies and fights behind closed doors. Years later, Bilandic refused to call the council during his term a rubber stamp. Rather he claimed it "had the opportunity to perform its tasks . . . but they did it backstage."[12]

Politically, Mayor Bilandic walked a tenuous narrow line. Unlike his predecessor, he could not consolidate his power in the county central committee. In simple terms, Bilandic was not a committeeman, and his future prospects of joining this elite, ruling party hierarchy were bleak. Blocking his political progress was the incumbent Eleventh Ward Democratic committeeman, State Senator Richard M. Daley—the eldest son of the "Mayor." Thus, Bilandic was forced to become a political broker who worked with (1) the traditional "old guard" (Daley's entrenched administrators and the party's warhorses like Alderman Vito Marzullo, County Commissioner Matthew Bieszczat, and Sewer Commissioner Edward Quigley); (2) the hungry "Young Turks" (led by Vrdolyak, Burke, Frost, and Chicago Park District Superintendent Edmund Kelly); and (3) the emerging dissidents (Poles, blacks, and lakefront liberals). It was to Bilandic's credit that in late 1978 few political commentators thought his upcoming 1979 reelection bid was in jeopardy.[13] Indeed, most praised Bilandic for keeping the city together and for successfully navigating the political tightrope that had appeared so slippery at the outset of his term.

How did Bilandic lose? Jane Byrne beat him. She combined an incredible streak of good luck with several costly Bilandic blunders to eke out a narrow 16,675 vote victory in the 1979 Democratic mayoral primary.

The overriding factors in Bilandic's defeat were threefold. First, Jane Byrne was his sole opponent. Second, she was able to unite the disenchanted behind her candidacy because, third, the now famous Chicago January snowstorms that closed down and covered the city also buried for the moment the divisive race issue. Unquestionably the blizzards eased and accelerated the movement of the divergent machine antagonists behind Byrne's candidacy, and she was also smart enough to take advantage of this heavenly gift and use it as entry into snow-clogged neighborhoods. Yet, with all her cleverness and the incumbent's ineptness, Bilandic still almost beat her one on one.

Bilandic's tale of woe following the record January snowstorms reveals a careful man finding himself suddenly in unknown territory. The city that supposedly worked stopped working. Garbage cluttered the alleys and remained uncollected, streets continued to be impassable, and parking spaces became prime real estate. Bilandic's public policy response to the snow was administratively inadequate and politically disastrous. His so-called snow removal plan, written by a former city-hall crony, turned out to be a joke. He alienated the black working class by having CTA (Chicago Transit Authority) commuter trains skip several large South and West Side stations; and perhaps most damaging, at the campaign's end Bilandic seemed out of control.

On St. Valentine's Day, two weeks before the primary, Bilandic spoke before a huge meeting of precinct captains at the downtown Bismarck Hotel. Under Daley, these traditional lunch gatherings were used both to fuel the organization's troops and to discourage the mayor's foes. Bilandic's performance on this occasion was described as bizarre and zany. Under a huge banner that read, "Keep Chicago Strong," the mayor for a time rattled off his accomplishments, then suddenly shifted gears and began answering critics of his snow-removal policy and mayoral performance. He compared the recent criticism of his administration to the crucifixion of Christ, the Nazi's persecution of the Jews, and the decline of democracy around the world. He concluded his rambling speech with a final astounding outburst: "In the early history of Christianity, you see a leader starting with twelve disciples. They crucified the leader and made martyrs of the others. It is our turn to be in the trenches and see if we are made of the same stuff as the early Christians, the persecuted Jews, the proud Poles, the Blacks and Latinos." [14]

Some in the audience listening to Bilandic giggled at his comments. Most were embarrassed. Few knew that the pressure of the campaign was not the only factor taking a toll on the mayor. A day before the meeting, Bilandic's elderly mother was rushed to the hospital; her death seemed imminent. His mother's illness, the unceasing criticism from the media, and the two-month battle against the unmeltable snow pushed Bilandic into reacting emotionally to his opponents.

Lost in the campaign's closing days was any mention of Bilandic's political strengths and election advantages. First, he had received strong newspaper endorsements from the Chicago *Tribune* and the Chicago *Sun-Times*. Both papers applauded the mayor's record and praised his efforts "to expand the city's economic base." [15] Second, nearly forgotten was the fact that his opponent, Jane Byrne, was an untested former city hall department head who had never held an elective office and whose philosophy and personality were virtually unknown to most Chicagoans. Finally, Bilandic had the Democratic organization; though admittedly it was not in the best condition, it still had not lost a contested mayoral primary since 1911. All of these Bilandic plus factors received scant public attention: the campaign ended as it began, centering on the snow and the mayor's snow-removal policy.

The blizzard of 1979 gave the three dissident voting groups in Chicago the leverage to beat the machine. Byrne won fourteen of the sixteen city's black wards, all seven independent lakefront wards, and several Northwest Side Polish wards. She won a total of twenty-nine city wards, leaving Bilandic the inner city and Southwest Side ethnic wards and a few remaining organization strongholds scattered throughout Chicago.

Bilandic's loss to the city's first woman mayor (for the record, Byrne did have to defeat another hapless Republican, Wallace Johnson, six weeks later to assume office) was a Chicago political revolution. The tradition of Democratic machine invincibility was broken. Four years later, another revolution would take place and a black would lead another successful battle against the once mighty machine.

In 1979, meteorological and political forces combined to oust Michael Bilandic. Chicago was receptive to these forces because it was undergoing dramatic demographic and lifestyle changes. Yet the question was and is still asked, "Could Bilandic have won even with the snow?"

The narrowness of his loss suggests an obvious yes answer to the above question. However, Bilandic's defeat was caused by more than just bad political luck and inclement weather. In retrospect, Bilandic was the wrong choice to carry on the policies of Cermak, Kelly, and Daley. Each of these organization legends reflected the city and the political machine they led. Bilandic did not. Wilson Frost or Cecil Partee (a long-time black organization stalwart and currently Chicago city treasurer) would have been much wiser choices than Bilandic. To be sure, their selection would have altered organization rule, but it would have been an evolutionary change that would have prevented the Byrne and Washington revolutions. Instead, the organization went with Bilandic, a shrewd and decent man, whose lasting legacy in the Chicago political tradition is that he was the last of the card-carrying machine regulars to serve as mayor.

12.

JANE M. BYRNE: TO THINK THE UNTHINKABLE AND DO THE UNDOABLE

Melvin G. Holli

When Jane M. Byrne won the Democratic Party's primary nomination for mayor in February 1979 in a stunning upset over incumbent mayor Michael Bilandic, a power surge of euphoria went through her. "I beat the whole goddamn Machine singlehanded," she uttered in an ecstatic moment.[1] It had been a David-and-Goliath contest pitting a diminutive, five-foot-three-inch, scrappy blonde against the political heavyweights and machine overlords who had not lost such a contest for half a century. The mighty had fallen, and most of Chicago cheered. The general election which followed in April was a cakewalk by comparison, for in one-party Chicago, winning the nomination in February has been tantamount to winning the general election in April. Jane Byrne handily beat her Republican opponent Wallace Johnson with the largest majority in Chicago's mayoral history, an astonishing 82 percent of the vote. Even Richard J. Daley in his peerless triumphs at the polls had never matched that percentage. From all appearances the new mayor had been put into office by a powerful, but evanescent mandate. This study of Jane Byrne is not intended to be a comprehensive story of every event of her four-year mayoral career, but rather a selective effort to separate the substance from the style and to take a hard look at the administration's record and the political meaning of Byrne's mayoralty.

Why the Machine?

Jane Byrne in her campaign caviled endlessly about the evils of machine politics and about the "cabal of evil men" who ran the city. She seemed to promise a new deal in politics and a reshuffling of the structure of power, at least in the city council. Don Rose, a political liberal and her consultant, ran her low budget, high decibel campaign, and he produced more bang for the buck than most of his high-priced rivals.

Martin Oberman, a lakeshore liberal councilman and certified reformer, was showered with flattery by the nominee during the interregnum between the February primary and the April general elections. According to Oberman, Byrne attributed her primary victory partly to the work of reform independents such as Oberman, Dick Simpson, and Bill Singer. Northwestern University Professor Louis Masotti, at Jane Byrne's behest, assembled a topnotch, blue-ribbon panel which authored the "transition report"—a voluminous four-year blueprint for reform and change that promised to do for Chicago what the first five-year plan did for a ramshackle Russia. Seldom had Chicago reformers been so sanguine. Like the spring tulips, hope for reform blossomed forth that April from the cold unyielding soil of twenty-five years of machine domination. It seemed almost too good to be true. On the eve of her election, candidate Jane Byrne paid a visit to independent leader Martin Oberman and congratulated him and a small band of liberals, saying that the people wanted an open, honest system. Oberman busied himself with the delightful prospects of organizing a new reformed committee structure in the council.[2]

Unexpectedly, immediately after her election, the new mayor slowly began to shift into a state of studied and uncharacteristic mayoral inaction. Masotti was treated with benign neglect, and his phone calls went unanswered. He and his committee, all volunteers and *pro bono,* were left to wither on the vine. Even the distilled wisdom of their "transition report" went unread. Mayor Jane's masterful inaction let the machine politicians and the "evil cabal," led by councilmen Edward "Fast Eddie" Vrdolyak and Edward Burke, organize the council committees and select their chairman. Oberman and the reformers had been left out in the cold seemingly without influence. The hopes for political reform died at the starting gate.[3]

Why did Jane Byrne abandon reform at such a critical moment? Many of her detractors later wrote it off as simply another example of her ficklessness, her "battiness," or her biology (it's a woman's prerogative to change her mind). Former mayoral aide Paul McGrath and the late Professor Milton Rakove argued on rational grounds that Mayor Byrne had nowhere else to turn. The reformers lacked the numbers and power to govern the council effectively, and no other public constituency was available in sufficient numbers and with passion enough to follow the mayor and turn the council into a popular assembly goaded to a reform agenda by a raging mob at its doors. The only plausible alternative was the machine regulars led by the "evil cabal." Thus Jane Byrne made a pragmatic compromise with Chicago's political reality. Seeing it somewhat differently, city budget director Donald Haider attributed Byrne's political about-face and her abandonment of her reformist ideas to the progressive deterioration of the city's financial situation. The period of high hopes and reform, according to Haider, lasted until about September 1979. When the financial crisis worsened, Byrne turned to the "evil cabal," the Old Guard, to tap their financial savvy and political potency. As Haider remembered it: "The Vrdolyaks and Burkes and others from the old regime returned. Suddenly the ins were out and the outs were in." About a year after the rapprochement with the machine, Mayor Byrne explained her actions or lack thereof in this manner: "I will have to work with these people. If I don't, nothing will move in the city council."[4]

In a more involved explanation of that turning point, Byrne explained in a 1986 interview that her single-handed toppling of the machine's mayor had sent seismic shock through the entire business-banking-labor nexus of city hall politics. Her aide, Don Rose, had warned her that her victory had threatened long-standing agreements, understandings, and ways of doing business dating to the Daley era. Unpredictability and destabilization are the nemesis of the banking and business world. Apparently, the newly elected mayor met with representatives of the banking community to calm their fears and may have sent similar assurances to Loop business interests and big labor. At this critical juncture, according to Byrne, an unrelated event occurred. Representatives of Richard M. Daley rudely intruded and began pushing Byrne to appoint a rival slate of Daley loyalists into key chairmanships (with the implied understanding that Daley junior was running the show). Evidently annoyed at Daley's cheekiness and aware of the weakness of the Byrne-backed group, she permitted the "evil cabal" to appoint the committees and chairman. Presumably this act symbolized that something less than radical reform was in the wings and that the machine Humpty Dumpty had been put back together again. Stability and predictability had been restored to their time-honored and rightful places in Chicago politics.[5]

When Jane Byrne assumed office in 1979, the second destructive wave of OPEC-driven inflation was lashing at the nation's vitals with 15 to 20 percent interest rates. Cities on the high-risk list had difficulty in selling their bonds, sometimes absorbing massive losses through deep discounts, and some bankers were even looking askance at short-term tax anticipation warrants which all cities needed to tide them over until taxes were paid. The doubling of interest rates meant that a massive transfer of money that formerly might have gone for raises to city workers would now be needed to borrow money from the bank. No or slow growth and the loss of industrial jobs and plants, a rustbelt-wide phenomenon, was felt most acutely at the time and aggravated Chicago's ability to pay its bills.

These were the grim fiscal realities that the vibrant new mayor faced during her first year in office. Unfortunately for Byrne, inflation as an objective measure of the consumer price index and as a built-in and emotional expectation would peak in 1980, calling forth escalating demands from the municipal unions and a time of troubles for the mayor.

In December 1979, Byrne became the first mayor to challenge the demands of the transit union. She entered into negotiations with the city's transit union hoping to pare back the expensive cost of living adjustments, high wage settlements, and overgenerous benefits package which neither the system nor the city could afford any longer. She also hoped to introduce other efficiencies which would moderate future fare increases and direct subsidies which the system regularly absorbed. The union's response was a threat to strike during the peak of the downtown and Loop Christmas shopping season. When Byrne refused to back down and announced a contingency plan which she said would keep the trains and buses running, the union struck. Byrne had no contingency backup plan to keep shoppers and workers moving into the Loop, and the downtown business community protested vehemently, placing fierce pressures on both the administration and the union to settle. The union returned to work. Some observers blamed the mayor and called her a union buster, and her rhetorical behavior lent some credence to that line of reasoning. Yet behind the smoke and fury lay the inescapable fact that Chicago simply could not afford the handshake giveaways to labor of former days.[6]

A second labor problem followed in January 1980 when the teachers' union went out on strike to recapture the jobs it had bargained away in the fall 1979 school talks. The school crisis which emerged in November 1979 had revealed that the board of education had illegally invaded capital funds to meet operating expenses and was nearing the end of its illicit resources. An audit showed that the board had misspent $47 million in school bond proceeds. The cumulative education deficit at the end of 1979 was $101 million. Moody's bond rating service dropped the Chicago schools from Municipal Investment Grade 2 to an unmarketable MIG 4, and the First National would no longer buy its bonds. School superintendent Joseph Hannon resigned in the middle of the revelations.

The city, with its own newly discovered deficit of $102 million, was drowning in its own red ink and was in no position to rescue the schools with a straight bailout. An agreement had to be worked out with the city putting in $50 million and the state putting in $50 million to meet the January payrolls and back pay for the teachers. The city then committed itself to interim financing until a new School Finance Authority—set up by the state and with powers over the budget—could straighten out the mess and sell $500 million in new bond issues. The board and the union also agreed to trim $60 million, to eliminate more than a thousand jobs from the budget, and to grant the Finance Authority veto power over the budget. In January, the teachers' union reneged on the spending cuts and job trimming and struck for two weeks, forcing the board to accept higher costs and to cut the losses out of the succeeding year's budget. Mayor Byrne took a large role in the final settlement; although it diminished the city's autonomy over its school and the mayor's influence over education matters, it did rescue the system from near-bankruptcy. And without the mayor's backing, the bailout could not have been achieved.[7]

The administration was on a strike-a-month schedule. A few weeks later on 14 February, Chicago firefighters went out on strike in what became an incredibly messy and nasty affair. The firemen, who had been promised union contracts by candidate Byrne, struck to force the issue. Since taking the oath of office, Mayor Byrne had apparently changed her mind on the issue of union contracts for public employees, but had never said so publicly. The editor of the Chicago *Tribune* upbraided her for this apparent duplicity and told her to come clean. The firefighters had chosen the dead of winter and the peak of the heating season when citizens are most likely to need fire protection. The union also brought in an "outside agitator" to lay out strategy and to call the tactics for the local union chief, who took a consistently belligerent, bellicose, and public-be-damned attitude on the nightly television news. The firemen won surprisingly little sympathy from the public for they were hardly charity cases, earning $21,000 for a 91-day year of 24-hour shifts. Many held second jobs, managed small businesses, and doubled their city income. Aggravating the issue in what appeared to be a bargaining ploy to make the union back down, the mayor promised as she had in the transit strike, that the firehalls would be fully staffed and fire protection would be available as usual in the city. Meanwhile nasty exchanges continued for several days between the mayor and the union. Some city hall aides openly suggested that some striking firemen were actually sabotaging fire protection and perhaps even engaging in arson. By the end of the winter, public opinion switched massively against the firefighters and over to the mayor, forcing the firemen to capitulate and return to work, but without a face-saving contract. The strike had taken a heavy toll on the close relationship that had long existed between the firemen and city hall.[8]

Although Byrne had beaten one of the toughest municipal unions in the city, she both then and later lamented that the strike was one of her biggest errors. Even though the mayor later agreed to a contract, the strike caused an irreparable tear in the municipal service fabric and would cost her future political support in one of the city's more politically active service units. Byrne later called it a "perceptual error," saying that she had intended to grant them a union contract all along.[9] It is difficult to follow the evidence trail of this incident and concur with that view. Jane Byrne's postmayoral remarks seem to be an effort to put the best face possible on the strike.

Yet in the long run her three major public employee strikes may have been necessary and possibly even unavoidable. The urban gravy train which had richly rewarded public employees such as transit workers and skilled craftsmen in the inflation ridden 1960s and 1970s had come to a halt in the austere, cash-short, and deflation-prone 1980s. Unions accustomed to riding the inflation escalator upward were not prepared psychologically and emotionally to adjust to the tax-conscious fiscal crunch of the 1980s. To her credit Jane Byrne faced this new reality. With few prospects for new transit money or to pay firefighters, she took two strikes. A third strike by the Chicago teachers' union, although a governmental unit less directly under her control was resolved only through her bargaining powers with the state government. To her discredit, Byrne handled all three strikes—transit, teachers, and firemen—in what to the public seemed to be a vacillating, then vindictive, and sometimes mean and small-minded manner. In all three affairs newsmen and the unions unflatteringly referred to her as "Attila the Hen" or "Calamity Jane" and a person who "shot from the lip." Her bombastic rhetoric and her oversell on preparedness to take on the strikes, tarnished and diminished somewhat the magnitude of her victory over the firefighters union.

In a larger sense and behind the smokescreen of rhetoric and verbal pyrotechnics, Byrne had shown a sense of fiscal responsibility in facing down powerful municipal unions and interest groups that no previous administration in modern times in Chicago had dared take on. Thereafter municipal unions and employee groups became more attentive to the burdens that their demands placed on taxpayers and more amenable to compromises, such as the transit workers agreements to slim down their fat cost-of-living adjustments and permit parttime drivers and other efficiencies. Politically Mayor Byrne had embarked on a high risk strategy in taking on three powerful employee groups and lost political support in all three. Whether the tradeoff of support in the public opinion polls was worth the loss of these interest groups would remain to be seen.

Budget and Fiscal Matters

On the fiscal front the mayor showed herself equally ready to bloody her lance. Fiscal policy is ultimately the lifeblood of any administration. Those dull numbers, that blizzard of figures that festoon the account books and ledgers, may numb the mind and glaze over the vision and certainly do lack political sex appeal. Yet ultimately they have the awesome power to topple the most popular mayoral regimes, as the political demise of New York City's John Lindsay so aptly illustrates, or to evoke huzzahs of praise as did Mayor Richard Daley's solid management in the mid-1970s when urban bankruptcies were threatening other big cities.

Candidate Byrne, during the twilight of Michael Bilandic's caretaker term (1976–79) and during her campaign for the Democratic nomination for mayor had been hinting that "hidden deficits," creative bookkeeping, and other irregularities were damaging the city's fiscal health. On 16 April 1979, only a few days after she took office, the city comptroller notified her that the city would have a cash storage of $64 million by the end of May. Instead of calling the chairman of the First National Bank of Chicago and the president of the Continental Illinois Bank, which had been standard operating procedure in the past, and quietly arranging to rollover the debt with another loan, Mayor Byrne called a press conference and blasted her spendthrift predecessors, and then went to the banks for loans.

Byrne brought in as budget director Donald H. Haider, a Northwestern University professor, who had spent the previous year monitoring the finances of near-bankrupt New York City and Cleveland. Haider was to work out a plan to liquidate whatever deficits a probing audit would reveal. An examination of the city's books uncovered a deficit of $102 million and the fact that previous administrations had dipped into specially marked state and federal funds and "trust and agency accounts" earmarked for special uses, such as neighborhood development, and had used such funds to pay ordinary city expenses. Mayors Daley and Bilandic had delayed payments to vendors, and as early as 1972 Daley began to use the trust and agency accounts as an "all purpose emergency fund," as well as using capital funds, such as bond proceeds, to meet ordinary expenses. Bilandic continued these practices and Chicago's peculiar bookkeeping methods kept the deficits from being noticed. Chicago meanwhile had a high bond rating.[10]

Mayor Byrne publicly damned the "political cowardice" of past administrations and vowed that as long as she was mayor, the city would not waste the "public money like a profligate welfare queen." She blistered her predecessors, charging that "good politics and good economics were at war in City Hall" and that the "city that worked was working largely—and surreptitiously—on next year's money, juggled books, and taxes on the next generation." These revelations caused Chicago's bond ratings to drop twice. Byrne put in an austerity budget for 1980 with a mere 1 percent spending increase, eliminated 1,500 jobs in city hall, raised taxes by $150 million, restructured $180 million in short-term debt, and vowed to run a tight ship and exert an iron grip on the city's purse strings. Meanwhile a falling out between the mayor and her budget director caused Donald Haider to quit, and the mayor brutalized him, publicly blaming him for an error that raised an extra $29 million in taxes. Byrne and her new budget director decided to keep the extra $29 million which persuaded Moody's bond rating service then to raise Chicago's rating. The higher ratings not only helped the city through its cash crises, but also enabled the School Finance Authority to now sell its bonds as well. Former budget director Donald Haider later claimed that Mayor Byrne had overdramatized the original crisis, that the actual inherited deficit was not more than $50 million, and furthermore that it could have been handled with less fanfare through some internal economies and modest tax increases.[11]

Whatever the case may be, Mayor Byrne did follow through with her promised fiscal responsibility and balanced the budget not only for 1980, but also for 1981, 1982, and finished up in 1983 with a small deficit (or surplus, depending on how one interprets the numbers.) Mayor Byrne's 1983 budget, although initiated by her, would be carried out by Harold Washington who assumed office in April of that year. Washington, in his campaign, in what now has become standard political rhetoric, lashed out at Byrne for reckless spending, giving away the store, and handing him a debt-ridden city with deficits that Washington feared would range into the high millions. The later budget figures showed only a $15 million deficit for 1983. And according to Byrne advisors, if Washington would have followed through on the city sale of cable franchises and parking garages as intended in the 1983 budget, there would have been a surplus of about $12 million.

Achievements

The measure of accomplishment for any mayoral administration is somewhat difficult to gauge, partly because no administration is completed within its formal office holding period and partly because of hostile successor administration. Since Jane Byrne's reign (1979–83) was an administration of motion and movement, perhaps her record should be looked at in motion or as it unfolded. At the end of her first year in 1980, when the honeymoon period had just drawn to a close, some observers perceived solid achievements. A Chicago *Tribune* review in June 1980, although deploring Byrne's "revolving door" policy of much hiring and firing of top staff, nonetheless cited as her "record of achievement": (1) trying to balance the budget, (2) increasing minority representation in government, (3) cracking down on worker inefficiency, and (4) making her administration more accountable to the public. The mayor had fired or laid off hundreds of employees (mostly from streets and sanitation) where, according to the "transition team" report, "bloated" street cleaning and pothole-patching crews operated without effective supervision. "Other reform areas," according to this first year report card included: changing the school board membership and giving minority representatives a majority voice, shaking up the Chicago Transit Authority leadership and appointing black Eugene Barnes as chairman, consolidating various categories of building inspectors, reorganizing the department of health with a new commissioner, an Hispanic, Dr. Hugo Muriel, and expanding special entertainment events including Chicagofest. The assessment concluded with "for better or worse, Mrs. Byrne has been more available to the media and the public than her predecessors."[13]

Jane Byrne's second year report card issued at the midpoint of her mayoralty was considerably less glowing. According to *Tribune* writer Robert Davis, friends and foes alternately described her administration as "creative, chaotic, dramatic, devastating, exciting, excrutiating . . . historic," although some claimed it was "hysteric." Mayor Byrne listed as her main accomplishments the restoration of financial and fiscal integrity to the city government. Her school rescue package, new taxes, and straightening of city bookkeeping had rescued the city's slumping bond ratings. She had also raised some $300 million in new taxes and fees and helped bring to the Chicago budget "user fee" real-ism. The mayor also pointed to her first year and the continuing austerity program that lopped off hundreds of superfluous workers from the city payroll. She announced, in 1981, plans to professionalize the upper levels of the bureaucracy by raising salaries to entice quality administrators, new initiatives for her "North Loop project," a massive O'Hare International Airport renovation and building program, and a new entertainment-business complex at Navy Pier. In closing, Davis lamented in his article that with few exceptions her "own staff of advisors is undistinguished at best and woefully inadequate at worst." Furthermore her substantive projects had been obscured by her "image as a mind-changing, impulse-directed chief administrator." Nevertheless the turmoil in the mayor's office had been much less in the preceeding few months and, as Davis saw it, "city government has quieted down." [14]

On the political side many negatives had accumulated. As *Tribune* reporter David Axelrod saw it, the administration was plagued with "errors in style— imprudent remarks and reversals, ill-conceived appointments, open battling within the administration, and heavy-handed attempts to derail her opponents or punish the news media." These had "obscured the mayor's substantive accomplishments." In 1979 she won kudos for appointing a majority black and minority school board and in 1980 incurred the wrath of the black community for dumping two blacks in favor of two white opponents of busing. Byrne's former campaign aide, Don Rose averred: "It's absolutely amazing how she managed in such a short time to antagonize both the black and whites." "There's just no way around the fact that the first two years have been a political disaster," added Rose who had masterminded her election. [15]

Part of the "battiness" and three-ring circus atmosphere derived from first husband Jay McMullen whom the press referred to as the "Rasputin in a turtleneck" and who needlessly inflamed relations with the press. He once banished a *Tribune* representative from the city press room and threatened a group of reporters that he would "bloody their noses." He referred to unfavorable coverage of his wife's administration as "more skunk juice from the Chicago *Tribune*." [16]

Moving on to Mayor Byrne's last year in office, 1983, Harry Golden of the *Sun-Times* summed up her record as a grand mix of public works, executive shakeups, civic celebrations, spats with the press, and some solid achievements. She started a $1 billion expansion project at O'Hare Airport, completed a new rapid transit system to the airport, positioned the city to consider bids for a new hotel-office complex in the North Loop, worked a redevelopment project for Navy Pier into the planning stages, was repairing the city's infrastructure of sewers and water mains at 15 to 20 miles per year, laid out plans for a new Southwest Side rapid transit system, reorganized the school board and set its finances on a firmer footing, installed a new personnel code that ended "temporary employment" of patronage works in civil service but exempted some 10,500 less skilled jobs from merit tests, reorganized the Chicago Housing Authority, took steps to convert Goldblatt's deserted downtown department store into a new public library, raised city revenues of some $400 million in new taxes and fees annually; rolled back real estate taxes by $30 million and turned in a balanced budget for each year of her administration (with the possible exception of 1983). To that list might be added a projected World's Fair for 1992.[17]

Political Socialization

Yet Jane Byrne's achievements were all but blurred and nearly erased by her peculiar mayoral style. Part of the answer to the enigma of Jane Byrne's mayoral career is to be found in her ability to think the unthinkable and to do the undoable. To understand this ability takes us to an odyssey of her political socialization. She was not the daughter of a working-class stiff or an aspiring precinct captain from the bungalow belt, but a debutante from a wealthy lace-curtain family from the Far Northwest Side. Unlike those who have carefully picked their way through the local political minefields, cajoled and dodged irate voters for years, spent most of their political lives as supplicants to some ward lord or boss, Jane Byrne had come through St. Scholastica, Barat College, J. F. Kennedy's football box at the Army Navy game,[18] and within less time than the normal politician takes to make it from ward heeler to precinct captain, landed an administrative appointment in the Daley family and a cochairmanship of the Cook County Democratic Committee. Starting more than two-thirds of the way up may not be as comforting as starting at the top, but it spares one those years of ankle busting, doorbell ringing, attending endless ward parties and minor events, and shelling out a goodly portion of a small pay each year to support your patron. It also spares the soul from that demeaning grovelling that political underlings put up with for most of their young working lives—unrecognized, unsung heroes whose most heroic acts are getting aging widows and disgruntled housewives to vote. None of the hurts, admonishments, and limitations that the lowly live through and which ultimately shape their adult character into what has become the quintessential Chicago politician—cautious, deferential to his political and economic betters (at least on the surface)—none of that long conditioning, soul-searing discipline, and humiliation was part of Jane Byrne's heritage. Jane Byrne did not fit the mold. She had sprung, as it were, in full political armament from the brow of Zeus (read Daley). She even looked different. She was physically small and shapely and had "gorgeous legs" (according to Jay McMullen), whereas most Chicago politicians looked like overstuffed armchairs or furniture movers.

Jane Byrne was *sui generis* in Chicago's recent mayoral history. She had no parallel in the half century following the Democratic machine's accession to power with Anton Cermak in 1933. Jane Byrne was *sui generis* because she could think the unthinkable (gambling casinos and world-class stock-car racing in the streets or rescuing an abandoned department store for a public library) and do the undoable (moving into crime-infested Cabrini-Green or taking on the toughest municipal unions such as the firefighters to restore fiscal soundness.[19] She had not been subjected to the socializing of regular Chicago Democratic politicians. Unorthodox and not brought up with the table manners and courting rituals of Democratic machine politics, she was refreshingly free not only of its restraints and its decorum, but also of its limitations. She was in some ways a political free spirit, a burning ember waiting to alight on the dry prairie grass, a stormy Robespierre ready to chop off heads, encouraged by her husband Jay McMullen.

In the end she obscured many of her achievements by giving way to that powerful impulse that Chicago politics ultimately is at its heart—street theater. Sometimes farce, sometimes high drama, and occasionally mere comic opera, Jane Byrne lightened the civic mood. She clearly had the best act in town. Few politicians in Chicago's history could match Byrne for her zaniness, madcap, and daring acts that were to mar the solid and substantive acts of her administration. Unfortunately for her, too many Chicagoans mistook her style for her substance.

13.

HAROLD WASHINGTON: THE ENIGMA OF THE BLACK POLITICAL TRADITION

William J. Grimshaw

Mayor Harold Washington is described in a biographical sketch by Robert McClory as "a remarkable man of paradoxes and enigmas."[1] McClory, a former reporter for the Chicago *Defender*, the principal black newspaper, certainly knows his way around black political circles; but he admits that Washington baffles him. Says McClory: "At times he seems as wise as a serpent and at others as simple as a dove."[2] I will argue that the paradoxical imagery of the serpent and the dove provides illuminating insight into the enigmatic Harold Washington and the equally perplexing black political tradition.

Since the Chicago Democratic machine's inception over a half century ago, blacks have been torn between a cultural antipathy to the machine's style of politics and a devastating array of social and economic circumstances which drive blacks into supporting the machine. The paradox is not well understood by students of Chicago's politics because no other ethnic group in the city's modern history has experienced the conflict to the extent blacks have. To speak of the black political tradition, then, is to speak of a unique political tradition in the city's recent history. It is a complex tradition to comprehend because it is at odds with itself; cultural values pull blacks in one direction while social and economic needs push them in an opposing direction. The tradition also is difficult to understand because it is so at odds with the political machine tradition which has so thoroughly dominated Chicago's politics until just recently.

Harold Washington personifies the torn black political tradition. His roots are deeply embedded in an intensely personal way in the torn tradition. Washington's own father, Roy, for many years had to manage the paradoxical roles of serving his community as a Protestant minister while serving the Democratic machine as one of its ward leaders, combining, as it were, the roles of the serpent and the dove.

The personal heritage is profoundly important because the bond between Washington and his father was extraordinarily warm and firm. The mayor had a relationship with his father that many fathers dream of but few achieve. He has described his father as his "one and only hero in life," as "a real man, a good man," and "my role model."[3] Thus, the path Washington has followed in his political career is essentially the footsteps his father laid down years ago in the Third Ward: to be a good man while working in the serpentine world of Chicago's politics.

At the cultural core of the torn black political tradition is the elemental fact that black politics is deeply rooted in the teachings of the church. During a long and arduous history of economic, social, and political segregation and discrimination, the one critical institution to which blacks had access was the church. The church was the sanctuary; it nurtured, and it instructed. The instruction included an extraordinary set of premises for political action. An elementary aspect of the creed is that action ought to be based on principle. Another basic aspect is the belief in universal brotherhood. These principles stand in the sharpest opposition to the machine tradition of politics. The machine tradition dictates that action ought to be taken on the basis of expediency. This requires a calculation of self-interest and consequences, instead of adherence to principle and leaving the outcome in ethereal hands. The machine is no less fundamentally committed to inequality. Those who support the machine are rewarded, while those who oppose it are punished.

It is a simple matter to see how the black community's social isolation and poverty figure in the machine's success. Machine politics has been described as a "system of organized bribery,"[4] an exchange of benefits for votes, and in communities of high need and low resources, the machine finds the largest number of takers. Yet for blacks, schooled politically by the church, machine politics presents a dilemma; cultural antipathy wrestles with economic necessity for control.

A compelling case can be made for the torn black political tradition by examining black political behavior over the past fifty years, beginning with the creation of the machine in 1931 and culminating in Mayor Washington's election in 1983. The evidence will be presented in terms of four distinctive stages of black political behavior.

Stage one is entitled Transformation and Contradiction, which encompasses the first twenty years of the political machine's hegemony, from 1931 through 1954. The second stage is called Exodus and Domination; it runs from 1955 through 1965, spanning the first decade of Daley's mayoralty. Stage three covers the second decade of Daley's reign and the succeeding mayoralties of Michael Bilandic and Jane Byrne; this stage runs from 1966 through 1982 and is entitled Disillusion and Revolt. The final stage, Victory and Resolution, covers the Washington mayoralty.

Some commentary on Harold Washington's progression and development as a politician will be woven into the four sections of the analysis. The objective is to identify certain critical junctures which have served to shape Washington's character and political career.

Two basic conclusions emerge from the analysis. First, the torn black political tradition has existed since the Democratic machine's inception, and while the shape of the paradox changed over the years, the content remained unchanged until the 1983 mayoral election. Thus, Washington's election represents a watershed in the black political tradition. It resolved the paradoxical character of black political behavior. For the first time, blacks stood in unified opposition to the political machine. The compelling question, of course, is whether the novel resolution can hold. In the balance swings the black political tradition: the new against the old.

Transformation and Contradiction

The conventional interpretation of why low-income voters readily support political machines rests upon a rational economic theory of motivation.[5] Because of their high degree of material need and social disorganization, the poor willingly give their votes to the machine in exchange for a combination of material and affectual benefits. This is the well-known favors-for-votes explanation which is said to account for the machine's high level of success in poor communities.

The ascendancy of the Democratic party during the Great Depression offers a valuable test of the conventional interpretation. President Franklin Roosevelt's Democratic New Deal established the modern welfare state, and it took the Republican party twenty years to regain the presidency. In Chicago, the Democratic machine rode Roosevelt's long coattails to victory and thoroughly eliminated the Republican party as a factor in the city's politics. Accordingly, we would expect to find a prompt and substantial shift of black voters in Chicago to the ascendant Democratic party.

Initially, the predicted shift occurred. After nearly a decade of Democratic dominance, Chicago's black wards cast 57 percent of their ballots for Democratic Mayor Edward Kelly in 1939, and President Roosevelt secured 53 percent of the black vote in 1940.[6] This constitutes a decisive shift inasmuch as Chicago's black voters had been overwhelmingly favorable to the Republican party just a decade earlier.

At this point, however, a wholly unanticipated development occurred. The black Democratic tide continued to rise at the national level. But at the local level, black support for the Democratic machine began to recede.

Mayor Kelly's black vote fell from 57 to 53 percent in 1943. His successor, the reform-minded Martin Kennelly, who received the largest popular vote of any mayoral candidate in the city's history, barely survived in the black wards. In both 1947 and 1951, Kennelly's black vote amounted to less than 51 percent. No less remarkable, the Republicans regained control over one of the two black wards. In 1943 the aged and once all-powerful Oscar DePriest was elected alderman of the Third Ward, and he was succeeded by Archibald Carey, a reform-oriented minister, who held the post for the Republicans until the great Democratic landslide of 1955 swept him under. Thus, even though the Democratic machine had thoroughly controlled the city's politics for two decades, the black vote was still altogether up for grabs.

What makes the situation even more perplexing is that at the national level the black Democratic vote continued to soar. Roosevelt's black vote reached 64 percent in 1944, and his successors did even better. Harry Truman picked up just over 70 percent of the vote in Chicago's black wards in 1948, and Adlai Stevenson raised the black Democratic margin to a record 75 percent four years later. Thus, Chicago's black voters were drawing a compelling distinction between the national Democratic party's New Deal and what many black voters perceived as the local Democratic machine's "raw deal."

Figure 1 capsulizes the black Democratic transformation and indicates the

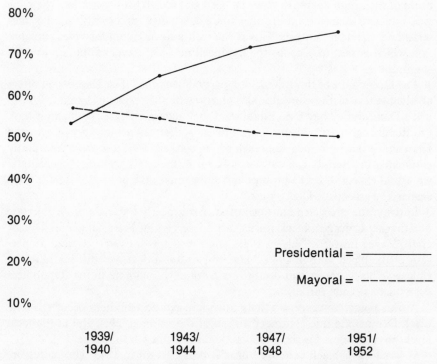

Figure 1. Black Democratic voting in presidential and mayoral elections, Chicago, 1939–1952

magnitude of the contradiction between national and local voting in the black wards during this period.

The massive electoral contradiction represents a strong piece of evidence for the existence of a torn black political tradition. Despite the Democratic machine's clear dominance and the black community's dire poverty, a substantial and rising proportion of the black electorate was unwilling to support the machine. There was a powerful countervailing force afoot in the black wards, which was sufficiently strong to overcome the Democratic machine's material inducements.

The core of the countervailing force is the cultural antipathy to the machine's style of politics.[7] The cultural antipathy was reinforced by the machine's racism. The machine honored the minor political quid pro quo in dealing with black voters, exchanging small favors for votes. But the machine did very little to ameliorate the racial segregation and discrimination which devastated the black community. Quite the contrary. The machine played a leading role in confining blacks to a second-class level of citizenship.

Ironically, the key to understanding the black rejection of the machine during this period is the machine's commitment to segregated housing. Over 70 percent of the black population was confined to a small, narrow, black belt, a patently illegal situation that nevertheless was enforced by the machine-controlled local courts.[8] The confinement created a community unlike any other in the city because it required the middle class to live among the poor, and this gave the generally poor black wards a decisive political advantage over their low-income white counterparts.

The unique social composition and structure of the black wards produced the unique political behavior. The middle class, being less dependent upon the machine's material inducements, was able to provide the poor with alternative political goals and leadership, and it possessed the wherewithal to construct organizations to counter the machine's ward organizations. Thus, the black wards, critically leavened by a politically active middle class, fought the powerful Democratic machine to a standoff.

Washington's Political Baptism

Harold Washington's first major campaign was not his own, but his father Roy's Third Ward aldermanic campaign in 1947.[9] Even by Chicago standards, it was an extraordinary political baptism for the twenty-five-year-old son. The campaign was befouled by layers of duplicity, eerily presaging Washington's mayoral campaign against Bernard Epton years later.

Roy Washington secured the nomination of the Third Ward Democratic organization; but the committeeman, Edward "Mike" Sneed, double-crossed Washington by quietly throwing the support of his forces to the Republican candidate, Archibald Carey, Jr. Sneed feared that if Washington won, he would use the aldermanic post as a launching pad to challenge Sneed for committeeman. Sneed's treachery paid off. Although Washington came in first, he lacked a majority of votes, and in a runoff election, he lost by just over two thousand votes to Carey.

In the following year, however, the tables were turned on Sneed. The committeemen were up for reelection, and Sneed was dumped. To begin with, his effectiveness was deplorable. He had twice failed to elect a Democratic alderman, and he committed the cardinal sin of failing to carry the machine's mayoral candidate in 1947, Martin Kennelly. The rumor of his double-dealing in the Washington election had also become widespread, making Sneed an acute embarrassment. Thus, while Sneed had won the aldermanic battle, he wound up losing the committeeman's war.

Washington was the reported frontrunner for the committeeman post; but the long arms of "Boss" Bill Dawson, committeeman of the neighboring Second Ward, reached into the Third Ward and grabbed the post. Dawson's chief aide, Christopher Wimbish, was slated. Dawson had gone before the slatemakers to argue that with the deep rift between the Sneed and Washington forces, an outside party was needed to restore order, and the slatemakers went along with his suggestion that Wimbish was the man for the job.

As it happened, Dawson had actually helped set Sneed up. Sneed had gone to Dawson for help in his aldermanic battle against Washington, and Dawson had discreetly sent over some of his best precinct captains to work for Carey.[10] The "policy wheels" tied to Dawson also assisted Sneed. Their wealth and array of "runners" (bet collectors) made them a potent campaign force. Needless to say, Dawson did not divulge his role in the conspiracy when he asked the slatemakers to dump Sneed and put in Wimbish.

With Wimbish in, Dawson became the de facto boss of two of the three black wards. At least, that was Dawson's intention; but Wimbish had other plans. He wanted to go into business for himself, dealing directly with the downtown bosses, instead of taking his orders from Dawson. The two conspirators promptly fell out, setting the Third Ward up for four more years of turmoil.

During the 1951 mayoral and aldermanic elections, Dawson once again crossed the political aisle, discreetly aiding Carey and Mayor Kennelly's Republican challenger, and Wimbish's Third Ward organization lost both elections. The turmoil and twin defeats set Wimbish up for the same fate Sneed had suffered four years earlier; he was dumped as committeeman.

This time a new figure on the scene designated the Third Ward committeeman. Carefully staging his run for party chairman, Richard Daley selected a political novice for the Third Ward post, Ralph Metcalfe.[11] Daley anticipated that Metcalfe would return the favor by backing him for chairman. Within the space of a few years, all of the black committeemen began dealing directly with

Daley, which left Dawson as little more than the ceremonial leader of the black wards.

The internecine warfare and duplicity had a profound impact on the young Harold Washington. Despite the ambiguity and treachery, the bottom line was easy to read. What the machine gave, it could just as easily take away, and the only way to combat it was to become a force in the community. Thus, while Washington worked hard within the machine, he also worked hard to develop ties outside the organization, with labor, church, and community groups. As it turned out, the hard-won knowledge and his high standing in the community saved him on more than one occasion when the machine sought to contain and destroy him.

Exodus and Domination

The 1955 mayoral election produced a critical political realignment in Chicago's black wards. Running in his first mayoral campaign, Richard Daley secured an unprecedented 72 percent of the vote in the black wards. Thus, the election finally resolved the massive electoral contradiction that had come to characterize black voting behavior. Under Daley, the black wards became so firmly Democratic that they displaced the poor white ethnic wards, which had carried the machine to success since its inception, as the machine's principal electoral stronghold. It would be wrong to assume, however, that the strong black Democratic shift was produced by either the machine's material resources or Daley's popularity. To borrow a distinction from Shakespeare, the machine did not achieve victory in the black wards so much as it had victory thrust upon it by two critical developments.

The first development was produced by the U.S. Supreme Court. In 1948 it overturned the racially restrictive housing covenants that had been used to confine black residents within a small and densely populated black belt. The decision opened a floodgate through which thousands of housing-hungry blacks poured. Within just two years the black belt, which had contained over 70 percent of the city's black population for decades, held less than half the population, and by 1960 the figure fell to 20 percent.[12] Yet it was not the exodus as such that produced the black political realignment. The realignment resulted from the class differentiation that was produced by the exodus. The vast proportion of those who fled the black belt were the economically able, the ones who could afford to take advantage of the new housing opportunities.[13] Thus, the poor remained in the black belt, and bereft of their middle-class political mentors, they quickly succumbed to the machine's material blandishments.

A second development augmented the political impact of the exodus and ensuing class differentiation. The volatile issue of race was injected into the 1955 mayoral campaign. The issue was used by Mayor Kennelly in an effort to de-

velop a white backlash against Daley's candidacy. The racist ploy boomer-
anged, however. Not much of a backlash developed. But black opposition to
the machine collapsed, losing its sense of purpose and legitimacy in the community through guilt-by-assocation with the racist forces. Consequently, Daley
became the prime beneficiary of Kennelly's strategy.

After he was dumped by the machine, Kennelly realized that he needed a
potent issue if he was going to successfully combat the machine's strong organizational edge; given his predilections, he seized the race issue. Kennelly
charged that the notorious black ward boss Congressman William Dawson had
been the chief architect of his dumping. He linked this charge to a characterization of Daley as a well-meaning but weak and naive fellow. Thus, Daley
would be a puppet mayor and Dawson and the other venal ward bosses would
be the ones jerking his strings.

Needless to say, the charge was electrifying, and the media, strongly committed to the reform-minded Kennelly, gave Kennelly's accusations extensive
coverage. The newspapers competed with each other to see which one could
produce the most sensational descriptions of the unsavory puppeteers, and
Dawson received the most prominent coverage. Shortly after the dumping, the
Chicago *Sun-Times*, in an editorial entitled "Policy, Narcotics, and Mayoral
Politics," had this to say:

> While Dawson did not singlehandedly execute the coup, there is no doubt
> that he wielded more influence than any other one man in the organization's
> decision to deny Kennelly the Democratic machine's support in the Febru-
> ary 22 mayoral primary. Dawson has long been a force for evil within the
> local Democratic organization. He is a political overlord of a district where
> policy rackets and narcotics peddling flourish as they do nowhere else in
> the city.[14]

The chief weakness of Kennelly's strategy was that the black media, notably
the Chicago *Defender*, which was heavily committed to the Democratic cause,
used the attack on Dawson to rally the black community around Dawson and
the Democratic machine. In a long and passionate front-page editorial, the *Defender* defended Dawson, called Mayor Kennelly a racist, and made Kennelly's
rejection a civic obligation.

> The tactics being used by Mayor Martin H. Kennelly to win the Democratic
> nomination for mayor are both dirty and dangerous. He charges that Rep.
> William L. Dawson, a Negro and a powerful Congressman, is primarily
> responsible for the fact that he has been dumped by the Democratic Party.
> Moreover, the Kennelly forces and the daily newspapers have found Con-
> gressman Dawson "guilty" of many crimes without benefit of any court of
> law. Congressman Dawson has not been indicted nor convicted for any crime
> by any judicial body. Kennelly's strategy is clearly designed to arouse the in-

dignation of whites against a powerful Negro leader and influence them to vote their prejudices rather than their well-founded convictions. After eight years as mayor with the entire police force at his command, Kennelly has suddenly discovered the policy racket. His own police department will tell him that this racket is owned and operated by the same syndicate gangsters who have been assassinating citizens on Chicago streets ever since the rise of Al Capone. Congressman Dawson does not now nor ever has had the power to prevent Mayor Kennelly from wiping out policy. The basic issue is not policy—it is politics. The majority of Negro voters are the same as voters in other wards: hardworking, law abiding citizens who want a clean, decent city, and who want, above all, to avoid racial bitterness. Hitler rose to power in Germany by accusing high-placed Jews of treason and whipping up anti-Semitism. Race-baiting in our own country has won victories in such states as Georgia and Mississippi. By building up a powerful Negro Congressman as a symbol of hatred, the Kennelly forces can exploit racial prejudice for all it is worth, while at the same time pretending to be crusading against corruption. This is a greater crime than any attributed to Dawson. It is the responsibility of all decent citizens of both races to make certain that race-baiting will produce no victories in Chicago.[15]

It is not difficult to imagine that with material such as this to distribute, the black Democratic ward organizations became the *Defender's* best delivery boys. The message the black machine precinct captains conveyed was simple and potent: Reject Racism, Dump Kennelly. The black antimachine forces, which had always relied on moral suasion to move voters against the machine, had the tables turned on them. The 1955 mayoral campaign turned politics in the black wards into a one-party affair. Table 4 indicates how radically the middle-class exodus and the race issue affected the performance of the three black-belt wards.

While the Daley machine was establishing its dominance in the old black-belt wards, it also was leaving nothing to chance in the new black areas. The new territory was carefully gerrymandered in order to minimize the political impact of the black middle class. Thus, while the city's black population stood

TABLE 4

Democratic Pluralities in the Black Belt Wards: Mayoral Elections, 1943–1963

Ward	1943	1947	1951	1955	1959	1963
2	1,134	1,325	2,110	13,416	13,733	12,890
3	2,804	− 35	−248	11,860	12,739	18,852
20	——	——	−795	10,459	12,652	15,020
Total	3,938	1,290	1,067	35,735	39,124	46,762

SOURCE: Chicago Board of Election Commissioners

at 23 percent in 1960, only six of the city's fifty wards—12 percent—had black representation in the city council.

The only dark cloud on the Daley machine's horizon did not appear until the end of Daley's first decade in office. In 1963 the six black wards gave Daley the largest black vote he had ever received, and it was instrumental in putting Daley over the top against the Polish Democratic renegade, Benjamin Adamowski. At the same time, however, a seventh black ward, the Seventeenth Ward, elected a black independent alderman, Charles Chew. Running against a white Democratic incumbent, the flamboyant Chew tore into the machine, making its "plantation style" of politics—denying representation to blacks—the centerpiece of his campaign.

Chew's victory marked a critical breakthrough because it represented the first crack in the Daley machine's seemingly invincible armor.[16] The impossible suddenly seemed possible, and black independents across the city drew hope from Chew's win. In the ensuing years, many black independent campaigns were launched against the machine, and several were successful. But at this point a critical distinction must be drawn. Virtually all of the significant black antimachine activity and success came in the new, more affluent black areas. South 63rd Street, which had once marked the southern border of the black belt, now marked the black community's class divide. The torn black political tradition was now torn along the new class divide. To the north of 63rd Street, where the poor resided, the machine prevailed. In the more affluent wards south of 63rd Street, the machine faced increasingly stiff opposition.

Washington's Entry into the Machine

Harold Washington was weaned on politics; but it was an odd style of politics. His allegiance was personal instead of political or organizational. He learned the craft from his father, Roy, by working as his assistant in the precincts in one campaign after another. He worked hard, and he was always around; but he was "Roy's boy" to those who knew him then, not a member of the organization. The organizational bond did not form until after his father's death in 1953. He joined the Third Ward Democratic organization in the fall of 1954, taking over his father's precinct and inheriting his city job in the corporation counsel's office.

Washington not only entered the machine late, he brought an unusual set of credentials with him. He had more practical experience than many of the organization's precinct captains, yet he was also a graduate of Northwestern University's prestigious law school. The Third Ward's newly elected ward committeeman, Ralph Metcalfe, a political novice appointed by Daley, knew just what to do with the unusual recruit. He gave Washington the responsibility for resuscitating the moribund Young Democrats organization.

The Young Democrats was an auxiliary of the Cook County Democratic organization, organized like the machine on a ward and township basis. The Young Democrats represented the high-minded side of the machine. Its principal purpose was to attract young businessmen and professionals into the machine by providing a forum for debating the issues of the times, raising money, and sponsoring various programs and activities. For those who were willing to "dirty their hands," the organization also conducted training sessions on how to work a precinct and win elections. Mayor Daley had asked the black committeemen to reestablish the Young Democrats as a means of containing and coopting the disaffected black middle class.

Washington made the most of the opportunity. He got the jump on the other black ward organizations, and the Third Ward Young Democrats organization was drawing young blacks from across the city and even the suburbs. By 1960 the auxiliary organization had grown twice as large as Metcalfe's parent ward organization, and the Young Democrats was by no means merely a debating society. By the mid-1960s, over half of Metcalfe's precinct captains had come up through the Young Democrats. Thus, when the Third Ward emerged during the 1960s as one of the crack ward organizations in the city—it gave Mayor Daley his largest plurality in the critical 1963 election—a large part of the Third Ward's success was attributable to Washington's efforts.

But Washington wound up reaping a peculiar reward for his success. In 1962 Mayor Daley sent word down to disband the Young Democrats. The civil rights movement was rearing its head, and the cautious Daley, fearful that the high-minded black Young Democrats might become a fifth column within the machine, decided to get rid of the Young Democrats before the movement fire swept north. When Metcalfe gave Washington the word to disband the Young Democrats, Washington straddled the line. Disinclined to draw Metcalfe's wrath, Washington formally withdrew from the organization. But he continued to serve informally as the Young Democrats' advisor, reluctant to give up the strong base he had developed outside the ward organization. The decision paid a handsome dividend. When the Third Ward's state representative, Kenneth Wilson, was elevated to a seat on the Cook County Board in 1963, the leadership of the Young Democrats recommended to Metcalfe that Washington be slated for the state legislative post. Metcalfe responded with alacrity for a couple of reasons. It would be easier to contain and coopt the Young Democrats with Washington in Springfield, and Springfield was a good place for Washington. The state legislature would occupy Washington's time and energy, and for Metcalfe, who had come to view Washington as a potential rival because of his success with the Young Democrats, this was no minor consideration.

Thus, Washington launched his legislative career by straddling the torn black political tradition. He played a major role in establishing the Third Ward Democratic organization as a dominant force in the increasingly lower-income old black belt. Here, as one of the organization's leading precinct captains, Washington became a master at trading on friendship and dispensing favors to secure votes. At the same time, as the principal leader of the Young Democrats, Washington had a solid foot in the black middle-class political camp. Here the issues were not merely favors and jobs, but racial equality, representation, and power. These were the issues on which the machine was willing to concede little ground.

Disillusion and Revolt

A third stage in black political behavior emerged during Mayor Daley's second decade in office. Once again, a critical external event—this time the civil rights movement—coupled with another outbreak of virulent racism at the local level, profoundly changed black political behavior.

The civil rights movement's dramatic moment in Chicago came when Dr. Martin Luther King's forces swept into the city in 1966 seeking open housing. King selected Chicago for his first northern foray because Chicago represented the greatest bastion of racism in the north. Thus, if King could bring Daley to heel, the movement would be established on a national instead of merely a southern regional basis. But Daley thoroughly outfoxed King. The movement depended upon confrontation; Daley artfully dodged King's grasp, offering cooperation instead of antagonism, greeting King by saying "Your goals are our goals."[17] Daley arranged summit conferences, publicly put his good offices at King's disposal, and deplored the violence that dogged King in the white ethnic areas. King seethed—"The people of Mississippi ought to come to Chicago to learn how to hate"[18]—but Daley's dancing trashed the movement's strategy and momentum.

Yet the outcome of the confrontation was not nearly so one-sided as it seemed at the time. King certainly did lose the open-housing battle to Daley. However, the movement won the political war by exposing the Daley machine's intransigent racism to the black community. One of Mayor Daley's aides, Earl Bush, recently summed it up this way: "What Daley did was smother King. What Daley couldn't smother was the civil rights movement."[19]

The movement's political impact turned up on the heels of King's foray into the city. The poor black wards, which had become the machine's electoral stronghold during Daley's first decade as mayor, displayed their first sign of disillusion with the machine in 1967, and the disenchantment grew progressively deeper during the 1970s. The political shift in the poor black wards from dominance by the machine to disillusion with it is indicated in table 5.

While the new disillusionment was festering in the poor black wards, the revolt was proceeding apace south of the 63rd Street class divide in the more affluent black wards. In 1967, two more black independent candidates defeated the machine: "Sammy" Rayner in the Sixth Ward and William Cousins in the Eighth Ward. Then in 1971 the revolt began spilling over the class divide. Anna Langford's independent candidacy was successful in the Sixteenth Ward,

TABLE 5

Dominance and Disillusion in the Poor Black Wards:
Citywide Ranking in Mayoral Elections, 1955–1975

Wards	1955	1959	1963	1967	1971	1975
Near South Side						
2	4	7	5	26	36	30
3	8	10	1	3	23	31
4	16	6	7	18	16	23
6	19	16	10	28	43	35
20	11	11	3	12	31	32
West Side						
24	1	1	2	7	4	25
28	7	23	20	37	40	44
29	6	4	4	6	24	41
Proportion in top ten wards for Daley	63%	63%	88%	38%	13%	none

SOURCE: Chicago Board of Election Commissioners. Ranking is based on the plurality for Daley in each of his six mayoral elections.

a ward straddling the class divide; and the once unthinkable happened in the Second Ward, the legendary "Boss" Dawson's ward. Dawson's organization, in a shambles following his death in 1970, was defeated by an ambitious social worker turned politician, Fred Hubbard.

There was trouble of sorts along the machine's mayoral front as well. Daley was confronted by two liberal independents in the 1975 primary: Alderman William Singer and a black state senator from the Hyde Park area, Richard Newhouse. Daley easily turned back both challenges; but the election revealed that black discontent with the machine had become pervasive. In the fourteen black wards, the combined Singer-Newhouse vote actually exceeded Daley's vote by a small margin. The greatest discontent was, of course, expressed by the more affluent black wards. However, Daley also trailed the combined Singer-Newhouse vote in two of the five poor Near South Side wards and in one of the three West Side wards. The black revolt was clearly running over the political demarcation lines of the social class divide.

The machine's downward spiral in the black community continued following Daley's death in 1976. The intriguing thing about Mayors Michael Bilandic and Jane Byrne is they both appear to have patterned their behavior after the aged and arrogant Daley in decline, instead of using the earlier, wily Daley as their model. Daley's dangerous arrogance was displayed, for example, in his lengthy feud with Congressman Ralph Metcalfe during the 1970s, a confrontation that transformed Metcalfe from a machine hack into an antimachine hero in the black community's eyes. Instead of seeing Daley's action for what it was, petulant personal politics, Bilandic and Byrne seem to have adopted it as their standard for dealing with the black political leadership.

Bilandic's arrogance was revealed shortly after he became mayor. He allowed some of the committeemen to work against Harold Washington's reelection to the state senate. This was widely seen as Washington's punishment for having challenged Bilandic in the 1977 mayoral election. When Bilandic's other challenger, Roman Pucinski, went unpunished, the black community viewed the discrimination as being racially motivated. Once Washington defeated the machine challenge, he emerged as the new champion of the black antimachine movement, and, more important, Washington himself became convinced that he had no future left in the machine. Thus, he stepped out, as Metcalfe never really had, to lead the black assault on the machine.

Bilandic compounded his problem in the black community by designating a notorious black hack, Bennett Stewart, to take the place of the deceased folk hero, Ralph Metcalfe, in Congress. The move drove the antimachine activists into a frenzy, and even some of the normally complacent black committeemen were offended by the decision. Congress was the highest office to which blacks could aspire, and Stewart did not begin to measure up to his predecessors: Oscar DePriest, William Dawson, and Ralph Metcalfe.

Bilandic's final display of insensitivity cost him the mayoralty. His fatal rash step came during the great snow storm that crashed down on his reelection bid. In an effort to speed the flow of traffic into the Loop during the storm, several black train stops along the Dan Ryan El were closed. The black hue and cry that ensued caused Bilandic to rescind the closings; but the damage could not be undone. Jane Byrne rode the crest of the black protest into the mayor's office.

Jane Byrne's mayoralty sated Chicago's gargantuan appetite for political folly as it had not been satisfied since the zany Roaring Twenties regime of "Big Bill" Thompson. Fear drove Byrne from the first days to the bitter end. The ghost of Mayor Daley always hovered around her: could she measure up? The mayoral aspirations of young Richard Daley dogged her: would she survive? The fears compelled her to get rid of the "dreamers"—Rose, Masotti, Haider, and finally McGrath—and embrace the "schemers" she had campaigned against—Vrdolyak, Burke, Roti, and Swibel. Blacks became her pawns in the match against young Daley for the white ethnic vote. Time and again she pitted black against white ethnic representation—in school, police, public housing, and ward boundary disputes—and came down heavily on the white ethnic side. The strategy was simple and brutal, and it openly divided the city along racial lines as it had not been divided since the 1960s.

Byrne apparently believed that two factors would keep a sufficient number of black votes behind her candidacy in 1983. The black Democratic ward organizations and their satellites, heavily dependent upon her good will and patronage, would work hard for her reelection, regardless of her racist actions. As well, no strong black mayoral candidate would emerge to challenge her. History supported the Byrne strategy. But her fears drove Byrne too far. The racial pot she had so furiously stirred spilled over, swamping both her expectations and her mayoralty.

Washington's Disillusionment and Revolt

Whatever high hopes Washington harbored on his way down to Springfield were soon dashed by the harsh realities of the general assembly. Chicago's legislators danced strictly to Mayor Daley's music. "Boss" William Dawson, a tireless dancer for Daley and the Democratic party in congress, explained why. "We must play the game according to the rules. I always play it that way and I play with my team. If you are on a baseball team you stick with your team or you may not be able to play much longer." [20] So the freshman legislator danced; but he kept falling out of step. Generally the missteps were minor. Yet by his second term he showed that he had both the skill and temerity to go beyond the pale. He assaulted the machine head-on by getting a bill out of committee calling for a civilian review board for the Chicago Police Department. Daley sent word down through Metcalfe that Washington had to be dumped. But before the ax fell, Washington appealed to Jack Touhy, the wily West Side ward boss who ran Daley's Springfield operation. Touhy had taken an avuncular interest in the bright, brash Washington, and he managed to pull Washington's neck off Daley's chopping block.

The near execution did not have the salutary effect on Washington that Daley expected. Instead, Washington started stepping out even further on his own. He developed a code of divided loyalty that he hoped would enable him to survive in the machine while operating outside of it when he had to. On legislative affairs, he insisted on being his own man when the occasion called for it. On electoral matters, he played strictly by the machine's rules. He managed Metcalfe's aldermanic and congressional campaigns, ran the Third Ward's training program, and supported the machine's ticket from top to bottom.

Washington's extraordinary code of honor did not endear him to the iron-willed Metcalfe. But Metcalfe's supreme caution—Washington once described him in a moment of pique as "a man who plotted every step in advance before he decided to cross a street" [21]—made him heavily dependent on Washington's electoral skill, and this bridged the breach between the two men. The fragile bridge finally collapsed, however, under the weight of the 1975 mayoral primary election. Washington saw the black community breaking away from the machine, pushed along in large part by the celebrated Metcalfe-Daley feud, and he urged Metcalfe to seize the momentum by running for mayor. He managed to push Metcalfe to the precipice; but all the cautious Metcalfe saw when he peered over the edge was few troops, little money, and no hope of winning. He pulled back, and the decision severed the thin bond that had held the two men together for twenty years.

Still, Washington was able to capitalize on the Daley-Metcalfe feud the following year and move up to the state senate. In a set of state elections that had more twists than a John LeCarré plot, Daley dumped Metcalfe for congress; Metcalfe then allied himself with the machine's arch enemy, Governor Dan Walker. Daley countered by putting up the black president of the state senate, Cecil Partee, as his candidate for Illinois attorney general. This was a classic Daley move. It appeared as if Daley was moving Partee up; but Partee stood no chance against the popular Republican incumbent William Scott. Daley was moving him out of the senate and out of the presidency.

Washington wanted Partee's senate seat; but getting it was no simple matter. Daley despised Washington's independence and he thought even less of his committeeman, Metcalfe. But by this time Washington had become a master at slipping through the few cracks in the monolithic machine. He asked his labor allies to intercede with Daley on his behalf, and the leadership of the United Auto Workers approached Daley with two compelling arguments. Washington had a superior labor record, and if he did not get Partee's seat, he was going over to the Walker-Metcalfe ticket. Revealing his fear and loathing of Walker and Metcalfe, Daley reluctantly agreed to slate Washington.

Washington sailed easily to victory; but the campaign convinced him that he was going to have to make a clean break with the machine. Despite his backing by the machine, his poorly organized and financed opponent still managed to get 43 percent of the vote merely by waving the independent flag and castigating Washington as a machine hack. The characterization infuriated Washington; but he understood its effect. Many voters simply did not know what to make of him, half in and half out of the machine.

The maverick went a long way toward clarifying his image by challenging Michael Bilandic in the 1977 special mayoral election. Washington did not renounce the machine; but he tore into it for failing to give blacks their due rewards for long years of support. At the same time, Washington was tearing into the machine in the state senate, working with the Black Caucus and the "Crazy Eight"—an independent band of legislators—and the media began to give recognition to his skill and independence.[22] Once again, Washington's neck was perilously close to the chopping block.

The chop came in his 1978 reelection campaign. In a hotly argued slating session, Washington won a bare majority of support; but two of the committeemen in his senatorial district were nevertheless allowed to oppose him. In an election settled by a few hundred votes, a strong independent force of volunteers proved to be the difference for Washington.

Washington's first full-blown independent campaign came in 1980 when he challenged Bennett Stewart for congress in the First District. Washington picked up the victory handily; but he also picked up a remarkable message during the course of the campaign. Everywhere he went word was coming up about a black mayor. An aide conducted straw polls, and the results were staggeringly positive. Washington spread the word, and other black organizations—which were springing up like mushrooms in response to Byrne's may-oralty—began polling and coming up with the same remarkable results.

A second set of polls was conducted to find the man to match the moment, and Washington's name invariably came out on top. But he proved to be a re-markably reluctant candidate. If he ran, he was determined that it would not be another symbolic gesture of black protest. It had to be a serious campaign, one that was well organized and well financed. Thus, the next step was a mas-sive voter registration drive, and black businessmen for the first time were brought into the independent political movement in a large way. The prospect of a black mayor was remote. But, on the other hand, the momentum was there and building, and never before had the black community been as united be-hind one man and one issue.

Victory and Resolution

The two most remarkable aspects of Washington's mayoral bid were the ex-ceptional prominence of religious symbolism in the campaign—reflecting the religious roots of the black political tradition—and the extraordinary sup-port Washington received from the traditionally machine-oriented poor black wards—an unprecedented phenomenon in mayoral politics.

Religious symbolism was present at the launching of the campaign. Washing-ton threw his hat into the ring surrounded by a host of black ministers who offered up prayers for the candidate's success. One of the political reporters covering the event remarked that he had never seen a campaign kicked off this way; it resembled a religious revival meeting.[23]

During the course of the primary campaign, a "truth squad" of Washington supporters emerged to prevent Mayor Byrne from using black churches for campaign appearances, contending that the conventional political practice desecrated the black church. Meanwhile, Washington rode the black church circuit hard, drawing upon the extensive clerical network he had formed over the years as a legislator.

Then came the mammoth rally at the University of Illinois Pavilion. Thir-teen thousand Washington supporters rocked for four hours to the politico-religious cadences of a group of black elected officials from across the country. Organized by Sid Ordower, who had hosted a black gospel music show on local television for many years, the rally resembled nothing less than a religious re-vival meeting at full swing.

On the day of the primary election, the Chicago *Sun-Times* carried a photo of the candidate that evoked the campaign's religious crusade dimension. Wash-ington was shown bowed down before his minister receiving a blessing before heading off to the final day of battle. From beginning to end, then, the Wash-ington campaign displayed a meld of the political and religious. It was a reli-gious movement as well as a political campaign, and the moral dimension of the crusade resonated throughout the black community, producing an unprecedented number of campaign workers as well as voters. A majority of the Washington campaign workers in the poor Near South Side wards, where the author coordinated election day activities, had never before worked in a political campaign.

The extraordinary transformation of the poor black wards was unprecedented in mayoral politics. Yet there was a clear basis for the political shift. During Daley's first decade as mayor, the poor black wards had been the machine's principal electoral stronghold. But, as we saw, a profound disillusion set in during the late 1960s, transforming the poor black wards into a lazy backwater of the machine; the machine was still supported by those who voted, but fewer and fewer blacks turned out to vote.

Thus, the problem for Washington was not so much to pull poor black voters away from the machine as to rekindle their faith in politics. This involved passing a qualification test—demonstrating that Washington possessed the capacity to govern—and a "win-ability" test—demonstrating that he could actually win.

The first test was essentially passed during the widely watched first television debate, which by virtually all accounts Washington won handily. Washington continued to demonstrate his superiority in the second debate, and he held his own in the other two debates. The debates were critically important because they transformed Washington from the black protest candidate into the most qualified candidate. His standing in the polls rose steadily throughout the debates period.[24]

The second test was not actually passed until the waning days of the primary campaign. The turning point came at the huge and wild rally at the Pavilion. The rally was an extraordinary gamble that paid off. It violated the political advance man's basic rule that events should always be held in the smallest room insurance against a low turnout. But the momentum from the debates was flagging, and the gamble had to be taken in order to catch the front-running Byrne.

The rally struck like a thunderbolt, convincing those who were there and those who saw it on television and read about it in the newspapers that the impossible had suddenly become possible. Washington could actually win. His standing in the polls began to soar once again as the last of the doubters were swept up by the enthusiasm displayed at the rally.

A simple comparison indicates the revolutionary effect that Washington's campaign had in the poor black wards. In 1977 Washington had carried four black wards (plus the racially mixed Fifth Ward), all of which were affluent wards south of the 63rd Street class divide. He fared poorly in all of the poor black wards, particularly in the so-called "plantation" wards on the West Side. Thus, we can gain a clear sense of the transformation that occurred in 1983 by seeing how Washington performed in these two areas (see table 6).

TABLE 6

Victory and Resolution: The Washington Vote in Affluent and Poor Black Wards

Wards	Primary Election		General Election	
	Vote	Turnout	Vote	Turnout
Affluent				
6	87%	79%	99%	84%
8	86%	76%	99%	83%
9★	80%	75%	94%	83%
21	88%	78%	99%	85%
Poor				
24	79%	73%	99%	81%
27★	72%	71%	93%	78%
28	81%	69%	99%	79%
29★	76%	71%	93%	80%

*A small white population resides in these three wards, accounting for the lower levels of support for Washington
SOURCE: Chicago Board of Election Commissioners

The campaign did not entirely remove the effects of social class and attendant ties to the machine in the poor black wards; but it came remarkably close to doing just that. Turnout in the poor wards was lower in both elections, and Washington received a lower vote in the primary election in the poor wards. Yet when the voting pattern is viewed in historical terms, the differences become trivial. For the first time black voters, affluent and poor, spoke with virtually one voice. The election resolved the long-standing torn black political tradition.

One election does not, of course, constitute a political realignment, and so the big question is what the future holds. Can the new unified black political tradition hold in the new maelstrom that has engulfed Chicago's politics since Washington's election? Washington has thus far—three years into his first term—remained true to the reform convictions he expressed during his campaign for office, and the voters approve. His black support remains firm across the board, and white opposition has subsided, according to both the private and public polls that have been conducted. Thus, if Washington can continue to avoid the serpents snapping at his heels, the political realignment should hold, affirming both the new black political tradition and a new course for Chicago politics.

14.

RANKING CHICAGO'S MAYORS: MIRROR, MIRROR, ON THE WALL, WHO IS THE GREATEST OF THEM ALL?

Melvin G. Holli

Ranking Politicians

Who is number one? Who has been the best mayor in Chicago's history? For years politicians, political junkies, and pundits have wrangled over this unresolved and seemingly unprovable issue. In an effort to shed some light on this question, a selected group of Chicago experts was asked to rank all Chicago's forty-one mayors, from the very first in 1837 to the incumbent, Harold Washington.

Expert rankings of politicians date back to a 1948 poll conducted by Professor Arthur H. Schlesinger, Sr., who asked fifty-five expert historians to rate the U.S. presidents on a scale from "failure" to "great," with each historian using his own criteria. Schlesinger repeated his exercise in 1962, polling some seventy-five experts with results largely confirming his earlier findings. More recently a Chicago *Tribune* reporter, Steve Neal, polled forty-nine prominent historians and authors, all of whom had published some "seminal work" on the presidency, for the purpose of ranking American presidents. His findings, with few exceptions, were similar to those of the earlier Schlesinger polls. One surprising result of these surveys is that the rankings, including even those of contemporary presidents, appear to become fixed in a relatively short period of time after they leave office.[1] Whether the same pattern will obtain for our mayors only subsequent polls will show. There exists then a parallel research base in academic ratings for grading elected political officials, but such measures have not been applied to Chicago mayors.

This first effort to rate Chicago's forty-one elected mayors who served since the city's incorporation in 1837 relied on a methodology similar to the presidential surveys and an analogous base of experts and scholars. The poll of experts was derived from academia, journalism (both print and electronic), and public affairs, all of whom had written, lectured, or broadcast extensively on the city of Chicago, its mayors, or urban politics. The pool of potential respondents was drawn from *A Directory of Chicago Area Historians, 1984* (ed. Rima Schultz) and more specifically from those persons who listed themselves as specialists in "Chicago," "Urban," and "Illinois" history. This was supplemented by a 1983 telephone survey by Melvin G. Holli, who searched the Chicago metropolitan area for professors who offered courses on sizable components of Chicago history or politics in their classes. To this historical core were added other scholars and writers who had published articles and chapters in books, such as the *Biographical Dictionary of American Mayors, 1820–1980* (ed. Melvin G. Holli and Peter d'A. Jones), *The Making of the Mayor, Chicago 1983* (ed. Melvin G. Holli and Paul M. Green), and *After Daley* (ed. Samuel K. Gove and Louis Masotti); those who had published single-authored books, such as Roger Biles (*Big City Boss in Depression and War: Edward J. Kelly*), Herman Kogan (*Big Bill of Chicago*), and Eugene Kennedy (*Himself . . . Richard J. Daley*); and dissertation writers, such as Dr. John R. Schmidt ("Dever of Chicago: A Political History," Ph.D. diss., University of Chicago, 1983). Also included were journalists and reporters covering politics in the Chicago Tribune, Sun-Times, and Defender as well as television and radio news analysts from the major Chicago stations. This resulted in a carefully selected list of 105 persons (see the Appendix to this essay), with 45 from history and the historical social sciences or research libraries, 20 from political and related social sciences; 30 from journalism including some free lance authors and a few persons in public affairs agencies, and 10 electronic journalists who are analysts for radio and television.

Rankings were solicited by a mailed questionnaire sent out in September and October of 1985 to the 105 potential respondents. This elicited a response from 45, of which 40 were complete and usable for a response level of 38 percent, which compares favorably to other polls of this type.[2] The 40 experts who returned and completed the poll clearly seemed to possess the credentials for the task, for as a group they had published a total of 32 books and 1,335 articles related to the topic of Chicago and its politics, for an average of 33 articles per expert. Only five had not published print articles or books, although even in this instance several had "published" analyses through the electronic media in broadcast form or in lecture forums. Our expert respondents seemed well suited by their formal credentials to rate Chicago mayors.

The survey instrument had three components. The first asked each respondent to rank by his own criteria Chicago's six mayors who served from 1933 to

1985. A second part of the questionnaire asked experts to rank the mayors since 1933 by three different dimensions—leadership, accomplishments, and political skill—thereby permitting a more refined judgment of the mayors of contemporary times. The third and final part of the poll asked respondents to rank the ten best of the forty-one mayors elected since the office was established in 1837. The mean, mode, and number of times selected first were also tallied for this segment, and the standard deviation was calculated for every ranking mayor in both parts one and three.

Results

Table 7, which ranks mayors since 1933, covered all six elected mayors beginning wth Edward Kelly, but excluded Anton Cermak, who died in 1933. As table 7 shows, Richard J. Daley (1955–76) was picked as the consensus number one by the experts and also gathered in the highest mean rank and the highest mode of the group. (The mean is the arithmetic average of all of the respondents' rankings and is found by adding all of the scores and dividing by the number of respondents; the mode is the rank named most often by the respondents). Chicago's six-term Daley was also selected for the "Times Ranked First" column by 26 ballots which was more frequent than any other mayor in the since 1933.

Mayor Edward J. Kelly (1933–47) was ranked second with a mean and a mode a full rank lower than Daley but also one full rank and a mode above the third-placed Martin J. Kennelly (1947–55). Ed Kelly was also picked by eight respondents as number one and is statistically a solid and clear second in our standings. The statistical differences narrow considerably for the third-, fourth-, and fifth-ranked mayors, with each one separated by only about one-third of a full rank. The only anomaly in the declension is that Harold Washington (1983–) was ranked first four times versus third-placed Martin Kennelly's being placed at the top of the list by only two respondents. Otherwise

TABLE 7
Ranking of Mayors since 1933

Mayor	Total Points	Mode	Mean Rank	Times Ranked First	S.D.
Daley	65	1	1.62	26	.94
Kelly	108	2	2.70	8	.70
Kennelly	150	3	3.75	2	1.06
Washington	162	4	4.05	4	1.43
Byrne	173	4	4.32	0	.76
Bilandic	208	5	5.20	0	.89

NOTE: N = 40. Mayors were ranked from 1 for the highest to 5 for the lowest, with a value of 6 assigned if not ranked.

TABLE 8

Mayors since 1933 Ranked on Three Dimensions

Leadership		Accomplishments		Political Skills		Composite Score	
Mayor	Mean	Mayor	Mean	Mayor	Mean	Mayor	Mean
Daley	4.25	Daley	3.97	Daley	4.47	Daley	4.23
Kelly	3.02	Kelly	2.67	Kelly	2.97	Kelly	2.87
Washington	2.55	Byrne	2.30	Washington	2.57	Washington	2.42
Byrne	2.12	Kennelly	2.22	Byrne	2.40	Byrne	2.24
Kennelly	1.85	Washington	2.15	Kennelly	1.40	Kennelly	1.82
Bilandic	1.10	Bilandic	1.12	Bilandic	0.95	Bilandic	1.05

NOTE: N = 40. Mayors were ranked on a scale of 5 for the highest and 1 for the lowest.

Washington's mode and mean are below those of Kennelly. Jane Byrne (1979–83) in fifth place is statistically much closer to Harold Washington than to last place Michael Bilandic (1976–79) who trails by almost a full rank. Neither of the latter two attracted any first place votes.[3]

Table 8, which asked the experts to rank the mayors since 1933 on three different dimensions, produced results that are largely compatible with table 7. In this section, each respondent was asked to judge the leadership, accomplishments, and political skills and to rank all six mayors on each dimension. This three-dimension test showed Daley rising to first place with almost a full number above the second-placed Ed Kelly. Harold Washington and Jane Byrne improved their standings in table 8 exchanging positions with Martin Kennelly. Our respondent-experts, when focusing on these three specific criteria, saw Washington and Byrne in a more favorable light. In addition, the statistical closeness between Byrne and Washington tightens considerably on two dimensions and Martin Kennelly slips one and two ranks below his earlier showing in the first table. The composite score, which is a summary of all three dimensions, dropped Kennelly to fifth place and accordingly moved up Washington and Byrne. Harold Washington's rankings should be read with a measure of caution since the poll was conducted before his first term was completed. The fact that table 8 differed slightly from table 7 in regard to Martin Kennelly's relative position may reflect in part the differences in the breadth and scope of the two measures. Table 7 asked the experts to rank mayors with no limits on the number of dimensions or criteria considered, whereas table 8 asked each respondent to focus specifically on only three dimensions of the mayoralty. Table 8 then should be perceived as a criteria-specific measure which probably measures less than the broad scope given in table 7.

Table 9, which ranks Chicago mayors from 1837 to 1985, increased enormously the number of mayors "at risk" from six to forty-one and also trebles the size of the historic hunting ground from 50 to approximately 150 years. We might hypothesize that by expanding the number of potential choices we should also statistically diminish the strength of the leaders in table 7. To some

TABLE 9

Ranking of Mayors, 1837–1985

Mayor	Mean	Mode	Times Ranked First	S.D.
1. Daley (1955–76)	2.07	1	23	1.97
2. Harrison I (1879–87, 1893)	5.25	2	6	2.41
3. Harrison II (1897–1905, 1911–15)	6.05	4	2	1.66
4. Cermak (1931–33)	6.40	3	1	2.18
5. Kelly (1933–47)	6.60	2	1	2.34
6. Wentworth (1857–58, 1860–61)	8.30	8	1	2.59
7. Dunne (1905–07)	8.55	—	0	2.16
8. Ogden (1837–38)	8.72	7	2	2.63
9. Dever (1923–27)	8.82	7	1	2.10
10. Medill (1871–73)	8.87	—	0	2.56
11. Washington (1983–)	9.37	10	1	3.16
12. Kennelly (1947–55)	9.97	10	0	2.18
13. Thompson (1915–23, 1927–31)	9.85	4	0	2.04
14. Busse (1907–11)	10.45	10	0	1.80
15. Byrne (1979–83)	10.47	9	0	1.19
16. Hopkins (1893–95)	10.47	6	0	0.82
17. Swift (1893, 1895–97)	10.60	10	0	1.41
18. Bilandic (1976–79)	10.85	—	0	2.00

NOTE: N = 40. Mayors were ranked on a scale of 1 to 10 with 1 the highest and 10 the lowest.

extent that does occur, for the addition of more choices did diminish slightly Daley's lead. But even more dramatically it pushed out of the ranks of Table 7's top group all but Daley and Kelly. New entrants from the historic list, the two Harrisons and Anton Cermak, pushed Ed Kelly down three notches, and historic mayors such as John Wentworth (1857–58, 1860–61), Edward F. Dunne (1905–07), William Ogden (1837–38), William Dever (1923–27), and Joseph Medill (1871–73) pushed Harold Washington, Martin Kennelly and Jane Byrne out of top contention.

More choices also signaled some erosion in the "Times Ranked First" column, whereas Daley, who garnered 26 in table 7, slips somewhat to 23 in table 9; Ed Kelly drops from 8 to 1; and Harold Washington slides from 4 to 1. Those losses are picked up by the Harrisons' father and son team with 6 and 2 "Times Ranked First" votes and the city's first mayor, William Ogden, who gleans 2 first-place ballots. The mean rank scores also show a statistically neat and gradual declension from Richard Daley's towering mean rank of 2 down to Michael Bilandic's unheroic 10.85.

Overall the most striking finding is that Daley's high rank almost isolates him into a class by himself—sui generis. His mean rank of 2 is more than 3 full ranks above the second-placed Carter Harrison I. The rest of the table suggests that other mayors are perceived as being more alike because of the close clustering of their mean rankings. Carter Harrison II, Anton Cermak, and Ed

Kelly are closely clustered about the mean rank of 6; Wentworth, Dunne, Ogden, Dever, and Medill gravitate about a mean rank of approximately 8; Harold Washington, Martin Kennelly, and Big Bill Thompson share a common orbit with the first digit of their mean rank which is 9; and Busse, Byrne, Bilandic et al. circle about in the mayoral cosmos in the outer ring of the 10 rank-range.

An unanticipated historical symmetry is also suggested by our top ten mayors: four came from the nineteenth century, Ogden, Wentworth, Medill, and Carter Harrison I; one shared both centuries, Carter Harrison II; and five came from the twentieth century, Dunne, Dever, Cermak, Kelly, and Daley.

Ranking contemporaries and incumbent leaders is not without its hazards.[4] Harold Washington's rank of 11th and Jane Byrne's position of 15th in the "since 1837" scale (see table 9) should not be viewed as permanent grade assignments, but positions likely to change in future polls. Washington's first term was not completed at the time of the poll, and it is very possible that administrative actions at the end of that term or subsequent terms could either raise or depress ratings. The same might be said for Jane Byrne, should she serve another term or terms. Unlike the case of Daley where opinion has jelled and where high rank seems probable in any subsequent polls, the likelihood that Harold Washington's rank may change is suggested by the high standard deviation around Washington's ranking, which shows there is more dispersion around the mean (S.D. 3.16) than for any other single mayor, as can been seen in tables 7 and 9. (The standard deviation is a measure of spread, dispersion, or scatter of the scores away from the mean whereby the standard deviation number increases in proportion to the spread or dispersion.) The standard deviation in this case can also be interpreted as disagreement among the experts which is much greater for Washington (S.D. 3.16) than in the case of Daley (S.D. 1.97) or Byrne, upon whom the experts are in even more agreement with an S.D. of 1.19. The low standard deviation scores for Daley and Byrne also indicate that expert opinion on these two mayors is crystallizing, perhaps completely in the case of Daley. It seems unlikely that new evidence will emerge about Daley's career which will significantly alter his status as first-ranked mayor. It bears repeating, however, that an additional term or terms for either Byrne or Washington could give the experts a new mayoral record to measure, with the possibility of either upward or downward mobility on the mayoral ladder.

Summary

Let us recapitulate the findings. Emerging as the overall winner in all three sections of the poll is Chicago's long-term office-holding champion, Richard J. Daley. The six-term Daley ranked first in mean rank in the "since 1933" test of 6 mayors and also first in the same composite score in the "since 1837 to present" segment. Daley held up well both as a short- and as a long-distance runner. By every statistical measure Daley emerged as the overwhelming favorite for the leader: he was ranked first by 26 respondent-experts in the "since 1933" poll, leading Edward Kelly, who got 8 first choices, and Harold Washington, who trailed with 4 (as shown in table 7).

In the 1837 to 1985 long-distance heat (which greatly expanded the number of choices from 6 to 41) Daley again emerged as undisputed leader, pulling 23 first-place votes to Carter Harrison II's 6, Carter Harrison I's and William B. Ogden's 2 each, and Harold Washington's 1. Thus, Daley's appeal should be viewed as more than merely a contemporary phenomenon in which he runs well only against his own class of ethnic and machine politicians, but as one where he more than holds his own and emerges as a winner against a sizable body of blue-ribbon founding fathers and nineteenth-century political worthies.

In light of the three post-Daley administrations' political turmoil, revolving door policies, falling bond ratings, forced austerity, and flagging leadership, the Daley administration, by contrast, may appear attractive. Even though Daley's actions sometimes belied his rhetorical ideals, he was a fervent booster of public consensus and unity in contrast to the strident divisiveness of recent administrations. Internecine council warfare, with no one person speaking for the city as a whole, may have taken its toll in lower rankings for Daley's successors and elevated opinion of Daley by our experts. Politics then does appear to be a zero-sum game where one politician's losses can be converted to another's gains.

Appendix
List of Experts Receiving Questionnaires

Terry Allen
College of DuPage

John Allswang
California State College

Sharon Alter
Harper Community College

David Axelrod
Oak Park, IL

Edward Banfield
Harvard University

Paul Barrett
Illinois Institute of Technology

Roger Biles
Oklahoma State University

John Binder
Evanston, IL

Henry Binford
Northwestern University

Bill Braden
Chicago *Sun-Times*

Charles Branham
Chicago

John Buenker
University of Wisconsin at Parkside

Douglas Bukowski
Oak Park, IL

Tom Bullard
Oak Park, IL

John Calloway
WTTW-TV

Patricia Chariss
Barat College

Richard Ciconne
Chicago *Tribune*

Terry Clark
University of Chicago

Charles Cleveland
Radio WIND

Peter Colby
University of Central Florida

William Crotty
Northwestern University

Irving Cutler
Chicago State University

Bob Davis
Chicago *Tribune*

Richard Day
Richard Day Associates

Victor DeGrazia
Chicago

Perry Duis
University of Illinois at Chicago

Bruce Dumont
WTTW-TV

Michael Ebner
Lake Forest College

Linda Evans
Chicago Historical Society

Mike Flannery
WBBM-TV

Michael Funchion
South Dakota State University

Tim Franklin
Chicago *Tribune*

Alan Gittelson
Loyola University

Alex Gottfried
University of Washington

Samuel Gove
University of Illinois

Doris Graber
University of Illinois at Chicago

Bill Granger
Chicago *Tribune*

Paul Green
Governors State University

J. David Greenstone
University of Chicago

William Grimshaw
Illinois Institute of Technology

Ron Grossman
Lake Forest College

Ray Hanania
Chicago *Sun-Times*

Joseph Hapek
Morraine Valley Community College

Kenan Heise
Chicago *Tribune*

Hugh Hill
WLS-TV

Arnold Hirsch
University of New Orleans

Walter Jacobson
WBBM-TV

Vernon Jarrett
Chicago *Sun-Times*

John Jentz
Newberry Library

Richard Jensen
University of Illinois at Chicago

Peter d'A. Jones
University of Illinois at Chicago

Edward Kantowicz
Chicago

Dick Kay
WMAQ-TV

Eugene Kennedy
Loyola University

Donald Klimovich
Chicago Magazine

Herman Kogan
New Buffalo

Marshall Kravitz
Chicago

Phil Krone
Winnetka, IL

Tom Lee
Arlington Heights *Daily Herald*

Florence Levinsohn
Chicago

Rev. Manceslaus Madaj
St. Mary of the Lake Seminary

David Maurer
Eastern Illinois University

Edward Mazur
Chicago City-Wide College

Joseph O'Malley
Lewis University

Dominic Pacyga
Columbia College

Clarence Page
Chicago *Tribune*

Joseph Parot
Northern Illinois University

Paul Peterson
University of Chicago

John McDermott
Chicago Reporter

John Madigan
WBBM radio

Louis Masotti
Northwestern University

Edward Marciniak
Loyola University

Robert McClory
Evanston, IL

Robert McCluggage
Loyola University

Paul McGrath
Chicago

Richard Meister
DePaul University

Robert Merriam
Chicago

Jim Merriner
Chicago *Sun-Times*

Mike Miner
Chicago *Reader*

Steve Neal
Chicago *Tribune*

Harold Platt
Loyola University

Michael Preston
University of Illinois

David Protess
Northwestern University

Andrew Prinz
Elmhurst College

Barbara Posades
Northern Illinois University

Steven Riess
Northeastern Illinois University

Don Rose
Chicago

Jim Piety
Wright College

Bill Raspberry
Chicago *Tribune*

Milton Rosenberg
WGN radio

Mike Royko
Chicago *Tribune*

Dick Simpson
University of Illinois at Chicago

John Schmidt
Chicago Board of Education

Rima Schultz
Newberry Library

Chinta Strasberg
Chicago *Defender*

Basil Talbott
Chicago *Sun-Times*

Arthur Thurner
DePaul University

Donald Tingley
Eastern Illinois University

Leslie Tischauser
Oak Park, IL

Warren Wade
North Park College

Larry Viskochil
Chicago Historical Society

Joel Weissman
WTTW-TV

Ralph Whitehead
Northeastern University

Don Whitney
Loop College

Evelyn Wilbanks
Chicago Historical Society

15.

THE CHICAGO POLITICAL TRADITION: A MAYORAL RETROSPECTIVE

Paul M. Green

A review of Chicago's modern mayors reveals a simple fact: There is no one way to win city hall. Some past Chicago mayors have been clever political strategists who outfought and outsmarted their mayoral rivals; some have been loyal party stalwarts who eased their way to the top; others have been nontraditional candidates whose leading attribute was their lack of political acumen. Through it all, city hall has been the ultimate political prize for Chicago politicians. Only one mayor, Edward Dunne, has ever gone on to higher political office following his stint as the city's chief executive.

Of all the themes that mark the landscape of Chicago politics, the pursuit and exercise of power towers above them all. In no other American city is the possession and dispensation of political power—or as Chicagoans call it, "clout"—as central to the operation of its government or to the daily lives of its citizens. Chicago's mayors have reflected this overriding theme despite governing the city under a weak mayor–strong council system. Successful mayors have used their political power to take command of the city and dominate the council while balancing the various interests of Chicago's diverse residents. Unsuccessful mayors were those who were unwilling to use their power and unable to deal with the council while taking positions that did not match their constituents' needs.

Prior to Anton Cermak, Chicago's mayors were personality-oriented leaders who represented political factions within a major party. Following Cermak and the emergence of the Chicago Democratic machine, the city's mayors were organization-oriented, either selected by the machine or allowed to administer with its acquiescence. In 1983, Harold Washington became the first mayor in the machine era to win and govern city hall without organization party support. In the long run, this fact may be far more important than the color of Washington's skin.

Given the total party involvement in Chicago's mayoral history, it is not surprising that no mayor has been able to bring true reform to the city. At the same time, no word in Chicago history has had more meanings, more champions, and more causes than *reform*. From Medill to Washington, no mayor has run for office without espousing major reforms to improve city life. However, once in office, Chicago's chief executives have found that most of their constituents were not "ready" to replace power politics with reform politics. From the civil service reforms in the 1890s to the Shakman decrees in the 1970s, Chicago's mayors have been able to sidestep laws and procedures aimed at reforming the governance process. It is important to note that the most impressive governmental/administrative reforms in Chicago history occurred in the terms of those mayors most associated with "boss politics." Cermak, Kelly, and Daley were professional politicians who sought total political control and yet were open to innovative improvements in governmental efficiency as long as it did not hinder their political activities.

Given the above logic, one sees how easily Chicagoans could accept machine domination in return for "a city that works." Early twentieth-century party factionalism that gave the people a city council filled with grey wolves and inconsistent mayoral leadership gave way to united Democratic party dominance that eventually curtailed council flamboyance and mayoral hijinks. The rhythm of Chicago politics became a relatively simple ins versus outs or professional versus amateur melody. The fight for power was the key element, and post-Cermakian mayors have stressed their executive competence based on balanced budgets, deliverance of outstanding city services, and a professional governmental demeanor. Even the periodic shouting matches, scandals, and sensational stories of waste and criminal wrongdoing have until recently made little difference to Chicago voters. A culture of comfort based on narrow neighborhood or ward interests and not the general welfare of all city residents has guided the decisions of Chicago's voters.

A corollary theme to the overriding issue of power is the historic diversity of Chicago's electorate. Ethnicity, religion, and race have been and still are key determinants of mayoral style and political behavior. Patrician mayors like Medill battled newly arrived immigrants for control of the city while a shrewd compromiser like Harrison was able to rally most of the different nationalities around his banner. Under Cermak, the various ethnic groups united to run the city themselves by forming a multinational political organization. This ethnically based machine ruled Chicago for over fifty years until another group of voters, blacks, unified and took over city hall.

As for religion, the old joke that "Republicans divide the city into wards while Democrats divide it into parishes" rang true for many years in Chicago. This strong Catholic influence has played havoc with mayoral policies on the issue of personal liberty—drinking, vice, gambling, and having a good time. From the segregated vice policies of Harrison, through the Capone era of Big Bill Thompson, down to the machine era of Daley, religion and revelry have battled it out for the city's soul. Stuffed-shirt mayors like Medill, Dunne, and Dever were too strict for the electorate while Kelly and Thompson were eventually ousted for letting the city become too wide open.

Chicago has had a growing black population throughout the twentieth century. Neither its government or its citizens have been able to change the "black belt mentality" that makes Chicago the most racially segregated city in America. However, persistent racial separation coupled with Chicago's ward-based politics has produced a tradition of black elected officials and party leaders in the city. These individuals have cut political deals whereby their black constituents have been the deciding factor in electing Thompson mayor in 1919, Daley mayor in 1955 and 1963, and, of course, Washington mayor in 1983. They were also crucial to Byrne's 1979 mayoral primary victory. Yet no mayor has ever come to grips with the underlying issue of how to incorporate racial integration into the ward and neighborhood lifestyle of the city.

Perhaps the notion of neighborhood identification is the one theme most persistent in the administration of past Chicago mayors. Clearly, individual loyalty to an ethnic community, a parish, a ward, or a street corner has meant Chicago has not been one huge city but rather a collection of little villages tied together politically but not culturally. Most of Chicago's mayors in this study have reflected this diversity in their governmental and political actions. Men like Daley and Kelly could overcome the label of boss and be revered and feared for their ability to centralize political authority while they decentralized city services. On the other hand, weak mayors were those who could not organize politically and were unable to deliver the goods to the neighborhoods. Chicagoans for generations have accepted city hall as its "fountain of clout," but it has been the clever mayor that has sprinkled the goodies to the various communities as well as downtown. Unlike the mayors of most other American cities, Chicago mayors have faced a tradition of neighborhood solidarity even while a powerful political machine dominated its governmental process. Short-term mayors were those who refused to accept the fact that almost any type of skullduggery could be justified and accepted as long as the sanctity of the neighborhood was not violated. Long-term mayors, even a buffoon like Thompson, were able to identify with neighborhood problems, to voice their concerns and echo their fears. In sum, this geographic parochialism may explain why good government independents with their city-wide concerns have historically been restricted to a narrow band along the city's lake shore while the rest of the city residents lived their lives inland in family-oriented communities.

APPENDIX

NOTES

CONTRIBUTORS

INDEX

APPENDIX: CHICAGO MAYORS, 1837–1987

Chicago Mayors

William Ogden (1837–38)
Buckner Morris (1838–39)
Benjamin Raymond (1839–40,
  1842–43)
Alexander Loyd (1840–41)
Francis Sherman (1841–42,
  1862–65)
Augustus Garrett (1843–44,
  1845–46)
Alson Sherman (1844)
John Chapin (1846–47)
James Curtiss (1847, 1850)
James Woodworth (1848–49)
Walter Gurnee (1851–52)
Charles Gray (1853)
Isaac Milliken (1854–55)
Levi Boone (1855)
Thomas Dyer (1856–57)
John Wentworth (1857–58,
  1860–61)
John Haines (1858–60)
Julian Rumsey (1861–62)
John Rice (1865–69)
Roswell Mason (1869–71)
Joseph Medill (1871–73)

Lester Legrant Bond (1873)
Harvey Colvin (1873–76)
Monroe Heath (1876–79)
Carter Harrison (1879–87, 1893)
John Roche (1887–89)
DeWitt Cregier (1889–91)
Hempstead Washburne (1891–93)
George Swift (1893, 1895–97)
John Hopkins (1893–95)
Carter Harrison, II (1897–1905,
  1911–15)
Edward Dunne (1905–1907)
Fred Busse (1907–11)
William H. Thompson (1915–23,
  1927–31)
William Dever (1923–27)
Anton Cermak (1931–33)
Frank Corr (1933)
Edward Kelly (1933–47)
Martin Kennelly (1947–55)
Richard Daley (1955–76)
Michael Bilandic (1976–79)
Jane Byrne (1973–1983)
Harold Washington, 1983–

Mayors Who Served in the Council

	Mayor	Alderman
Ogden, William Butler	1837–1838	1840–1841
		1847–1848
Morris, Buckner Stith	1838–1839	1839–1840
		1844

Raymond, Benjamin W.	1839–1840	1847–1848
	1842–1843	
Loyd, Alexander	1840–1841	1850–1851
Sherman, Francis C.	1841–1842	1837–1838
	1862–1865	
Garrett, Augustus	1843–1844	1840–1841
	1845–1846	
Sherman, Alson S.	1844–1845	1842–1843
		1849–1851
Chapin, John P.	1846–1847	1844–1845
Curtiss, James	1847–1848	1838–1839
	1850–1851	1846–1847
Woodworth, James H.	1848–1850	1845–1846
		1847–1848
Milliken, Isaac	1854–1855	1850–1854
Boone, Dr. Levi D.	1855–1856	1846–1847
		1847–1848
		1854–1855
Dyer, Thomas	1856–1857	1853
Haines, John C.	1858–1860	1848–1854
Heath, Monroe	1876–1879	1871–1875
Swift, George B.	1895–1897	1879–1882
		1892–1894
Thompson, William Hale	1915–1923	1900–1902
	1927–1931	
Dever, William E.	1923–1927	1902–1910
Cermak, Anton J.	1931–1933	1909–1912
		1919–1922
Bilandic, Michael A.	1976–1979	1969–1976

Source: Holli, Jones, *Biographical Dictionary of American Mayors, 1820–1980.*

NOTES

1. Joseph Medill: Chicago's First Modern Mayor

1. Medill may be described as a "class reformer," part of a group of patrician Republicans concerned with promoting governmental efficiency. This distinguishes him from "party reformers," whose concern is with increasing political representation, and "status reformers," who promote socioeconomic equality. See William J. Grimshaw, "Is Chicago Ready for Reform?—or, A New Agenda for Harold Washington," in Melvin G. Holli and Paul M. Green, eds., *The Making of the Mayor, Chicago 1983* (Grand Rapids, Michigan: Eerdmans Pub. Co., 1984), 141–65.

2. In their seminal article on the mayors of Chicago, Bradley and Zald labelled Medill as a "transition" mayor between the "commercial elite" and the first machine mayors. See Donald S. Bradley and Mayer N. Zald, "From Commercial Elite to Political Administrator: The Recruitment of the Mayors of Chicago," *American Journal of Sociology* (Fall 1965), 153–67.

3. Letter from Joseph Medill to R. W. Patterson (Medill's son-in-law), 4 November 1871 Chicago *Tribune* Archives collection.

4. Ibid.

5. In the 1870s, Chicago had twenty wards with two aldermen serving from each ward. For an analysis of the demographic composition of the wards, see Wayne Andrews, *The Battle for Chicago* (New York: Harcourt and Brace, 1946).

6. State of Illinois, "An Act concerning the appointment and removal of city officers . . . , conferring additional powers upon Mayors . . . , and concerning appropriation bills and ordinances passed. . . ." Passed 9 March 1872; implemented 1 July 1872.

7. *Journal of the Proceedings of the Common Council of the City of Chicago*, 4 December 1871. (hereafter, *Journal*).

8. Ferdinand Rex, *The Mayors of Chicago* (Chicago: Municipal Reference Library mimeograph, 1933), 55–56.

9. Letter form Joseph Medill to U.S. Vice-President Schuyler Colfax, 5 February 1872, Chicago Historical Society Archives Collection.

10. Rex, 56.

11. *Journal*, 2 December 1872.

12. One historian described Medill as "sick at the thought of compromise with immigrant voters." (See Andrews, 67.) This is perhaps unfair, given his repeated efforts to reach such compromises during the first year of his administration. Still, there is little question that the official explanation of fatigue and

"ill-health" (see John Moses and Joseph Kirkland, eds., *History of Chicago,* vol. 1, Chicago: Munsell & Co., 1895, 216) is incomplete. The absence of primary historical documents on this subject will cause it to remain somewhat of a mystery.

13. *Journal,* 18 August 1873.

14. Ibid., 26 January 1874.

15. Ibid., 4 December 1871.

16. Moses and Kirkland, 216.

17. *Journal,* 26 February 1872.

18. On 11 March 1872, Alderman Charles C. Holden (10th), who Medill had defeated for mayor the previous year, introduced a resolution to the city council demanding that the Chicago Relief and Aid Society give to the city treasury more than one million dollars it had collected to provide assistance to victims of the fire. The council passed the resolution and Medill signed it reluctantly on 3 May 1872. State of Illinois, Secretary of State Archives Division. (Springfield, Illinois: Records of official city business prior to 1875, n.d.)

19. Rex, 55.

20. *Journal,* 29 July 1872. On 25 September 1872 Alderman Holden responded to Medill's demand that "the practice of appointing police on the recommendation of aldermen must stop." He claimed that Medill's allegation was largely unfounded and provided a list of "sponsors" of policemen for six months to support his contention. State of Illinois, Secretary of State Archives Division.

21. *Journal,* 4 December 1871.

22. Chicago *Tribune,* 15 January 1881.

23. On 15 July 1872 the complaint of a private citizen that "Irish [have been] excluded from nominees to the Board of Education" was introduced to the city council as a Remonstrance measure. No action was taken on the complaint, and all of Medill's nominees were approved. State of Illinois, Secretary of State Archives Division.

24. J. Robert Nash, *People to See* (New Century Publishers, 1981), 5.

25. Alfred Theodore Andreas, *History of Chicago,* vol. 3 (New York: Arno Press, 1975), 855.

26. Quoted from a resolution adopted by a mass meeting of German citizens, 24 October 1872, which was submitted to the city council as a "Communication Relative to the Enforcement of the Sunday law" on 28 October 1872. Secretary of State, Archives Division.

27. Andreas, 855.

28. On 7 February 1874, the Chicago *Tribune* republished the allegation made by the *Staats-Zeitung* and provided evidence that it was incorrect.

29. Andrews, 49.

30. Nash, 19.

31. Lincoln responded by calling Medill a "coward. You and your Tribune

have had more influence than any paper in the Northwest in making this war. . . . Go home and send us these men." Medill admitted afterwards that "it was the first time I was ever whipped, and I didn't have an answer." Quoted in Ida M. Tarbell, *The Life of Abraham Lincoln,* vol. 2 (New York: Lincoln History Society, 1903), 218–19.

32. Quoted in Nash, 9.

33. Medill was not the first newspaperman to serve as a mayor of Chicago. "Long John" Wentworth, publisher of the Chicago *Democrat,* was elected mayor in 1857. However, Wentworth was completely unconcerned with the press's coverage of his administration. According to Nash, Wentworth "grew tired of his newspapering" and sold the *Democrat* to the Chicago *Tribune.* Nash, 3.

34. "Colonel" Robert R. McCormick ultimately became the dominant influence in the management of the *Tribune* from 1911 to 1955. See Gwen Morgan and Arthur Veysey, *Poor Little Rich Boy* (Carpentersville, Illinois: Crossroads Communications, 1985).

35. *Journal,* 20 March 1899.

2. Carter H. Harrison II: The Politics of Balance

1. Jon Teaford, *The Unheralded Triumph: City Government in America, 1870–1900* (Baltimore: Johns Hopkins University Press, 1984) overturns James Lord Bryce's oft-quoted dictum that city government in America was a "conspicuous failure." I would like to consider my essay on Carter Harrison a part of this large reevaluation of city politics at the turn of the century. Teaford discusses Harrison briefly on pages 49–50, 52–53, 59–60.

2. G. K. Chesterton, *Orthodoxy* (Garden City, NY: Doubleday, 1959), 99.

3. The basic sources on the Harrisons are: Claudius O. Johnson, *Carter Henry Harrison I: Political Leader* (Chicago: University of Chicago Press, 1928); Carter H. Harrison, Jr., *Stormy Years* (Indianapolis: Bobbs-Merrill Co., 1935); Carter H. Harrison, Jr., *Growing Up with Chicago* (Chicago: Ralph Fletcher Seymour, 1944). A highly sanitized collection of Harrison papers resides at Newberry Library.

4. A city census of 1878 recorded 436,739 residents; in 1880, the city census counted 491,516 and the U.S. Census 503,298 (*Chicago City Manual* [1913] 188). For the growth of Chicago's geographic boundaries, see Harold M. Mayer, Richard C. Wade, *Chicago: Growth of a Metropolis* (Chicago: University of Chicago Press, 1969), 177.

5. Harrison, *Stormy Years,* 18, 26; "Message of Carter H. Harrison, Mayor, 1887," Chicago Historical Society.

6. *Chicago City Manual* (1913) 205; (1912) 208.

7. Edward R. Kantowicz, "The Ghetto Experience: Chicago as a Case Study," (paper delivered at the National Archives Conference on State and Local History, May 1975); Kantowicz, "Church and Neighborhood," *Ethnicity*

7 (December 1980), 349–66; John M. Allswang, *A House for All Peoples* (Lexington: University Press of Kentucky, 1971).

8. For a perceptive study of Chicago's "moral geography," see Perry R. Duis, *The Saloon* (Urbana: University of Illinois Press, 1983).

9. *Chicago City Manual* (1912) 209.

10. All biographical information on Harrison, Sr., is from Johnson, *Carter Henry Harrison I,* and from Frederick Rex, *The Mayors of the City of Chicago, 1837–1933* (Chicago: Municipal Reference Library, 1947).

11. "Last Speech of Carter H. Harrison, 28 October 1893," Chicago Historical Society.

12. *Skandinaven,* quoted in Johnson, *Carter Henry Harrison I,* 119.

13. See Harrison's two autobiographies: *Stormy Years* and *Growing Up with Chicago.*

14. "Scrapbook of Articles under Pen Name Cecil Harcourt," Chicago Historical Society.

15. Theodore Roosevelt, *Autobiography* (New York: Macmillan, 1913), 63.

16. Paul M. Green, "The Chicago Democratic Party, 1840–1920," (Ph.D. diss., University of Chicago, 1975), 85ff.

17. The historical literature on progressivism is immense. My thinking on progressivism has been shaped by Richard Hofstadter, *The Age of Reform* (New York: Vintage, 1955); Robert Wiebe, *The Search for Order* (New York: Hill and Wang, 1967); and Richard Abrams, *The Burdens of Progress 1900–1929* (New York: Scott Foresman, 1978); Melvin Holli, *Reform in Detroit* (New York: Oxford University Press, 1969) is an admirable study of Hazen Pingree, a "reform boss" similar in many ways to Harrison.

18. Chapter 3, "Anatomy of a Reform Movement," in Steven J. Diner, *A City and Its Universities* (Chapel Hill: University of North Carolina Press, 1980) provides a good overview of reform in Chicago.

19. Joseph Bush Kingsbury, "Municipal Personnel Policy in Chicago, 1895–1915," (Ph.D. diss., University of Chicago, 1925), 4–7.

20. William T. Stead, *If Christ Came to Chicago* (Chicago: Laird and Lee, 1894); Lloyd Wendt and Herman Kogan, *Lords of the Levee* (Garden City, NY: Garden City Publishing Co., 1944), 91–96.

21. Ibid., 117–20; Green, "Chicago Democratic Party," 55–57; "Ogden Gas Company—Legal Research, Dated August 4, 1939," in Harrison Papers, Newberry Library.

22. Harrison, *Stormy Years,* 304–14; Harrison to Major Clifton P. Williamson (undated), in Harrison Papers; Wendt and Kogan, *Lords of the Levee,* 159–60.

23. Lincoln Steffens, *The Shame of the Cities,* (New York: Hill and Wang, 1957), 162–94; Kingsbury, "Municipal Personnel Policy," 57–68; Ralph Russell Tingley, "From Carter Harrison II to Fred Busse," (Ph.D. diss., Univer-

sity of Chicago, 1950), 32–33; "Mayor's Annual Message, April 10, 1905," Chicago Historical Society.

24. "Mayor's Annual Message, April 10, 1905"; "The Truth About Harrison," March 1901 campaign pamphlet; Green, "Chicago Democratic Party," 57.

25. "The Truth about Harrison," March 1901; "Mayor's Annual Message, April 10, 1905"; Rex, *Mayors of Chicago*, 88.

26. "The Truth about Harrison," March 1901; "Mayor's Message, 1900."

27. For background on Chicago traction, see John A. Fairlie, "The Street Railway Question in Chicago," *The Quarterly Journal of Economics* 21 (May 1907), 371–404; and Paul Barrett, *The Automobile and Mass Transit* (Philadelphia: Temple University Press, 1983).

28. Sidney I. Roberts, "Portrait of a Robber Baron: Charles T. Yerkes," *Business History Review* 35 (Autumn 1961), 344–71; and, for a more favorable view of Yerkes, Robert D. Weber, "Rationalizers and Reformers: Chicago Local Transportation in the Nineteenth Century," (Ph.D. diss., University of Wisconsin, 1971).

29. Roberts, "Portrait of a Robber Baron," 356–70; Harrison, *Stormy Years*, 136–75; Fairlie, "Street Railway Question," 380.

30. Roberts, "Portrait of a Robber Baron," 368, 371.

31. "Mayor's Message to the City Council, Outlining the Provisions of a Street Railway Franchise Renewal Ordinance, January 6, 1902"; and "Carter H. Harrison to the Citizens of Chicago, April 4, 1903," both in Harrison Papers. I believe that Paul Barrett, in *The Automobile and Mass Transit*, misinterpreted Harrison's policy, when he stated: "Harrison had no clear position on the transportation issue" (22).

32. Fairlie, "Street Railway Question," 388–400.

33. "Report of the Committee on Local Transportation to the City Council of the City of Chicago, January 15, 1907," Chicago Historical Society; Barrett, *The Automobile and Mass Transit*, 37–44.

34. *Chicago Times-Herald*, 14 July 1897, quoted in "The Truth About Harrison," March 1901, Chicago Historical Society.

35. Edward R. Kantowicz, *Polish-American Politics in Chicago* (Chicago: University of Chicago Press, 1972), 75–76.

36. Ibid., 77–83; Michael McCarthy, "Prelude to Armageddon: Charles E. Merriam and the Chicago Mayoral Election of 1911," *Journal of the Illinois State Historical Society* 67 (November 1974), 505–18; Harrison, *Stormy Years*, 291–95; Charles E. Merriam, *Chicago: A More Intimate View of Urban Politics* (New York: Macmillan, 1929), 283–86.

37. Wendt and Kogan, *Lords of the Levee*, 294–304; Harrison, *Stormy Years*, 304–14; John Landesco, *Organized Crime in Chicago* (Chicago: University of Chicago Press, 1929), 26–31; Chicago Vice Commission, *The Social Evil in Chicago* (Chicago, 1911).

38. Green, "Chicago Democratic Party," 172–241; William Jennings Bryan to Carter Harrison, 17 September 1914, and 9 November 1914, in Harrison Papers.

39. Carter Harrison to Graham Taylor, 7 January 1936, in Graham Taylor Papers, Newberry Library.

40. Wendt and Kogan, *Lords of the Levee*, 229.

41. Carter Harrison to Major Clifton P. Williamson (undated), in Harrison Papers.

42. "Mayor's Message to the City Council, Outlining the Provisions of a Street Railway Franchise Renewal Ordinance, January 6, 1902," in Harrison Papers.

43. For Tom Johnson, Frederic Howe, and the idea of a civic renaissance, see chapter 10, "The City Republic," in Frederic C. Howe, *The City: Hope of Democracy* (New York: Charles Scribners Sons, 1905).

44. See, for example, Green, "Chicago Democratic Party," 75, and Nick A. Komos, "Chicago, 1893–1907: The Politics of Reform," (Ph.D. diss., George Washington University, 1961), 243.

45. "Mayor's Annual Message," 3 April 1915, Chicago Historical Society.

46. *Chicago City Manual*, 1913, 99.

47. Harrison, *Stormy Years*, 339.

3. Edward F. Dunne: The Limits of Municipal Reform

1. The charges of radicalism were typical of those found in most Republican newspapers of the day, especially the *Tribune* the *Daily News*, and the *Record-Herald*. Dunne's version of his mayoral career can be found primarily in Edward F. Dunne, *Illinois: The Hearst of the Nation*, (Chicago: The Lewis Publishing Company, 1933) v. 2, 188–207 and in William Sullivan, comp., *Dunne: Judge, Mayor, Governor*, Chicago: The Lewis Publishing Company, 1916). The Illinois History Survey at the University of Illinois-Urbana/Champaign also has a collection of Dunne scrapbooks that contain mostly newspaper clippings. I am grateful to John Hoffman, director of the survey, for his cooperation.

2. The best sources for Dunne's intellectual development are his own works cited in note 1 and Richard E. Becker, "Edward Dunne, Reform Mayor Chicago; 1905, 1907," (Ph.D. dissertation, University of Chicago, 1971) 1–24. On "Catholic social liberalism" see Aaron I. Abell, American Catholic Thought on Social Questions, (Indianapolis: Bobbs-Merrill, 1968), 143–264. On social reformers see Melvin G. Holli, *Reform in Detroit: Hazen S. Pingree and Urban Politics*, (New York: Oxford University Press, 1969), 157–84. On "urban liberalism," see John D. Buenker, *Urban Liberalism and Progressive Reform*, (New York: Charles Scribners' Sons, 1973). On the significance of being "co-ethnic" see Edgar Litt, *Beyond Pluralism: Ethnic Politics in America*, (Glenview, Illinois: Scott, Foresman and Company; 1970), 1–74, 127–41. No less an authority than Carter H. Harrison II observed that it was taking one's life in one's

hands to campaign against Dunne in such Irish Catholic strongholds as Bridge-port or Back-of-the-Yards. See note 6.

3. John A. Fairlie, "The Street Railway Question in Chicago," *Quarterly Journal of Economics* 21 (1907): 371–404.

4. Dunne, *Illinois*, 227–35; Sullivan, *Dunne*, 177–85, 188–218.

5. Dunne, *Illinois*, v. 2, 228–39; Sullivan, *Dunne*, 197–218.

6. Dunne, *Illinois*, v. 2, 242–48; Chicago *Record-Herald*, 26 February 1905.

7. Sullivan, *Dunne*, 205–18.

8. Dunne, *Illinois*, v. 2, 244–45.

9. Becker, "Edward Dunne," 1–24; Nick A. Komons "Chicago, 1893–1907; The Politics of Reform," (Ph.D. diss. George Washington University, 1961), 310–25; Ralph Tingley, "From Carter Harrison to Fred Busse . . ." (Ph.D. diss. University of Chicago, 1950), 170–78; Paul M. Green, "The Chicago Democratic Party, 1840–1920," (Ph.D. diss., University of Chicago, 1975), 89–90.

10. Chicago *Tribune*, 27 June and 14 December 1904; Sullivan, *Dunne*, 170–75; Chicago *Evening Post*, 19 December 1904.

11. Chicago *Tribune*, 23 January 1905; Dunne, *Illinois*, v. 2, 255; Becker, "Edward Dunne," 31–35: Chicago *Chronicle*, 26 February 1905; Sullivan, *Dunne*, 177–85.

12. Linda J. Lear, *Harold L. Ickes: The Aggressive Progressive, 1874–1933* (New York: Garland Publishing Company, 1981), 56–64. In Ickes's view, "the formerly fierce traction opponent and IMO advocate had become bland and timid—safe and sound—dull and conservative," with ideas that were "more or less of a hodge podge."

13. Green, "Chicago Democratic Party," 103–10; Becker, "Edward Dunne," 35–38; Sullivan, *Dunne*, 186–87. Green styles Dunne's campaign a "brilliant combination of politics and reform zeal."

14. Becker, "Edward Dunne," 49–57; Komons, "Chicago, 1893–1907," 325–37; Green, "Chicago Democratic Party," 114–18; Lear, *Harold Ickes*, 58–62. Green concludes that Dunne handled the Traeger incident "with the ease and polish of a party professional."

15. Becker, "Edward Dunne," 37–49. Typical of Dunne's volunteer organizations were the Women's, Austin, Southside Women's, Scandinavian, and German-American Municipal Ownership Clubs, and the E. F. Dunne Workingman's Club, the Chicago Teacher's Federation Dunne Club, the Northwestern Law School Club, and the Ben Franklin Club.

16. *Tribune*, 5–6 April 1905. The voting analysis is based upon the comparison of the returns found in the *Tribune* with the ward map of the city and data found in U.S. Bureau of the Census, *Thirteenth Census of the United States*, 1910, v. 2, *Population*, 512–14. Especially useful in understanding the city's geographical makeup were Harold M. Mayer, Richard C. Wade, and Glen E. Holt, *Chicago: Growth of a Metropolis*, (Chicago: University of Chicago Press,

1969); Harvey Warren Zorbaugh, *The Gold Coast and the Slum: A Sociological Study of Chicago's Near North Side,* (Chicago: University of Chicago Press, 1929); and Glen E. Holt and Dominic A. Pacygca, *Chicago: A Historical guide to the Neighborhoods; The Loop and the South Side,* (Chicago: Chicago Historical Society, 1979).

17. *Tribune,* 6 April 1905. The Socialist candidate John Collins received 23,034, most of which presumably might have gone to Dunne if he had not been in the race.

18. Fairlie, "Chicago Railway question," 390–92; *Barrett, Automobile and Urban Transit,* 33–35; *Tribune,* 6 April 1905.

19. Becker, "Edward Dunne," 61–84; Komons, "Chicago, 1893–1907," 342–44; Jane Addams, *Twenty Years at Hull House,* (New York: Macmillan Co., 1910), 330–38; Dunne, *Illinois,* v. 2, 297–98.

20. On his European tour, Dunne had been impressed with the Glasgow system managed by A. C. Young. The man that he unwittingly invited to Chicago was James Dalrymple, Young's successor. Dalrymple accepted Dunne's hospitality and repaid him by writing a report that emphasized the political and financial difficulties of achieving MO. Dunne's attempt to suppress the report and its subsequent release by his opponents caused the mayor considerable embarrassment. See Fairlie, "Street Railway Question," 392; Komons, "Chicago, 1893–1907," 355–56.

21. Fairlie, "Street Railway Question," 390–98; Barrett, *Automobile and Urban Transit,* 33–36; Dunne, *Illinois,* v. 2, 270–89.

22. Charles E. Merriam, *Chicago: A More Intimate View of Urban Politics,* (New York: Macmillan Co., 1929), 90–133; Harrison, *Stormy Years,* 240–57; Green "Chicago Democratic Party," 117–9; Chicago *Record-Herald,* 3 April 1905.

23. Komons, "Chicago, 1893–1907," 346–54; Becker, "Edward Dunne," 69–73; Dunne, *Illinois,* v. 2, 268.

24. Dominic Candeloro, "The Chicago School Board Crisis of 1907," *Journal of the Illinois State Historical Society* 68 (1975): 396–406; *Tribune,* 10 October 1906; *Chronicle,* 4 April 1907.

25. Becker, "Edward Dunne," 165–97; Komons, "Chicago, 1893–1907," 366–68; *Record-Herald,* 30 May, 30 September, and 4 May 1905; 6, 7, and 24 March and 4 April 1906.

26. Alex Gottfried, *Boss Cermack of Chicago: A Study of Urban Political Leadership,* Seattle: University of Washington Press, 1962) 48–61; John M. Allswag, *A House for All Peoples: Ethnic Politics in Chicago, 1890–1936,* (Lexington: University Press of Kentucky, 1971), 3–36; *Tribune,* 19 March 1906; Dunne, *Illinois,* v. 2, 295.

27. Chicago *Inter-Ocean,* 22 February 1907.

28. Arthur F. Bentley, "Municipal Ownership Interest Groups in Chicago: A Study of Referendum Votes, 1902–1907," (Typescript in Regenstein Library, University of Chicago, n.d.); *Tribune,* 9 January 1907. A *Colliers* edi-

torial concluded that the voters had chosen "immediate seats in the cars rather than immediate municipal ownership."

29. Green, "Chicago Democratic Party," 117–21; Becker, "Edward Dunne," 184–97; Komons, "Chicago, 1893–1907," 378–98; *Tribune*, 22 February 1907.

30. Becker, "Edward Dunne," 197–211; *Tribune*, 12, 21, and 25 March 1907. The MO cause was carried by such Chicagoans as William Dever, Louis F. Post, and George Hooker and by such nationally recognized advocates as Tom Johnson and Brand Whitlock, with the latter calling Dunne a "co-partner in municipalization." For a discussion of William Randolph Hearst's role see Herbert S. Rosenthal, "William Randolph Hearst and Municipal Ownership," *Tamkang Journal of American Studies* 1 (1984): 6–36.

31. Becker, "Edward Dunne," 197–204. Dunne, *Illinois*, v. 2, 294–307. Busse was a member of the Lorimer faction of the GOP which had close ties to the traction companies and which the moderates regularly condemned for its alleged corruption, machine tactics, and preference for a wide-open city. Presumably, the combination of their antipathy toward the Dunne administration and the support of settlement was powerful enough to overcome their normal aversion. See Joel A. Tarr, *A Study in Boss Politics: William Lorimer of Chicago*, (Urbana: University of Illinois Press, 1971).

32. Lear, *Harold Ickes*, 69–70; Barrett, *Automobile and Urban Transit*, 38–45; Fairlie, "Street Railway Questions," 399–401. Dunne later claimed that he was indirectly offered a $50,000 campaign contribution if he would keep open the brothels on Custom House Place and that "in the river wards where money counts most, my candidacy was literally slaughtered at the polls." See Dunne, *Illinois*, v. 2, 294–97; and Becker, "Edward Dunne," 190–201.

33. *Tribune*, 3 April 1907. The electoral analysis was accomplished by the same sources cited in note 20 above. The Socialist candidate, George Koop, received 13,429 votes, slightly more than Busse's margin over Dunne. See also Edward R. Kantowicz, *Polish-American Politics in Chicago, 1880–1940*, (Chicago: University of Chicago Press, 1975).

34. *Tribune*, 3 April 1907; Becker, "Edward Dunne," 205–11; Bentley, "Municipal Ownership Interest Groups in Chicago," n.p.

35. See Dunne, *Illinois*, v. 2, 268–88. For a view that Dunne bungled MO and produced a "mottled victory," see Ginger, *Altgeld's America*, 295–303. Just two weeks after the election, the Supreme Court ruled that the street car certificates counted against the city's total bonded indebtedness, thus rendering the Mueller Law virtually useless.

36. Dunne, *Illinois*, v. 2, 290–92; Becker, "Edward Dunne," 74–75; Sullivan, *Dunne*, 315–23; *Daily News*, 22 April 1905.

37. Dunne, *Illinois*, v. 2, 290–91; Becker, "Edward Dunne," 165–78; *Tribune*, 10 February, 14 March, 12 April 1906.

38. Becker, "Edward Dunne," 170–77; Sullivan, *Dunne*, 315–23, 336–49;

Tribune, 18 April 1906; *Daily News,* 11 December 1965, 30 June 1906.

39. Becker, "Edward Dunne," 170–71; Sullivan, *Dunne,* 336–49; *Tribune,* 14 and 22 December 1906.

40. Dunne, *Illinois,* v. 2, 300–304; Becker, "Edward Dunne," 80–82; *Daily News,* 22 April 1905.

41. Candeloro, "School Board Crisis," 397–405; Dunne, *Illinois,* v. 2, 293, 304–5; *Tribune,* 10 October 1906, 13 November 1908; *Chronicle,* 28 May 1907.

42. Becker, "Edward Dunne," 212–17. Dunne narrowly lost the Democratic mayoral nomination to Harrison in 1911 and was elected governor of Illinois in 1912. His administration, although handicapped by lack of a legislative majority, made an impressive progressive record in labor, welfare, regulatory, and penal legislation and enacted limited woman suffrage. Defeated for reelection in 1916, Dunne devoted the rest of his life to his family, Democratic politics, and Irish-American causes. In 1919, he led an Irish-American delegation to the Versailles Conference pleading Irish independence, and in 1933 at the age of 80, he published his five volume *Illinois: Heart of the Nation.* He died in Chicago on 24 May 1937 at the age of 83.

4. Fred A. Busse: A Silent Mayor in Turbulent Times

1. George C. Sikes, "Chicago's New Mayor," *The American Monthly Review of Reviews* (May 1907), 585.

2. See Maureen A. Flanagan, "Charter Reform in Chicago: Political Culture and Urban Progressive Reform," *Journal of Urban History* (February 1986).

3. Nick A. Komons, "Chicago, 1893–1907: The Politics of Reform" (Ph.D. Dissertation, George Washington University, 1961) provides a detailed description of the role of the traction issue in municipal politics. See especially 295–96 and 311–26.

4. Chicago *Tribune,* 22 March 1907, 2; 23 March 1907, 3; and 29 March 1907, 4.

5. Ibid., 26 March 1907, 2.

6. At all the Chicago Federation of Labor meetings in January 1907 and 3 and 17 February 1907 this issue was of particular concern. See Chicago Federation of Labor, *Minutes* (Chicago Historical Society).

7. *Tribune,* 29 March 1907, 4.

8. See Carter Harrison, *Stormy Years: The Autobiography of Carter H. Harrison, Five Times Mayor of Chicago* (Indianapolis: Bobbs-Merrill, 1935), 110–12; Lloyd Wendt and Herman Kogan, *Bosses in Lusty Chicago* (Bloomington: University of Indiana, 1943), 38 for accounts of Yerkes; see Sikes, 588 and the *Tribune,* 20 March 1907, 2 for Busse and traction.

9. *Tribune,* 23 March 1907, 4; 26 March, 1; 28 March, 3; 27 March, 1; 26 March, 3; and 24 March, 1.

10. Ibid., 23 March 1907, 2; 26 March 1907, 3; and 23 March 1907, 1.

11. Ibid., 23 March 1907, 3; 26 March, 2; and 30 March, 2.

12. In the same way, Busse's Republican support from elsewhere in the

country was *ipso facto* good, Edward Dunne's outside Democratic support was bad. Because of his stand on municipal ownership, Republicans linked Dunne with the political aspirations of the notorious "outside agitator" William Randolph Hearst, accusing the Mayor of taking orders directly from "carpetbagger" Hearst and his "mud-slinging" cronies who would descend upon Chicago, determined to put it under the thumb of New York City. That the Republicans were quite willing to place Chicago under the control of Theodore Roosevelt and the Republican party in Washington, was beside the point. Or rather, once again, it seems to have been a case of the other guy's partisanship being wrong, while the Republicans' was of course right. For examples, see the *Tribune,* 27 March 1907, 1; 28 March, 2; 29 March, 1; 23 March, 1; and 28 March, 1.

13. In the municipal elections of 1900, for example, when the Republicans won control of the city council, the Municipal Voters League discarded its hitherto sacred call for nonpartisan constitution of council committees. They backed the Republican plan to form committees along strict party lines saying "it is understood, however, that most, even of the more prominent reform members, do not regard the [nonpartisan] pledge as binding in the event it can be shown that better results can be accomplished by the majority party having control of the committees and working machinery of the Council." The notorious democratic alderman Johnny Powers, looking through the jaundiced eye of a seasoned politician, pronounced the situation for what it was: "to the victor belong the spoils." See the *Tribune,* 4 April 1900, 1–2 and 8 April 1900, 1.

14. *Tribune,* editorial 22 March 1907, 2 and 31 March 1907, 5.

15. For further accounts of the history of the conflict and the arguments of each position, see especially the *Public,* 17 November 1906; Chicago Federation of Labor, *Minutes,* 2 December 1906; Chicago *Record-Herald,* 3 December 1906; Adade Wheeler and Marlene Wortman, *The Roads They Made: Women in Illinois History,* (Chicago: Charles Kerr, 1977), 87–89; Mary E. Dreier, *Margaret Dreier Robins: Her Life, Letters, and Work* (New York, 1950); and Chicago *Daily News Almanac* (1905) 358.

16. *Tribune,* 18 May 1907, 1.

17. *Tribune,* 28 May 1907, 1–2; CFL, *Minutes,* 16 June, 21 July, and 4 August 1907; *Record-Herald,* 5 August 1907.

18. See Maureen A. Flanagan, "Charter Reform in Chicago, 1890–1915: Community and Government in the Progressive Era" (Ph.D. Dissertation, Loyola University of Chicago, 1980).

19. Flanagan, "The Ethnic Entry into Chicago Politics: The United Society for Local Self-Government and the Reform Charter of 1907," *Journal of the Illinois State Historical Society* (Spring 1982).

20. *Abendpost,* 3 April 1907.

21. *Abendpost,* 6 and 7 September 1907; Illinois *Staats-Zeitung,* 7 and 8 September 1907; *Record-Herald,* 6 September 1907.

22. *Record-Herald,* 14 September 1907.

23. *Record-Herald*, 29 April 1909 and 12 May 1909.
24. See *Tribune*, 21 May 1907, 2.
25. *Union Labor Advocate*, February 1911, 6–11.
26. Michael P. McCarthy, "Prelude to Armageddon: Charles E. Merriam and the Chicago Mayoral Election of 1911," *Journal of the Illinois State Historical Society*, (November 1975), 505–18.

5. Big Bill Thompson: The "Model" Politician

1. Article reprinted in *Congressional Record*, Senate, 70th Cong., 1st sess., 1928. vol. 69, pt. 4, 3697–3700; Washington, D.C.: U.S. Government Printing Office, 1928 (copy of pamphlet on file at Chicago Historical Society). Senator Thomas Heflin of Alabama followed Watson and inserted "The Law of Eligibility" from the *Protestant* magazine. The article contended canon law made it virtually impossible for a Catholic to hold the presidency.
2. Federal Bureau of Investigation, Subject: William Hale Thompson, File: 87–3286.
3. For the standard treatment of Thompson, see Reinhard H. Luthin, *American Demagogues* (Boston: 1954). Journalists have been the most fascinated by Thompson. William Stuart, *Twenty Incredible Years* (Chicago: 1935), treats his subject as a prophet scorned, which is not surprising since Stuart was a Hearst newspaperman and Thompson confidant. More balanced is Herman Kogan and Lloyd Wendt's *Big Bill of Chicago* (Indianapolis: 1953). As working reporters, the two had access to newspaper clipping files now destroyed or denied public use. Daniel J. Boorstin, *The Americans: The Democratic Experience* (New York: 1973), 83; FBI, Subject: William Hale Thompson, File: references, page stamped "60305"; Joel Tarr, *A Study in Boss Politics: William Lorimer of Chicago* (Urbana: 1971), chs. 4 and 7.
4. Chicago *Tribune*, 23 January 1915; Kogan and Wendt, *Big Bill*, 92; *Tribune*, 5, 14, 24, and 25 February 1915.
5. Chicago *Tribune*, 3, 12, 18, and 31 March 1915.
6. Chicago *Tribune*, 28 January and 17 February 1915; Arthur W. Thurner, "The Impact of Ethnic Groups on the Democratic Party, 1920–1928" (Ph.D. diss., University of Chicago, 1966), 13; *Tribune*, 26 January 1915; Kogan and Wendt, *Big Bill*, 108. A copy of the handbill is in the graphics collection of the Chicago Historical Society.
7. Edward H. Mazur, "Minyans for a Prairie City: The Politics of Chicago Jewry, 1850–1940" (Ph.D. diss., University of Chicago, 1974), 235. In all, Sweitzer lost the Bohemian, German, Jewish, and Swedish as well as the black vote. See John Allswang, *A House for All People: Ethnic Politics in Chicago* (Lexington: 1971), Table A-2.
8. *Daily News Almanac and Yearbook* (1916) at Chicago Historical Society; *Chicago Tribune*, 7 and 16 April 1915; Thomas E. Vadney, *The Wayward Liberal: A Political Biography of Donald Richberg* (Lexington: 1970), 32–34; *Tri-

bune, 25 April 1915; on economy drive and Eastland, *Tribune*, 5 and 30 June and 29 July to 1 August 1915.

9. Chicago *Tribune*, 15–17 June 1915; *Chicago Commerce*, vol. 11, no. 7, 18 June 1915, at Chicago Historical Society (CHS); *Tribune*, 2 October 1915; Howard Barton Myers, "The Policing of Labor Disputes in Chicago: A Case Study" (Ph.D. diss., University of Chicago, 1929), 813 and 837; *Tribune*, 30 November 1915.

10. James W. Errant, "Trade Unionism in the Civil Service of Chicago, 1895 to 1930" (Ph.D. diss. University of Chicago, 1939), 113–14 and Chicago *Tribune*, 11, 17, and 19 July 1916; for Loeb Rule, *Tribune*, 26 August 1915, and Mary J. Herrick, *The Chicago Schools* (Beverly Hills: 1971), 122.

11. Open letter of the Illinois Manufacturers' Association, 9 September 1915, Box 162, Illinois Manufacturers Association Collection, CHS; Herrick, *Schools*, 128 and 135.

12. Perry Duis, *The Saloon: Public Drinking in Chicago and Boston, 1880–1920* (Urbana: 1983), 286–87; Chicago *Tribune*, 5 and 6 October 1915.

13. Chicago *Tribune*, 29 May to 8 June 1916; William T. Hutchinson, *Lowden of Illinois: The Life of Frank O. Lowden* (Chicago, 1957), vol. 1, 104, 263–66; Charles Gates Dawes to Lawrence Y. Sherman, 1 July 1915, Lawrence Y. Sherman Papers, Illinois State Historical Library, Springfield.

14. Kogan and Wendt, *Big Bill*, 133–34 and 137–43; Chicago *Tribune*, 22 February, 21 March, and 3 April 1916; "The Truth About Civil Service," CHS; *Tribune*, 19 March 1916.

15. Chicago *Tribune*, 14 and 17 September 1915; for rally and leaflet, *Tribune*, 16 and 30 September 1915.

16. Chicago *Tribune*, 11 and 24 October 1916, and 19 January 1917. The trials are covered in Kogan and Wendt, *Big Bill*, 147–48, and Harold F. Gosnell, *Negro Politicians* (Chicago: 1935), 172–74. On wiretaps, *Tribune*, 15 and 28 November 1917.

17. Chicago *Tribune*, 12 September 1915; on preparedness, *Tribune*, 4 June 1916.

18. Kogan and Wendt, *Big Bill*, 153; *Congressional Record*, House, 65th Cong., 1st sess., 1917. vol. 55, pt. 1, 413. The "no" votes were cast by Fred A. Britten, Charles E. Fuller, Edward J. King, William E. Mason, William A. Rodenberg, and Loren E. Wheeler. Britten represented a Chicago district; Mason resided in Chicago as a congressman-at-large. The others represented downstate districts. According to William Stuart, Thompson worked for Lowden in 1916 in exchange for support of his Senate ambitions. William Hutchinson argues there was no clear understanding between the two. See Stuart, *Twenty Incredible Years*, 27 and Hutchinson, *Lowden*, vol. 1, 265 and vol. 2, 383–84.

19. For Thompson's problems with the press, see Kogan and Wendt, *Big Bill*, 149–60. "Food Shortage Warning," 26 April 1917, Chicago Municipal

Reference Library (CMR); *The Republican,* 2 and 23 June and 28 July 1917, CHS.

20. Chicago *Tribune,* 2 and 9 March 1917.

21. Chicago *Tribune,* 3 August 1917; *Chicago Plan Commission Proceedings,* 953, CHS.

22. Address of William Hale Thompson, *Proceedings of the Chicago City Council,* 1918–1919, 13 May 1918, 90–98; for Thompson's versions of the incidents, "The Truth About William Hale Thompson," CMR; on People's Council, Chicago *Tribune,* 1 to 5 September 1917, and Hutchinson, *Lowden,* vol. 1, 378–80; *Tribune,* 26 August 1917, and 25 March, 8 April, and 7 May 1918.

23. Copy of letter marked "personal," Samuel Graham to Charles F. Clyne, U.S. district attorney for northern Illinois, 17 May 1917, and explanation by Joseph B. Fleming to Clyne, 29 May 1917, correspondence numbered 9-5-390-1 and 2, Record Group 60, National Archives; Department of Justice Central Files, Record Group 60, no. 9-19-1206, National Archives; Melvin G. Holli, "The Great War Sinks Chicago's German Kultur," in Melvin G. Holli and Peter d'A. Jones eds., *Ethnic Chicago,* (Grand Rapids: 1984), revised and expanded edition, 501–2; Chicago *Tribune,* 8 August 1917.

24. Chicago *Tribune,* 29 August 1917; Emerson Hough, *The Web* (Chicago: 1919), 182–85, 491, CHS.

25. Chicago *Tribune,* 4 September 1917; Holli, "Great War," 501–2; "A Year of Americanization Work, July 1918–July 1919," CHS. The individual lessons were collected and turned into a text, *A First Book in English for Non-English Speaking Adults* (Chicago: 1920), by Frances K. Wetmore. Lessons included Goggles—"Wear goggles at work and save your eyes."—and Time (on the dangers of buying a defective watch)—"The timekeeper docked me for lost time."

26. "The Truth About William Hale Thompson," CMR.

27. Chicago *Tribune,* 7, 8, and 12 September 1918; *Daily News Almanac and Yearbook* (1919) CHS.

28. *The Republican,* 15 February 1919; Charles E. Merriam, Spencer D. Parrott, Albert Lepawsky, *The Government of the Metropolitan Region of Chicago* (Chicago: 1933), 10. Ickes lived in the Hubbard Woods section of Winnetka; his law partner Richberg lived in south suburban Palos Park.

29. Chicago *Tribune,* 17 February 1919; for Olson's views on eugenics, *Tribune,* 4 September 1915; pamphlets "Win With Merriam" and "Chicago's Hope is Its Free Men and Women" in Charles E. Merriam Papers, University of Chicago.

30. Chicago *Tribune,* 12 and 14 February 1919; on vigilantes, *Tribune,* 18, 19, 20 and 25 February 1919; *Tribune,* 19 and 26 February 1919. Barry D. Karl in his *Charles E. Merriam and the Study of Politics* (Chicago: 1974) makes no mention of Merriam's campaign tactics. See pp. 97–98.

31. Kogan and Wendt, *Big Bill*, p. 167; Chicago *Tribune*, 10 and 11 March 1919; "How Sweitzer and Thompson Appealed to Race Prejudice for Votes," CMR; *Daily News Almanac and Yearbook*, 1920. The campaign included a fourth candidate, John Fitzpatrick, president of the Chicago Federation of Labor, who polled 56,000 votes.

32. Chicago *Tribune*, 29 March 1915. A Thompson speaker made the Sweitzer-Johnson charge. Charles Branham, "The Transformation of Black Political Leadership in Chicago, 1864–1942" (Ph.D. diss., University of Chicago, 1981), 154–57. Movie ads for "Birth" are in *Tribune*, 14 July 1915; 16 November 1916; and 8 June 1917. Here, too, the Democrats failed to capitalize. When the film again played in Chicago in 1924, the administration of William Dever cited state law to ban it but then quickly reversed itself in fear of a possible lawsuit by exhibitors. See Chicago *Defender*, 2, 9, and 16 February 1924. Michael Wallace Homel, "Negroes in the Chicago Public Schools, 1910–1941" (Ph.D. diss., University of Chicago, 1972), 38–40.

33. The reports were not confined to the press. See undated statement by Merriam on the "support of patriotic colored people" for his 1919 candidacy, Merriam Papers, and a letter form Raymond Robins to "Dear Captain-General," 12 March 1927, in the Raymond Robins Papers, Wisconsin State Historical Society, Madison. A social reformer, Robins hoped that the opposition of Edward H. Wright to Thompson could be used to sway black voters to Dever in the 1927 mayoral election. Six years earlier, when Wright was allied with Thompson, he was the object of press criticism for a $30,000 legal bill he sent city hall. See Chicago *Tribune*, 14 and 16 April 1921. Chicago *Defender*, 16 June and 30 October 1926.

34. Gosnell, *Negro Politicians*, pp. 200 and 250; Leonard D. White to Charles E. Merriam, 11 July 1931, in Merriam Papers.

35. William M. Tuttle Jr.'s *Race Riot: Chicago in the Red Summer of 1919* (New York: 1975) and Allan H. Spear's *Black Chicago: The Making of a Negro Ghetto, 1890–1920* (Chicago: 1967) both view the riot largely as a clash over public facilities, housing, and jobs. Thomas Lee Philpott's *The Slum and The Ghetto: Neighborhood Deterioration and Middle-Class Reform, Chicago, 1880–1930* (New York: 1978) ignores environmental and ethnic factors and emphasizes the role of racism. *Dziennik Zwiazkowy*, 27 May 1918, in I-C Polish of Chicago Foreign Press Survey, Works Progress Administration (Foreign Press Survey); *Lietuva*, 31 May 1918, in III-H Lithuanian, Foreign Press Survey, Chicago *Tribune*, 10 June 1919.

36. *Narod Polski*, 28 May 1919, in I-C Polish, Foreign Press Survey; *Jewish Courier*, 19 May and 14 July 1919, in II-D-10 Jewish, Foreign Press Survey; Chicago *Tribune*, 22 May and 8 and 9 June 1919; *Courier*, 25 July 1919, in I-C Jewish, Foreign Press Survey.

37. For Dunne, Chicago *Tribune*, 12 and 18 April, 30 May, 2 and 8 June,

and 9 July 1919; on rallies, *Tribune,* 8 and 25 June and 14 and 15 July 1919.

38. Tuttle, *Race Riot,* 141; Chicago *Tribune,* 28 June and 12 July 1919; on Star Order incident, *Tribune,* 21 June 1920.

39. Chicago *Tribune,* 24–28 July 1919; Hutchinson, *Lowden,* vol. 2, 456–57, and *Tribune,* 6–13 June 1920; Kogan and Wendt, *Big Bill,* 184.

40. Chicago *Tribune,* 1 November 1920. M. A. Michaelson to Warren G. Harding, 27 June 1921; Harry Daughtery to Harding, 29 June 1921; and Andrew Mellon to Harding, 6 July 1921, are all on microfilm roll 195, presidential case file Illinois, Warren G. Harding Papers, Ohio Historical Society. Copy of letter William M. Offey to Mac Gregor Bond, 28 January 1922, and handwritten note by Daughtery on bottom of summary of his phone conversation with Bond are in Department of Justice Central Files, Record Group 60, no. 220285, National Archives. The state supreme court in 1930 reversed a lower court ruling that Thompson was personally liable for the funds in the experts' fee suits. See Kogan and Wendt, *Big Bill,* 194, 310–11, and 320. *Tribune,* 21 June 1922; copy of letter William Hale Thompson to Herbert Hoover, 21 October 1921, in John Fitzpatrick Papers, CHS.

41. Kogan and Wendt, *Big Bill,* 210–13.

42. Sprague's name appears on a list of those accepting appointment to the committee, in John Fitzpatrick Papers, CHS. Chicago *Tribune,* 8 September 1921; Royal E. Montgomery, *Industrial Relations in the Chicago Building Trades* (Chicago: 1927), 275–81; undated leaflet in pamphlets for Citizens' Committee to Enforce the Landis Award, CHS.

43. "The Landis Award: Its Purpose and Accomplishments," CHS. Dever's union membership is cited in "Dever Did Deliver," in Box 3 of Agnes Nestor Papers, CHS. *Landis Award Journeyman,* vol. 1, no. 7, 1 May 1924, CHS. Both Samuel Insull and Col. William Pelouze, Thompson's political supporter and brother-in-law, respectively, were committee members, a connection the Democrats did not exploit in the 1927 election.

44. Stephen D. London, "Business and the Chicago Public School System, 1890–1966" (Ed.D., University of Chicago, 1968), 99; Herrick, *Chicago Schools,* 144–54. The "platoon" system increased the number of children an individual school could handle.

45. William Hale Thompson to William W. Borah, 1 February 1926, Illinois Invitations, William Borah Papers, Library of Congress; Carroll Hill Wooddy, *The Chicago Primary of 1926: A Study in Election Methods* (1974 Arno reprint of 1926 edition), 64–67, particularly Thompson speech contained in footnote.

46. Chicago *Tribune,* 9 January 1927; Kogan and Wendt, *Big Bill,* 253–54, and *Tribune,* 9 March 1927; Thurner, "Impact of Ethnic Groups," 248; on music, *Tribune,* 3 April 1927; for Hoyne and Robins, *Tribune,* 24 March 1927.

47. Chicago *Tribune,* 23 and 30 March and 1 April 1927.

48. Chicago *Tribune,* 17 and 19 March 1927; Thompson speech dated 31 March 1927 in Merriam Papers; *Tribune,* 26 February and 10 April 1927.

49. Chicago *Tribune*, 6 April 1927; Orville James Taylor to Julius Rosenwald, 11, 18, and 19 March 1927, Julius Rosenwald Papers, University of Chicago; for ad by Independent Republicans, *Tribune*, 31 March 1927; Alice Reichel to Julius Rosenwald, 18 May 1927, Rosenwald Papers.

50. Errant, "Trade Unionism," 118–19; Herrick, *Chicago Schools*, 168–70; Kogan and Wendt, *Big Bill*, 340, and Chicago *Tribune*, 8 August 1927; on the new labor-political relationship, Errant, 170–72.

51. Estimates in Kogan and Wendt, *Big Bill*, 268–69; M. R. Werner, *Julius Rosenwald: The Life of a Practical Humanitarian* (New York: 1939), 295–315.

52. Serritella's trial coincided with the 1931 general election. His conviction was overturned on appeal. See Harold F. Gosnell, *Machine Politics: Chicago Model* (1968 Greenwood reprint of 1937 edition), footnote, p. 12. The link between the syndicate and politics is detailed in Len O'Connor, *Clout: Mayor Daley and His City* (New York: 1975), and Mike Royko, *Boss: Richard J. Daley of Chicago* (New York: 1971).

53. Chicago *Tribune*, 22–27 April and 3 June 1927; "America First-Farm Relief-Inland Waterways-National Flood Control to Prevent Disaster," CMR; San Francisco *Examiner*, 16 September 1927, Thompson Clipping file.

54. Chicago *Tribune*, editorial, 8 June 1920: Chicago *Herald-Examiner*, 27 January 1923. San Francisco *Examiner*, 21 July 1926 and 8 April 1927 and undated New York *American* editorial are all contained in Thompson clipping file, courtesy of the San Francisco *Examiner*. Hearst editorial in the Baltimore *American*, 5 November 1927, courtesy of the Baltimore *New-American*.

55. Chicago *Defender*, 24 April and 8 May 1926; copy of letter marked "personal," Victor Olander to Oscar F. Nelson, 16 April 1927, in Box 10, Victor Olander Papers, CHS.

56. Herrick, Chicago Schools, 168–70. McAndrew was charged with insubordination and tainting the school histories with pro-British propaganda. His contract expired before a "guilty" verdict was reached. See Chicago *Tribune*, 22 March 1928. Thompson sent a letter to the school board, 22 November 1927, on ethnic heroes of the Revolution. See George S. Courts, *School and Society in Chicago* (1971 Arno reprint of 1928 edition), 280–83. Chicago *Tribune*, 1 December 1927, and Rupert Costo, ed., *Textbooks and the American Indian* (San Francisco: 1970), 2–3.

57. On Pineapple Primary and Thompson breakdown, Kogan and Wendt, *Big Bill*, 304–8 and 312–14; Chicago *Tribune*, 10 October 1930.

58. Clarence Darrow to Donald Richberg, 15 June 1930, in Box 9, Donald Richberg Papers, CHS; Karl, Merriam, 235; Harold Ickes, *Autobiography of a Curmudgeon* (New York: 1943), 267–70 and 281; Vadney, *Wayward Liberal*, 120.

59. Chicago *Defender*, 4 April 1931; on St. Patrick's Day Meeting, *Defender*, 20 March 1926.

60. Chicago *Tribune*, 6 April 1931; Alex Gottfried, *Boss Cermak of Chicago: A Study of Political Leadership* (Seattle: 1962), 180–200; on Cermak and Jar-

ecki, Douglas Bukowski, "Judge Edmund K. Jarecki: A Rather Regular Independent," *Chicago History*, vol. 8, no. 4, Winter 1979–1980; Allswang, *House for All Peoples*, Table 8: 2, p. 161.

61. The most comprehensive treatment of the public works of Thompson's successor is Carl W. Condit's *Chicago, 1930–1970: Building, Planning, and Urban Technology* (Chicago: 1974).

62. Chicago *Tribune*, 7 April 1931; on Citizens' Committee, *Tribune*, 14 March 1929; O'Connor, *Clout*, 17.

63. Ickes, *Autobiography*, 173.

6. William E. Dever: A Chicago Political Fable

1. Dever's background and early career are detailed by the writer in "Dever of Chicago: A Political Biography" (Ph.D. dissertation, University of Chicago, 1983). See also the William E. Dever Papers and the William E. Dever Scrapbooks, both at the Chicago Historical Society.

2. The best contemporary study of Chicago politics in the early twentieth century is Charles E. Merriam, *Chicago: A More Intimate View of Urban Politics* (New York: The Macmillan Co., 1929). For the evolution of the Democratic organization, consult Paul M. Green, "The Chicago Democratic Party, 1840–1920: From Factionalism to Political Organization" (Ph.D. diss., University of Chicago, 1975).

3. Chicago *Daily News*, 19 December 1922, 4 January 1923; Chicago *Tribune*, 7, 11 January 1923.

4. Brennan's selection of Dever is described in Parke Brown, "Brennan of Illinois," *Century Magazine* 112 (September 1926): 596–97. See also Harold L. Ickes, *The Autobiography of a Curmudgeon* (New York: Reynal and Hitchcock, 1943), 247–48; George Sikes to Martin J. O'Brien, 11 November 1922, Dever Papers.

5. Chicago *Journal*, 2 March 1923.

6. Chicago *Herald and Examiner*, Chicago *Tribune*, both 17 April 1923.

7. At least one contemporary magazine essay on Dever's beer war was published in booklet form: Neil McCullough Clark, *Mayor Dever and Prohibition: The Story of a Dramatic Fight to Enforce the Law* (Westerville, OH: American Issue Publishing Co., 1925).

8. Chicago *Tribune*, 8, 15 January 1925.

9. Dever wrote his own account of the cleanup for the New York *Herald*, 25 November 1923; the article was syndicated and appeared in other papers. See also Chicago *Tribune*, 8 October 1923.

10. Chicago *Herald and Examiner*, 10 April 1925.

11. Chicago *Tribune*, 10 January 1925.

12. The McAndrew controversy is described in George S. Counts, *School and Society in Chicago* (New York: Harcourt, Brace, 1928).

13. U.S., Congress, Senate Subcommittee of the Committee on the Judi-

ciary, *The National Prohibition Law.* Hearings on bills to amend the National Prohibition Act, 5–24 April 1926, 69th Cong., 1st sess., 1926, 1377–78, 1384–85.

14. Chicago *Herald and Examiner*, 3 October 1926; William E. Dever, "Get at the Facts." *Atlantic Monthly* 138 (October 1926): 518–24.

15. Chicago *Herald and Examiner*, 5 January 1927.

16. Chicago *Daily News*, 23 February 1927; John Bright, *Hizzoner Big Bill Thompson: An Idyll of Chicago* (New York: Jonathon Cape and Harrison Smith, 1930), 250–51.

17. Quoted in Elmer Davis, "Portrait of an Elected Person," *Harper's Magazine* 155 (July 1927): 183.

18. Besides the Davis article cited above, other national magazine commentaries on the 1927 election include: Nels Andersen, "Democracy in Chicago," *Century Magazine* 115 (November 1927): 71–78; Kate Sargent, "Chicago: Hands Down!" *The Forum* 78 (November 1927): 708–24; William Allen White, "They Can't Beat My Big Boy!" *Collier's* 79 (18 June 1927): 8–9, 46–47; "What 'Big Bill's' Victory Means," *Literary Digest* 93 (6 April 1927): 5–7; "Why Chicago Did It," *New Republic* 50 (20 April 1927): 234–36.

19. Chicago *Herald and Examiner*, 18 March 1924; Arthur W. Thurner, "The Impact of Ethnic Groups on the Democratic Party in Chicago, 1920–1928," (Ph.D. diss., University of Chicago, 1966), 263–64.

7. Anton J. Cermak: The Man and His Machine

1. Alex Gottfried, *Boss Cermak of Chicago: A Study of Political Leadership* (Seattle: University of Washington Press, 1962), viii.

2. H. K. Barnard, *Anton the Martyr* (Chicago: Marion Publishing, 1933), 20.

3. Gottfried, 369.

4. Personal Interview. Chicago, 1985.

5. Personal Interview. Chicago, 1970.

6. Chicago *Tribune*, 7 May 1915.

7. See Paul M. Green's "Irish Chicago: The Multi-Ethnic Road to Machine Success," in Melvin G. Holli and Peter d'A. Jones, eds., *Ethnic Chicago* (Grand Rapids: Eerdman's Publishing Company, 1984), 434–39.

8. Personal Interview. Chicago, 1970.

9. Chicago *Herald and Examiner*, 13 February 1927.

10. See Gottfried, 169–99. Mike Royko, *Boss: Richard J. Daley of Chicago* (New York: E. P. Dutton, 1971), 36. Andrew Greeley, *That Most Distressed Nation* (Chicago: Quadrangle Books, 1972), 206. Eugene Kennedy, *Himself! The Life and Times of Mayor Richard J. Daley* (New York: The Viking Press, 1978), 51.

11. Chicago *Herald and Examiner*, 30 October 1929.

12. Ibid. 7 October 1929.

13. Ibid. 25 April 1929.
14. Chicago *Tribune*, 24 March 1931.
15. Ibid. 14 May 1931.
16. Personal Interview. Chicago, 1971.
17. See Kip Sullivan, "Politics and Educational Policy: The Control of Chicago Public Schools During the Administration of Anton J. Cermak" (Unpublished Ph.D. diss., Loyola University of Chicago, 1985).
18. Chicago *Tribune*, 13 July 1931.
19. Chicago *Tribune*, 21 May 1931.
20. *Public Service Leader*, 5 December 1932.
21. See Green, *Ethnic Chicago*, 451–52.

8. Edward J. Kelly: New Deal Machine Builder

1. Roger Biles, *Big City in Depression and War: Mayor Edward J. Kelly of Chicago* (DeKalb: Northern Illinois University Press, 1984), 13–19. On Cermak, see Alex Gottfried, *Boss Cermak of Chicago: A Study in Political Leadership* (Seattle: University of Washington Press, 1962). Prior to selecting Kelly, Nash chose Alderman Francis J. Corr as "acting" mayor. He served from March 10 to April 14.
2. "Mayor Kelly's Own Story," Chicago *Herald-American*, 5 May 1947; Donald S. Bradley and Mayer N. Zald, "From Commercial Elite to Political Administrator: The Recruitment of the Mayors of Chicago," *American Journal of Sociology* 71 (September 1965): 153–67.
3. Broadus Mitchell, *Depression Decade* (New York: Rinehart and Co., 1947), 105; Irving Bernstein, *The Lean Years: A History of the American Worker, 1920–1933* (Boston: Houghton Mifflin, 1966), 297–98.
4. Paul Douglas, "Chicago's Financial Muddle," *New Republic* 61 (12 February 1930): 324–26; Lyman B. Burbank, "Chicago Public Schools and the Depression Years of 1928–1937," *Journal of the Illinois State Historical Society* 64 (Winter 1971): 365–81; *New York Times*, 27 November 1932.
5. *Newsweek* 5 (13 April 1935): 7; Charles T. Holman, "Chicago Elects a New Mayor," *Christian Century* 50 (26 April 1933): 567–68; New York *Times*, 16 April 1933; Chicago *Tribune*, 26 April 1933; John T. Flynn, "These Our Rulers," *Collier's* 106 (20 July 1940): 18, 19.
6. *Lightnin'* (July 1933): 10; Burbank, 375; Chicago *Tribune*, 28 April 1933.
7. "Elected to Fill Former Mayor Cermak's Unexpired Term," *Newsweek* 1 (22 April 1933): 19; New York *Times*, 16 April 1933; Harold M. Mayer and Richard C. Wade, *Chicago: Growth of a Metropolis* (Chicago: University of Chicago Press, 1969), 362–64; Arthur G. Lindell, *City Hall Chronology, 1966*, Municipal Reference Library of Chicago, vol. 2.
8. Chicago *Tribune*, 24 February 1935 (quote); *Newsweek* 5 (13 April 1935): 7; *Chicago American*, 3 April 1935 (Wetten quote).
9. New York *Times*, 4 March 1935 (first quote), 20 October 1936 (Krock

quote); "Chicago's Record of Accomplishment Under Mayor Edward J. Kelly," 1940, Chicago Historical Society (Sutherland quote).

10. Gottfried, 207; John M. Allswang, *A House For All Peoples: Ethnic Politics in Chicago, 1890–1936* (Lexington: University Press of Kentucky, 1971), 42–43; Edward R. Kantowicz, "American Politics in Polonia's Capital: 1888–1940," Ph.D. diss., University of Chicago, 1972, 429–30.

11. Henry F. Gosnell, *Machine Politics: Chicago Model* (Chicago: University of Chicago Press, 1937); Sonya Forthal, *Cogwheels of Democracy: A Study of the Precinct Captain* (New York: William-Frederick Press, 1946).

12. "Mayor Kelly's Chicago," *Life* 17 (17 July 1944), 75; "The Kelly-Nash Political Machine," *Fortune* 14 (August 1936), 126–39.

13. Donald G. Sofchalk, "The Chicago Memorial Day Incident: An Episode of Mass Action," *Labor History* 6 (Winter 1965): 17; U.S. Congress, Senate Committee on Education and Labor, "The Chicago Memorial Day Incident: Hearings before a Subcommittee of the Senate Committee on Education and Labor," 75th Cong., 1st sess., 1937, 37–40; Barbara Newell, *Chicago and the Labor Movement: Metropolitan Unionism in the 1930s* (Urbana: University of Illinois Press, 1961), 178–79, 224–25, 250.

14. Roger Biles, "'Big Red in Bronzeville': Mayor Ed Kelly Reels in the Black Vote," *Chicago History* 10 (Summer 1981), 99–111.

15. Ibid.

16. Perry R. Duis, "Arthur W. Mitchell, New Deal Negro in Congress," M.A. thesis, University of Chicago, 1966, 26–38; John M. Allswang, "The Chicago Negro Voter and the Democratic Consensus: A Case Study, 1918–1936," *Journal of the Illinois State Historical Society* 60 (Summer 1967), 172.

17. James Q. Wilson, "Negro Leaders in Chicago," Ph.D. diss., University of Chicago, 1959, 102 (quote); James Q. Wilson, *Negro Politics: The Search for Leadership* (Glencoe, IL: Free Press of Glencoe, 1960), 50.

18. Mike Royko, *Boss: Richard J. Daley of Chicago* (New York: E. P. Dutton, 1971), 132; Len O'Connor, *Clout: Mayor Daley and His City* (New York: Avon Books, 1975), 178–79.

19. William H. Stuart, *The Twenty Incredible Years* (Chicago: M. A. Donahue, 1935), 536; Virgil W. Peterson, *Barbarians in Our Midst: A History of Chicago Crime and Politics* (Boston: Little, Brown, and Co., 1952), 165; Warren H. Pierce, "Chicago: Unfinished Anomaly" in Robert S. Allen, ed., *Our Fair City* (New York: Vanguard Press, 1947), 177; Chicago *Daily News*, 30 October 1934; John Bartlow Martin, "Al Capone's Successors," *American Mercury* 68 (June 1949): 733; Biles, *Big City Boss*, 107.

20. Chicago *Daily News*, 30 October 1934; Paul Douglas, *In the Fullness of Time* (New York: Harcourt Brace Jovanovich, 1971), 90; Pierce, 177; John T. Flynn, "Too Much Fun," *Collier's* 104 (7 October 1939): 35–36; Martin, 733; Peterson, 165.

21. Chicago *Daily News*, 30 October 1934.

22. Biles, *Big City Boss*, 8–11, 107–8; Pierce, 177; Douglas, *In the Fullness of Time*, 91; Eugene Kennedy, *Himself!: The Life and Times of Mayor Richard J. Daley* (New York: Viking Press, 1978), 62 (quote).

23. Harold L. Ickes, *The Secret Diary of Harold L. Ickes: The First Thousand Days, 1933–1936* (New York: Simon and Schuster, 1954), 246, 494, 557; Arthur M. Schlesinger, Jr., *The Age of Roosevelt: The Politics of Upheaval* (Boston: Houghton Mifflin, 1960), 442–43; Edward J. Kelly to Harry Hopkins, memo of telephone conversation, 10 September 1935, Harry Hopkins Papers, Box 93, Franklin D. Roosevelt Library, Hyde Park, New York.

24. James A. Farley, *Jim Farley's Story: The Roosevelt Years* (New York: McGraw-Hill, 1948), 92; Ickes, 463; Jim Farley to Edward J. Kelly, 17 September 1936, Democratic National Committee Papers, Illinois File, FDR Library.

25. Edward J. Kelly to Franklin D. Roosevelt, received 30 August 1932, Franklin D. Roosevelt Papers, Personal File 3166, FDR Library; Franklin D. Roosevelt to Edward J. Kelly, 12 September 1932, ibid.; Samuel I. Rosenman, *Working With Roosevelt* (New York: Harper and Row, 1952), 123; Biles, *Big City Boss*, 80–83.

26. Lyle W. Dorsett, *Franklin D. Roosevelt and the City Bosses* (Port Washington, New York: Kennikat Press, 1977), 93; Ralph Madison, "Letter from Chicago," *New Republic* 112 (23 April 1945): 549–51.

27. Dorsett, 93; Biles, *Big City Boss*, 83–85.

28. On Roosevelt's role in the 1936 Illinois gubernatorial race, see: Thomas B. Littlewood, *Horner of Illinois* (Evanston: Northwestern University Press, 1969).

29. Gene Delon Jones, "The Local Political Significance of New Deal Relief Legislation in Chicago: 1933–1940," (Ph.D. diss., Northwestern University, 1970), 244; City of Chicago, *Chicago's Report to the People, 1933–1946*, (March 1947), 7, 9; Carl W. Condit, *Chicago, 1930–1970: Building, Planning, and Urban Technology* (Chicago: University of Chicago Press, 1974), 24, 30, 34, 48n.

30. Jones, 206 (quote); Biles, *Big City Boss*, 71–80.

31. Walter Davenport, "From Whom All Blessings Flow," *Collier's* 96 (20 July 1935), 7, 8, 34–36; Lorena Hickok to Harry Hopkins, 18 July 1936, Lorena Hickok Papers, FERA Reports, Box 11, FDR Library (quote); Gosnell, 78; Chicago *Tribune*, 26 April 1937; Speech of Wayne McMillen, 25 January 1938, Records of the National Association of Social Workers, Chicago Chapter, Box 5, Chicago Historical Society; Leo M. Lyons, "Illinois Investigates the Relief Situation," *National Municipal Review* 27 (January 1938): 26 (quote).

32. Edwin O'Connor, *The Last Hurrah* (Boston: Little, Brown, and Co., 1956), especially 101, 329–31. In agreement with this critique of the Last Hurrah thesis are: Bruce M. Stave, *The New Deal and the Last Hurrah: Pittsburgh Machine Politics* (Pittsburgh: University of Pittsburgh Press, 1970); Lyle

W. Dorsett, *The Pendergast Machine* (New York: Oxford University Press, 1968); and Jones, "Local Political Significance of New Deal Relief Legislation."

33. Littlewood, 208–11; Flynn, "Too Much Fun," 36; Chicago *Tribune*, 1 March 1939; Chicago *Herald and Examiner*, 2 March 1939; New York *Times*, 5 April 1939. The only biography of Dwight Green is Robert J. Casey and W. A. S. Douglas, *The Midwesterner: The Story of Dwight H. Green* (Chicago: Wilcox and Follett, 1948).

34. Chicago *Tribune*, 23 February 1943 (McKibbin quote), 7 April 1943; Chicago *Sun*, 8 April 1943.

35. Paul F. Barrett, "Mass Transit, the Automobile, and Public Policy in Chicago, 1900–1930," Ph.D. diss., University of Illinois at Chicago Circle, 1976, 72, 95, 108, 230; Lindell, 248.

36. "Millenium for Straphangers," *Time* 50 (8 September 1947): 24–25; City of Chicago, *Chicago's Report to the People*, 192, 196; Paul F. Barrett, "Public Policy and Private Choice: Mass Transit and the Automobile in Chicago Between the Wars," *Business History Review* 49 (Winter 1975): 473–97.

37. Biles, *Big City Boss*, 47 (quote); O'Connor, 56–58; Kennedy, 79–80; Chicago *Sun*, 17 April 1947.

38. Ralph Whitehead, Jr., "The Ward Boss Who Saved the New Deal," *Chicago* 26 (May 1977): 179 (quote); Milburn P. Akers, "Twilight of Boss Kelly," *Nation* 162 (April 13, 1946): 425–26; "Protected Gambling in Chicago," *Criminal Justice* 74 (May 1947): 20–23.

39. Biles, *Big City Boss*, 147; Melvin G. Holli interview with J. Greenough, 14 April 1985, River Forest, Illinois.

40. Ibid., 147–48; O'Connor, 58–59; Milburn P. Akers, "Chicago Dumps Kelly," *Nation* 164 (4 January 1947): 8; Chicago *Tribune*, 16 April 1947, 21, 24 October 1950; "Funeral of a Boss," *Life* (6 November 1950): 40–41.

41. Ibid.

42. Walter Johnson and Carol Evans, eds., *The Papers of Adlai E. Stevenson* (Boston: Little, Brown, and Company, 1973), vol. 3, 311 (Stevenson quote); Alfred Steinberg, *The Bosses* (New York: Macmillan, 1972), 8 (first Kelly quote); Victor Rubin, "You've Gotta Be a Boss," *Collier's* 116 (25 September 1945): 36 (second Kelly quote).

9. Martin H. Kennelly: The Mugwump and the Machine

1. Perry R. Duis and Glen E. Holt, "The Real Legacy of 'Poor Martin' Kennelly," *Chicago* 27 (July 1978): 162–65; Charles B. Cleveland, "Look What He's Doing to Chicago," *Saturday Evening Post* 221 (July 3, 1948): 15ff.

2. Cleveland, "Look What He's Doing to Chicago," 16 and passim.; "Biographical Sketch of Mayor Martin H. Kennelly," (n.p., n.d.) in the Martin H. Kennelly Papers, Department of History, University of Illinois at Chicago; Interview with Leon Despres, Chicago, Illinois, 19 August 1985.

3. New York *Times*, 22 December 1946.

4. Despres interview, 19 August 1985; Len O'Connor, *Clout: Mayor Daley and His City* (New York: Avon Books, 1975), 85.

5. "Biographical Sketch of Martin H. Kennelly"; "Martin H. Kennelly, Chicago's Thirty-ninth Mayor: Biography—History," (n.p., n.d.); The Greater Chicago Committee for the Re-Election of Mayor Kennelly, "Meet Martin Kennelly," (n.p., n.d.), all in the Kennelly Papers. Peter J. O'Malley, "Mayor Martin H. Kennelly of Chicago: A Political Biography," (Ph.D. diss., University of Illinois at Chicago, 1980), ch. 1.

6. Duis and Holt, "The Real Legacy," 164; O'Malley, "Mayor Martin H. Kennelly," ch. 1.

7. O'Malley, "Mayor Martin H. Kennelly," ch. 1.

8. Roger Biles, *Big City Boss in Depression and War: Mayor Edward J. Kelly of Chicago* (DeKalb, IL: Northern Illinois University Press, 1984), 148–50; O'Malley, "Mayor Martin H. Kennelly," 36.

9. Biles, Kelly's biographer, doubts this version of events. In addition to the sources cited in note 8, above, see also Milton L. Rakove, *We Don't Want Nobody Nobody Sent* (Bloomington: Indiana University Press, 1979), 12.

10. New York *Times*, 22 December 1946. While there is no firsthand account of the bargain struck between Arvey and Kennelly, John Bartlow Martin provides some insight with his account of Arvey's dealings with gubernatorial candidate Adlai Stevenson. According to Martin's reconstruction, Arvey said: "I will tell you the same thing I told Kennelly in 1947. The only thing I ask of you is that you help the Democratic Party as much as you can in a decent way. We want the patronage when a Democrat can fill the job. I am not talking about cabinet appointments or your own personal appointments. Get the best men you can for those. We want you to get the best. That's the way you can help the party the most. You're our showcase. If you do well, then we'll look good. All I ask is that you be loyal to the party—don't make an alliance with the Republicans." See John Bartlow Martin, *Adlai Stevenson of Illinois* (Garden City, NY: Doubleday and Company, Inc., 1976), 279. If, in fact, Arvey made such a deal with Kennelly, it was a shrewd one that protected the Cook County Democratic organization's interests at a time when the Republicans controlled a significant minority in the city council. See above, 000–000.

11. Statement of Martin H. Kennelly to the members of the Democratic Central Committee, 20 December 1946, in the Kennelly Papers.

12. Speech by Russell W. Root over radio station WLS, 18 February 1947; Address by George B. McKibben over radio station WENR, 10 March 1947, both in the Kennelly Papers; Independent Voters of Illinois, Minutes of the State Central Committee Meeting, 9 December 1946, in the Independent Voters of Illinois Papers, Chicago Historical Society (CHS).

13. Martin H. Kennelly for Mayor, press releases, 7 and 24 March 1947; Martin H. Kennelly, radio address no. 1, "Chicago Is My Home Town," all in the Kennelly Papers.

14. O'Malley, "Mayor Martin H. Kennelly," ch. 2.

15. Inaugural Address of Mayor Martin H. Kennelly, Council Chambers, City Hall, 15 April 1947, in the Kennelly Papers.

16. O'Malley, "Mayor Martin H. Kennelly," ch. 3; Leon Despres interview, 19 August 1985.

17. Martin H. Kennelly, "State of the City" address, 2 February 1954, in the Kennelly Papers; O'Malley, "Mayor Martin H. Kennelly," ch. 5.

18. Mary J. Herrick, *The Chicago Schools: A Social and Political History* (Beverly Hills: Sage Publications, 1971), 259–77.

19. Herrick, *The Chicago Schools*, 277–78; Margaret Hancock to Mitchell McKeown, 13 March 1951, in the Kennelly Papers.

20. Herrick, *The Chicago Schools*, 279–300.

21. Chicago *Tribune*, 7 March 1954.

22. O'Malley, "Mayor Martin H. Kennelly," 81–83; A Democratic precinct captain to Mr. Mayor, 12 March 1951, in the Kennelly Papers; Chicago *Tribune*, 7, 8 March 1954; Chicago *Sun-Times*, 8 March 1954; Chicago *Daily News*, 5 March 1954; O'Connor, *Clout*, 84.

23. Duis and Holt, "The Real Legacy," 162–65; O'Malley, "Mayor Martin H. Kennelly," ch. 4.

24. Kennelly, "State of the City" address, 2 February 1954.

25. O'Connor, *Clout*, 91; O'Malley, "Mayor Martin H. Kennelly," ch. 5.

26. In addition to the sources cited in note 25 above, see also Chicago *Tribune*, 24 January 1951.

27. O'Malley, "Mayor Martin H. Kennelly," ch. 5; Statement of Mayor Martin H. Kennelly left with Senate Crime Investigation Committee, 5 October 1950; Memorandum Re Organized Syndicated Vice and Gambling (n.d.), both in the Kennelly Papers; "News on the Spot," 14 November 1950, in the Len O'Connor Papers, CHS.

28. The Greater Chicago Committee, Martin H. Kennelly for Mayor, press release, 14 February 1947 and n.d., both in the Kennelly Papers.

29. Interview with Robert E. Merriam, Chicago, Illinois, 23 September 1985.

30. O'Connor, *Clout*, 89; Stephen E. Hurley to J. H. Dillard, 31 August 1954 and "Requested Increase in Civil Service Budget Rejected Up To Now," 6 December 1954, both in the Kennelly Papers; O'Malley, "Mayor Martin H. Kennelly," ch. 3; Merriam interview, 23 September 1985.

31. Merriam interview, 23 September 1985.

32. Chicago *Sun-Times*, 27 March 1950; Rakove, *We Don't Want Nobody Nobody Sent*, 276.

33. Biles, *Big City Boss*, 152; Chicago *Sun Times*, 8 March 1954; Francis W. McPeek to Mayor Kennelly, 20 October 1954, in the Kennelly Papers; O'Connor, *Clout*, 13, 86; Rakove, *We Don't Want Nobody Nobody Sent*, 299; Merriam interview, 23 September 1985.

34. O'Malley, "Mayor Martin H. Kennelly," ch. 3.

35. Milton C. Mumford to Hughston McBain, 16 May 1947, in the Holman D. Pettibone Papers, CHS; Metropolitan Housing and Planning Council, Minutes of the Executive Committee, 29 October 1953; Sydney Stein, Jr. to Edward Eagle Brown, 27 April 1953; Metropolitan Housing and Planning Council, Minutes of the Board of Governors Meeting, 3 April 1953, all in the Metropolitan Housing and Planning Council Papers, Special Collections, University of Illinois at Chicago; Interview with Julian Levi, Chicago, Illinois, 29 July 1980; Interview with Ferd Kramer, Chicago, Illinois, 4 August 1980. For a detailed examination of the legislative background to slum clearance and renewal in Chicago, see Arnold R. Hirsch, *Making the Second Ghetto: Race and Housing Chicago, 1940–1960* (New York: Cambridge University Press, 1983), 100–170.

36. Interview with Ira J. Bach, Chicago, Illinois, 24 July 1980.

37. Martin Meyerson and Edward C. Banfield, *Politics, Planning, and the Public Interest* (New York: The Free Press, 1955), 171–72.

38. Martin, *Adlai Stevenson of Illinois*, 450–51, 460; O'Malley, "Mayor Martin H. Kennelly," ch. 7.

39. Rakove, *We Don't Want Nobody Nobody Sent,* 13; Herrick, *The Chicago Schools,* 277; Chicago *Sun-Times,* 15, 17 April 1953; 22 July 1953; and unidentified clippings in the Daniel M. Cantwell Papers, CHS.

40. For Kelly's record on racial issues, see Biles, *Big City Boss,* 89–102; Interview with Vernon Jarrett, Chicago, Illinois, 28 August 1985.

41. Chicago *Defender,* 22, 29 March 1947; Chicago *Bee,* 5 January 1947.

42. Rakove, *We Don't Want Nobody Nobody Sent,* 12; Eugene Kennedy, *Himself! The Life and Times of Richard J. Daley* (New York: Viking Press, 1978), 80–81; Biles, *Big City Boss,* 146–48.

43. Chicago Commission on Human Relations, "Memorandum on the Fernwood Park Homes" (mimeo., n.d.), Chicago Urban League Papers (CUL Papers), Special Collections, University of Illinois at Chicago; "The Peoria Street Incident" (mimeo., n.d.), Municipal Reference Library (MRL), City Hall, Chicago, Illinois.

44. Sidney Williams to Homer Jack, December 1949, in the Archibald J. Carey, Jr. Papers, CHS; Sidney Williams to Mayor Martin H. Kennelly, 29 November 1949, in the Catholic Interracial Council Papers (CIC Papers), CHS; Arvarh E. Strickland, *History of the Chicago Urban League* (Urbana, IL: University of Illinois Press, 1966), 172–74; Hirsch, *Making the Second Ghetto,* 61–62, 246–47.

45. Chicago Council Against Racial and Religious Discrimination to Martin H. Kennelly, 24 February 1949 and Archibald J. Carey to Val J. Washington, 27 April 1949, both in the Carey Papers; Chicago *Defender,* 5 March 1949.

46. Elizabeth Wood to the Commissioners, 28 July 1947, Business and Pro-

fessional People in the Public Interest Papers (BPI Papers), CHS; Meyerson and Banfield, *Politics, Planning, and the Public Interest,* passim.; Address by Elizabeth Wood, Executive Secretary of the Chicago Housing Authority at "A Tribute to Good Government" dinner given in her honor by Chicago citizens at the Red Lacquer Room of the Palmer House on Thursday, 9 October 1952, CUL Papers; *Southeast Economist,* 26 May 1949, clipping in the Cantwell Papers.

47. Address by Elizabeth Wood; Institute for Community Design Analysis, "Review and Analysis of the Chicago Housing Authority and Implementation of Recommendations; Final Report of Phase I: Recommended Changes and Resulting Savings," 31 March 1982, MRL: Wood's firing is discussed in greater detail in Hirsch, *Making the Second Ghetto,* 234–38.

48. O'Malley, "Mayor Martin H. Kennelly," 147, 222–23; Willard Townsend to J. S. Knowlson, 9 April 1951; Willard Townsend to Mayor Kennelly, 16 April 1951; J. S. Knowlson to Martin H. Kennelly, 7 June 1951; [Olive M.] Diggs, Memo, 13 March 1951, all in the Kennelly Papers.

49. O'Malley, "Mayor Martin H. Kennelly," 192; Timothy J. O'Connor to Martin H. Kennelly, 13 January 1955, n.p.; Patrolman C. Ryan to Aide to the Commissioner, n.d.; Summary of Gambling Arrests Made for the Year 1951, n.d., all in the Kennelly Papers, Mike Royko, *Boss: Richard J. Daley of Chicago* (New York: Signet Books, 1971), 62; Bach interview, 24 July 1980.

50. Jarrett interview, 28 August 1985; Chicago *Tribune,* 13 January 1952, 6 February 1955; Chicago *Sun-Times,* 31 December 1953; unidentified clipping in the C. C. Wimbish Papers, CHS.

51. O'Malley, "Mayor Martin H. Kennelly," 222; Chicago *Defender,* 7 April 1951.

52. Merriam interview, 23 September 1985.

53. Report on the Community Forum's Meeting on Trumbull Park, 23 May 1954, in the Irene McCoy Gaines Papers, CHS; Chicago *Defender,* 15 May 1954, 26 March 1955; Elizabeth Wood to Members of the CHA Advisory Committee on Race Relations, 27 April 1954, in the BPI Papers; Duckett-Lawrence Associates, et al., "A Specialized Public Relations and Promotional Program Proposed for Robert E. Merriam, Candidate for Mayor of Chicago (Aimed at the Negro Community)," n.d., in the Carey Papers.

54. Kennelly campaign press release, 30 January 1955, in the Kennelly Papers, Chicago *Sun-Times,* 28 January 1955; Chicago *Defender,* 5, 19 February 1955, 26 March 1955; Claude A. Barnett to Frederick D. Jordan, 21 February 1955 in the Claude A. Barnett Papers, CHS.

55. The South Deering Improvement Association employed a sound truck to drum up votes for Daley in the Trumbull Park area. See Illinois Division, American Civil Liberties Union, Executive Committee Minutes, 7 April 1955, 16 June 1955, in the Illinois Division-American Civil Liberties Union Papers,

Special Collections, Regenstein Library, University of Chicago; see also *Daily Calumet*, 21 February 1955; Chicago *Defender*, 19 February 1955; O'Malley, "Mayor Martin H. Kennelly," ch. 8; O'Connor, *Clout*, 106–25.

56. Chicago *Sun-Times*, 24 February 1955.

10. Richard J. Daley: America's Last Boss

1. We wish to thank Johns Hopkins University Press for permission to publish this chapter, which will appear in revised form in a Hopkins book. Len O'Connor, *Clout: Mayor Daley and His City* (Chicago, 1975), chs. 2, 3; Mike Royko, *Boss: Richard J. Daley of Chicago* (New York, 1971), ch. 2.

2. Chicago *Tribune*, 27 March 1955, 8; 30 March 1955, 7; 5 March 1955, 2.

3. Chicago *Tribune*, 25 March 1955, 2; Royko, *Boss*, 89.

4. Chicago *Tribune*, 5 April 1959, 24; 1 April 1959, part 2, 2; 28 March 1959, 12.

5. Chicago *Tribune*, 2 April 1959, 1ff; 6 April 1959, 6; 5 April 1959, 1ff, 24.

6. E.g., Chicago *Tribune*, 22 March 1963, 6.

7. Leon Despres, "Corruption in Chicago," *The Nation* (12 March 1960), 220–23.

8. Chicago *Tribune*, 15 March 1963, 17; 31 March 1963, 22.

9. Tom Wicker, "The Place Where All America Was Radicalized," New York *Times Magazine* (24 August 1969): 26ff.; John P. Robinson, "Public Reaction to Political Protest: Chicago, 1968," *Public Opinion Quarterly* (Spring 1970): 1–3, 5.

10. Chicago *Tribune*, 24 March 1971, 8.

11. Chicago *Defender*, 5 March 1955, 1ff.

12. Chicago *Defender*, 1 April 1959, 1ff.; 16 March 1959, 11.

13. Chicago *Defender*, 2 April 1963, 1, 3; 1 March 1967, 3.

14. Chicago *Defender*, 16 March 1971, 1, 3ff.; 17 March 1971, 4ff.

15. Chicago *Defender*, 22 February 1975. See also Chicago *Defender*, 29 March 1975, 2; Chicago *Tribune*, 27 March 1975, part 2, 1.

16. Quoted in Royko, *Boss*, 164–65.

17. David Halberstam, "Daley of Chicago," *Harper's* (August 1968): 31, 34–35.

18. Chicago *Defender*, 25 March 1971, 3ff.; 16 March 1971, 1, 3ff.; 17 March 1971, 4ff.; Chicago *Tribune*, 6 April 1971, 2.

19. O'Connor, *Clout*, 4, ch. 12; Chicago *Tribune*, 1 April 1975, part 2, 1.

11. Michael A. Bilandic: The Last of the Machine Regulars

1. Chicago *Tribune*, 23 December 1976.

2. Ibid., 26 December 1976.

3. Ibid., 29 December 1976.

4. Personal interview, May 1986.

5. From 1933 to the early 1940s Chicago Mayor Edward J. Kelly shared power with Cook County Democratic party chairman Pat Nash.

6. Chicago *Tribune,* 18 April 1977.

7. Ibid., 19 April 1977.

8. After losing to Bilandic, Block joined most of his former Chicago Republicans by moving to the suburbs. In short, he got out of town.

9. Personal interview, June 1986.

10. Personal Interview, June 1986.

11. Milton Rakove, "Jane Byrne and the New Chicago Politics," in Samuel Gove and Louis Masotti, eds., *After Daley: Chicago Politics in Transition* (Urbana: University of Illinois Press, 1982), p. 227.

12. Michael Bilandic speaking at the Milton Rakove Memorial Seminar, University of Illinois, Chicago, November 1985.

13. Peter W. Colby and Paul M. Green, "The Consolidation of Clout: The Vote Power of Chicago Democrats from Cermak to Bilandic," *Illinois Issues* (February 1979). Reprinted in Paul M. Green, David Everson, Peter Colby, and Joan Parker, eds., *Illinois Elections,* 3d ed. (Springfield: Sangamon State University, 1986).

14. Chicago *Tribune,* 25 February 1979.

15. Chicago *Sun-Times,* 18 February 1979.

12. Jane M. Byrne: To Think the Unthinkable and Do the Undoable

1. Bill and Lori Granger, *Fighting Jane: Mayor Jane Byrne and the Chicago Machine* (New York, 1980), 19.

2. Ibid., 221–22.

3. Robert Davis, "Evil Cabal to a Crew of Haters," Chicago *Tribune,* 2 September 1980; David Axelrod, "City Transition Team Transits," Chicago *Tribune,* 29 April 1979.

4. Eugene Kennedy, "An Opinionated Psychobiography of Mayor Jane Byrne," Chicago *Sun Times,* 9 February 1983; Paul McGrath at the Chicago Political Tradition Conference, Chicago Historical Society, 2 December 1985; Milton Rokave, "Jane Byrne and the New Chicago Politics," in Samuel Gove and Louis Masotti, eds., *After Daley* (Urbana: University of Illinois Press, 1982), 234–35; Haider cited in Alfredo Lanier, "Jane Byrne's High Hopes and Hard Times," *Chicago* (December 1981): 198; Byrne cited in Chicago *Tribune,* 6 April 1980.

5. Interview with Jane Byrne, 4 March 1986.

6. Chicago *Tribune,* 28 December 1979; Bob Wiedrich, "Byrne's Strident Strike Rhetoric," Chicago *Tribune,* 21 December 1979; Sidney Lens, "What CTA Workers are Asking For," Ibid.

7. A. F. Ehrbar, "Financial Probity: Chicago Style," *Fortune* 101 (2 June 1980): 100–105; "Byrne Tells New Plan for Schools," Chicago *Tribune,* 25

January 1980; N. Shepperd, Jr., "It's Mayor Byrne vs. the Rest," New York *Times*, 7 January 1980.

8. "Byrne Halts Strike Talks," Chicago *Tribune*, 19 February 1980; see also editorial, ibid.; "Byrne Vows to End Strike," ibid., 15 February 1980; Granger, *Fighting Jane*, 227–29.

9. "Reflective Byrne," Palm Beach *Post*, 17 April 1983.

10. Ehrbar, "Financial Probity: Chicago Style," 100–105.

11. Ibid.; "Byrne Hits Past Mayors for City's Financial Woes," Chicago *Tribune*, 31 December 1980; "City Bond Rating . . . ," Chicago *Tribune*, 9 February 1980; Haider cited in Lanier, "Jane Byrne's High Hopes . . . ," 198.

12. Interview with Jane Byrne, 4 March 1986; Donald Haider, "A Multi-Year Financial Projection of and Options for the Corporate Budget, City of Chicago, 1985–1989" (Prepared for the Committee on Finance, City Council, November 1985), 14, 16.

13. "Mayor's Record of Achievement," Chicago *Tribune*, 22 June 1980.

14. Robert Davis, "Byrne's Crusade," Chicago *Tribune*, 5 April 1981.

15. David Axelrod, "The Battles," Chicago *Tribune*, 5 April 1981.

16. McMullen quoted in "Byrne, McMullen Hit Abusive Press," Chicago *Tribune*, 19 January 1980, and in Christopher Willcox "Chicago: How the City Works," Detroit *News Magazine* (20 July 1980): 18.

17. Harry Golden, "Byrne's Mercurial Record of Feats, Fests," Chicago *Sun Times*, 15 February 1983; Ira Bach, "Byrne Has Been Good for the City," Chicago *Tribune*, 19 February 1983.

18. Granger, *Fighting Jane*, 27–31; "Jane Byrne," *Current Biography 1980*, 33. For early life see also Kathleen Whalen Fitzgerald, *Brass: Jane Byrne and the Pursuit of Power* (Chicago 1980).

19. On her move to Cabrini-Green see Anne Keegan, "I Can't Wait Till She Moves In," Chicago *Tribune*, 23 March 1981. McMullen on Mayor Byrne's legs cited in Granger, *Fighting Jane*, 102.

13. Harold Washington: The Enigma of the Black Political Tradition

1. Robert McClory, "Up from Obscurity: Harold Washington," in Melvin G. Holli and Paul M. Green, eds., *The Making of the Mayor: Chicago, 1983* (Grand Rapids: Eerdmans Press, 1984), 3.

2. Ibid., 3.

3. Ibid., 4.

4. Edward C. Banfield and James O. Wilson, *City Politics* (Cambridge, MA: Harvard University Press and M.I.T. Press).

5. Ibid.

6. Election returns are from the Chicago Board of Election Commissioners.

7. An earlier version of this argument is in my article, "Is Chicago Ready for Reform?" in Holli and Green, *The Making of the Mayor*.

8. Population data are from the *Local Community Fact Book* series published by the University of Chicago Press.

9. The material for this and the other sections on Harold Washington comes from interviews with him and other politicians who were involved in the incidents discussed.

10. Interview with Edison Love, one of Dawson's top precinct captains. On Love, see Milton L. Rakove, *We Don't Want Nobody Nobody Sent,* (Bloomington: Indiana University Press, 1979), 37–45.

11. Dawson vehemently opposed Metcalfe's nomination behind the scenes, but he was no match for Daley. Interview with Corneal Davis, President of the Second Ward organization.

12. An excellent and densely detailed discussion of this period can be found in Arnold R. Hirsch, *Making the Second Ghetto* (Cambridge: Cambridge University Press, 1983).

13. Ibid. Realtors regularly charged blacks exhorbitant prices for housing beyond the black belt.

14. Chicago *Sun-Times,* 1 February 1955.

15. Chicago *Defender,* 5 February 1955.

16. An interesting discussion of this period is contained in Joe Mathewson, *Up Against Daley* (LaSalle, IL: Open Court Press, 1974), 121–34.

17. Chicago *Sun-Times,* 19 January 1986.

18. Ibid.

19. Ibid.

20. Edward T. Clayton, *The Negro Politician,* (Chicago: Johnson Publishing Co., 1964), 73.

21. Interview with Mayor Washington.

22. *Chicago* magazine selected Washington as one of the top ten legislators, and the Chicago *Sun-Times* ranked him "the most capable black in the legislature." Both citations came in 1977.

23. Basil Talbott, Chicago *Sun-Times,* n.d.

24. Polling in the 1983 mayoral campaign is discussed by a pollster, Richard Day, "Polling in the 1983 Mayoral Election," in Holli and Green, *The Making of The Mayor.*

14. Ranking Chicago's Mayors: Mirror, Mirror, on the Wall, Who Is the Greatest of Them All?

1. Arthur M. Schlesinger, Sr. *Life,* 1 November 1948, 65–66, 73–74; New York *Times Magazine,* 29 July 1962, 12–13, 40–43; Steve Neal, "Our Best and Worst Presidents," Chicago *Tribune Magazine,* 10 January 1982, 9–18.

2. For example see Robert K. Murray and Tim H. Blessing, "The Presidential Performance Study: A Progress Report," *Journal of American History* 70 (December 1983): 538.

3. For biographical information, see Peter O'Malley, "Edward J. Kelly" in *The Biographical Dictionary of American Mayors, 1820–1980*, eds., Melvin G. Holli and Peter d'A. Jones (Westport, CT, 1981), (hereafter cited as BDAM). See also Roger Biles, *Big City Boss in Depression and War: Edward J. Kelly of Chicago* (DeKalb, IL, 1984) and Arnold Hirsch, *Making the Second Ghetto: Race and Housing in Chicago, 1940–1960* (Cambridge, 1984); Edward H. Mazur, "Carter Harrison I," and Andrew K. Prinz, "Carter Harrison II" in BDAM, 151–52; Peter J. O'Malley, "Anton J. Cermak," in BDAM, 60–61; Alex Gottfried, *Boss Cermak of Chicago* (Seattle, 1962); Roger Biles, "John Wentworth," in BDAM, 387; see also Don Fehrenbacher, *A Biography of Long John Wentworth* (Madison, WI, 1957); Andrew K. Prinz, "Edward F. Dunne," BDAM, 106–7; John D. Buenker, "Edward F. Dunne: The Urban New Stock Democrat as Progressive," Mid-America (January 1968); Paul M. Green, "The Chicago Democratic Party, 1840–1920," (Ph.D. thesis, University of Chicago, 1975); and Richard Becker, "Edward Dunne: Reform Mayor of Chicago," (Ph.D. thesis, University of Chicago, 1971); John R. Schmidt, "Mayor Dever of Chicago," (Ph.D. diss., University of Chicago, 1984); Douglas Bukowski, "William Dever and Prohibition," *Chicago History*, (Summer 1984); Paul Barrett, "Joseph Medill," in BDAM, 251–52; Thomas R. Bullard, "William B. Ogden," in BDAM, 251–52.

4. For example, ex-President Eisenhower was placed on the ten-worst list in 1962 by his contemporaries, but after his successors had stumbled through Bay of Pigs, the Vietnam War, burning cities, Watergate, and "malaise" speeches, Eisenhower skyrocketed to ninth-best in the 1982 Neal-*Tribune* poll.

CONTRIBUTORS

JOHN M. ALLSWANG is Professor of History at California State University, Los Angeles and the author of several studies including the forthcoming *Bosses, Machines, and Urban Voters* (Johns Hopkins University Press).

ROGER BILES is Associate Professor of History at Oklahoma State University, Stillwater and the author of *Big City Boss in Depression and War: Mayor Edward J. Kelly of Chicago* (1984).

JOHN D. BUENKER is Professor of History at the University of Wisconsin-Parkside and is the author of several works including *Urban Liberalism and Progressive Reform* (1977).

DOUGLAS BUKOWSKI is completing a doctoral study of Chicago Mayor William "Big Bill" Thompson at the University of Illinois–Chicago and has written several articles related to politics.

MAUREEN A. FLANAGAN has recently completed a book-length study of Chicago Charter Reform and was a scholar in residence at the American Academy of Rome in 1985–86.

PAUL M. GREEN is Professor and Director of the Institute for Public Policy and Administration at Governors State University and is the author and co-editor of *The Making of the Mayor, Chicago 1983* (with Melvin G. Holli, 1984).

WILLIAM J. GRIMSHAW is Associate Professor of Political Science at Illinois Institute of Technology and has in print a number of studies including *Black Politics in Chicago: The Quest for Leadership, 1939–1979* (1980).

ARNOLD HIRSCH is Associate Professor of History at the University of New Orleans and is the author of *Making the Second Ghetto: Race and Housing in Chicago, 1940–1960* (1983).

MELVIN G. HOLLI is Professor of History at the University of Illinois–Chicago and is the author and editor of several books including *Ethnic Chicago* (with Peter d'A. Jones, 1981, 1984).

EDWARD R. KANTOWICZ is a resident of Chicago and the author most recently of *Corporation Sole: Cardinal Mundelein and Chicago Catholicism* (1983).

DAVID L. PROTESS of Northwestern University Journalism School is the author of numerous articles on Chicago politics and urban reform.

JOHN R. SCHMIDT of the Chicago Board of Education completed his dissertation on Mayor William E. Dever at the University of Chicago.

INDEX

Adamowski, Benjamin, 134, 135, 142, 143; and 1955 mayoral election, 144, 146, 149; as state's attorney, 147–48
Addams, Jane, 40
Alter, Sharon, ix
American Protective League, 68
Anderson, Louis B. (alderman), 79
Arvey, Jacob, 106, 114, 124, 127, 137
Axelrod, David, 180

Bach, Ira, 136, 140
Barnes, Eugene, 179
Bauler, Mathias "Paddy," 82, 114; on council honesty, 135
"Beer War," 89, 90, 91
Bilandic, Michael: becomes mayor, 164–68; defeats Dennis Block, 168; as mayor, 168–69; and 1979 mayoral primary, 169–71; newspaper endorsements of, 170
Blacks, 38, 65, 70, 71, 79, 142; and Democrats, 116, 185, 214. *See also individual mayoral elections*
Bohemian-Americans, 100, 101
Bond, Lester (acting mayor), 7
Brennan, George: as Democratic leader, 85–87, 90–91, 93; death of, 103
Burke, Edward, 164, 166, 173
Bush, Earl, 162, 194
Busse, Fred A.: early life of, 50–51; and 1907 mayoral campaign, 50–56; and traction, 52; fires school board members, 57; and charter reform, 58–59; and temperance, 58–59; and leadership, 59; and 1911 mayoral election, 60
Byrne, Jane M.: and 1979 mayoral election, 172; and reforms, 173; shifts to Vrdolyak, 173–74; and transit, teachers', and firemen's strikes, 174–75; and fiscal responsibility, 177–79; and budget, 178–79; achievements of, 179–81; and political socialization, 181

Capone, Al, 77
Carey, Archibald, Jr., 139, 186
Cermak, Anton J.: early life of, 99–100; as antiprohibitionist, 101; and multi-ethnic politics, 103–4; as mayor, 105–9; disciplines Democrats, 106; and civil service, 109; assassination of, 109–10
Chew, Charles, 156, 192
Chicago Board of Education, 57
Chicago *Defender*, 138, 142
Chicago Federation of Labor, and public schools, 57–58
Chicago Federation of Teachers, 64
Chicago Fire, 2, 6
Chicago Police Department reforms, 88. *See also* Daley, Richard J.
Chicago Public Library, 5, 15
Chicago Relief and Aid Society, 9
Chicago *Staats Zeitung*, 13
Chicago *Tribune*, 2, 7, 15; and 1907 mayoral campaign, 54–55
Chicago Urban League, 138
Citizens Fire-Proof Ticket, 2, 3
Colvin, Harvey, 12
Coughlin, John, 22, 26, 30, 64
Cousins, William, 194
Crowe, Timothy, 101; and "Whoopee" scandal, 103–4

Daley, Richard J.: and 1955 mayoral election, 144, 146–47; and 1959 mayoral election, 147–48; Leon Despres' assessment of, 148; and 1959 police scandal, 148; and 1963 and 1967 mayoral elections, 149–50; and 1968 convention riots, 150; and 1971 and 1973 mayoral elections, 151, 158; and black voter support, 153–56, 158; and King riots, 157; and administration scandals, 161–62; suffers stroke, 162; and site for University of Illinois at Chicago campus, 163
Danaher, Matthew, 162